"*Basic Writings of Existentialism* will be, for many, a reminder of what first drew them to existentialism and, simply, to philosophy. Marino's introductory essays—taut, instructive, well tuned to the drumbeat of each thinker's passions and concerns—along with the substantial selections from the foremost representatives of the movement, are a benediction. In defiance of Hegel's pronouncements, the thinkers included here introduce us to a philosophy in present tense, and preferably in the active voice. Readers new to existentialism have as reliable a guide as the subject matter permits. Those familiar with movement have an occasion for recollection and more."

—Vanessa Rumble,
associate professor of philosophy, Boston College

"This book is a perfect choice for all who wonder what existentialism is all about. The key writers are included—Kierkegaard, Nietzsche, and Dostoevsky from the nineteenth century, and Heidegger, Sartre, and Camus from the twentieth century. It's good to see selections from Simone de Beauvoir and Ralph Ellison as well. Marino has a sharp eye for picking telling passages from often long and complex works. It's now clear that existentialism is one of the enduring traditions in Western philosophy, art, and religion, a perspective that articulates and responds to the deepest human needs. These fresh selections lay out the issues, from alienation to reconciliation, from despair to joyful wisdom, that make this world perspective so compelling. Marino's introductions to each writer, and his introductory overview, are lively and capture the spirit of the chosen texts. A profound adventure awaits those readers ready to immerse themselves in this jewel of a book."

—Edward F. Mooney,
professor of philosophy and religion,
Syracuse University

BASIC WRITINGS OF

EXISTENTIALISM

BASIC WRITINGS OF
EXISTENTIALISM

*Edited and with an Introduction
by Gordon Marino*

THE MODERN LIBRARY

NEW YORK

2004 Modern Library Paperback Edition

Introduction Copyright © 2004 by Gordon D. Marino

Grateful acknowledgment is made for the permission to reprint the enclosed
excerpts. Please see the first page of each section for permission
acknowledgments.

LIBRARY OF CONGRESS CATALOGING-IN-PUBLICATION DATA

Basic writings of existentialism / edited and with
an introduction by Gordon Marino.
p. cm.
ISBN 0-375-75989-1
1. Existentialism. I. Marino, Gordon.

B819.B37 2004
142'.78—dc22   2003061060

Modern Library website address: www.modernlibrary.com

Printed in the United States of America

12 14 16 18 19 17 15 13 11

To Susan Ellis Marino,

THE LOVE OF MY LIFE

Acknowledgments

I would like to thank my friend David Possen for his sagacious advice on this volume. Gratitude is also due my editor, Evelyn O'Hara, for her patience and perspicuity.

Contents

BASIC WRITINGS OF
EXISTENTIALISM

SØREN KIERKEGAARD

FRIEDRICH NIETZSCHE

FYODOR DOSTOEVSKY

MIGUEL DE UNAMUNO Y JUGO

INTRODUCTION

Gordon Marino

I came to existentialism on my knees, after a youthful divorce and in the cold grip of a withering depression. As a professor of philosophy, I realize that it is not fashionable and, philosophically speaking, almost vulgar to begin an anthology with a confession, but existentialism is a much more personal form of philosophizing than any other. In fact, some of the existential philosophers whom you will shake hands with in this book insist on working from the first-person perspective. And so I am within the tradition that I am presenting to confess that either by chance or grace, in the depths of a benumbing funk, I encountered the individual who is widely regarded as the father of existentialism, Søren Kierkegaard. I was in a used-book store, nervously flipping through texts, when I opened page one of Kierkegaard's *Works of Love:*

> If it were so, as conceived sagacity, proud of not being deceived, thinks, that we should believe nothing which we cannot see with our eyes, then first and foremost we ought to give up believing in love. If we were to do so and do it out of fear lest we be deceived, would we not then be deceived? We can, of course, be deceived in many ways. We can be deceived by believing what is untrue, but we certainly

are also deceived by not believing what is true. We can be deceived by appearances, but we can also be deceived by shrewdness, by the flattering conceit which is absolutely certain it cannot be deceived. Which deception is more dangerous? Whose recovery is more doubtful, that of one who does not see, or that of the person who sees and yet does not see? What is more difficult—to awaken someone who is sleeping or to awaken someone who awake, is dreaming that he is awake? Which is sadder, the sight that promptly and unconditionally moves one to tears, the sight of someone unhappily deceived in love, or the sight that in a certain sense could tempt laughter, the sight of the self-deceived, whose fatuous conceit of not being deceived would indeed be ridiculous and laughable if the ridiculousness of it were not an even stronger expression for horror, since it shows that he is unworthy of tears.

Today, orthodoxy has it that sudden psychological changes are chemical in nature, but there was a time when we still believed that an idea, or an interpretation of your experience, could turn the page of that experience. Kierkegaard's *Works of Love* did that for me. In his *Journals and Papers*, Kierkegaard notes that "there is nothing worse than thinking of your own emotional life as twaddle." And yet that is precisely how I felt on the long march under the black sun of depression—indifferent to almost everything, as though I had been struck by a meaningless kind of psychological leprosy. The famously depressive Dane went on to draw a distinction between despair and depression that has been paved over in the present age. While Kierkegaard would agree with modern psychology that depression is marked by inexplicable sadness and self-loathing, he explains that the depressed individual who is also in despair "sees quite clearly that this depression . . . is of no great significance but precisely that fact, that it neither has nor acquires any great significance, is despair." And that is where I was calling from when Kierkegaard helped me to make the turn from thinking of suffering as a fever to regarding it as an action that could be carried out with dignity.

I was a graduate student in philosophy on leave from the university when I had this initial encounter with existentialism. It was the late seventies, a period in which most philosophy departments were controlled by the analytic tradition. Analytic philosophy placed great stress on clarity, precision, and logical form. Topics that could not be rigorously defined—and that was just about everything meaningful—were dismissed as pseudoproblems. Most philosophical talk during this era was about the way we talk. If you wanted to discuss the nature of the self you would first have to spend a couple of decades discussing the way we discuss the self, or so it seemed to me and many of my fellow students. It was, at the time, fashionable for analytic-type professors to begin a seminar by making a negative object lesson of one of the existentialists. The professor might read a line such as, "The self is a relation that relates itself to itself" and then chortle, "Can you imagine anyone taking this gobbledygook for philosophy?" Comically enough, the professor might then go on to passionately treat some trivial academic footnote battle for the remainder of the seminar. I went into philosophy smitten with Socrates and the fantasy that intellectual reflection might actually make an important difference in my life. After all, the word "philosophy" derives from the Greek expression for love of wisdom. But much of the academic philosophy that I was muddling through as a graduate student was bloodless and far removed from both experience and wisdom. Kierkegaard, however, flung open the window and convinced me that at least the existential movement resonated with the ancient view of philosophy as a way of life, as a guide for the perplexed.

Like some of the films that young people admire today and assimilate into their self-understanding, existentialism does not dodge the fact that there is something disturbing going on in the basement of our cozy middle-class world. While there is a long tradition in philosophy of believing that knowledge must be grounded in experience, existentialism tries to get at experience from the inside out. For instance, listen to the gears of Kierkegaard's mind clicking in his philosophical magnum opus, *Concluding Unscientific Postscript*. Kierkegaard is pressing the difference between an objective and a subjective perspective. He reflects on what it means to die. Kierkegaard explains that he knows "what people ordinarily know: that if I swallow a dose of sulfuric acid I will die, likewise by drowning myself or sleeping in coal gas etc. I know that Napoleon always carried poison with him, that Juliet took it." The text continues, "I know that the tragic hero dies in the fifth act and that death here gains infinite reality in pathos but has no such pathos when an ale house keeper dies. I know that the poet interprets death in a variety of moods to the point of verging on the comic. I know what the clergy usually say. . . ." The catalog continues until Kierkegaard concludes, "Despite this almost extraordinary knowledge or proficiency of knowledge, I am by no means able to regard death as something I have understood. So before I go on to world history, about which I still must always say: God knows if it actually does concern you; I think it would be better to consider this, lest existence mock me for having become so erudite that I had forgotten to understand what will happen to me and every human being sometime—sometime, but what am I saying! Suppose death were insidious enough to come tomorrow!" And from there our urexistentialist goes on to discuss the task of subjectively appropriating the uncertain certainty of your own demise. Whereas other philosophers might have tried to formulate a general theory of personal identity, or perhaps a definition of death, Kierkegaard and then Martin Heidegger after him try to fathom the individual meaning of our mortality. In short, existentialism works at the level of personal meaning in contrast to general theory.

Consensus has it that the term "existentialism" did not come into currency until the mid-1940s. Though borrowing from Kierkegaard, the existential philosopher and psychiatrist Karl Jaspers was using the term "existence philosophy" after the First World War, but it was not until a couple of decades later that existentialism was officially baptized. Simone de Beauvoir recounts the day in 1945 that she believes existentialism was born:

> During a discussion organized during the summer ... Sartre had refused to allow Gabriel Marcel to apply this adjective [existentialist] to him: "My philosophy is a philosophy of existence; I don't even know what existentialism is." I shared his irritation. . . . But our protests were in vain. In the end, we took the epithet that everyone used for us and used it for our own purposes.

Now, one of the problems with defining existentialism is the fact that almost everyone who was labeled an existentialist went to great lengths to deny that he or she was an existentialist. A member of the same café circle as Jean-Paul Sartre, Albert Camus insisted that as a novelist he was doing something quite different from the more highfalutin philosophy of Sartre and Heidegger and so was not an existentialist. Heidegger wrote an essay in which he denounced the suggestion that he was an existentialist as Sartre conceived of it.

On the other hand, Sartre took up the banner and formulated an existential creed. In his famous essay "Existentialism," Sartre argues that if there were a God, it would be plausible to think that the essence of everything in creation inhered in the mind of the creator. Sartre, however, believes that it is obvious that God does not exist but claims that there is still

> at least one being in whom existence precedes essence, a being who exists before he can be defined by any concept, and that this being is man, or, as Heidegger says, human reality. What is meant here by saying that existence precedes essence? It means that, first of all, man exists, turns up, appears on the scene, and, only afterwards, defines himself. . . . Not only is man what he conceives himself to be, but he is also only what he wills himself to be after this thrust toward existence.

Whereas a table is a table is a table, humans have no preexisting essence and so define themselves. According to Sartre, existentialists believe that we are all forced to sit for the final exam, "What does it mean to be a human being?" We answer this parent question of life in the ink of our choices and actions. Now,

Kierkegaard, Gabriel Marcel, Miguel de Unamuno y Jugo, and other non-atheist existentialists would disagree with Sartre's claim that there is no underlying plan in our lives, but all the existentialists concur that it is through our choices that we become who we are.

———

Though they may disagree about the details, the existentialists are linked by their commitment to the common themes of freedom, choice, authenticity, alienation, and rebellion. A distant teacher of Karl Marx, the German philosopher G.W.F. Hegel argued that our states of minds are conditioned by historical circumstances. While the existentialists and especially Kierkegaard were inclined to argue against Hegel, who with his unconditional faith in reason was the great wizard of philosophical systematizers, there can be no doubt that the roots of an existential approach were grounded during the Enlightenment, at a time when the faith of people turned in varying degrees from God to reason and humanity itself. As the philosopher Charles Guignon (drawing on the work of Max Weber) has noted, the existential movement is a response to the disenchantment of the world, that is, to the sense that the history and social structure of the world are not God sanctioned. The Lord is not out there as in a theater, watching and giving meaning to our every move. Put in Sartrean terms, existentialism is born of the experience that we are, as it were, forlorn castaways, or as the guitar-strumming existentialist Bob Dylan has put it, "I was born here and I'll die here against my will."

And yet, it was not until the twentieth century that existentialism was recognized as a movement. After two world wars, everyone was ready for a philosophy that could nod to the irrational elements in life; hence, perhaps the immense popularity of both psychoanalysis and existentialism after the abattoir of the twentieth century. Thanks in large part to the fame that Sartre and Camus achieved in the post–World War II years, existentialism took flame in America in the late forties and fifties. Recognizing the influence that Kierkegaard and Friedrich Nietzsche worked on Heidegger and Heidegger on Sartre, the backward process of sanctification began. Scholars began to argue over whether or not this author or that was an existentialist. Some historians of philosophy followed the lineage of existentialists back as far as St. Augustine. Other scholars classified William Shakespeare, Blaise Pascal, and even St. Thomas Aquinas under the new rubric.

———

Existentialism is an interdisciplinary movement that finds expression in three genres: philosophy, literature, and psychotherapy. As a purely philosophical movement, the taproot of existentialism can be traced to the phenomenological work of Edmund Husserl. In his search for certitude, Husserl tried to take philosophy back to the analysis of concrete experience. Husserl's phenomenology brackets the question of whether or not our experience points to anything beyond itself and sticks to the analysis of experience itself. While Heidegger was also drawing upon the work of Kierkegaard and Nietzsche (both of whom became popular in Germany after World War I), his early work shows the impress of his teacher, Husserl. Examples of existential phenomenology can be found in the selections from *Being and Time* (Heidegger) and *Being and Nothingness* (Sartre). On the other hand, existentialism is a literary movement. Fyodor Dostoevsky, Ralph Ellison, Camus, and Franz Kafka have all been classified as existentialists in part because of their profound influence on thinkers whom we have come to associate with existentialism, but also because they hammer out existential themes with existential presuppositions. Of course some existentialists, namely Marcel, Unamuno, Sartre, de Beauvoir, and Camus, wrote both novels and plays as well as philosophical tracts. Finally, the sixties saw the emergence of an existential school of psychology. The works of Rollo May, Viktor Frankl, and Ludwig Binswanger are the most representative of this movement, which focuses on helping the individual to own his or her own choices. Existentialism has even found a presence on the silver screen. Many of Ingmar Bergman's films stand as studies in existentialism, and the same could well be said about *Fight Club* and *The Matrix*.

Before the curtain opens, a word of caution: Today we often connect the idea of education with an almost cozy notion of enlightenment and progress. Sometimes we forget that ideas can be dynamite. Plato and his teacher Socrates taught us that anything that has the power to help also has the power to harm. Depending on your existential coordinates, the voices collected in this book may unsettle your self-understanding and lead to a new awakening or they may simply produce more of the angst that attracted you to this cadre of thinkers to begin with. Take for unnerving example the Nietzchean question, what exactly is the value of value? Or put another way, are Western morals salutary or debilitating? Or again, for those cocksure of their faith, beware of Kierkegaard, who argues that Christians have made a point of forgetting what it really means to be a Christian. For Kierkegaard, most of the people who cross themselves at night and shake their heads over the poor nonbelievers are Christians in much the same way as country club members. In short, caveat emptor: The existentialists are not for people looking to read themselves to sleep.

Basic Writings of

Existentialism

SØREN KIERKEGAARD

Widely regarded as the father of existentialism, Søren Aabye Kierkegaard was born in Copenhagen on May 5, 1813. For those who wonder what's in a name, Kierkegaard's surname means "churchyard" in Danish (with all the familiar connotations of "graveyard"). He was the youngest child of Michael Pedersen Kierkegaard and his second wife, Anne Sørensdatter Lund. Kierkegaard's father was both a Pietist and member of the Copenhagen nouveau riche. A brilliant dialectician, the old man exercised an enormous influence on the life and work of his genial son.

Kierkegaard entered the University of Copenhagen in 1830, but it took more than a decade and the deathbed wishes of his father for him to finish his degree. He passed his exams in 1840 and a year later completed his remarkable dissertation, *On the Concept of Irony: With Constant Reference to Socrates.*

In 1837, when Kierkegaard was twenty-four, he met and fell in love with Regine Olsen. Three years later, they became engaged, but despite the loud protests of both his and her families, Kierkegaard broke off the relationship. In his *Journals,* Kierkegaard gave two different explanations for the break. On the one hand, he claimed that he did not want to bring Regine into the severe melancholy that afflicted virtually his entire family, and on the other, he said that he did not think that he could be the religious author that he felt called to be and a husband at the same time. After emotionally struggling for more than a year, Regine became engaged and married another. However, Kierkegaard would remain obsessed with her for the remainder of his days, even to the point of leaving her the little that he had upon his death.

Kierkegaard started writing in earnest around the time of the break with Regine. From the early 1840s until his death in 1855, Kierkegaard poured forth an amazing number of works. Some were attributed to pseudonyms and were deemed to be part of what he termed his indirect authorship, e.g., *The Concept of Anxiety* and *Concluding Unscientific Postscript.* Others, such as the more straightforwardly religious tracts, e.g., *Works of Love* and *Edifying Discourses,* were written under his own name. There is much debate among Kierkegaard scholars as to how to interpret Kierkegaard's use of pen names, but all agree that the reader should by no means assume that the author behind the authors held the same views as those expressed by his pseudonyms.

Kierkegaard wrote during a tumultuous period in Danish history. The empire was rapidly shrinking, the economy was in shambles, and the state was involved in the peaceful but still difficult transition from a monarchy to a democracy. At the same time, however, it was the golden age of art and literature in Denmark, and Kierkegaard was very much influenced by the Danish romantic poets and novelists of his day. He was a Lutheran, and it is easy to detect the presence of Martin Luther in his religious reflections. Philosophers such as Socrates, Plato, Aristotle, St. Augustine, René Descartes, and Immanuel Kant also left deep impresses on Kierkegaard's thinking. Moreover, Kierkegaard wrestled intensely with the speculative philosophy of G.W.F. Hegel. Indeed, many historians of philosophy see Hegel and Kierkegaard as locked in immortal combat, with Kierkegaard defending the sovereignty of the individual against the Hegelian notion that the significance of the individual derives from his or her participation in the universal or community.

In his *From the Point of View of My Work as an Author,* Kierkegaard explains that his entire authorship was from beginning to end taken up with the question of what it means to have faith. While there are scholars who do not accept Kierkegaard's self-interpretations, there can be no doubt that Kierkegaard gave serious consideration to the issue of what it means to be a Christian. By the end of his own life and perhaps long before, Kierkegaard came to the conclusion that believing in Christ involved the attempt to follow Christ in his self-denial, his suffering, and ultimately in his humiliation. So far as Kierkegaard was concerned, the imitation of Christ was about the furthest thing possible from the mind-set of institutionalized Christianity. Toward the terminus of his life, Kierkegaard stopped going to church, saying that he no longer wanted to participate in "making a fool of God."

In 1854, Kierkegaard began publishing a series of powerful articles that were to become known as his *Attack on Christendom.* In September of 1855, he collapsed on the street and was taken to the hospital, where he died six weeks later from unknown causes.

The first selection that you have before you is from *Fear and Trembling*, which was written early in Kierkegaard's literary career. It raises questions about the relation between ethics and religion and, I think, is intended to remind the bourgeois churchgoer of the primitive and radical dimension of faith. The second selection is from *The Sickness unto Death*, which may be Kierkegaard's most polished and mature work. It is a timely meditation on the nature and structure of despair. As intimated in the introduction to this book, we now live in a world where the distinction between psychological and spiritual maladies has been effaced. In *The Sickness unto Death*, Kierkegaard retrieves this important distinction.

For readers eager to continue along the psychological current of Kierkegaard's thought, I suggest doubling back to a work that Kierkegaard published in 1844, *The Concept of Anxiety*. This text also informs the Heidegger selection contained in the present volume. For those who want to trace the more purely philosophical lines of Kierkegaard's authorship, I suggest reading his *Philosophical Fragments* and then his *Concluding Unscientific Postscript*. Finally, if you are looking to Kierkegaard for Christian edification and/or as a dialogue partner on matters of faith, consider reading his *Works of Love, For Self-Examination,* and his *Upbuilding Discourses.*

FROM

FEAR AND TREMBLING

Problema I

IS THERE A TELEOLOGICAL SUSPENSION OF THE ETHICAL?

The ethical as such is the universal,[1] and as the universal it applies to everyone, which from another angle means that it applies at all times. It rests immanent in itself, has nothing outside itself that is its τέλος [end, purpose] but is itself the τέλος for everything outside itself, and when the ethical has absorbed this into itself, it goes not further. The single individual,[2] sensately and

1. See, for example, G.W.F. Hegel, *Grundlinien der Philosophie des Rechts,* para. 104, 139, 142–57, *Georg Wilhelm Friedrich Hegel's Werke. Vollständige Ausgabe,* I–XVIII, ed. Philipp Marheineke et al. (Berlin: 1832–41), VIII, pp. 210–21; *Jubiläumsausgabe [J.A.],* I–XXVI, ed. Hermann Glockner (Stuttgart: 1927–40), VII, pp. 226–37; *Hegel's Philosophy of Right* (tr. of *Philosophie des Rechts,* 1 ed., 1821; Kierkegaard had 2 ed., 1833), tr. T. M. Knox (Oxford: Clarendon Press, 1962), pp. 108–10.

2. On the important categories "individual" and "the single individual," see *Journals and Papers,* tr. Howard V. and Edna H. Hong (Princeton: Princeton University Press, 1978–2000), II, 1964–2086 and pp. 597–99; *JP* VII, pp. 49–50. See also, for example, *Eigh-*

psychically qualified in immediacy, is the individual who has his τέλος in the universal, and it is his ethical task continually to express himself in this, to annul his singularity in order to become the universal. As soon as the single individual asserts himself in his singularity before the universal, he sins, and only by acknowledging this can he be reconciled again with the universal. Every time the single individual, after having entered the universal, feels an impulse to assert himself as the single individual, he is in a spiritual trial [*Anfægtelse*], from which he can work himself only by repentantly surrendering as the single individual in the universal. If this is the highest that can be said of man and his existence, then the ethical is of the same nature as a person's eternal salvation, which is his τέλος forevermore and at all times, since it would be a contradiction for this to be capable of being surrendered (that is, teleologically suspended), because as soon as this is suspended it is relinquished, whereas that which is suspended is not relinquished but is preserved in the higher, which is its τέλος.

If this is the case, then Hegel is right in "The Good and Conscience,"[3] where he qualifies man only as the individual and considers this qualification as a "moral form of evil"[4] (see especially *The Philosophy of Right*), which must be annulled [*ophævet*] in the teleology of the moral in such a way that the single individual who remains in that stage either sins or is immersed in spiritual trial. But Hegel is wrong in speaking about faith; he is wrong in not protesting loudly and clearly against Abraham's enjoying

---

teen Upbuilding Discourses, Kierkegaard's Writings, I–XVI, tr. Howard V. and Edna H. Hong (Bloomington: Indiana University Press, 1967–78), V; *Fragments, KW* VII; *Anxiety,* pp. 111–13, *KW* VIII; *Postscript, KW* XII; *Two Ages,* pp. 84–96, *KW* XIV; *Discourses in Various Spirits, KW* XV; *Sickness unto Death,* pp. 119–24, *KW* XIX; *Practice, KW* XX; *Armed Neutrality, KW* XXII; *On My Work as an Author, KW* XXII; *The Point of View for My Work as an Author, KW* XXII.

3. Hegel, *Werke,* VIII, pp. 171–209; *J.A.,* VII, pp. 187–225; *Philosophy of Right,* pp. 86–103 (*aufgehoben* is translated as "annulled," para. 139, 141).

4. Hegel, *Werke,* VIII, p. xix; *J.A.,* VII, p. 16 (ed. tr.). "Moral Forms of Evil. Hypocrisy, Probabilism, Good Intentions, Conviction, Irony, Note to para. 140." The rubrics are omitted in the table of contents of *Philosophy of Right;* see note 1 above.

honor and glory as a father of faith when he ought to be sent back to a lower court and shown up as a murderer.

Faith is namely this paradox that the single individual is higher than the universal—yet, please note, in such a way that the movement repeats itself, so that after having been in the universal he as the single individual isolates himself as higher than the universal. If this is not faith, then Abraham is lost, then faith has never existed in the world precisely because it has always existed.[5] For if the ethical—that is, social morality[6]—is the highest and if there is in a person no residual incommensurability in some way such that this incommensurability is not evil (i.e., the single individual, who is to be expressed in the universal), then no categories are needed other than what Greek philosophy had or what can be deduced from them by consistent thought. Hegel should not have concealed this, for, after all, he had studied Greek philosophy.

5. See, for example, Hegel, *Encyclopädie der philosophischen Wissenschaften, Erster Theil, Die Logik,* para. 63, *Werke,* VI, p. 128; *J.A.,* VIII, p. 166; *Hegel's Logic* (tr. of *Encyclopädie,* 3 ed., 1830; the text of the edition Kierkegaard had was of the 3 ed.), tr. William Wallace (Oxford: Clarendon Press, 1975), p. 97: "But, seeing that derivative knowledge is restricted to the compass of facts, Reason is knowledge underivative, or Faith." See p. 69 and note 6.

6. Danish *det sædelige* or *Sædelighed,* corresponding to the German *Sittlichkeit,* is here translated as "social morality," whereas the translation of *Sittlichkeit* in Hegel is usually "ethical life." See, for example, Hegel, *Philosophie des Rechts,* para. 141, *Werke,* VIII, p. 207; *J.A.,* VII, p. 223; *Philosophy of Right,* p. 103:

Transition from Morality to Ethical Life

141. For the good as the substantial universal of freedom, but as something still abstract, there are therefore required determinate characteristics of some sort and the principle for determining them, though a principle identical with the good itself. For conscience similarly, as the purely abstract principle of determination, it is required that its decisions shall be universal and objective. If good and conscience are each kept abstract and thereby elevated to independent totalities, then both become the indeterminate which ought to be determined.—But the integration of these two relative totalities into an absolute identity has already been implicitly achieved in that this very subjectivity of pure self-certainty, aware in its vacuity of its gradual evaporation, is identical with the abstract universality of the good. The identity of the good with the subjective will, an identity which therefore is concrete and the truth of them both, is Ethical Life.

On morality and the ethical in Kierkegaard's thought, see *JP* I, pp. 530–32.

People who are profoundly lacking in learning and are given to clichés are frequently heard to say that a light shines over the Christian world, whereas a darkness enshrouds paganism. This kind of talk has always struck me as strange, inasmuch as every more thorough thinker, every more earnest artist still regenerates himself in the eternal youth of the Greeks. The explanation for such a statement is that one does not know what one should say but only that one must say something. It is quite right to say that paganism did not have faith, but if something is supposed to have been said thereby, then one must have a clearer understanding of what faith is, for otherwise one falls into such clichés. It is easy to explain all existence, faith along with it, without having a conception of what faith is, and the one who counts on being admired for such an explanation is not such a bad calculator, for it is as Boileau[7] says: *Un sot trouve toujours un plus sot, qui l'admire* [One fool always finds a bigger fool, who admires him].

Faith is precisely the paradox that the single individual as the single individual is higher than the universal, is justified before it, not as inferior to it but as superior—yet in such a way, please note, that it is the single individual who, after being subordinate as the single individual to the universal, now by means of the universal becomes the single individual who as the single individual is superior, that the single individual as the single individual stands in an absolute relation to the absolute. This position cannot be mediated, for all mediation takes place only by virtue of the universal; it is and remains for all eternity a paradox, impervious to thought. And yet faith is this paradox, or else (and I ask the reader to bear these consequences *in mente* [in mind] even though it would be too prolix for me to write them all down) or else faith has never existed simply because it has always existed, or else Abraham is lost.

7. Boileau, *L'Art poétique*, I, 232, *Œuvres de Boileau*, I–IV (Paris: 1830), II, p. 190; *The Art of Poetry*, tr. Albert S. Cook (Boston: Ginn, 1892), p. 172: "And in all times a forward scribbling fop / Has found some greater fool to cry him up."

It is certainly true that the single individual can easily confuse this paradox with spiritual trial [*Anfægtelse*], but it ought not to be concealed for that reason. It is certainly true that many persons may be so constituted that they are repulsed by it, but faith ought not therefore to be made into something else to enable one to have it, but one ought rather to admit to not having it, while those who have faith ought to be prepared to set forth some characteristics whereby the paradox can be distinguished from a spiritual trial.

The story of Abraham contains just such a teleological suspension of the ethical. There is no dearth of keen minds and careful scholars who have found analogies to it. What their wisdom amounts to is the beautiful proposition that basically everything is the same. If one looks more closely, I doubt very much that anyone in the whole wide world will find one single analogy, except for a later one, which proves nothing if it is certain that Abraham represents faith and that it is manifested normatively in him, whose life not only is the most paradoxical that can be thought but is also so paradoxical that it simply cannot be thought. He acts by virtue of the absurd, for it is precisely the absurd that he as the single individual is higher than the universal. This paradox cannot be mediated, for as soon as Abraham begins to do so, he has to confess that he was in a spiritual trial, and if that is the case, he will never sacrifice Isaac, or if he did sacrifice Isaac, then in repentance he must come back to the universal. He gets Isaac back again by virtue of the absurd. Therefore, Abraham is at no time a tragic hero but is something entirely different, either a murderer or a man of faith. Abraham does not have the middle term that saves the tragic hero. This is why I can understand a tragic hero but cannot understand Abraham, even though in a certain demented sense I admire him more than all others.

In ethical terms, Abraham's relation to Isaac is quite simply this: the father shall love the son more than himself. But within its own confines the ethical has various gradations. We shall see whether this story contains any higher expression for the ethical that can ethically explain his behavior, can ethically justify his suspending the ethical obligation to the son; but without moving beyond the teleology of the ethical.

When an enterprise of concern to a whole nation[8] is impeded, when such a project is halted by divine displeasure, when the angry deity sends a dead calm that mocks every effort, when the soothsayer carries out his sad task and announces that the deity demands a young girl as sacrifice—then the father must heroically bring this sacrifice. He must nobly conceal his agony, even though he could wish he were "the lowly man who dares to weep"[9] and not the king who must behave in a kingly manner. Although the lonely agony penetrates his breast and there are only three persons[10] in the whole nation who know his agony, soon the whole nation will be initiated into his agony and also into his deed, that for the welfare of all he will sacrifice her, his daughter, this lovely young girl. O bosom! O fair cheeks, flaxen hair.[11] And the daughter's tears will agitate him, and the father will turn away his face, but the hero must raise the knife. And when the news of it reaches the father's house, the beautiful Greek maidens will blush with enthusiasm, and if the daughter was engaged, her betrothed will not be angry but will be proud to share in the father's deed, for the girl belonged more tenderly to him than to the father.

8. The Trojan War.

9. Euripides, *Iphigenia in Aulis*, ll. 446–48; *Euripides*, tr. Christian Wilster (Copenhagen: 1840), p. 116; *The Complete Greek Tragedies*, I–IV, ed. David Grene and Richmond Lattimore (Chicago: University of Chicago Press, 1958–60), IV, p. 316 (tr. Charles R. Walker):

> [*Agamemnon speaking*]
> O fortunate men of mean,
> Ignoble birth, freely you may weep and
> Empty out your hearts, but the highborn—
> Decorum rules our lives. . . .

10. Menelaus, Calchas, and Ulysses, ibid., l. 107; *Euripides*, tr. Wilster, p. 104; *Greek Tragedies*, IV, p. 301.

11. Line reference to *Iphigenia in Aulis*, *Euripides*, tr. Wilster, p. 125.

When the valiant judge[12] who in the hour of need saved Israel binds God and himself in one breath by the same promise, he will heroically transform the young maiden's jubilation, the beloved daughter's joy to sorrow, and all Israel will sorrow with her over her virginal youth. But every freeborn man will understand, every resolute woman will admire Jephthah, and every virgin in Israel will wish to behave as his daughter did, because what good would it be for Jephthah to win the victory by means of a promise if he did not keep it—would not the victory be taken away from the people again?

When a son forgets his duty,[13] when the state entrusts the sword of judgment to the father, when the laws demand punishment from the father's hand, then the father must heroically forget that the guilty one is his son, he must nobly hide his agony, but no one in the nation, not even the son, will fail to admire the father, and every time the Roman laws are interpreted, it will be remembered that many interpreted them more learnedly but no one more magnificently than Brutus.

But if Agamemnon, while a favorable wind was taking the fleet under full sail to its destination, had dispatched that messenger who fetched Iphigenia to be sacrificed; if Jephthah, without being bound by any promise that decided the fate of the nation, had said to his daughter: Grieve now for two months over your brief youth, and then I will sacrifice you; if Brutus had had a righteous son and yet had summoned the lictors to put him to death—who would have understood them? If, on being asked why they did this, these three men had answered: It is an ordeal in which we are being tried [*forsøges*]—would they have been better understood?

---

12. Jephthah. See Judges 11:30–40.

13. Brutus (Junius) had led the Romans in expelling the Tarquins after the rape of Lucrece. He then executed his sons for plotting a Tarquinian restoration. See Livy, *From the Founding of a City* (*History of Rome*), II, 3–5; T. Livii Patavini, *Historiarum libri, quæ supersunt omnia*, I–V, ed. Augusto Guil. Ernesti (Leipzig: n.d.), I, pp. 75–77; *Livy*, I–XIV, tr. B. O. Foster (Loeb Classics, Cambridge: Harvard University Press, 1939–59), I, pp. 227–35.

· When in the crucial moment Agamemnon, Jephthah, and Brutus heroically have overcome the agony, heroically have lost the beloved, and have only to complete the task externally, there will never be a noble soul in the world without tears of compassion for their agony, of admiration for their deed. But if in the crucial moment these three men were to append to the heroic courage with which they bore the agony the little phrase: But it will not happen anyway—who then would understand them? If they went on to explain: This we believe by virtue of the absurd— who would understand them any better, for who would not readily understand that it was absurd, but who would understand that one could then believe it?

The difference between the tragic hero and Abraham is very obvious. The tragic hero is still within the ethical. He allows an expression of the ethical to have its τέλος in a higher expression of the ethical; he scales down the ethical relation between father and son or daughter and father to a feeling that has its dialectic in its relation to the idea of moral conduct. Here there can be no question of a teleological suspension of the ethical itself.

Abraham's situation is different. By his act he transgressed the ethical altogether and had a higher τέλος outside it, in relation to which he suspended it. For I certainly would like to know how Abraham's act can be related to the universal, whether any point of contact between what Abraham did and the universal can be found other than that Abraham transgressed it. It is not to save a nation, not to uphold the idea of the state that Abraham does it; it is not to appease the angry gods. If it were a matter of the deity's being angry, then he was, after all, angry only with Abraham, and Abraham's act is totally unrelated to the universal, is a purely private endeavor. Therefore, while the tragic hero is great because of his moral virtue,[14] Abraham is great because of a purely personal virtue. There is no higher expression for the ethical in Abraham's life than that the father shall love

14. See Hegel, *Philosophie des Rechts*, para. 150, *Werke*, VIII, pp. 214–16; *J.A.*, VII, pp. 230–32; *Philosophy of Right*, pp. 107–08.

the son. The ethical in the sense of the moral is entirely beside the point. Insofar as the universal was present, it was cryptically in Isaac, hidden, so to speak, in Isaac's loins, and must cry out with Isaac's mouth: Do not do this, you are destroying everything.

Why, then, does Abraham do it? For God's sake and—the two are wholly identical—for his own sake. He does it for God's sake because God demands this proof of his faith; he does it for his own sake so that he can prove it. The unity of the two is altogether correctly expressed in the word already used to describe this relationship. It is an ordeal, a temptation. A temptation—but what does that mean? As a rule, what tempts a person is something that will hold him back from doing his duty, but here the temptation is the ethical itself, which would hold him back from doing God's will. But what is duty? Duty is simply the expression for God's will.

Here the necessity of a new category for the understanding of Abraham becomes apparent. Paganism does not know such a relationship to the divine. The tragic hero does not enter into any private relationship to the divine, but the ethical is the divine, and thus the paradox therein can be mediated in the universal.

Abraham cannot be mediated; in other words, he cannot speak. As soon as I speak, I express the universal, and if I do not do so, no one can understand me. As soon as Abraham wants to express himself in the universal, he must declare that his situation is a spiritual trial [*Anfægtelse*], for he has no higher expression of the universal that ranks above the universal he violates.

Therefore, although Abraham arouses my admiration, he also appalls me. The person who denies himself and sacrifices himself because of duty gives up the finite in order to grasp the infinite and is adequately assured; the tragic hero gives up the certain for the even more certain, and the observer's eye views him with confidence. But the person who gives up the universal in order to grasp something even higher that is not the universal—

what does he do? Is it possible that this can be anything other than a spiritual trial? And if it is possible, but the individual makes a mistake, what salvation is there for him? He suffers all the agony of the tragic hero, he shatters his joy in the world, he renounces everything, and perhaps at the same time he barricades himself from the sublime joy that was so precious to him that he would buy it at any price. The observer cannot understand him at all; neither can his eye rest upon him with confidence. Perhaps the believer's intention cannot be carried out at all, because it is inconceivable. Or if it could be done but the individual has misunderstood the deity—what salvation would there be for him? The tragic hero needs and demands tears, and where is the envious eye so arid that it could not weep with Agamemnon, but where is the soul so gone astray that it has the audacity to weep for Abraham? The tragic hero finishes his task at a specific moment in time, but as time passes he does what is no less significant: he visits the person encompassed by sorrow, who cannot breathe because of his anguished sighs, whose thoughts oppress him, heavy with tears. He appears to him, breaks the witchcraft of sorrow, loosens the bonds, evokes the tears, and the suffering one forgets his own sufferings in those of the tragic hero. One cannot weep over Abraham. One approaches him with a *horror religiosus,* as Israel approached Mount Sinai.[15] What if he himself is distraught, what if he had made a mistake, this lonely man who climbs Mount Moriah, whose peak towers sky-high over the flatlands of Aulis, what if he is not a sleepwalker safely crossing the abyss while the one standing at the foot of the mountain looks up, shakes with anxiety, and then in his deference and horror does not even dare to call to him?—Thanks, once again thanks, to a man who, to a person overwhelmed by life's sorrows and left behind naked, reaches out the words, the leafage of language by which he can conceal his misery. Thanks to you, great Shakespeare, you who can say everything, everything, everything just

15. See Exodus 19:12.

as it is—and yet, why did you never articulate this torment? Did you perhaps reserve it for yourself, like the beloved's name that one cannot bear to have the world utter, for with his little secret that he cannot divulge the poet buys this power of the word to tell everybody else's dark secrets. A poet is not an apostle; he drives out devils only by the power of the devil.[16]

But if the ethical is teleologically suspended in this manner, how does the single individual in whom it is suspended exist? He exists as the single individual in contrast to the universal. Does he sin, then, for from the point of view of the idea, this is the form of sin. Thus, even though the child does not sin, because it is not conscious of its existence as such, its existence, from the point of view of the idea, is nevertheless sin, and the ethical makes its claim upon it at all times. If it is denied that this form can be repeated in such a way that it is not sin, then judgment has fallen upon Abraham. How did Abraham exist? He had faith. This is the paradox by which he remains at the apex, the paradox that he cannot explain to anyone else, for the paradox is that he as the single individual places himself in an absolute relation to the absolute. Is he justified? Again, his justification is the paradoxical, for if he is, then he is justified not by virtue of being something universal but by virtue of being the single individual.

How does the single individual reassure himself that he is legitimate? It is a simple matter to level all existence to the idea of the state or the idea of a society. If this is done, it is also simple to mediate, for one never comes to the paradox that the single individual as the single individual is higher than the universal, something I can also express symbolically in a statement by Pythagoras to the effect that the odd number is more perfect than the even number.[17] If occasionally there is any response at

16. See Mark 3:15–22.

17. See W. G. Tennemann, *Geschichte der Philosophie,* I–XI (Leipzig: 1798–1819), I, p. 106. The Pythagoreans gave a number of reasons, not wholly satisfying, for this distinction. Odd numbers added successively to the number one give square numbers; even

all these days with regard to the paradox, it is likely to be: One judges it by the result. Aware that he is a paradox who cannot be understood, a hero who has become a σκάνδαλον [offense] to his age will shout confidently to his contemporaries: The result will indeed prove that I was justified. This cry is rarely heard in our age, inasmuch as it does not produce heroes—this is its defect— and it likewise has the advantage that it produces few carica- tures. When in our age we hear these words: It will be judged by the result—then we know at once with whom we have the honor of speaking. Those who talk this way are a numerous type whom I shall designate under the common name of assistant professors.[18] With security in life, they live in their thoughts: they have a *per- manent* position and a *secure* future in a well-organized state. They have hundreds, yes, even thousands of years between them and the earthquakes of existence; they are not afraid that such things can be repeated, for then what would the police and the news- papers say? Their life task is to judge the great men, judge them according to the result. Such behavior toward greatness betrays a strange mixture of arrogance and wretchedness—arrogance because they feel called to pass judgment, wretchedness because they feel that their lives are in no way allied with the lives of the great. Anyone with even a smattering *erectioris ingenii* [of nobil- ity of nature] never becomes an utterly cold and clammy worm, and when he approaches greatness, he is never devoid of the thought that since the creation of the world it has been custom- ary for the result to come last and that if one is truly going to

---

numbers added to the number two give "oblong" numbers. The whole universe is iden- tified with the number one. Even numbers are "unlimited" and therefore are endless (no τέλος) and incomplete. See *JP* V 5616.

18. *Docenter* (pl.) literally means tutors in the university setting of the time, university teachers who assisted the professors in the teaching of the discipline. The root *docere* (Latin and Danish) emphasizes the didactic. Here Johannes de Silentio uses the term broadly to include specifically the professors with their detached objectivity, their pontifical evaluations of the past, and their lifetime appointments. See *The Point of View, KW* XXII.

learn something from greatness one must be particularly aware of the beginning. If the one who is to act wants to judge himself by the result, he will never begin. Although the result may give joy to the entire world, it cannot help the hero, for he would not know the result until the whole thing was over, and he would not become a hero by that but by making a beginning.

Moreover, in its dialectic the result (insofar as it is finitude's response to the infinite question) is altogether incongruous with the hero's existence. Or should Abraham's receiving Isaac by a *marvel* be able to prove that Abraham was justified in relating himself as the single individual to the universal? If Abraham actually had sacrificed Isaac, would he therefore have been less justified?

But we are curious about the result, just as we are curious about the way a book turns out. We do not want to know anything about the anxiety, the distress, the paradox. We carry on an esthetic flirtation with the result. It arrives just as unexpectedly but also just as effortlessly as a prize in a lottery, and when we have heard the result, we have built ourselves up. And yet no manacled robber of churches is so despicable a criminal as the one who plunders holiness in this way, and not even Judas, who sold his Lord for thirty pieces of silver, is more contemptible than someone who peddles greatness in this way.

It is against my very being to speak inhumanly about greatness, to make it a dim and nebulous far-distant shape or to let it be great but devoid of the emergence of the humanness without which it ceases to be great, for it is not what happens to me that makes me great but what I do, and certainly there is no one who believes that someone became great by winning the big lottery prize. A person might have been born in lowly circumstances, but I would still require him not to be so inhuman toward himself that he could imagine the king's castle only at a distance and ambiguously dream of its greatness, and destroy it at the same time he elevates it because he elevated it so basely. I require him to be man enough to tread confidently and with

dignity there as well. He must not be so inhuman that he insolently violates everything by barging right off the street into the
king's hall—he loses more thereby than the king. On the contrary, he should find a joy in observing every bidding of propriety with a happy and confident enthusiasm, which is precisely
what makes him a free spirit. This is merely a metaphor, for that
distinction is only a very imperfect expression of the distance
of spirit. I require every person not to think so inhumanly of
himself that he does not dare to enter those palaces where the
memory of the chosen ones lives or even those where they
themselves live. He is not to enter rudely and foist his affinity
upon them. He is to be happy for every time he bows before
them, but he is to be confident, free of spirit, and always more
than a charwoman, for if he wants to be no more than that, he
will never get in. And the very thing that is going to help him is
the anxiety and distress in which the great were tried, for otherwise, if he has any backbone, they will only arouse his righteous
envy. And anything that can be great only at a distance, that
someone wants to make great with empty and hollow phrases—
is destroyed by that very person.

Who was as great in the world as that favored woman, the
mother of God, the Virgin Mary?[19] And yet how do we speak of
her? That she was the favored one among women does not make
her great, and if it would not be so very odd for those who listen to be able to think just as inhumanly as those who speak,
then every young girl might ask: Why am I not so favored? And
if I had nothing else to say, I certainly would not dismiss such a
question as stupid, because, viewed abstractly, vis-à-vis a favor,
every person is just as entitled to it as the other. We leave out

---

19. The Virgin Mary is celebrated also in other writings. See, for example, *Irony,*
KW II; *Either/Or,* I, *KW* III; *Eighteen Discourses, KW* V; *Fragments, KW* VII; *Postscript, KW* XII;
Discourses in Various Spirits, KW XV; *Christian Discourses, KW* XVII; *Practice, KW* XX; *An Up-*
building Discourse, in *Without Authority, KW* XVIII; *Judge for Yourselves!, KW* XXI; *The Moment*
and Late Writings, KW XXIII. See also *JP* III 2669–74 and p. 814; VII, p. 60.

the distress, the anxiety, the paradox. My thoughts are as pure as anybody's, and he who can think this way surely has pure thoughts, and, if not, he can expect something horrible, for anyone who has once experienced these images cannot get rid of them again, and if he sins against them, they take a terrible revenge in a silent rage, which is more terrifying than the stridency of ten ravenous critics. To be sure, Mary bore the child wondrously, but she nevertheless did it "after the manner of women,"[20] and such a time is one of anxiety, distress, and paradox. The angel was indeed a ministering spirit, but he was not a meddlesome spirit who went to the other young maidens in Israel and said: Do not scorn Mary, the extraordinary is happening to her. The angel went only to Mary, and no one could understand her. Has any woman been as infringed upon as was Mary, and is it not true here also that the one whom God blesses he curses in the same breath? This is the spirit's view of Mary, and she is by no means—it is revolting to me to say it but even more so that people have inanely and unctuously made her out to be thus—she is by no means a lady idling in her finery and playing with a divine child. When, despite this, she said: Behold, I am the handmaid of the Lord[21]—then she is great, and I believe it should not be difficult to explain why she became the mother of God. She needs worldly admiration as little as Abraham needs tears, for she was no heroine and he was no hero, but both of them became greater than these, not by being exempted in any way from the distress and the agony and the paradox, but became greater by means of these.

It is great when the poet in presenting his tragic hero for public admiration dares to say: Weep for him, for he deserves it. It is great to deserve the tears of those who deserve to shed tears. It is great that the poet dares to keep the crowd under restraint,

20. See Genesis 18:11.
21. See Luke 1:38.

dares to discipline men to examine themselves individually to see if they are worthy to weep for the hero, for the slop water of the snivellers is a debasement of the sacred.—But even greater than all this is the knight of faith's daring to say to the noble one who wants to weep for him: Do not weep for me, but weep for yourself.[22]

We are touched, we look back to those beautiful times. Sweet sentimental longing leads us to the goal of our desire, to see Christ walking about in the promised land. We forget the anxiety, the distress, the paradox. Was it such a simple matter not to make a mistake? Was it not terrifying that this man walking around among the others was God? Was it not terrifying to sit down to eat with him? Was it such an easy matter to become an apostle? But the result, the eighteen centuries—that helps, that contributes to this mean deception whereby we deceive ourselves and others. I do not feel brave enough to wish to be contemporary[23] with events like that, but I do not for that reason severely condemn those who made a mistake, nor do I depreciate those who saw what was right.

But I come back to Abraham. During the time before the result, either Abraham was a murderer every minute or we stand before a paradox that is higher than all mediations.

The story of Abraham contains, then, a teleological suspension of the ethical. As the single individual he became higher than the universal. This is the paradox, which cannot be mediated. How he entered into it is just as inexplicable as how he remains in it. If this is not Abraham's situation, then Abraham is not even a tragic hero but a murderer. It is thoughtless to want to go on calling him the father of faith, to speak of it to men who have an interest only in words. A person can become a tragic hero through his own strength—but not the knight of faith. When a person walks what is in one sense the hard road of

22. See Luke 23:28.
23. On the theme of contemporaneity, see especially *Fragments, KW* VII.

the tragic hero, there are many who can give him advice, but he who walks the narrow road of faith has no one to advise him—no one understands him. Faith is a marvel, and yet no human being is excluded from it; for that which unites all human life is passion,* and faith is a passion.

---

* Lessing has somewhere said something similar from a purely esthetic point of view. He actually wants to show in this passage that grief, too, can yield a witty remark. With that in mind, he quotes the words spoken on a particular occasion by the unhappy king of England, Edward II. In contrast he quotes from Diderot a story about a peasant woman and a remark she made. He goes on to say: Auch das war Witz, und noch dazu Witz einer Bäuerin; aber die Umstände machten ihn unvermeidlich. Und folglich auch muss man die Entschuldigung der witzigen Ausdrücke des Schmerzes und der Betrübniss nicht darin suchen, dass die Person, welche sie sagt, eine vornehme, wohlerzogene, verständige, und auch sonst witzige Person sey; *denn die Leidenschaften machen alle Menschen wieder gleich:* sondern darin, dass wahrscheinlicher Weise ein jeder Mensch ohne Unterschied in den nämlichen Umständen das nämliche sagen würde. Den Gedanken der Bäuerin hätte eine Königin haben können und haben müssen: so wie das, was dort der König sagt, auch ein Bauer hätte sagen können und ohne Zweifel würde gesagt haben [That also was wit, and the wit of a peasant woman, besides; but the situation made it inevitable. And consequently one must not seek the excuse for the witty expressions of pain and sorrow in the fact that the person who said them was a distinguished, well-educated, intelligent, and also witty person; *for the passions make all men equal again:* but in this, that in the same situation probably every person, without exception, would have said the same thing. A queen could have had and must have had the thought of a peasant woman, just as a peasant could have said and no doubt would have said what the king said there]. See *Sämmtliche Werke,* XXX, p. 223.[24]

24. *Auszüge aus Lessing's Antheil an den Litteratur-briefen,* Letter 81, *Schriften,* XXX, pp. 221–23 (ed. tr.).

PROBLEMA II

IS THERE AN ABSOLUTE DUTY TO GOD?[1]

The ethical is the universal, and as such it is also the divine. Thus it is proper to say that every duty is essentially duty to God, but if no more can be said than this, then it is also said that I actually have no duty to God. The duty becomes duty by being traced back to God, but in the duty itself I do not enter into relation to God. For example, it is a duty to love one's neighbor. It

1. See Immanuel Kant, *Grundlegung zur Metaphysik der Sitten* (2 ed., Riga: 1786), for example, pp. 29, 73–74, 85–86; *Kant's gesammelte Schriften,* I–XXIII (Berlin: 1902–55), IV, pp. 409–10, 433–34, 439; *Foundations of the Metaphysics of Morals,* tr. Lewis White Beck (Indianapolis: Bobbs-Merrill, 1969), pp. 25, 51, 58:

> Even the Holy One of the Gospel must be compared with our ideal of moral perfection before He is recognized as such; even He says of Himself, "Why call ye Me (whom you see) good? None is good (the archetype of the good) except God only (whom you do not see)." But whence do we have the concept of God as the highest Good? Solely from the idea of moral perfection which reason formulates a priori and which it inseparably connects with the concept of a free will.
>
> If we now look back upon all previous attempts which have ever been undertaken to discover the principle of morality, it is not to be wondered at that they all had to fail. Man was seen to be bound to laws by his duty, but it was not seen that he

is a duty by its being traced back to God, but in the duty I enter into relation not to God but to the neighbor I love. If in this connection I then say that it is my duty to love God, I am actually pronouncing only a tautology, inasmuch as "God" in a totally abstract sense is here understood as the divine—that is, the universal, that is, the duty. The whole existence of the human race rounds itself off as a perfect, self-contained sphere, and then the ethical is that which limits and fills at one and the same time. God comes to be an invisible vanishing point, an impotent thought; his power is only in the ethical, which fills all of existence. Insofar, then, as someone might wish to love God in any other sense than this, he is a visionary, is in love with a phantom, which, if it only had enough power to speak, would say to him: I do not ask for your love—just stay where you belong. Insofar as someone might wish to love God in another way, this love would be as implausi-

is subject only to his own, yet universal, legislation, and that he is only bound to act in accordance with his own will, which is, however, designed by nature to be a will giving universal laws. For if one thought of him as subject only to a law (whatever it may be), this necessarily implied some interest as a stimulus or compulsion to obedience because the law did not arise from his will. Rather, his will was constrained by something else according to a law to act in a certain way. By this strictly necessary consequence, however, all the labor of finding a supreme ground for duty was irrevocably lost, and one never arrived at duty but only at the necessity of action from a certain interest. This might be his own interest or that of another, but in either case the imperative always had to be conditional and could not at all serve as a moral command. This principle I will call the principle of *autonomy* of the will in contrast to all other principles which I accordingly count under *heteronomy*.

The essence of things is not changed by their external relations, and without reference to these relations a man must be judged only by what constitutes his absolute worth; and this is true whoever his judge is, even if it be the Supreme Being. Morality is thus the relation of actions to the autonomy of the will, i.e., to possible universal lawgiving by maxims of the will. The action which can be compatible with the autonomy of the will is permitted; that which does not agree with it is prohibited. The will whose maxims necessarily are in harmony with the laws of autonomy is a holy will or an absolutely good will.

Kant's denial of an absolute duty to God transcending rational morality (or a conflation of divine will and the autonomy of man's rational will) is shared with variations by Fichte, Schleiermacher, and Hegel. In raising the question, Johannes de Silentio runs counter to the dominant ethical thought of the time.

ble as the love Rousseau mentions, whereby a person loves the Kaffirs instead of loving his neighbor.[2]

Now if this train of thought is sound, if there is nothing in-commensurable in a human life, and if the incommensurable that is present is there only by an accident from which nothing results insofar as existence is viewed from the idea, then Hegel was right. But he was not right in speaking about faith or in per-mitting Abraham to be regarded as its father, for in the latter case he has pronounced judgment both on Abraham and on faith. In Hegelian philosophy,[3] *das Äussere* (*die Entäusserung*) [the outer (the externalization)] is higher than *das Innere* [the inner]. This is frequently illustrated by an example. The child is *das Innere*, the adult *das Äussere*, with the result that the child is determined by the external and, conversely, the adult as *das Äussere* by the inner. But faith is the paradox that interiority is higher than exteriority, or, to call to mind something said earlier, the uneven number is higher than the even.

Thus in the ethical view of life, it is the task of the single in-dividual to strip himself of the qualification of interiority and to express this in something external. Every time the individual shrinks from it, every time he withholds himself in or slips down again into the qualifications of feeling, mood, etc. that belong to interiority, he trespasses, he is immersed in spiritual trial [*Anfæg-telse*]. The paradox of faith is that there is an interiority that is incommensurable with exteriority, an interiority that is not identical, please note, with the first but is a new interiority.[4] This must not be overlooked. Recent philosophy has allowed itself

2. The source has not been located.

3. See Hegel, *Wissenschaft der Logik, Erster Theil, Die objective Logik, Zweites Buch*, II, 3, C, *Werke*, IV, pp. 177–83; *J.A.*, IV, pp. 655–61; *Hegel's Science of Logic* (tr. of *W.L.*, Lasson ed., 1923), tr. A. V. Miller (New York: Humanities Press, 1969), pp. 523–28; Hegel, *Encyclopädie, Logik*, para. 140, *Werke*, VI, pp. 275–81; *J.A.*, VIII, pp. 313–19; *Hegel's Logic*, pp. 197–200. See *Either/Or*, I, *KW* III.

4. See faith as second immediacy (spontaneity), immediacy after reflection, in *Stages, KW* XI; *Postscript, KW* XII; *Works of Love, KW* XVI; *JP* II 1123 and pp. 594–95; VII, pp. 48–49, 90.

simply to substitute the immediate for "faith."[5] If that is done, then it is ridiculous to deny that there has always been faith. This puts faith in the rather commonplace company of feelings, moods, idiosyncrasies, *vapeurs* [vagaries], etc. If so, philosophy may be correct in saying that one ought not to stop there. But nothing justifies philosophy in using this language. Faith is preceded by a movement of infinity; only then does faith commence, *nec opinate* [unexpected], by virtue of the absurd. This I can certainly understand without consequently maintaining that I have faith. If faith is nothing more than philosophy makes it out to be, then even Socrates went further, much further, instead of the reverse—that he did not attain it. In an intellectual sense, he did make the movement of infinity. His ignorance is the infinite resignation. This task alone is a suitable one for human capabilities, even though it is disdained these days; but only when this has been done, only when the individual has emptied himself in the infinite, only then has the point been reached where faith can break through.

The paradox of faith, then, is this: that the single individual is higher than the universal, that the single individual—to recall a distinction in dogmatics rather rare these days—determines his relation to the universal by his relation to the absolute, not his relation to the absolute by his relation to the universal. The paradox may also be expressed in this way: that there is an absolute duty to God, for in this relationship of duty the individual relates himself as the single individual absolutely to the absolute. In this connection, to say that it is a duty to love God means something different from the above, for if this duty is absolute, then the ethical is reduced to the relative. From this it

5. See Hegel, *Encyclopädie, Logik,* para. 63, *Werke,* VI, pp. 128–31; *J.A.,* VIII, pp. 166–69; *Hegel's Logic,* pp. 97–99, especially, p. 99: "With what is here called faith or immediate knowledge must also be identified inspiration, the heart's revelations, the truths implanted in man by nature, and also in particular, healthy reason or Common Sense, as it is called. All these forms agree in adopting as their leading principle the immediacy, or self-evident way in which a fact or body of truths is presented in consciousness." See also Hegel, *Philosophische Propädeutik,* para. 72, *Werke,* XVIII, p. 75; *J.A.,* III, p. 97. See *JP* I 49; II 1096; the latter includes a reference to Hegel.

does not follow that the ethical should be invalidated; rather, the ethical receives a completely different expression, a paradoxical expression, such as, for example, that love to God may bring the knight of faith to give his love to the neighbor—an expression opposite to that which, ethically speaking, is duty.

If this is not the case, then faith has no place in existence, then faith is a spiritual trial and Abraham is lost, inasmuch as he gave in to it.

This paradox cannot be mediated, for it depends specifically on this: that the single individual is only the single individual. As soon as this single individual wants to express his absolute duty in the universal, becomes conscious of it in the universal, he recognizes that he is involved in a spiritual trial, and then, if he really does resist it, he will not fulfill the so-called absolute duty, and if he does not resist it, then he sins, even though his act *re-aliter* [as a matter of fact] turns out to be what was his absolute duty. What should Abraham have done, for instance? If he had said to someone: I love Isaac more than anything in the world and that is why it is so hard for me to sacrifice him—the other person very likely would have shaken his head and said: Why sacrifice him, then? Or, if the other had been smart, he probably would have seen through Abraham and perceived that he was manifesting feelings that glaringly contradicted his action.

The story of Abraham contains such a paradox. The ethical expression for his relation to Isaac is that the father must love the son. This ethical relation is reduced to the relative in contradistinction to the absolute relation to God. To the question "Why?" Abraham has no other answer than that it is an ordeal, a temptation that, as noted above, is a synthesis of its being for the sake of God and for his own sake. In fact, these two determinants correspond in ordinary language. For instance, if we see someone doing something that does not conform to the universal, we say that he is hardly doing it for God's sake, meaning thereby that he is doing it for his own sake. The paradox of faith has lost the intermediary, that is, the universal. On the one side, it has the expression for the highest egotism (to do the terrible act, do it for one's own sake), on the other side, the expression for the most absolute devotion, to do it for God's sake. Faith itself cannot be mediated into the universal, for thereby it is canceled. Faith is this paradox, and the single individual simply cannot make himself understandable to anyone. People fancy that the single individual can make himself understandable to another single individual in the same situation. Such a view would be unthinkable if in our day we were not trying in so many ways to sneak slyly into greatness. The one knight of faith cannot help the other at all. Either the single individual himself becomes the knight of faith by accepting the paradox or he never becomes one. Partnership in these areas is utterly unthinkable. Only the single individual can ever give himself a more explicit explanation of what is to be understood by Isaac. And even though an ever so precise determination could be made, generally speaking, of what is to be understood by Isaac (which, incidentally, would be a ridiculous self-contradiction—to bring the single individual, who in fact stands outside the universal, under universal categories when he is supposed to act as the single individual who is outside the universal), the single individual would never be able to be convinced of this by others, only by himself as the single individual. Thus, even if a person were craven and base enough to want to become a knight of faith on someone else's responsibility, he would never come to be one, for only the single individual becomes that as the single individual, and this is the greatness of it—which I certainly can understand without becoming involved in it, since I lack the courage—but this is also the terribleness of it, which I can understand even better.

As we all know, Luke 14:26 offers a remarkable teaching on the absolute duty to God: "If any one comes to me and does not hate his own father and mother and wife and children and brothers and sisters, yes, and even his own life, he cannot be my disciple." This is a hard saying. Who can bear to listen to it?[6] This is the reason, too, that we seldom hear it. But this silence is only an

6. See John 6:60.

escape that is of no avail. Meanwhile, the theological student learns that these words appear in the New Testament, and in one or another exegetical resource book[7] he finds the explanation that μισεῖν [to hate] in this passage and in a few other passages *per* μείωσιν [by weakening] means: *minus diligo, posthabeo, non colo, nihili facio* [love less, esteem less, honor not, count as nothing]. The context in which these words appear, however, does not seem to confirm this appealing explanation. In the following verse we are told that someone who wants to erect a tower first of all makes a rough estimate to see if he is able to finish it, lest he be mocked later. The close proximity of this story and the verse quoted seems to indicate that the words are to be taken in their full terror in order that each person may examine himself to see if he can erect the building.

If that pious and accommodating exegete, who by dickering this way hopes to smuggle Christianity into the world, succeeded in convincing one person that grammatically, linguistically, and κατ' ἀναλογίαν [by analogy] this is the meaning of that passage, then it is to be hoped that he at the same time would succeed in convincing the same person that Christianity is one of the most miserable things in the world. The teaching that in one of its most lyrical outpourings, in which the consciousness of its eternal validity overflows most vigorously, has nothing to offer except an overblown word that signifies nothing but only suggests that one should be less kind, less attentive, more indifferent, the teaching that in the moment it gives the appearance of wanting to say something terrible ends by slavering instead of terrifying—that teaching certainly is not worth standing up for.[8]

The words are terrible, but I dare say that they can be understood without the necessary consequence that the one who has understood them has the courage to do what he has understood. One ought to be sufficiently honest, however, to admit what it

7. See C. G. Bretschneider, *Lexicon Manuale Graeco-Latinum in Libros Novi Testamenti,* I–II (Leipzig: 1829), II, p. 87.

8. The reference is to the practice of standing for the reading of the Gospel text for the day.

says, to admit that it is great even though one himself lacks the courage to do it. Anyone who acts thus will not exclude himself from participation in this beautiful story, for in a way it does indeed have a kind of comfort for the person who does not have the courage to begin construction of the tower. But honest he must be, and he must not speak of this lack of courage as humility, since, on the contrary, it is pride, whereas the courage of faith is the one and only humble courage.

It is easy to see that if this passage is to have any meaning it must be understood literally. God is the one who demands absolute love. Anyone who in demanding a person's love believes that this love is demonstrated by his becoming indifferent to what he otherwise cherished is not merely an egotist but is also stupid, and anyone demanding that kind of love simultaneously signs his own death sentence insofar as his life is centered in this desired love. For example, a man requires his wife to leave her father and mother, but if he considers it a demonstration of her extraordinary love to him that she for his sake became an indifferent and lax daughter etc., then he is far more stupid than the stupid. If he had any idea of what love is, he would wish to discover that she was perfect in her love as a daughter and sister, and he would see therein that she would love him more than anyone in the kingdom. Thus what would be regarded as a sign of egotism and stupidity in a person may by the help of an exegete be regarded as a worthy representation of divinity.

But how to hate them [Luke 14:26]? I shall not review here the human distinction, either to love or to hate, not because I have so much against it, for at least it is passionate, but because it is egotistic and does not fit here. But if I regard the task as a paradox, then I understand it—that is, I understand it in the way one can understand a paradox. The absolute duty can lead one to do what ethics would forbid, but it can never lead the knight of faith to stop loving. Abraham demonstrates this. In the moment he is about to sacrifice Isaac, the ethical expression for what he is doing is: he hates Isaac. But if he actually hates Isaac, he can rest assured that God does not demand this of him, for

Cain[9] and Abraham are not identical. He must love Isaac with his whole soul. Since God claims Isaac, he must, if possible, love him even more, and only then can he *sacrifice* him, for it is indeed this love for Isaac that makes his act a sacrifice by its paradoxical contrast to his love for God. But the distress and the anxiety in the paradox is that he, humanly speaking, is thoroughly incapable of making himself understandable. Only in the moment when his act is in absolute contradiction to his feelings, only then does he sacrifice Isaac, but the reality of his act is that by which he belongs to the universal, and there he is and remains a murderer.

Furthermore, the passage in Luke must be understood in such a way that one perceives that the knight of faith can achieve no higher expression whatsoever of the universal (as the ethical) in which he can save himself. Thus if the Church were to insist on this sacrifice from one of its members, we would have only a tragic hero. The idea of the Church is not qualitatively different from the idea of the state. As soon as the single individual can enter into it by a simple mediation, and as soon as the single individual has entered into the paradox, he does not arrive at the idea of the Church; he does not get out of the paradox, but he must find therein either his salvation or his damnation. A Church-related hero such as that expresses the universal in his act, and there will be no one in the Church, not even his father and mother, who does not understand him. But a knight of faith he is not, and in fact he has a response different from Abraham's; he does not say that this is an ordeal [*Prøvelse*] or a temptation [*Fristelse*] in which he is being tried [*forsøges*].

As a rule, passages such as this one in Luke are not quoted. We are afraid to let people loose; we are afraid that the worst will happen as soon as the single individual feels like behaving as the single individual. Furthermore, existing as the single individual is considered to be the easiest thing in the world, and thus people must be coerced into becoming the universal. I can share neither that fear nor that opinion, and for the same reason. Any

9. See Genesis 4:2–16.

one who has learned that to exist as the single individual is the most terrible of all will not be afraid to say that it is the greatest of all, but he must say this in such a way that his words do not become a pitfall for one who is confused but instead help him into the universal, although his words could create a little room for greatness. Anyone who does not dare to mention such passages does not dare to mention Abraham, either. Moreover, to think that existing as the single individual is easy enough contains a very dubious indirect concession with respect to oneself, for anyone who actually has any self-esteem and concern for his soul is convinced that the person who lives under his own surveillance alone in the big wide world lives more stringently and retired than a maiden in her virgin's bower. It may well be that there are those who need coercion, who, if they were given free rein, would abandon themselves like unmanageable animals to selfish appetites. But a person will demonstrate that he does not belong to them precisely by showing that he knows how to speak in fear and trembling, and speak he must out of respect for greatness, so that it is not forgotten out of fear of harm, which certainly will not come if he speaks out of a knowledge of greatness, a knowledge of its terrors, and if one does not know the terrors, one does not know the greatness, either.

Let us consider in somewhat more detail the distress and anxiety in the paradox of faith. The tragic hero relinquishes himself in order to express the universal; the knight of faith relinquishes the universal in order to become the single individual. As said previously, everything depends on one's position. Anyone who believes that it is fairly easy to be the single individual can always be sure that he is not a knight of faith, for fly-by-nights and itinerant geniuses are not men of faith. On the contrary, this knight knows that it is glorious to belong to the universal. He knows that it is beautiful and beneficial to be the single individual who translates himself into the universal, the one who, so to speak, personally produces a trim, clean, and, as far as possible, faultless edition of himself, readable by all. He knows that it is refreshing to become understandable to himself in the universal in such a way that he understands it, and every individual who understands him in turn understands the universal in him, and both rejoice in the security of the universal. He knows it is beautiful to be born as the single individual who has his home in the universal, his friendly abode, which immediately receives him with open arms if he wants to remain in it. But he also knows that up higher there winds a lonesome trail, steep and narrow; he knows it is dreadful to be born solitary outside of the universal, to walk without meeting one single traveler. He knows very well where he is and how he relates to men. Humanly speaking, he is mad and cannot make himself understandable to anyone. And yet "to be mad" is the mildest expression. If he is not viewed in this way, then he is a hypocrite, and the higher he ascends this path, the more appalling a hypocrite he is.

The knight of faith knows that it is inspiring to give up himself for the universal, that it takes courage to do it, but that there also is a security in it precisely because it is a giving up for the universal. He knows that it is glorious to be understood by everyone of noble mind and in such a way that the observer himself is ennobled thereby. This he knows, and he feels as if bound; he could wish that this was the task that had been assigned to him. In the same way, Abraham now and then could have wished that the task were to love Isaac as a father would and should, understandable to all, memorable for all time; he could have wished that the task were to sacrifice Isaac to the universal, that he could inspire fathers to laudable deeds—and he is almost shocked at the thought that for him such wishes constitute a spiritual trial [*Anfægtelse*] and must be treated as such, for he knows that he is walking a lonesome path and that he is accomplishing nothing for the universal but is himself only being tried [*forsøges*] and tested [*prøves*]. What did Abraham accomplish for the universal? Let me speak humanly about it, purely humanly! It takes him seventy years to have the son of old age.[10] It takes him seventy years to get what others get in a hurry and enjoy

10. Johannes de Silentio reckons that Abraham was married at the age of thirty and that Isaac was born when Abraham was one hundred.

for a long time. Why? Because he is being tested and tempted [*fristes*]. Is it not madness! But Abraham had faith, and only Sarah vacillated and got him to take Hagar as concubine, but this is also why he had to drive her away. He receives Isaac—then once again he has to be tested. He knew that it is glorious to express the universal, glorious to live with Isaac. But this is not the task. He knew that it is kingly to sacrifice a son like this to the universal; he himself would have found rest therein, and everybody would have rested approvingly in his deed, as the vowel rests in its quiescent letter.[11] But that is not the task—he is being tested. That Roman commander widely known by his nickname Cunctator[12] stopped the enemy by his delaying tactics—in comparison with him, what a procrastinator Abraham is—but he does not save the state. This is the content of 130 years. Who can endure it? Would not his contemporaries, if such may be assumed, have said, "What an everlasting procrastination this is; Abraham finally received a son, it took long enough, and now he wants to sacrifice him—is he not mad? If he at least could explain why he wants to do it, but it is always an ordeal [*Prøvelse*]." Nor could Abraham explain further, for his life is like a book under divine confiscation and never becomes *publice juris* [public property].

This is the terrifying aspect of it. Anyone who does not perceive this can always be sure that he is no knight of faith, but the one who perceives it will not deny that even the most tried of tragic heroes dances along in comparison with the knight of faith, who only creeps along slowly. Having perceived this and

11. The allusion is to certain Hebrew consonants that can serve also to indicate certain vowel sounds. Kierkegaard, following Jacob Christian Lindberg, *Hovedreglerne af den hebraiske Grammatik* (2 ed., Copenhagen: 1835), pp. 8, 17–18, and the interpretation given in Ludvig Beatus Meyer, *Fremmed Ordbog* (Copenhagen: 1837), uses metaphorically the Danish version of *matres lectionis* or *literae quiescibiles: Hvile-Bogstaver*. According to Lindberg and Meyer, such a consonant may be sounded as a consonant, or, quiescent, it may "rest" [*hvile*] in the vowel indicated while it remains unsounded as a consonant. Here Johannes de Silentio seems to have inverted the relationship. See *Either/Or,* I, *KW* III; *JP* II 2263; V 5378.

12. Fabius Maximus (d. 203 B.C.), who in 217 B.C. fought against Hannibal and was named Cunctator (Latin: delayer) because of his deliberate tactic of harassing Hannibal's troops but never joining battle.

made sure that he does not have the courage to understand it, he may then have an intimation of the wondrous glory the knight attains in becoming God's confidant, the Lord's friend, if I may speak purely humanly, in saying "You"[13] to God in heaven, whereas even the tragic hero addresses him only in the third person.

The tragic hero is soon finished, and his struggles are soon over; he makes the infinite movement and is now secure in the universal. The knight of faith, however, is kept in a state of sleeplessness, for he is constantly being tested [prøves], and at every moment there is the possibility of his returning penitently to the universal, and this possibility may be a spiritual trial [Anfægtelse] as well as the truth. He cannot get any information on that from any man, for in that case he is outside the paradox.

First and foremost, then, the knight of faith has the passion to concentrate in one single point the whole of the ethical that he violates, in order that he may give himself the assurance that he actually loves Isaac with his whole soul.* If he cannot, he is undergoing spiritual trial. Next, he has the passion to produce this assurance instantaneously and in such a way that it is fully as valid as in the first moment. If he cannot do this, then he never moves from the spot, for then he always has to begin all over again. The tragic hero also concentrates in one point the ethical

---

13. Danish *Du*, the familiar second-person singular pronoun, used (as in German) in addressing family members and close friends. In English, "thou" is a relic of the same form, but current ecclesiastical usage endows it with the distance and solemnity of the old formal second-person plural form.

* May I once again throw some light on the distinction between the collisions of the tragic hero and of the knight of faith. The tragic hero assures himself that the ethical obligation is totally present in him by transforming it into a wish. Agamemnon, for example, can say: To me the proof that I am not violating my fatherly duty is that my duty is my one and only wish. Consequently we have wish and duty face to face with each other. Happy is the life in which they coincide, in which my wish is my duty and the reverse, and for most men the task in life is simply to adhere to their duty and to transform it by their enthusiasm into their wish. The tragic hero gives up his wish in order to fulfill this duty. For the knight of faith, wish and duty are also identical, but he is required to give up both. If he wants to relinquish by giving up his wish, he finds no rest, for it is indeed his duty. If he wants to adhere to the duty and to his wish, he does not become the knight of faith, for the absolute duty specifically demanded that he should give it up. The tragic hero found a higher expression of duty but not an absolute duty.

he has teleologically overstepped, but in that case he has a stronghold in the universal. The knight of faith has simply and solely himself, and therein lies the dreadfulness. Most men live in adherence to an ethical obligation in such a way that they let each day have its cares,[14] but then they never attain this passionate concentration, this intense consciousness. In achieving this, the tragic hero may find the universal helpful in one sense, but the knight of faith is alone in everything. The tragic hero does it and finds rest in the universal; the knight of faith is constantly kept in tension. Agamemnon gives up Iphigenia and thereby finds rest in the universal, and now he proceeds to sacrifice her. If Agamemnon had not made the movement, if at the crucial moment his soul, instead of being passionately concentrated, had wandered off into the usual silly talk about having several daughters and that *vielleicht das Ausserordentliche* [perhaps the extraordinary] still could happen—then, of course, he is no hero but a pauper. Abraham, too, has the concentration of the hero, although it is far more difficult for him, since he has no stronghold at all in the universal, but he makes one movement more, whereby he gathers his soul back to the marvel. If Abraham had not done this, he would have been only an Agamemnon, insofar as it can be otherwise explained how wanting to sacrifice Isaac can be justified when the universal is not thereby benefited.

Whether the single individual actually is undergoing a spiritual trial or is a knight of faith, only the single individual himself can decide. But from the paradox itself several characteristic signs may be inferred that are understandable also to someone not in it. The true knight of faith is always absolute isolation; the spurious knight is sectarian. This is an attempt to jump off the narrow path of the paradox and become a tragic hero at a bargain price. The tragic hero expresses the universal and sacrifices himself for it. In place of that, the sectarian Punchinello has a private theater, a few good friends and comrades who represent

14. See Matthew 6:34.

the universal just about as well as the court observers in *Gulddaasen*[15] represent justice. But the knight of faith, on the other hand, is the paradox; he is the single individual, simply and solely the single individual without any connections and complications. This is the dreadfulness the sectarian weakling cannot endure. Instead of learning from this that he is incapable of doing the great and then openly admitting it—naturally something I cannot but approve, since it is what I myself do—the poor wretch thinks that by joining up with other poor wretches he will be able to do it. But it does not work; in the world of spirit cheating is not tolerated. A dozen sectarians go arm in arm with one another; they are totally ignorant of the solitary spiritual trials that are in store for the knight of faith and that he dares not flee precisely because it would be still more dreadful if he presumptuously forced his way forward. The sectarians deafen one another with their noise and clamor, keep anxiety away with their screeching. A hooting carnival crowd like that thinks it is assaulting heaven, believes it is going along the same path as the knight of faith, who in the loneliness of the universe never hears another human voice but walks alone with his dreadful responsibility.

The knight of faith is assigned solely to himself; he feels the pain of being unable to make himself understandable to others, but he has no vain desire to instruct others. The pain is his assurance; vain desire he does not know—for that his soul is too earnest. The spurious knight quickly betrays himself by this expertise that he has acquired instantly. He by no means grasps what is at stake: that insofar as another individual is to go the same path he must become the single individual in the very same way and then does not require anyone's advice, least of all the advice of one who wants to intrude. Here again, unable to endure the martyrdom of misunderstanding, a person jumps off this path and conveniently enough chooses the worldly admiration of expertise. The true knight of faith is a witness, never the

---

15. Christian Olufsen, *Gulddaasen,* II, 10 (Copenhagen: 1793), p. 64.

teacher, and therein lies the profound humanity, which has much more to it than this trifling participation in the woes and welfare of other people that is extolled under the name of sympathy, although, on the contrary, it is nothing more than vanity. He who desires only to be a witness confesses thereby that no man, not even the most unimportant man, needs another's participation or is to be devalued by it in order to raise another's value. But since he himself did not obtain at bargain price what he obtained, he does not sell it at bargain price, either. He is not so base that he accepts the admiration of men and in return gives them his silent contempt; he knows that true greatness is equally accessible to all.

Therefore, either there is an absolute duty to God—and if there is such a thing, it is the paradox just described, that the single individual as the single individual is higher than the universal and as the single individual stands in an absolute relation to the absolute—or else faith has never existed because it has always existed, or else Abraham is lost, or else one must interpret the passage in Luke 14 as did that appealing exegete and explain the similar and corresponding passages[16] in the same way.

16. Deuteronomy 13:6–7, 33:9; Matthew 10:37, 19:29. The final copy has 1 Corinthians 7:11 in parentheses.

THE SICKNESS UNTO DEATH

A
Despair Is the Sickness unto Death

A.
DESPAIR IS A SICKNESS OF THE SPIRIT, OF THE SELF, AND ACCORDINGLY CAN TAKE THREE FORMS: IN DESPAIR NOT TO BE CONSCIOUS OF HAVING A SELF (NOT DESPAIR IN THE STRICT SENSE); IN DESPAIR NOT TO WILL TO BE ONESELF; IN DESPAIR TO WILL TO BE ONESELF

A human being is spirit. But what is spirit? Spirit is the self. But what is the self? The self is a relation that relates itself to itself or is the relation's relating itself to itself in the relation; the self is not the relation but is the relation's relating itself to itself. A human being is a synthesis of the infinite and the finite, of the temporal and the eternal, of freedom and necessity, in short, a synthesis.[1] A

---

1. On the conception of man as a synthesis of the temporal and the eternal, see, for example, *The Concept of Irony, KW* II; *Either/Or,* II, *KW* IV; *The Concept of Anxiety, KW* VIII; *Stages, KW* XI; *Postscript, KW* XII; *The Point of View, KW* XXII; *JP* I 55; VI 5792.

---

synthesis is a relation between two. Considered in this way, a human being is still not a self.

In the relation between two, the relation is the third as a negative unity,[2] and the two relate to the relation and in the relation to the relation; thus under the qualification of the psychical the relation between the psychical and the physical is a relation. If, however, the relation relates itself to itself, this relation is the positive third, and this is the self.[3]

Such a relation that relates itself to itself, a self, must either have established itself or have been established by another.

If the relation that relates itself to itself has been established by another, then the relation is indeed the third, but this relation, the third, is yet again a relation and relates itself to that which established the entire relation.

The human self is such a derived, established relation, a relation that relates itself to itself and in relating itself to itself relates itself to another. This is why there can be two forms of despair in the strict sense. If a human self had itself established itself, then there could be only one form: not to will to be oneself, to will to do away with oneself, but there could not be the form: in despair to will to be oneself. This second formulation is specifically the expression for the complete dependence of the relation (of the self), the expression for the inability of the self to arrive at or to be in equilibrium and rest by itself, but only, in relating itself to itself, by relating itself to that which has established the entire relation. Yes, this second form of despair (in despair to will to be oneself) is so far from designating merely a distinctive kind of despair that, on the contrary, all despair ultimately can be traced back to and be resolved in it. If the despairing person is aware of his despair, as he thinks he is, and does not speak meaninglessly of it as of something that is happening to him (somewhat as one suffering from dizziness[4] speaks

2. See "the first self," *Eighteen Upbuilding Discourses, KW* V.

3. See "the deeper self," ibid.

4. See *The Concept of Anxiety, KW* VIII; *Three Discourses at the Communion on Fridays, KW* XVIII. See Historical Introduction, p. xii.

in nervous delusion of a weight on his head or of something that has fallen down on him, etc., a weight and a pressure that nevertheless are not something external but a reverse reflection of the internal) and now with all his power seeks to break the despair by himself and by himself alone—he is still in despair and with all his presumed effort only works himself all the deeper into deeper despair. The misrelation of despair is not a simple misrelation but a misrelation in a relation that relates itself to itself and has been established by another, so that the misrelation in that relation which is for itself [*for sig*]⁵ also reflects itself infinitely in the relation to the power that established it.

The formula that describes the state of the self when despair is completely rooted out is this: in relating itself to itself and in willing to be itself, the self rests transparently in the power that established it.

B.

THE POSSIBILITY AND THE ACTUALITY OF DESPAIR

Is despair an excellence or a defect? Purely dialectically, it is both. If only the abstract idea of despair is considered, without any thought of someone in despair, it must be regarded as a surpassing excellence. The possibility of this sickness is man's superiority over the animal, and this superiority distinguishes him in quite another way than does his erect walk, for it indicates infinite erectness or sublimity, that he is spirit. The possibility of this sickness is man's superiority over the animal; to be aware of this sickness is the Christian's superiority over the natural man; to be cured of this sickness is the Christian's blessedness.

Consequently, to be able to despair is an infinite advantage, and yet to be in despair is not only the worst misfortune and misery— no, it is ruination. Generally this is not the case with the relation

---

5. An individual as a psycho-somatic duality is "in himself"; in relating itself to itself, the duality is "for itself." See pp. 13–14. Cf. Sartre's *en soi* and *pour soi*. Jean-Paul Sartre, *Being and Nothingness*, tr. Hazel E. Barnes (New York: Philosophical Library, 1956), pp. 73–220, 617–28.

between possibility and actuality.[6] If it is an excellence to be able to be this or that, then it is an even greater excellence to be that; in other words, to be is like an ascent when compared with being able to be. With respect to despair, however, to be is like a descent when compared with being able to be; the descent is as infinitely low as the excellence of possibility is high. Consequently, in relation to despair, not to be in despair is the ascending scale. But here again this category is ambiguous. Not to be in despair is not the same as not being lame, blind, etc. If not being in despair signifies neither more nor less than not being in despair, then it means precisely to be in despair. Not to be in despair must signify the destroyed possibility of being able to be in despair; if a person is truly not to be in despair, he must at every moment destroy the possibility. This is generally not the case in the relation between actuality and possibility. Admittedly, thinkers say that actuality is annihilated possibility, but that is not entirely true; it is the consummated, the active possibility.[7] Here, on the contrary, the actuality (not to be in despair) is the impotent, destroyed possibility, which is why it is also a negation; although actuality in relation to possibility is usually a corroboration, here it is a denial.

Despair is the misrelation in the relation of a synthesis that relates itself to itself. But the synthesis is not the misrelation; it is merely the possibility, or in the synthesis lies the possibility of the misrelation. If the synthesis were the misrelation, then despair would not exist at all, then despair would be something that lies in human nature as such. That is, it would not be despair; it would be something that happens to a man, something he suffers, like a disease to which he succumbs, or like death, which is everyone's fate. No, no, despairing lies in man himself. If he were not a synthesis, he could not despair at all; nor could he despair if the synthesis in its original state from the hand of God were not in the proper relationship.

Where, then, does the despair come from? From the relation in which the synthesis relates itself to itself, inasmuch as God,

6. See *JP* IV 4030.
7. See *Fragments, KW* VII.

who constituted man a relation, releases it from his hand, as it were—that is, inasmuch as the relation relates itself to itself. And because the relation is spirit, is the self, upon it rests the responsibility for all despair at every moment of its existence, however much the despairing person speaks of his despair as a misfortune and however ingeniously he deceives himself and others, confusing it with that previously mentioned case of dizziness, with which despair, although qualitatively different, has much in common, since dizziness corresponds, in the category of the psychical, to what despair is in the category of the spirit, and it lends itself to numerous analogies to despair.

Once the misrelation, despair, has come about, does it continue as a matter of course? No, it does not continue as a matter of course; if the misrelation continues, it is not attributable to the misrelation but to the relation that relates itself to itself. That is, every time the misrelation manifests itself and every moment it exists, it must be traced back to the relation. For example, we say that someone catches a sickness, perhaps through carelessness. The sickness sets in and from then on is in force and is an *actuality* whose origin recedes more and more into the *past.* It would be both cruel and inhuman to go on saying, "You, the sick person, are in the process of catching the sickness right now." That would be the same as perpetually wanting to dissolve the actuality of the sickness into its possibility. It is true that he was responsible for catching the sickness, but he did that only once; the continuation of the sickness is a simple result of his catching it that one time, and its progress cannot be traced at every moment to him as the cause; he brought it upon himself, but it cannot be said that he *is bringing* it upon himself. To despair, however, is a different matter. Every actual moment of despair is traceable to possibility; every moment he is in despair he *is bringing* it upon himself. It is always the present tense; in relation to the actuality there is no pastness of the past: in every actual moment of despair the person in despair bears all the past as a present in possibility. The reason for this is that to despair is a qualification of spirit and relates to the eternal in man. But he cannot rid himself of the eternal—no, never in all eternity. He cannot throw it away once and for all, nothing is more impossible; at any moment that he does not have it, he must have thrown it or is throwing it away—but it comes again, that is, every moment he is in despair he is bringing his despair upon himself. For despair is not attributable to the misrelation but to the relation that relates itself to itself. A person cannot rid himself of the relation to himself any more than he can rid himself of his self, which, after all, is one and the same thing, since the self is the relation to oneself.

C.
DESPAIR IS "THE SICKNESS UNTO DEATH"

This concept, the sickness unto death, must, however, be understood in a particular way. Literally it means a sickness of which the end and the result are death. Therefore we use the expression "fatal sickness" as synonymous with the sickness unto death. In that sense, despair cannot be called the sickness unto death. Christianly understood, death itself is a passing into life. Thus, from a Christian point of view, no earthly, physical sickness is the sickness unto death, for death is indeed the end of the sickness, but death is not the end. If there is to be any question of a sickness unto death in the strictest sense, it must be a sickness of which the end is death and death is the end. This is precisely what despair is.

But in another sense despair is even more definitely the sickness unto death. Literally speaking, there is not the slightest possibility that anyone will die from this sickness or that it will end in physical death. On the contrary, the torment of despair is precisely this inability to die. Thus it has more in common with the situation of a mortally ill person when he lies struggling with death and yet cannot die. Thus to be sick *unto* death is to be unable to die, yet not as if there were hope of life; no, the hopelessness is that there is not even the ultimate hope, death. When death is the greatest danger, we hope for life; but when we learn to know the even greater danger, we hope for death. When the danger is so great that death becomes the hope, then despair is the hopelessness of not even being able to die.

It is in this last sense that despair is the sickness unto death, this tormenting contradiction, this sickness of the self, perpetually to be dying, to die and yet not die, to die death. For to die signifies that it is all over, but to die death means to experience dying, and if this is experienced for one single moment, one thereby experiences it forever. If a person were to die of despair as one dies of a sickness, then the eternal in him, the self, must be able to die in the same sense as the body dies of sickness. But this is impossible; the dying of despair continually converts itself into a living. The person in despair cannot die; "no more than the dagger can slaughter thoughts" can despair consume the eternal, the self at the root of despair, whose worm does not die and whose fire is not quenched.[8] Nevertheless, despair is veritably a self-consuming, but an impotent self-consuming that cannot do what it wants to do. What it wants to do is to consume itself, something it cannot do, and this impotence is a new form of self-consuming, in which despair is once again unable to do what it wants to do, to consume itself; this is an intensification, or the law of intensification. This is the provocativeness or the cold fire in despair, this gnawing that burrows deeper and deeper in impotent self-consuming. The inability of despair to consume him is so remote from being any kind of comfort to the person in despair that it is the very opposite. This comfort is precisely the torment, is precisely what keeps the gnawing alive and keeps life in the gnawing, for it is precisely over this that he despairs (not as having despaired): that he cannot consume himself, cannot get rid of himself, cannot reduce himself to nothing. This is the formula for despair raised to a higher power, the rising fever in this sickness of the self.

An individual in despair despairs over *something*. So it seems for a moment, but only for a moment; in the same moment the

8. See Mark 9:48.

true despair or despair in its true form shows itself. In despairing over *something,* he really despaired over *himself,* and now he wants to be rid of himself. For example, when the ambitious man whose slogan is "Either Caesar or nothing"[9] does not get to be Caesar, he despairs over it. But this also means something else: precisely because he did not get to be Caesar, he now cannot bear to be himself. Consequently he does not despair because he did not get to be Caesar but despairs over himself because he did not get to be Caesar. This self, which, if it had become Caesar, would have been in seventh heaven (a state, incidentally, that in another sense is just as despairing), this self is now utterly intolerable to him. In a deeper sense, it is not his failure to become Caesar that is intolerable, but it is this self that did not become Caesar that is intolerable; or, to put it even more accurately, what is intolerable to him is that he cannot get rid of himself. If he had become Caesar, he would despairingly get rid of himself, but he did not become Caesar and cannot despairingly get rid of himself. Essentially, he is just as despairing, for he does not have his self, is not himself. He would not have become himself by becoming Caesar but would have been rid of himself, and by not becoming Caesar he despairs over not being able to get rid of himself. Thus it is superficial for someone (who probably has never seen anyone in despair, not even himself) to say of a person in despair: He is consuming himself. But this is precisely what he in his despair [wants] and this is precisely what he to his torment cannot do, since the despair has inflamed something that cannot burn or be burned up in the self.

Consequently, to despair over something is still not despair proper. It is the beginning, or, as the physician says of an illness, it has not yet declared itself. The next is declared despair, to despair over oneself. A young girl despairs of love, that is, she despairs over the loss of her beloved, over his death or his unfaithfulness to her. This is not declared despair; no, she despairs over herself. This self of hers, which she would have been rid of

9. *Aut* Caesar *aut nihil,* the motto of Caesar Borgia. See *Stages, KW* XI.

or would have lost in the most blissful manner had it become "his" beloved, this self becomes a torment to her if it has to be a self without "him." This self, which would have become her treasure (although, in another sense, it would have been just as despairing), has now become to her an abominable void since "he" died, or it has become to her a nauseating reminder that she has been deceived. Just try it, say to such a girl, "You are consuming yourself," and you will hear her answer, "O, but the torment is simply that I cannot do that."

To despair over oneself, in despair to will to be rid of oneself— this is the formula for all despair. Therefore the other form of despair, in despair to will to be oneself, can be traced back to the first, in despair not to will to be oneself, just as we previously resolved the form, in despair not to will to be oneself, into the form, in despair to will to be oneself (see A). A person in despair despairingly wills to be himself. But if he despairingly wills to be himself, he certainly does not want to be rid of himself. Well, so it seems, but upon closer examination it is clear that the contradiction is the same. The self that he despairingly wants to be is a self that he is not (for to will to be the self that he is in truth is the very opposite of despair), that is, he wants to tear his self away from the power that established it. In spite of all his despair, however, he cannot manage to do it; in spite of all his despairing efforts, that power is the stronger and forces him to be the self he does not want to be. But this is his way of willing to get rid of himself, to rid himself of the self that he is in order to be the self that he has dreamed up. He would be in seventh heaven to be the self he wants to be (although in another sense he would be just as despairing), but to be forced to be the self he does not want to be, that is his torment—that he cannot get rid of himself.

Socrates proved the immortality of the soul from the fact that sickness of the soul (sin) does not consume it as sickness of the body consumes the body.[10] Similarly, the eternal in a person can

10. Plato, *Republic*, X, 608 c–610; *Platonis quae extant opera*, I–IX, ed. F. Astius (Leipzig: 1819–32), V, pp. 79–85.

be proved by the fact that despair cannot consume his self, that precisely this is the torment of contradiction in despair. If there were nothing eternal in a man, he could not despair at all; if despair could consume his self, then there would be no despair at all.

Such is the nature of despair, this sickness of the self, this sickness unto death. The despairing person is mortally ill. In a completely different sense than is the case with any illness, this sickness has attacked the most vital organs, and yet he cannot die. Death is not the end of the sickness, but death is incessantly the end. To be saved from this sickness by death is an impossibility, because the sickness and its torment—and the death—are precisely this inability to die.

This is the state in despair. No matter how much the despairing person avoids it, no matter how successfully he has completely lost himself (especially the case in the form of despair that is ignorance of being in despair) and lost himself in such a manner that the loss is not at all detectable—eternity nevertheless will make it manifest that his condition was despair and will nail him to himself so that his torment will still be that he cannot rid himself of his self, and it will become obvious that he was just imagining that he had succeeded in doing so. Eternity is obliged to do this, because to have a self, to be a self, is the greatest concession, an infinite concession, given to man, but it is also eternity's claim upon him.

B
THE UNIVERSALITY OF THIS
SICKNESS (DESPAIR)

Just as a physician might say that there very likely is not one single living human being who is completely healthy, so anyone who really knows mankind might say that there is not one single living human being who does not despair a little, who does not secretly harbor an unrest, an inner strife, a disharmony, an anxiety about an unknown something or a something he does not even dare to try to know, an anxiety about some possibility in existence or an anxiety about himself, so that, just as the physician speaks of going around with an illness in the body, he walks around with a sickness, carries around a sickness of the spirit that signals its presence at rare intervals in and through an anxiety he cannot explain. In any case, no human being ever lived and no one lives outside of Christendom who has not despaired, and no one in Christendom if he is not a true Christian, and insofar as he is not wholly that, he still is to some extent in despair.

No doubt this observation will strike many people as a paradox, an overstatement, and also a somber and depressing point of view. But it is none of these things. It is not somber, for, on the contrary, it tries to shed light on what generally is left somewhat obscure; it is not depressing but instead is elevating, inasmuch as it views every human being under the destiny of the highest claim upon him, to be spirit; nor is it a paradox but, on the contrary, a consistently developed basic view, and therefore neither is it an overstatement.

However, the customary view of despair does not go beyond appearances, and thus it is a superficial view, that is, no view at all. It assumes that every man must himself know best whether he is in despair or not. Anyone who says he is in despair is regarded as being in despair, and anyone who thinks he is not is therefore regarded as not. As a result, the phenomenon of despair is infrequent rather than quite common. That one is in despair is not a rarity; no, it is rare, very rare, that one is in truth not in despair.

The common view has a very poor understanding of despair. Among other things, it completely overlooks (to name only this, which, properly understood, places thousands and thousands and millions in the category of despair), it completely overlooks that not being in despair, not being conscious of being in despair, is precisely a form of despair. In a much deeper sense, the position of the common view in interpreting despair is like that of the common view in determining whether a person is sick—in a much deeper sense, for the common view understands far less well what spirit is (and lacking this understanding, one cannot understand despair, either) than it understands sickness and health. As a rule, a person is considered to be healthy when he himself does not say that he is sick, not to mention when he himself says that he is well. But the physician has a different view of sickness. Why? Because the physician has a defined and developed conception of what it is to be healthy and ascertains a man's condition accordingly. The physician knows that just as there is merely imaginary sickness there is also merely imaginary health, and in the latter case he first takes measures to disclose the sickness. Generally speaking, the physician, precisely because he is a physician (well informed), does not have complete confidence in what a person says about his condition. If everyone's statement about his condition, that he is healthy or sick, were completely reliable, to be a physician would be a delusion. A physician's task is not only to prescribe remedies but also, first and foremost, to identify the sickness, and consequently his first task is to ascertain whether the supposedly sick person is actually sick or whether the supposedly healthy person is perhaps actually sick. Such is also the relation of the physician of the soul to despair. He knows what despair is; he recognizes it and therefore is satisfied neither with a person's declaration that he is not in despair nor with his declaration that he is. It must be pointed out that in a certain sense it is not even always the case that those who say they despair are in despair. Despair can be affected, and as a qualification of the spirit it may also be mistaken for and confused with all sorts of transitory states, such as dejection, inner conflict, which pass without developing into despair. But the physician of the soul properly regards these also as forms of despair; he sees very well that they are affectation. Yet this very affectation is despair: he sees very well that this dejection etc. are not of great significance, but precisely this—that it has and acquires no great significance—is despair.

The common view also overlooks that despair is dialectically different from what is usually termed a sickness, because it is a sickness of the spirit. Properly understood, this dialectic again brings thousands under the definition of despair. If at a given time a physician has made sure that someone is well, and that person later becomes ill, then the physician may legitimately say that this person at one time was healthy but now is sick. Not so with despair. As soon as despair becomes apparent, it is manifest that the individual was in despair. Hence, at no moment is it possible to decide anything about a person who has not been saved by having been in despair, for whenever that which triggers his despair occurs, it is immediately apparent that he has been in despair his whole life. On the other hand, when someone gets a fever, it can by no means be said that it is now apparent that he has had a fever all his life. Despair is a qualification of the spirit, is related to the eternal, and thus has something of the eternal in its dialectic.

Despair is not only dialectically different from a sickness, but all its symptoms are also dialectical, and therefore the superficial view is very easily deceived in determining whether or not despair is present. Not to be in despair can in fact signify precisely to be in despair, and it can signify having been rescued from being in despair. A sense of security and tranquillity can signify being in despair; precisely this sense of security and tranquillity can be the despair, and yet it can signify having conquered despair and having won peace. Not being in despair is not similar to not being sick, for not being sick cannot be the same as being sick, whereas not being in despair can be the very same as being in despair. It is not with despair as with a sickness, where feeling indisposed is the sickness. By no means. Here again the indisposition is dialectical. Never to have sensed this indisposition is precisely to be in despair.

This means and has its basis in the fact that the condition of man, regarded as spirit (and if there is to be any question of despair, man must be regarded as defined by spirit), is always critical. We speak of a crisis in relation to sickness but not in relation to health. Why not? Because physical health is an immediate qualification that first becomes dialectical in the condition of sickness, in which the question of a crisis arises. Spiritually, or when man is regarded as spirit, both health and sickness are critical; there is no immediate health of the spirit.

As soon as man ceases to be regarded as defined by spirit (and in that case there can be no mention of despair, either) but only as psychical-physical synthesis, health is an immediate qualification, and mental or physical sickness is the only dialectical qualification. But to be unaware of being defined as spirit is precisely what despair is. Even that which, humanly speaking, is utterly beautiful and lovable—a womanly youthfulness that is perfect peace and harmony and joy—is nevertheless despair. To be sure, it is happiness, but happiness is not a qualification of spirit, and deep, deep within the most secret hiding place of happiness there dwells also anxiety, which is despair; it very much wishes to be allowed to remain there, because for despair the most cherished and desirable place to live is in the heart of happiness. Despite its illusory security and tranquillity, all immediacy is anxiety and thus, quite consistently, is most anxious about nothing. The most gruesome description of something most terrible does not make immediacy as anxious as a subtle, almost carelessly, and yet deliberately and calculatingly dropped allusion to some indefinite something—in fact, immediacy is made most anxious by a subtle implication that it knows very well what is being talked about. Immediacy probably does not know it, but reflection never snares so unfailingly as when it fashions its snare out of nothing, and reflection is never so much itself as when it is—nothing. It requires extraordinary reflection, or, more correctly, it requires great faith to be able to endure reflection upon nothing—that is, infinite reflection. Consequently, even that which is utterly beautiful and lovable, womanly youthfulness, is still despair, is happiness. For that reason, it is impossible to slip through life on this immediacy. And if this happiness does succeed in slipping through, well, it is of little use, for it is despair. Precisely because the sickness of despair is totally dialectical, it is the worst misfortune never to have had that sickness: it is a true godsend to get it, even if it is the most dangerous of illnesses, if one does not want to be cured of it. Generally it is regarded as fortunate to be cured of a sickness; the sickness itself is the misfortune.

Therefore, the common view that despair is a rarity is entirely wrong; on the contrary, it is universal. The common view, which assumes that everyone who does not think or feel he is in despair is not or that only he who says he is in despair is, is totally false. On the contrary, the person who without affectation says that he is in despair is still a little closer, is dialectically closer, to being cured than all those who are not regarded as such and who do not regard themselves as being in despair. The physician of souls will certainly agree with me that, on the whole, most men live without ever becoming conscious of being destined as spirit[11]—hence all the so-called security, contentment with life, etc., which is simply despair. On the other hand, those who say they are in despair are usually either those who have so deep a nature that they are bound to become conscious as spirit or those whom bitter experiences and dreadful decisions have assisted in becoming conscious as spirit: it is either the one or the other; the person who is really devoid of despair is very rare indeed.

There is so much talk about human distress and wretchedness— I try to understand it and have also had some intimate acquaintance with it—there is so much talk about wasting a life, but only that person's life was wasted who went on living so deceived by life's joys or its sorrows that he never became decisively and eternally conscious as spirit, as self, or, what amounts to the same thing, never became aware and in the deepest sense never gained the impression that there is a God and that "he," he himself, his self, exists before this God—an infinite benefaction that is never gained except through despair. What wretchedness that so many go on living this way, cheated of this most blessed of thoughts! What wretchedness that we are engrossed in or encourage the human throng to be engrossed in everything else, using them to supply the energy for the drama of life but never reminding them of this blessedness. What wretchedness that they are lumped together and deceived instead of being split apart so that each individual may gain the highest, the only thing worth living for and enough to live in for an eternity. I think that I could weep an eternity over the existence of such wretchedness! And to me an even more horrible expression of this most terrible sickness and misery is that it is hidden—not only that the person suffering from it may wish to hide it and may succeed, not only that it can so live in a man that no one, no one detects it, no, but also that it can be so hidden in a man that he himself is not aware of it! And when the hourglass has run out, the hourglass of temporality, when the noise of secular life has grown silent and its restless or ineffectual activism has come

11. *JP* III 3567.

to an end, when everything around you is still, as it is in eternity, then—whether you were man or woman, rich or poor, dependent or independent, fortunate or unfortunate, whether you ranked with royalty and wore a glittering crown or in humble obscurity bore the toil and heat of the day, whether your name will be remembered as long as the world stands and consequently as long as it stood or you are nameless and run nameless in the innumerable multitude, whether the magnificence encompassing you surpassed all human description or the most severe and ignominious human judgment befell you—eternity asks you and every individual in these millions and millions about only one thing: whether you have lived in despair or not, whether you have despaired in such a way that you did not realize that you were in despair, or in such a way that you covertly carried this sickness inside of you as your gnawing secret, as a fruit of sinful love under your heart, or in such a way that you, a terror to others, raged in despair. And if so, if you have lived in despair, then, regardless of whatever else you won or lost, everything is lost for you, eternity does not acknowledge you, it never knew you—or, still more terrible, it knows you as you are known and it binds you to yourself in despair.

C
THE FORMS OF THIS SICKNESS
(DESPAIR)

The forms of despair may be arrived at abstractly by reflecting upon the constituents of which the self as a synthesis is composed. The self is composed of infinitude and finitude. However, this synthesis is a relation, and a relation that, even though it is derived, relates itself to itself, which is freedom.[12] The self is freedom. But freedom is the dialectical aspect of the categories of possibility and necessity.

However, despair must be considered primarily within the category of consciousness; whether despair is conscious or not constitutes the qualitative distinction between despair and despair. Granted, all despair regarded in terms of the concept is conscious, but this does not mean that the person who, according to the concept, may appropriately be said to be in despair is conscious of it himself. Thus, consciousness is decisive. Generally speaking, consciousness—that is, self-consciousness—is decisive with regard to the self. The more consciousness, the more self; the more consciousness, the more will; the more will, the

---

12. On derivation and freedom, see *JP* II 1251.

more self. A person who has no will at all is not a self; but the more will he has, the more self-consciousness he has also.

A.
DESPAIR CONSIDERED WITHOUT REGARD TO ITS BEING CONSCIOUS OR NOT, CONSEQUENTLY ONLY WITH REGARD TO THE CONSTITUENTS OF THE SYNTHESIS

a. Despair as Defined by Finitude/Infinitude

The self is the conscious synthesis of infinitude and finitude that relates itself to itself, whose task is to become itself, which can be done only through the relationship to God. To become oneself is to become concrete. But to become concrete is neither to become finite nor to become infinite, for that which is to become concrete is indeed a synthesis. Consequently, the progress of the becoming must be an infinite moving away from itself in the infinitizing of the self, and an infinite coming back to itself in the finitizing process. But if the self does not become itself, it is in despair, whether it knows that or not. Yet every moment that a self exists, it is in a process of becoming, for the self κατὰ δύναμιν [in potentiality] does not actually exist, is simply that which ought to come into existence. Insofar, then, as the self does not become itself, it is not itself; but not to be itself is precisely despair.

α. Infinitude's Despair Is to Lack Finitude

That this is so is due to the dialectic inherent in the self as a synthesis, and therefore each constituent is its opposite. No form of despair can be defined directly (that is, undialectically), but only by reflecting upon its opposite. The condition of the person in despair can be described directly, as the poet in fact does by giving him lines to speak.[13] But the despair can be defined only by way of its opposite, and if the lines are to have any poetic value,

---

13. On the significance of speaking, see, for example, *Fear and Trembling, KW* VI.

the coloring of the expression must contain the reflection of the dialectical opposite. Consequently, every human existence that presumably has become or simply wants to be infinite, in fact, every moment in which a human existence has become or simply wants to be infinite, is despair. For the self is the synthesis of which the finite is the limiting and the infinite the extending constituent. Infinitude's despair, therefore, is the fantastic, the unlimited, for the self is healthy and free from despair only when, precisely by having despaired, it rests transparently in God.

The fantastic, of course, is most closely related to the imagination [*Phantasien*], but the imagination in turn is related to feeling, knowing, and willing; therefore a person can have imaginary feeling, knowing, and willing. As a rule, imagination is the medium for the process of infinitizing; it is not a capacity, as are the others—if one wishes to speak in those terms, it is the capacity *instar omnium* [for all capacities]. When all is said and done, whatever of feeling, knowing, and willing a person has depends upon what imagination he has, upon how that person reflects himself— that is, upon imagination. Imagination is infinitizing reflection, and therefore the elder Fichte[14] quite correctly assumed that even in relation to knowledge the categories derive from the imagination. The self is reflection, and the imagination is reflection, is the rendition of the self as the self's possibility. The imagination is the possibility of any and all reflection, and the intensity of this medium is the possibility of the intensity of the self.

The fantastic is generally that which leads a person out into the infinite in such a way that it only leads him away from himself and thereby prevents him from coming back to himself.

When feeling becomes fantastic in this way, the self becomes only more and more volatilized and finally comes to be a kind

14. J. G. Fichte, *Grundriss des Eigenthümlichen der Wissenschaftslehre, Sämmtliche Werke,* I–XI (Berlin, Bonn: 1834–46), I, 1, pp. 386–87. Fichte regarded the "productive power of the imagination" as the source of the concept of the external world (the *Not-I*) and of the basic categories of thought.

See Anti-Climacus, *Practice in Christianity, KW* XX, where *Indbildningskraft* (also "imagination" in English) is used to stress the relation of the ethical and imagination, "the capacity for perfecting (idealizing)" (p. 178).

of abstract sentimentality that inhumanly belongs to no human being but inhumanly combines sentimentally, as it were, with some abstract fate—for example, humanity *in abstracto.* Just as the rheumatic is not master of his physical sensations, which are so subject to the wind and weather that he involuntarily detects any change in the weather etc., so also the person whose feeling has become fantastic is in a way infinitized, but not in such a manner that he becomes more and more himself, for he loses himself more and more.

So also with knowing, when it becomes fantastic. The law for the development of the self with respect to knowing, insofar as it is the case that the self becomes itself, is that the increase of knowledge corresponds to the increase of self-knowledge, that the more the self knows, the more it knows itself. If this does not happen, the more knowledge increases, the more it becomes a kind of inhuman knowledge, in the obtaining of which a person's self is squandered, much the way men were squandered on building pyramids, or the way men in Russian brass bands are squandered on playing just one note, no more, no less.[15]

The self is likewise gradually volatilized when willing becomes fantastic. Willing, then, does not continually become proportionately as concrete as it is abstract, so that the more infinite it becomes in purpose and determination, the more personally present and contemporary it becomes in the small part of the task that can be carried out at once, so that in being infinitized it comes back to itself in the most rigorous sense, so that when furthest away from itself (when it is most infinite in purpose and determination), it is simultaneously and personally closest to carrying out the infinitely small part of the work that can be accomplished this very day, this very hour, this very moment.

When feeling or knowing or willing has become fantastic, the entire self can eventually become that, whether in the more active form of plunging headlong into fantasy or in the more passive form of being carried away, but in both cases the person is

15. Each of the sixty members had a horn fashioned for a particular note, which was played only at appropriate times.

responsible. The self, then, leads a fantasized existence in abstract infinitizing or in abstract isolation, continually lacking its self, from which it only moves further and further away. Take the religious sphere, for example. The God-relationship is an infinitizing, but in fantasy this infinitizing can so sweep a man off his feet that his state is simply an intoxication. To exist before God may seem unendurable to a man because he cannot come back to himself, become himself. Such a fantasized religious person would say (to characterize him by means of some lines): "That a sparrow can live is comprehensible; it does not know that it exists before God. But to know that one exists before God, and then not instantly go mad or sink into nothingness!"

But to become fantastic in this way, and thus to be in despair, does not mean, although it usually becomes apparent, that a person cannot go on living fairly well, seem to be a man, be occupied with temporal matters, marry, have children, be honored and esteemed—and it may not be detected that in a deeper sense he lacks a self. Such things do not create much of a stir in the world, for a self is the last thing the world cares about and the most dangerous thing of all for a person to show signs of having. The greatest hazard of all, losing the self, can occur very quietly in the world, as if it were nothing at all. No other loss can occur so quietly; any other loss—an arm, a leg, five dollars, a wife, etc.—is sure to be noticed.

β. *Finitude's Despair Is to Lack Infinitude*

That this is so is due, as pointed out under α, to the dialectic inherent in the self as a synthesis, and therefore each constituent is its opposite.

To lack infinitude is despairing reductionism, narrowness. Of course, what is meant here is only ethical narrowness and limitation. As a matter of fact, in the world there is interest only in intellectual or esthetic limitation or in the indifferent (in which there is the greatest interest in the world), for the secular mentality is nothing more or less than the attribution of infinite worth to the indifferent. The secular view always clings tightly to the difference between man and man and naturally does not have any understanding of the one thing needful[16] (for to have it is spirituality), and thus has no understanding of the reductionism and narrowness involved in having lost oneself, not by being volatilized in the infinite, but by being completely finitized, by becoming a number instead of a self, just one more man, just one more repetition of this everlasting *Einerlei* [one and the same].

Despairing narrowness is to lack primitivity or to have robbed oneself of one's primitivity, to have emasculated oneself in a spiritual sense. Every human being is primitively intended to be a self, destined to become himself, and as such every self certainly is angular, but that only means that it is to be ground into shape, not that it is to be ground down smooth, not that it is utterly to abandon being itself out of fear of men, or even simply out of fear of men not to dare to be itself in its more essential contingency (which definitely is not to be ground down smooth), in which a person is still himself for himself. But whereas one kind of despair plunges wildly into the infinite and loses itself, another kind of despair seems to permit itself to be tricked out of its self by "the others." Surrounded by hordes of men, absorbed in all sorts of secular matters, more and more shrewd about the ways of the world—such a person forgets himself, forgets his name divinely understood, does not dare to believe in himself, finds it too hazardous to be himself and far easier and safer to be like the others, to become a copy, a number, a mass man.

Now this form of despair goes practically unnoticed in the world. Just by losing himself this way, such a man has gained an increasing capacity for going along superbly in business and social life, indeed, for making a great success in the world. Here there is no delay, no difficulty with his self and its infinitizing; he is as smooth as a rolling stone, as *courant* [passable] as a circulating coin. He is so far from being regarded as a person in despair that he is just what a human being is supposed to be. As is natu-

16. See Luke 10:42.

ral, the world generally has no understanding of what is truly appalling. The despair that not only does not cause one any inconvenience in life but makes life cozy and comfortable is in no way, of course, regarded as despair. That this is the world's view is borne out, for example, by practically all the proverbs, which are nothing more than rules of prudence. For example, we say that one regrets ten times for having spoken to once for having kept silent—and why? Because the external fact of having spoken can involve one in difficulties, since it is an actuality. But to have kept silent! And yet this is the most dangerous of all. For by maintaining silence, a person is thrown wholly upon himself; here actuality does not come to his aid by punishing him, by heaping the consequences of his speaking upon him. No, in this respect it is easy to keep silent. But the person who knows what is genuinely appalling fears most of all any mistake, any sin that takes an inward turn and leaves no outward trace. The world considers it dangerous to venture in this way—and why? Because it is possible to lose. Not to venture is prudent. And yet, precisely by not venturing it is so terribly easy to lose what would be hard to lose, however much one lost by risking, and in any case never this way, so easily, so completely, as if it were nothing at all—namely, oneself. If I have ventured wrongly, well, then life helps me by punishing me. But if I have not ventured at all, who helps me then? Moreover, what if by not venturing at all in the highest sense (and to venture in the highest sense is precisely to become aware of oneself) I cowardly gain all earthly advantages—and lose myself![17]

So it is with finitude's despair. Because a man is in this kind of despair, he can very well live on in temporality, indeed, actually all the better, can appear to be a man, be publicly acclaimed, honored, and esteemed, be absorbed in all the temporal goals. In fact, what is called the secular mentality consists simply of such men who, so to speak, mortgage themselves to the world. They use their capacities, amass money, carry on secular enterprises,

17. See Matthew 16:26.

calculate shrewdly, etc., perhaps make a name in history, but themselves they are not; spiritually speaking, they have no self, no self for whose sake they could venture everything, no self before God—however self-seeking they are otherwise.

b. Despair as Defined by Possibility/Necessity

Possibility and necessity are equally essential to becoming (and the self has the task of becoming itself in freedom). Possibility and necessity belong to the self just as do infinitude and finitude (ἄπειρον/πέρας [the unlimited/limited]).[18] A self that has no possibility is in despair, and likewise a self that has no necessity.

α. *Possibility's Despair Is to Lack Necessity*

That this is so is due, as pointed out previously, to the dialectic [inherent in the self as a synthesis].

Just as finitude is the limiting aspect in relation to infinitude, so also necessity is the constraint in relation to possibility. Inasmuch as the self as a synthesis of finitude and infinitude is established, is κατὰ δύναμιν [potential], in order to become itself it reflects itself in the medium of imagination, and thereby the infinite possibility becomes manifest. The self is κατὰ δύναμιν [potentially] just as possible as it is necessary, for it is indeed itself, but it has the task of becoming itself. Insofar as it is itself, it is the necessary, and insofar as it has the task of becoming itself, it is a possibility.

But if possibility outruns necessity so that the self runs away from itself in possibility, it has no necessity to which it is to return; this is possibility's despair. This self becomes an abstract possibility, it flounders around in possibility until it is exhausted, but it neither moves from the place where it is nor arrives anywhere, for necessity is literally the place where it is. To become is a movement away from that place, but to become oneself is a movement in that place.

Thus possibility seems greater and greater to the self; more

18. See, for example, Plato, *Philebus,* 30 a; *Platonis opera,* III, p. 316.

and more becomes possible because nothing becomes actual. Eventually everything seems possible, but this is exactly the point at which the abyss swallows up the self. It takes time for each little possibility to become actuality. Eventually, however, the time that should be used for actuality grows shorter and shorter; everything becomes more and more momentary. Possibility becomes more and more intensive—but in the sense of possibility, not in the sense of actuality, for the intensive in the sense of actuality means to actualize some of what is possible. The instant something appears to be possible, a new possibility appears, and finally these phantasmagoria follow one another in such rapid succession that it seems as if everything were possible, and this is exactly the final moment, the point at which the individual himself becomes a mirage.

What the self now lacks is indeed actuality, and in ordinary language, too, we say that an individual has become unreal. However, closer scrutiny reveals that what he actually lacks is necessity. The philosophers are mistaken when they explain necessity as a unity of possibility and actuality—no, actuality is the unity of possibility and necessity.[19] When a self becomes lost in possibility in this way, it is not merely because of a lack of energy; at least it is not to be interpreted in the usual way. What is missing is essentially the power to obey, to submit to the necessity in one's life, to what may be called one's limitations. Therefore, the tragedy is not that such a self did not amount to something in the world; no, the tragedy is that he did not become aware of himself, aware that the self he is is a very definite something and thus the necessary. Instead, he lost himself, because this self fantastically reflected itself in possibility. Even in seeing one*self* in a mirror it is necessary to recognize oneself, for if one does not, one does not see one*self* but only a human being. The mirror of possibility is no ordinary mirror; it must be used with extreme

19. "Necessity has been defined, and rightly so, as the union of possibility and actuality" (Hegel, *Encyclopädie der philosophischen Wissenschaften, Erster Theil, Die Logik, Werke,* VI, para. 147, p. 292; *J.A.,* VIII, p. 330; *Hegel's Logic,* tr. William Wallace [Oxford: Clarendon Press, 1975], p. 208).

caution, for, in the highest sense, this mirror does not tell the truth. That a self appears to be such and such in the possibility of itself is only a half-truth, for in the possibility of itself the self is still far from or is only half of itself. Therefore, the question is how the necessity of this particular self defines it more specifically. Possibility is like a child's invitation to a party; the child is willing at once, but the question now is whether the parents will give permission—and as it is with the parents, so it is with necessity.

In possibility everything is possible. For this reason, it is possible to become lost in possibility in all sorts of ways, but primarily in two. The one takes the form of desiring, craving; the other takes the form of the melancholy-imaginary (hope/fear or anxiety). Legends and fairy tales tell of the knight who suddenly sees a rare bird and chases after it, because it seems at first to be very close; but it flies again, and when night comes, he finds himself separated from his companions and lost in the wilderness where he now is. So it is also with desire's possibility. Instead of taking the possibility back into necessity, he chases after possibility—and at last cannot find his way back to himself.—In melancholy the opposite takes place in much the same way. Melancholically enamored, the individual pursues one of anxiety's possibilities, which finally leads him away from himself so that he is a victim of anxiety or a victim of that about which he was anxious lest he be overcome.

β. *Necessity's Despair Is to Lack Possibility*

If losing oneself in possibility may be compared with a child's utterance of vowel sounds, then lacking possibility would be the same as being dumb. The necessary is like pure consonants, but to express them there must be possibility. If this is lacking, if a human existence is brought to the point where it lacks possibility, then it is in despair and is in despair every moment it lacks possibility.

Generally it is thought that there is a certain age that is especially rich in hope, or we say that at a certain time, at a particular moment of life one is or was so rich in hope and possibility. All this, however, is merely a human manner of speaking that does not get at the truth; all this hope and all this despair are as yet neither authentic hope nor authentic despair.

What is decisive is that with God everything is possible.[20] This is eternally true and consequently true at every moment. This is indeed a generally recognized truth, which is commonly expressed in this way, but the critical decision does not come until a person is brought to his extremity, when, humanly speaking, there is no possibility. Then the question is whether he will believe that for God everything is possible, that is, whether he will *believe*. But this is the very formula for losing the understanding; to believe is indeed to lose the understanding in order to gain God. Take this analogy. Imagine that someone with a capacity to imagine terrifying nightmares has pictured to himself some horror or other that is absolutely unbearable. Then it happens to him, this very horror happens to him. Humanly speaking, his collapse is altogether certain—and in despair his soul's despair fights to be permitted to despair, to attain, if you please, the composure to despair, to obtain the total personality's consent to despair and be in despair; consequently, there is nothing or no one he would curse more than an attempt or the person making an attempt to hinder him from despairing, as the poet's poet so splendidly and incomparably expresses it (*Richard II*, III, 3):

> *Verwünscht sei Vetter, der mich abgelenkt*
> *Von dem bequemen Wege zur Verzweiflung.*
> [Beshrew thee, cousin, which didst lead me forth
> Of that sweet way I was in to despair!]

At this point, then, salvation is, humanly speaking, utterly impossible; but for God everything is possible! This is the battle of *faith*, battling, madly, if you will, for possibility, because possibility is the only salvation. When someone faints, we call for water, eau de Cologne, smelling salts; but when someone wants

20. See Matthew 19:26; Mark 10:27, 14:36; Luke 1:37.

to despair, then the word is: Get possibility, get possibility, possibility is the only salvation. A possibility—then the person in despair breathes again, he revives again, for without possibility a person seems unable to breathe. At times the ingeniousness of the human imagination can extend to the point of creating possibility, but at last—that is, when it depends upon *faith*—then only this helps: that for God everything is possible.

And so the struggle goes on. Whether or not the embattled one collapses depends solely upon whether he obtains possibility, that is, whether he will believe. And yet he understands that, humanly speaking, his collapse is altogether certain. This is the dialectic of believing. As a rule, a person knows only that this and that probably, most likely, etc. will not happen to him. If it does happen, it will be his downfall. The foolhardy person rushes headlong into a danger with this or that possibility, and if it happens, he despairs and collapses. The *believer* sees and understands his downfall, humanly speaking (in what has happened to him, or in what he has ventured), but he believes. For this reason he does not collapse. He leaves it entirely to God how he is to be helped, but he believes that for God everything is possible. To *believe* his downfall is impossible. To understand that humanly it is his downfall and nevertheless to believe in possibility is to believe. So God helps him also—perhaps by allowing him to avoid the horror, perhaps through the horror itself—and here, unexpectedly, miraculously, divinely, help does come. Miraculously, for it is a peculiar kind of pedantry to maintain that only 1,800 years ago did it happen that a person was aided miraculously. Whether a person is helped miraculously depends essentially upon the passion of the understanding whereby he has understood that help was impossible and depends next on how honest he was toward the power that nevertheless did help him. As a rule, however, men do neither the one nor the other; they cry out that help is impossible without once straining their understanding to find help, and afterward they ungratefully lie.

The believer has the ever infallible antidote for despair—

possibility—because for God everything is possible at every moment. This is the good health of faith that resolves contradictions. The contradiction here is that, humanly speaking, downfall is certain, but that there is possibility nonetheless. Good health generally means the ability to resolve contradictions. For example, in the realm of the bodily or physical, a draft is a contradiction, for a draft is disparately or undialectically cold and warm, but a good healthy body resolves this contradiction and does not notice the draft. So also with faith.

To lack possibility means either that everything has become necessary for a person or that everything has become trivial.

The determinist, the fatalist, is in despair and as one in despair has lost his self, because for him everything has become necessity. He is like that king who starved to death because all his food was changed to gold.[21] Personhood is a synthesis of possibility and necessity. Its continued existence is like breathing (*re*spiration), which is an inhaling and exhaling. The self of the determinist cannot breathe, for it is impossible to breathe necessity exclusively, because that would utterly suffocate a person's self. The fatalist is in despair, has lost God and thus his self, for he who does not have a God does not have a self, either. But the fatalist has no God, or, what amounts to the same thing, his God is necessity; since everything is possible for God, then God is this—that everything is possible. Therefore the fatalist's worship of God is at most an interjection, and essentially it is a muteness, a mute capitulation: he is unable to pray. To pray is also to breathe, and possibility is for the self what oxygen is for breathing. Nevertheless, possibility alone or necessity alone can no more be the condition for the breathing of prayer than oxygen alone or nitrogen alone can be that for breathing. For prayer there must be a God, a self—and possibility—or a self and possibility in a pregnant sense, because the existence of God means that everything is possible, or that everything is possible means

---

21. King Midas. Ovid, *Metamorphoses,* XI, 85–145; *Opera quæ extant* (Leipzig: 1828).

the existence of God; only he whose being has been so shaken that he has become spirit by understanding that everything is possible, only he has anything to do with God. That God's will is the possible makes me able to pray; if there is nothing but necessity, man is essentially as inarticulate as the animals.

It is quite different with the philistine-bourgeois mentality, that is, triviality, which also essentially lacks possibility. The philistine-bourgeois mentality is spiritlessness; determinism and fatalism are despair of spirit, but spiritlessness is also despair. The philistine-bourgeois mentality lacks every qualification of spirit and is completely wrapped up in probability, within which possibility finds its small corner; therefore it lacks the possibility of becoming aware of God. Bereft of imagination, as the philistine-bourgeois always is, whether alehouse keeper or prime minister, he lives within a certain trivial compendium of experiences as to how things go, what is possible, what usually happens. In this way, the philistine-bourgeois has lost his self and God. In order for a person to become aware of his self and of God, imagination must raise him higher than the miasma of probability, it must tear him out of this and teach him to hope and to fear—or to fear and to hope—by rendering possible that which surpasses the *quantum satis* [sufficient standard] of any experience. But the philistine-bourgeois mentality does not have imagination, does not want to have it, abhors it. So there is no help to be had here. And if at times existence provides frightful experiences that go beyond the parrot-wisdom of routine experience, then the philistine-bourgeois mentality despairs, then it becomes apparent that it was despair; it lacks faith's possibility of being able under God to save a self from certain downfall.

Fatalism and determinism, however, do have sufficient imagination to despair of possibility, sufficient possibility to discover impossibility; the philistine-bourgeois mentality reassures itself with the trite and obvious and is just as much in despair whether things go well or badly. Fatalism and determinism lack possibility for the relaxing and mitigating, for the tempering of necessity, and thus lack possibility as mitigation. The philistine-bourgeois mentality thinks that it controls possibility, that it has tricked this prodigious elasticity into the trap or madhouse of probability, thinks that it holds it prisoner; it leads possibility around imprisoned in the cage of probability, exhibits it, imagines itself to be the master, does not perceive that precisely thereby it has imprisoned itself in the thralldom of spiritlessness and is the most wretched of all. The person who gets lost in possibility soars high with the boldness of despair; he for whom everything became necessity overstrains himself in life and is crushed in despair; but the philistine-bourgeois mentality spiritlessly triumphs.

B.
DESPAIR AS DEFINED BY CONSCIOUSNESS

The ever increasing intensity of despair depends upon the degree of consciousness or is proportionate to its increase: the greater the degree of consciousness, the more intensive the despair. This is everywhere apparent, most clearly in despair at its maximum and minimum. The devil's despair is the most intensive despair, for the devil is sheer spirit and hence unqualified consciousness and transparency; there is no obscurity in the devil that could serve as a mitigating excuse. Therefore, his despair is the most absolute defiance. This is despair at its maximum. Despair at its minimum is a state that—yes, one could humanly be tempted almost to say that in a kind of innocence it does not even know that it is despair. There is the least despair when this kind of unconsciousness is greatest; it is almost a dialectical issue whether it is justifiable to call such a state despair.

a. The Despair That Is Ignorant of Being Despair,
or the Despairing Ignorance of Having a Self
and an Eternal Self

That this condition is nevertheless despair and is properly designated as such manifests what in the best sense of the word may be called the obstinacy of truth. *Veritas est index sui et falsi* [Truth is the criterion of itself and of the false].[22] But this obstinacy of truth certainly is not respected; likewise, it is far from being the case that men regard the relationship to truth, relating themselves to the truth, as the highest good, and it is very far from being the case that they Socratically regard being in error in this manner as the worst misfortune[23]—the sensate in them usually far outweighs their intellectuality. For example, if a man is presumably happy, imagines himself to be happy, although considered in the light of truth he is unhappy, he is usually far from wanting to be wrenched out of his error. On the contrary, he becomes indignant, he regards anyone who does so as his worst enemy, he regards it as an assault bordering on murder in the sense that, as is said, it murders his happiness. Why? Because he is completely dominated by the sensate and the sensate-psychical, because he lives in sensate categories, the pleasant and the unpleasant, waves goodbye to spirit, truth, etc., because he is too sensate to have the courage to venture out and to endure being spirit. However vain and conceited men may be, they usually have a very meager conception of themselves nevertheless, that is, they have no conception of being spirit, the absolute that a human being can be; but vain and conceited they are—on the basis of comparison. Imagine a house with a basement, first floor, and second floor planned so that there is or is supposed to be a social distinction between the occupants according to floor. Now, if what it means to be a human being is compared with such a house, then all too regrettably the sad and ludicrous truth about the majority of people is that in their own house they prefer to live in the basement. Every human being is a psychical-physical synthesis intended to be spirit; this is the building, but he prefers to live in the basement, that is, in sensate categories.

22. Freely quoted from Benedict de Spinoza, *Ethics,* II, *Scholium* to *Propositio* 43; *Opera philosophica omnia,* ed. A. Gfroerer (Stuttgart: 1830). See *Fragments, KW* VII; *Prefaces, KW* IX.

23. See Diogenes Laertius, II, 5, 31; *Diogen Laërtses vitis philosophorum* (Leipzig: 1833; *ASKB* 1109), p. 75; *Diogen Laërtses filosofiske Historie,* I–II, tr. Børge Riisbrigh (Copenhagen: 1812; *ASKB* 1110–11), I, p. 70; *Stages, KW* XI; *Postscript, KW* XII; *Two Ages,* p. 10, *KW* XIV; *JP* IV 4267.

Moreover, he not only prefers to live in the basement—no, he loves it so much that he is indignant if anyone suggests that he move to the superb upper floor that stands vacant and at his disposal, for he is, after all, living in his own house.

No, to be in error is, quite un-Socratically, what men fear least of all.[24] There are amazing examples that amply illustrate this. A thinker erects a huge building, a system, a system embracing the whole of existence, world history, etc., and if his personal life is considered, to our amazement the appalling and ludicrous discovery is made that he himself does not personally live in this huge, domed palace but in a shed alongside it, or in a doghouse, or at best in the janitor's quarters. Were he to be reminded of this by one single word, he would be insulted. For he does not fear to be in error if he can only complete the system—with the help of being in error.

Therefore, it makes no difference whether the person in despair is ignorant that his condition is despair—he is in despair just the same. If the despair is perplexity [*Forvildelse*], then the ignorance of despair simply adds error [*Vildfarelse*] to it. The relation between ignorance and despair is similar to that between ignorance and anxiety (see *The Concept of Anxiety*[25] by Vigilius Haufniensis); the anxiety that characterizes spiritlessness is recognized precisely by its spiritless sense of security. Nevertheless, anxiety lies underneath; likewise, despair also lies underneath, and when the enchantment of illusion is over, when existence begins to totter, then despair, too, immediately appears as that which lay underneath.

Compared with the person who is conscious of his despair, the despairing individual who is ignorant of his despair is simply a negativity further away from the truth and deliverance. De-

24. The paragraph is a token of Kierkegaard's polemic against Hegelianism and other system building that dissolves the individual into the whole and is thereby indifferent to individual existence, that of the thinker himself and of others. See, for example, *Fragments, KW* VII; *Postscript, KW* XII; on Socrates, *JP* IV 4267.

25. See "The Anxiety of Spiritlessness," *The Concept of Anxiety, KW* VIII (*SV* IV 363–66).

spair itself is a negativity; ignorance of it, a new negativity. However, to reach the truth, one must go through every negativity, for the old legend about breaking a certain magic spell is true: the piece has to be played through backwards or the spell is not broken.[26] However, it is in only one sense, in a purely dialectic sense, that the individual who is ignorant of his despair is further from the truth and deliverance than one who knows it and yet remains in despair, for in another sense, an ethical-dialectical sense, the person who is conscious of his despair and remains in it is further from deliverance, because his despair is more intensive. Yet ignorance is so far from breaking the despair of changing despair to nondespair that it can in fact be the most dangerous form of despair. To his own demoralization, the individual who in ignorance is in despair is in a way secured against becoming aware—that is, he is altogether secure in the power of despair.

An individual is furthest from being conscious of himself as spirit when he is ignorant of being in despair. But precisely this—not to be conscious of oneself as spirit—is despair, which is spiritlessness, whether the state is a thoroughgoing moribundity, a merely vegetative life, or an intense, energetic life, the secret of which is still despair. In the latter case, the individual in despair is like the consumptive: when the illness is most critical, he feels well, considers himself to be in excellent health, and perhaps seems to others to radiate health.

This form of despair (ignorance of it) is the most common in the world; indeed, what we call the world, or, more exactly, what Christianity calls the world—paganism and the natural man in Christendom, paganism as it was historically and is (and paganism in Christendom is precisely this kind of despair) is despair but is ignorant of the fact. To be sure, paganism and likewise the natural man make the distinction between being in despair and not being in despair—that is, they talk about despair as if only some individuals despaired. Nevertheless, this distinction is just as misleading as the distinction that paganism and the natural

26. See *Irische Elfenmärchen* (T. C. Croker, *Fairy Tales and Traditions of the South of Ireland*, I–III [London: 1825–28]), tr. Jakob and Wilhelm Grimm (Leipzig: 1826), p. lxxxiii.

man make between love and self-love, as if all this love were not essentially self-love. Beyond this misleading distinction, however, paganism and also the natural man cannot possibly go, because to be ignorant of being in despair is the specific feature of despair.

It is easy to see from all this that the esthetic conception of spiritlessness by no means provides the criterion for judging what is despair and what is not, which, incidentally, is quite in order, for if what is spirit cannot be defined esthetically, how can the esthetic answer a question that simply does not exist for it! It would also be very stupid to deny that individual pagans as well as pagan nations *en masse* have accomplished amazing feats that have inspired and also will inspire poets, to deny that paganism boasts examples of what esthetically cannot be admired enough. It would also be foolish to deny that in paganism the natural man can and does lead a life very rich in esthetic enjoyment, using in the most tasteful manner every favor granted him, and even letting art and science serve to heighten, enhance, and refine his pleasure. No, the esthetic category of spiritlessness does not provide the criterion for what is and what is not despair; what must be applied is the ethical-religious category: spirit or, negatively, the lack of spirit, spiritlessness. Every human existence that is not conscious of itself as spirit or conscious of itself before God as spirit, every human existence that does not rest transparently in God but vaguely rests in and merges in some abstract universality (state, nation, etc.) or, in the dark about his self, regards his capacities merely as powers to produce without becoming deeply aware of their source, regards his self, if it is to have intrinsic meaning, as an indefinable something—every such existence, whatever it achieves, be it most amazing, whatever it explains, be it the whole of existence, however intensively it enjoys life esthetically—every such existence is nevertheless despair. That is what the ancient Church Fathers[27] meant when they said that the virtues of the pagans were glittering vices:

27. See Augustine, *The City of God*, XIX, 25; *Sancti Aurelii Augustini . . . opera*, I–XVII (Bassani: 1797–1804); *Fragments, KW* VII.

they meant that the heart of paganism was despair, that paganism was not conscious before God as spirit. That is why the pagan (to cite this as an example, although it touches this whole investigation in a much more profound way) judged suicide with such singular irresponsibility, yes, praised suicide, which for spirit is the most crucial sin, escaping from existence in this way, mutinying against God. The pagan lacked the spirit's definition of a self, and therefore it judged *sui*cide [*S e l v mordet: self-murder*] in that way; and the same pagan who judged suicide in that way passed severe moral judgment on stealing, unchastity, etc. He lacked the point of view for suicide, he lacked the God-relationship and the self; in purely pagan thinking, suicide is neutral, something entirely up to the pleasure of each individual, since it is no one else's business. If an admonition against suicide were to be given from the viewpoint of paganism, it would have to be in the long, roundabout way of showing that suicide breaks the relation of obligation to other men. The point that suicide is basically a crime against God completely escapes the pagan.[28] Therefore, it cannot be said that the suicide is despair, for such a remark would be a thoughtless hysteron-proteron;[29] but it may be said that such a judging of suicide by the pagan was despair.

Yet there is and remains a difference, and it is a qualitative difference, between paganism in the stricter sense and paganism in Christendom, the distinction that Vigilius Haufniensis[30] pointed out with respect to anxiety, namely, that paganism does indeed lack spirit but that it still is qualified in the direction of spirit, whereas paganism in Christendom lacks spirit in a departure from spirit or in a falling away and therefore is spiritlessness in the strictest sense.

---

28. This view of suicide holds for the Stoics but not, for example, for Socrates and Plato. See *Phaedo,* 61-62.

29. Anachronism.

30. See *The Concept of Anxiety, KW* VIII.

b. The Despair That Is Conscious of Being Despair and Therefore Is Conscious of Having a Self in Which There Is Something Eternal and Then Either in Despair Does Not Will to Be Itself or in Despair Wills to Be Itself

Here, of course, the distinction must be made as to whether or not the person who is conscious of his despair has the true conception of what despair is. Admittedly, he can be quite correct, according to his own idea of despair, to say that he is in despair; he may be correct about being in despair, but that does not mean that he has the true conception of despair. If his life is considered according to the true conception of despair, it is possible that one must say: You are basically deeper in despair than you know, your despair is on an even profounder level. So it is also with the pagan (to recall the previous reference). When he regarded himself as being in despair by comparing himself with others, he was probably correct about his being in despair but wrong in regarding the others as not being in despair—that is, he did not have the true conception of despair.

On the one hand, then, the true conception of despair is indispensable for conscious despair. On the other hand, it is imperative to have clarity about oneself—that is, insofar as simultaneous clarity and despair are conceivable. To what extent perfect clarity about oneself as being in despair can be combined with being in despair, that is, whether this clarity of knowledge and of self-knowledge might not simply wrench a person out of despair, make him so afraid of himself that he would stop being in despair, we will not determine here; we will not even make an attempt in that direction, since this whole investigation will be taken up later. Without pursuing the idea to this dialectical extreme, we merely point out here that just as the level of consciousness of what despair is can vary exceedingly, so also can the level of consciousness of one's own state that it is despair. Actual life is too complex merely to point out abstract contrasts such as that between a despair that is completely unaware of being so and a despair that is completely aware of being so. Very often the person in despair probably has a dim idea of his own state, although here again the nuances are myriad. To some degree, he is aware of being in despair, feels it the way a person does who walks around with a physical malady but does not want to acknowledge forthrightly the real nature of the illness. At one moment, he is almost sure that he is in despair; the next moment, his indisposition seems to have some other cause, something outside of himself, and if this were altered, he would not be in despair. Or he may try to keep himself in the dark about his state through diversions and in other ways, for example, through work and busyness as diversionary means, yet in such a way that he does not entirely realize why he is doing it, that it is to keep himself in the dark. Or he may even realize that he is working this way in order to sink his soul in darkness and does it with a certain keen discernment and shrewd calculation, with psychological insight; but he is not, in a deeper sense, clearly conscious of what he is doing, how despairingly he is conducting himself, etc. There is indeed in all darkness and ignorance a dialectical interplay between knowing and willing, and in comprehending a person one may err by accentuating knowing exclusively or willing exclusively.

As pointed out earlier, the level of consciousness intensifies the despair. To the extent that a person has the truer conception of despair, if he still remains in despair, and to the extent that he is more clearly conscious of being in despair—to that extent the despair is more intensive. The person who, with a realization that suicide is despair and to that extent with a true conception of the nature of despair, commits suicide is more intensively in despair than one who commits suicide without a clear idea that suicide is despair; conversely, the less true his conception of despair, the less intensive his despair. On the other hand, a person who with a clearer consciousness of himself (self-consciousness) commits suicide is more intensively in despair than one whose soul, by comparison, is in confusion and darkness.

I shall now examine the two forms of conscious despair in such a way as to point out also a rise in the consciousness of the nature of despair and in the consciousness that one's state is despair, or, what amounts to the same thing and is the salient point, a rise in the consciousness of the self. The opposite to being in despair is to have faith. Therefore, the formula set forth above, which describes a state in which there is no despair at all, is entirely correct, and this formula is also the formula for faith: in relating itself to itself and in willing to be itself, the self rests transparently in the power that established it (cf. A, A).

α. *In Despair Not to Will to Be Oneself: Despair in Weakness*
To call this form despair in weakness already casts a reflection on the second form, β, in despair to will to be oneself. Thus the opposites are only relative. No despair is entirely free of defiance; indeed, the very phrase "not to will to be" implies defiance. On the other hand, even despair's most extreme defiance is never really free of some weakness. So the distinction is only relative. The one form is, so to speak, feminine despair, the other, masculine despair.*

---

* An occasional psychological observation of actual life will confirm that this idea, which is sound in thought and consequently shall and must prove to be correct, does in fact prove to be correct, and it will confirm that this classification embraces the entire actuality of despair; for only bad temper, not despair, is associated with children, because we are entitled only to assume that the eternal is present in the child κατὰ δύναμιν [potentially], not to demand it of him as of the adult, for whom it holds that he is meant to have it. I am far from denying that women may have forms of masculine despair and, conversely, that men may have forms of feminine despair, but these are exceptions. And of course the ideal is also a rarity, and only ideally is this distinction between masculine and feminine despair altogether true. However much more tender and sensitive woman may be than man, she has neither the egotistical concept of the self nor, in a decisive sense, intellectuality. But the feminine nature is devotedness, givingness, and it is unfeminine if it is not that. Strange to say, no one can be as coy (and this word was coined especially for women), so almost cruelly hard to please as a woman—and yet by nature she is devotedness, and (this is precisely the wonder of it) all this actually expresses that her nature is devotedness. For precisely because she carries in her being this total feminine devotedness, nature has affectionately equipped her with an instinct so sensitive that by comparison the most superior masculine reflection is as nothing. This devotedness on the part of woman, this, to speak as a Greek, divine gift and treasure, is too great a good to be tossed away blindly, and yet no clear-sighted human reflection is capable of seeing sharply enough to use it properly. That is why nature has looked after her: blindfolded, she instinctively sees more clearly than the most clear-sighted reflection; instinctively she sees what she should admire, that to which she should give herself. Devotedness is the one unique quality that woman has, and that is also why nature took it upon itself to be her

(1) DESPAIR OVER THE EARTHLY OR OVER SOMETHING EARTHLY

This is pure immediacy or immediacy containing a quantitative reflection.—Here there is no infinite consciousness of the self, of what despair is, or of the condition as one of despair. The despair is only a suffering, a succumbing to the pressure of external factors; in no way does it come from within as an act. The appearance of such words as "the self" and "despair" in the language of immediacy is due, if you will, to an innocent abuse of language, a playing with words, like the children's game of playing soldier.

The *man of immediacy* is only psychically qualified (insofar as there really can be immediacy without any reflection at all); his self, he himself, is an accompanying something within the dimensions of temporality and secularity, in immediate connection with "the other" (τοἕτερον), and has but an illusory appearance of having anything eternal in it. The self is bound up in immediacy with the other in desiring, craving, enjoying, etc., yet passively; in its craving, this self is a dative, like the "me" of a child. Its dialectic is: the pleasant and the unpleasant; its concepts are: good luck, bad luck, fate.

---

guardian. That is the reason, too, why womanliness comes into existence only through a metamorphosis; it comes into existence when woman's illimitable coyness expresses itself as feminine devotedness. By nature, however, woman's devotedness also enters into despair, is again a mode of despair. In devotion she loses herself, and only then is she happy, only then is she herself; a woman who is happy without devotion, that is, without giving her self, no matter to what she gives it, is altogether unfeminine. A man also gives himself—and he is a poor kind of man who does not do so—but his self is not devotion (this is the expression for feminine substantive devotion), nor does he gain his self by devotion, as woman in another sense does; he has himself. He gives himself, but his self remains behind as a sober awareness of devotion, whereas woman, with genuine femininity, abandons herself, throws her self into that to which she devotes herself. Take this devotion away, then her self is also gone, and her despair is: not to will to be oneself. The man does not give himself in this way, but the second form of despair also expresses the masculine form: in despair to will to be oneself.

The above pertains to the relation between masculine and feminine despair. But it is to be borne in mind that this does not refer to devotion to God or to the God-relationship, which will be considered in Part Two. In the relationship to God, where the distinction of man-woman vanishes, it holds for men as well as for women that devotion is the self and that in the giving of oneself the self is gained. This holds equally for man and woman, although it is probably true that in most cases the woman actually relates to God only through the man.

Now something *happens* that impinges (*upon* + *to strike*) upon this immediate self and makes it despair. In another sense, it cannot happen at this point; since the self has no reflection, there must be an external motivation for the despair, and the despair is nothing more than a submitting. By a "stroke of fate" that which to the man of immediacy is his whole life, or, insofar as he has a minuscule of reflection, the portion thereof to which he especially clings, is taken from him; in short, he becomes, as he calls it, unhappy, that is, his immediacy is dealt such a crushing blow that it cannot reproduce itself: he despairs. Or—and although this is rarely seen in actuality, it is dialectically quite in order—this despair on the part of immediacy is occasioned by what the man of immediacy calls extraordinary good luck, for immediacy as such is so extremely fragile that every *quid nimis* [excess] that requires reflection of it brings it to despair.

So he despairs—that is, in a strange reversal and in complete mystification about himself, he calls it despairing. But to despair is to lose the eternal—and of this loss he does not speak at all, he has no inkling of it. In itself, to lose the things of this world is not to despair; yet this is what he talks about, and this is what he calls despairing. In a certain sense, what he says is true, but not in the way he understands it; he is conversely situated, and what he says must be interpreted conversely: he stands and points to what he calls despair but is not despair, and in the meantime, sure enough, despair is right there behind him without his realizing it. It is as if someone facing away from the town hall and courthouse pointed straight ahead and said: There is the town hall and courthouse. He is correct, it is there—if he turns around. He is not in despair—this is not true—and yet he is correct in saying it. He claims he is in despair, he regards himself as dead, as a shadow of himself. But dead he is not; there is still, one might say, life in the person. If everything, all the externals, were to change suddenly, and if his desire were fulfilled, then there would be life in him again, then spontaneity and immediacy would escalate again, and he would begin to live all over again. This is the only way immediacy knows how to strive, the only thing it knows: to despair and faint—and yet, that about which he knows the least is despair. He despairs and faints, and after that lies perfectly still as if he were dead, a trick like "playing dead"; immediacy resembles certain lower animals that have no weapon or means of defense other than to lie perfectly still and pretend that they are dead.

Meanwhile, time passes. If help arrives from the outside, the person in despair comes alive again, he begins where he left off; a self he was not, and a self he did not become, but he goes on living, qualified only by immediacy. If there is no external help, something else frequently happens in actual life. In spite of everything, there is still life in the person, but he says that "he will never be himself again." He now acquires a little understanding of life, he learns to copy others, how they manage their lives—and he now proceeds to live the same way. In Christendom he is also a Christian, goes to church every Sunday, listens to and understands the pastor, indeed, they have a mutual understanding; he dies, the pastor ushers him into eternity for ten rix-dollars—but a self he was not, and a self he did not become.

This form of despair is: in despair not to will to be oneself. Or even lower: in despair not to will to be a self. Or lowest of all: in despair to will to be someone else, to wish for a new self. Immediacy actually has no self, it does not know itself; thus it cannot recognize itself and therefore generally ends in fantasy. When immediacy despairs, it does not even have enough self to wish or dream that it had become that which it has not become. The man of immediacy helps himself in another way: he wishes to be someone else. This is easily verified by observing immediate persons; when they are in despair, there is nothing they desire more than to have been someone else or to become someone else. In any case, it is difficult to keep from smiling at one who despairs in this way, who, humanly speaking and despite being in despair, is so very innocent. As a rule, one who despairs in this way is very comical. Imagine a self (and next to God there is nothing as eternal as a self), and then imagine that it suddenly occurs to a self that it might become someone other—than itself. And yet one in despair this way, whose sole desire is this most lunatic of lunatic metamorphoses, is infatuated with the illusion that this change can be accomplished as easily as one changes clothes. The man of immediacy does not know himself, he quite literally identifies himself only by the clothes he wears, he identifies having a self by externalities (here again the infinitely comical). There is hardly a more ludicrous mistake, for a self is indeed infinitely distinct from an externality. So when the externals have completely changed for the person of immediacy and he has despaired, he goes one step further; he thinks something like this, it becomes his wish: What if I became someone else, got myself a new self. Well, what if he did become someone else? I wonder whether he would recognize himself. There is a story about a peasant who went barefooted to town with enough money to buy himself a pair of stockings and shoes and to get drunk, and in trying to find his way home in his drunken state, he fell asleep in the middle of the road. A carriage came along, and the driver shouted to him to move or he would drive over his legs. The drunken peasant woke up, looked at his legs and, not recognizing them because of the shoes and stockings, said: "Go ahead, they are not my legs." When the man of immediacy despairs, it is impossible to give a true description of him outside of the comic; if I may put it this way, it is already something of a feat to speak in that jargon about a self and about despair.

When immediacy is assumed to have some reflection, the despair is somewhat modified; a somewhat greater consciousness of the self comes about, and thereby of the nature of despair and of one's condition as despair. It means something for such an individual to talk about being in despair, but the despair is essentially despair in weakness, a suffering, and its form is: in despair not to will to be oneself.

The advance over pure immediacy manifests itself at once in the fact that despair is not always occasioned by a blow, by something happening, but can be brought on by one's capacity for reflection, so that despair, when it is present, is not merely a suffering, a succumbing to the external circumstance, but is to a certain degree self-activity, an act. A certain degree of reflection is indeed present here, consequently a certain degree of pondering over one's self. With this certain degree of reflection begins the act of separation whereby the self becomes aware of itself as essentially different from the environment and external events and from their influence upon it. But this is only to a certain degree. When the self with a certain degree of reflection in itself wills to be responsible for the self, it may come up against some difficulty or other in the structure of the self, in the self's necessity. For just as no human body is perfect, so no self is perfect. This difficulty, whatever it is, makes him recoil. Or something happens to him that breaks with the immediacy in him more profoundly than his reflection had done, or his imagination discovers a possibility that, if it eventuated, would thus become the break with immediacy.

So he despairs. In contrast to the despair of self-assertion, his despair is despair in weakness, a suffering of the self; but with the aid of the relative reflection that he has, he attempts to sustain his self, and this constitutes another difference from the purely immediate man. He perceives that abandoning the self is a transaction, and thus he does not become apoplectic when the blow falls, as the immediate person does; reflection helps him to understand that there is much he can lose without losing the self. He makes concessions; he is able to do so—and why? Because to a certain degree he has separated his self from externalities, because he has a dim idea that there may even be something eternal in the self. Nevertheless, his struggles are in vain; the difficulty he has run up against requires a total break with immediacy, and he does not have the self-reflection or the ethical reflection for that. He has no consciousness of a self that is won by infinite abstraction from every externality, this naked abstract self, which, compared with immediacy's fully dressed self, is the first form of the infinite self and the advancing impetus in the whole process by which a self infinitely becomes responsible for its actual self with all its difficulties and advantages.

So he despairs, and his despair is: not to will to be himself. But he certainly does not entertain the ludicrous notion of wanting to be someone else; he keeps up the relation to his self—reflection has attached him to the self to that extent. His relation to the self is like the relation a person may have to his place of residence (the comic aspect is that the self certainly does not have as contingent a relation to itself as one has to a place of residence), which becomes an abomination because of smoke fumes or something else, whatever it might be. So he leaves it, but he does not move away, he does not set up a new residence; he continues to regard the old one as his address, he assumes that the problem will disappear. So also with the person in despair. As long as the difficulty lasts, he does not dare, as the saying so trenchantly declares, "to come to himself," he does not will to be himself; presumably this will pass, perhaps a change will take place, this gloomy possibility will probably be forgotten. So as long as it lasts, he visits himself, so to speak, only occasionally, to see whether the change has commenced. As soon as it commences, he moves home again, "is himself once again," as he says; but this simply means that he begins where he left off—he was a self up to a point and he went no further than that.

If there is no change, he seeks another remedy. He turns away completely from the inward way along which he should have advanced in order truly to become a self. In a deeper sense, the whole question of the self becomes a kind of false door with nothing behind it in the background of his soul. He appropriates what he in his language calls his self, that is, whatever capacities, talents, etc. he may have; all these he appropriates but in an outward-bound direction, toward life, as they say, toward the real, the active life. He behaves very discreetly with the little bit of reflection he has within himself, fearing that what he has in the background might emerge again. Little by little, he manages to forget it; in the course of time, he finds it almost ludicrous, especially when he is together with other competent and dynamic men who have a sense and aptitude for real life. Charming! He has been happily married now for several years, as it says in novels, is a dynamic and enterprising man, a father and citizen, perhaps even an important man; at home in his own house the servants call him "He Himself"; downtown he is among those addressed with "His Honor"; his conduct is based on respect of persons or on the way others regard one, and others judge according to one's social position. In Christendom he is a Christian[31] (in the very same sense as in paganism he would be a pagan and in Holland a Hollander), one of the cultured Christians. The question of immortality has often occupied him, and more than once he has asked the pastor whether there is such an immortality, whether one would actually recognize himself again—something that certainly must be of very particular interest to him, since he has no self.

It is impossible to depict this kind of despair accurately without a certain touch of satire. It is comical that he wants to talk about having been in despair; it is appalling that after the conquering of despair, according to his view, his condition is in fact despair. Ideally understood, it is extremely comical that underlying the worldly wisdom that is so celebrated in the world, underlying all that diabolical profusion of good advice and clever clichés—"Wait and see," "Don't worry," "Forget it"—there is utter stupidity about where and what the danger actually is. Again, it is this ethical stupidity that is appalling.

Despair over the earthly or over something earthly is the most common form of despair, and especially in the second form, that is, immediacy with a quantitative reflection. The more despair is thought through, the more rarely it is seen or the more rarely it appears in the world. This by no means proves that the majority have not despaired; it proves only that they have not gone particularly deep in despairing. There are very few persons who live even approximately within the qualification of spirit; indeed, there are not many who even try this life, and most of those who do soon back out of it. They have not learned to fear, have not learned "to have to" without any dependence, none at all, upon whatever else happens. Therefore, they are unable to

31. See, for example, *Postscript, KW* XII; *JP* I 372, 407.

bear what already appears to them to be a contradiction, what in reflection in the surroundings looks all the more glaring, so that to be concerned about one's soul and to will to be spirit seems to be a waste of time in the world, indeed, an indefensible waste of time that ought to be punished by civil law if possible, one that is punished in any case with scorn and contempt as a kind of treason against the human race, as a defiant madness that insanely fills out time with nothing. Then comes a moment in their lives—alas, this is their best time—when they begin to turn inward. Then, when they encounter their first difficulties, they turn away; it seems to them that this path leads to a dismal desert—*und rings umher liegt schöne grüne Weide* [while all about lie meadows fresh and green].[32] And so they take off and soon forget that time, the best time of their lives—alas, forget it as if it were a piece of childishness. They are also Christians, reassured by the pastors of their salvation. As stated, this despair is the most common, so common that this alone explains the common notion that despair is part of being young, something that appears only in the early years but is not found in the mature person who has reached the age of discretion. This is a desperate error or, more correctly, a desperate mistake that disregards— yes, and what is even worse, disregards the fact that what it disregards is almost the best that can be said about people, because very often something far worse happens—disregards the fact that, fundamentally, most people virtually never advance beyond what they were in their childhood and youth: immediacy with the admixture of a little dash of reflection. No, despair certainly is not something that appears only in the young, something one outgrows as a matter of course—"just as one outgrows illusion." This is not the case, even though one may be foolish enough to believe it. On the contrary, we can often enough meet men and women and older people who have illusions just as childish as any young person's. We disregard the fact that illu-

32. Goethe, *Faust,* Part I, Sc. IV (Mephistopheles); *Goethe's Werke,* I-LV (Stuttgart, Tübingen: 1828–33), XII, p. 91.

sion essentially has two forms: the illusion of hope and the illusion of recollection. Youth has the illusion of hope; the adult has the illusion of recollection, but precisely because he has this illusion, he also has the utterly biased idea of illusion that there is only the illusion of hope. The adult, of course, is not troubled by the illusion of hope but instead by the quaint illusion, among others, of looking down on the illusions of youth, presumably from a higher point free of illusion. The youth has illusions, hopes for something extraordinary from life and from himself; the adult, in recompense, is often found to have illusions about his memories of his youth. An older woman who presumably has left all illusions behind her is often found to be just as fantastically deluded as any young girl when it comes to her recollection of herself as a young girl, how happy she was then, how beautiful, etc. This *fuimus* [we have been],[33] which is common to older people, is just as great an illusion as the illusions of young people about the future: they both lie or fictionalize.

The mistaken notion that despair belongs only to youth is also desperate and despairing in quite another way. Moreover, it is very foolish and simply shows a lack of judgment as to what spirit is—along with a failure to appreciate that man is spirit and not merely animal—to think that faith and wisdom come that easily, that they come as a matter of course over the years like teeth, a beard, etc. No, whatever a man may arrive at as a matter of course, whatever things may come as a matter of course— faith and wisdom are definitely not among them. As a matter of fact, from a spiritual point of view, a man does not arrive at anything as a matter of course over the years; this concept is precisely the uttermost opposite of spirit. On the contrary, it is very easy to leave something behind as a matter of course over the years. And over the years, an individual may abandon the little bit of passion, feeling, imagination, the little bit of inwardness he

33. "We Trojans, with Ilium and all its Teucrian glory, / Are things of the past" (Virgil, *Aeneid*, II, 325; *The Aeneid of Virgil*, I–II, tr. C. Day Lewis [London: Hogarth Press, 1954], I, p. 40).

had and embrace as a matter of course an understanding of life in terms of trivialities (for such things come as a matter of course). This—improved—condition, which, to be sure, has come with the years, he now in despair considers a good thing; he easily reassures himself (and in a certain satirical sense nothing is more sure) that now it could never occur to him to despair—no, he has secured himself. But he is in despair, devoid of spirit and in despair. Why, I wonder, did Socrates love youth if it was not because he knew man!

If over the years an individual does not happen to sink into this most trivial kind of despair, it still by no means follows that despair belongs merely to youth. If a person really does develop over the years, if he becomes mature in an essential consciousness of the self, then he may despair in a higher form. And if he does not develop essentially over the years, although he still does not sink completely into triviality—that is, if he never advances any further than being a young man, a youth, even though he is an adult, a father, and a gray-head, consequently retaining some of the good in youth—he will be just as liable as a youth to despair over the earthly or over something earthly.

There may well be a difference between the despair of an adult like that and a youth's despair, but it is purely incidental, nothing essential. The youth despairs over the future as the present *in futuro* [in the future]; there is something in the future that he is not willing to take upon himself, and therefore he does not will to be himself. The adult despairs over the past as a present *in præterito* [in the past] that refuses to recede further into the past, for his despair is not such that he has succeeded in forgetting it completely. This past may even be something that repentance really should have in custody. But if repentance is to arise, there must first be effective despair, radical despair, so that the life of the spirit can break through from the ground upward. But in despair as he is, he does not dare to let it come to such a decision. There he stands still, time passes—unless, even more in despair, he succeeds in healing it by forgetting it, and thus instead of becoming a penitent, he becomes his own receiver of stolen goods [*Hæler*].³⁴ But essentially the despair of a youth and of an adult remains the same; there is never a metamorphosis in which consciousness of the eternal in the self breaks through so that the battle can begin that either intensifies the despair in a still higher form or leads to faith.

Is there, then, no essential difference between the two expressions used identically up to now: to despair over the earthly (the category of totality) and to despair over something earthly (the particular)? Indeed there is. When the self in imagination despairs with infinite passion over something of this world, its infinite passion changes this particular thing, this something, into the world *in toto;* that is, the category of totality inheres in and belongs to the despairing person. The earthly and the temporal as such consist precisely of particular things, and some particular thing may be regarded as the whole. The loss or deprivation of every earthly thing is actually impossible, for the category of totality is a thought category. Consequently, the self infinitely magnifies the actual loss and then despairs over the earthly *in toto.* However, as soon as this distinction (between despairing over the earthly and over something earthly) is to be maintained essentially, there is also a genuine advance in consciousness of the self. This formula, to despair over the earthly, is then a dialectical initial expression for the next form of despair.

(2) DESPAIR OF THE ETERNAL OR OVER ONESELF

Despair over the earthly or over something earthly is in reality also despair of the eternal and over oneself, insofar as it is despair, for this is indeed the formula for all despair.* But the individual

---

34. In the Danish there is a play on the two expressions: *at hele* (to heal) and *Hæler.*

* And therefore it is linguistically correct to say: to despair *over* the earthly (the occasion), *of* the eternal, but *over* oneself. For this again is another expression for the occasion of despair, which, according to the concept, is always *of* the eternal, whereas *that which* is despaired *over* can be very diverse. We despair *over* that which binds us in despair—over a misfortune, over the earthly, over a capital loss, etc.—but we despair *of* that which, rightly understood, releases us from despair: of the eternal, of salvation, of our own strength, etc. With respect to the self, we say both: to despair *over* and *of* oneself,

in despair depicted above is not aware, so to speak, of what is going on behind him. He thinks he is despairing over something earthly and talks constantly of that over which he despairs, and yet he is despairing of the eternal, for the fact that he attributes such great worth to something earthly—or, to carry this further, that he attributes to something earthly such great worth, or that he first makes something earthly into the whole world and then attributes such great worth to the earthly—this is in fact to despair of the eternal.

This despair is a significant step forward. If the preceding despair was *despair in weakness,* then this is *despair over his weakness,* while still remaining within the category: despair in weakness as distinct from despair in defiance (β). Consequently, there is only a relative difference, namely, that the previous form has weakness's consciousness as its final consciousness, whereas here the consciousness does not stop with that but rises to a new consciousness—that of his weakness. The person in despair himself understands that it is weakness to make the earthly so important, that it is weakness to despair. But now, instead of definitely turning away from despair to faith and humbling himself under his weakness, he entrenches himself in despair and despairs over his weakness. In so doing, his whole point of view is turned around: he now becomes more clearly conscious of his despair, that he despairs of the eternal, that he despairs over himself, over being so weak that he attributes such great significance to the earthly, which now becomes for him the despairing sign that he has lost the eternal and himself.

The progression is as follows. First comes the consciousness of the self, for to despair of the eternal is impossible without having a conception of the self, that there is something eternal

---

because the self is doubly dialectical. And the haziness, particularly in all the lower forms of despair and in almost every person in despair, is that he so passionately and clearly sees and knows *over* what he despairs, but *of* what he despairs evades him. The condition for healing is always this repenting *of,* and, purely philosophically, it could be a subtle question whether it is possible for one to be in despair and be fully aware of that *of* which one despairs.

in it, or that it has had something eternal in it. If a person is to despair over himself, he must be aware of having a self; and yet it is over this that he despairs, not over the earthly or something earthly, but over himself. Furthermore, there is a greater consciousness here of what despair is, because despair is indeed the loss of the eternal and of oneself. Of course, there is also a greater consciousness that one's state is despair. Then, too, despair here is not merely a suffering but an act. When the world is taken away from the self and one despairs, the despair seems to come from the outside, even though it always comes from the self; but when the self despairs over its despair, this new despair comes from the self, indirectly-directly from the self, as the counter-pressure (reaction), and it thereby differs from defiance, which comes directly from the self. Ultimately, this is still a step forward, although in another sense; simply because this despair is more intensive, it is in a certain sense closer to salvation. It is difficult to forget such despair—it is too deep; but every minute that despair is kept open, there is the possibility of salvation as well.

Nevertheless, this despair is classified under the form: in despair not to will to be oneself. Like a father who disinherits a son, the self does not want to acknowledge itself after having been so weak. In despair it cannot forget this weakness; it hates itself in a way, will not in faith humble itself under its weakness in order thereby to recover itself—no, in despair it does not wish, so to speak, to hear anything about itself, does not itself know anything to say. Nor is there any question of being helped by forgetting or of slipping, by means of forgetting, into the category of the spiritless and then to be a man and a Christian like other men and Christians—no, for that the self is too much self. As is often the case with the father who disinherits his son, the external circumstance is of little help; he does not thereby rid himself of his son, at least not in his thought. It is often the case when a lover curses the one he detests (his beloved) that it does not help very much; it captivates him almost more—and so it goes with the despairing self in regard to itself.

This despair is qualitatively a full level deeper than the one described earlier and belongs to the despair that less frequently appears in the world. That false door mentioned previously, behind which there is nothing, is here a real door, but a carefully closed door, and behind it sits the self, so to speak, watching itself, preoccupied with or filling up time with not willing to be itself and yet being self enough to love itself. This is called inclosing reserve [*Indesluttethed*]. And from now on we shall discuss inclosing reserve, which is the very opposite of immediacy and in terms of thought, among other things, has a great contempt for it.

Is there no one with such a self in the world of actuality, has he taken flight from actuality into the desert, the monastery, the madhouse; is he not an actual human being, dressed like others, wearing ordinary outer garments? Of course, why not! But this matter of the self he shares with no one, not a soul; he feels no urge to do so, or he has learned to subdue it. Just listen to what he himself says of it: "In fact, it is only purely immediate man— who in the category of spirit is just about on the same level as the young child, who, with utterly lovable unconstraint, tells all—it is only purely immediate people who are unable to hold anything back. It is this kind of immediacy that often with great pretension calls itself 'truth, being honest, an honest man telling it exactly as it is,' and this is just as much a truth as it is an untruth when an adult does not immediately yield to a physical urge. Every self with just a minuscule of reflection still knows how to constrain the self." And our man in despair is sufficiently self-inclosed to keep this matter of the self away from anyone who has no business knowing about it—in other words, everyone— while outwardly he looks every bit "a real man." He is a university graduate, husband, father, even an exceptionally competent public officeholder, a respectable father, pleasant company, very gentle to his wife, solicitude personified to his children. And Christian?—Well, yes, he is that, too, but prefers not to talk about it, although with a certain wistful joy he likes to see that his wife is occupied with religion to her upbuilding. He rarely attends church, because he feels that most pastors really do not know what they are talking about. He makes an exception of one particular pastor and admits that he knows what he is talking about, but he has another reason for not wanting to listen to him, since he fears being led too far out. On the other hand, he not infrequently longs for solitude, which for him is a necessity of life, at times like the necessity to breathe, at other times like the necessity to sleep. That this is a life-necessity for him more than for most people also manifests his deeper nature. On the whole, the longing for solitude is a sign that there still is spirit in a person and is the measure of what spirit there is. "Utterly superficial nonpersons and group-people" have so little longing for solitude that, like lovebirds, they promptly die the moment they have to be alone. Just as a little child has to be lulled to sleep, so these people need the soothing lullaby of social life in order to be able to eat, drink, sleep, fall in love, etc. In antiquity as well as in the Middle Ages there was an awareness of this longing for solitude and a respect for what it means; whereas in the constant sociality of our day we shrink from solitude to the point (what a capital epigram!) that no use for it is known other than as a punishment for criminals. But since it is a crime in our day to have spirit, it is indeed quite in order to classify such people, lovers of solitude, with criminals.

The self-inclosing despairing person goes on living *horis succesivis* [hour after hour]; even if not lived for eternity,[35] his hours have something to do with the eternal and are concerned with the relation of his self to itself—but he never really gets beyond that. When it is done, when his longing for solitude is satisfied, he goes out, as it were—even when he goes in to or is involved with his wife and children. Aside from his natural good nature and sense of duty, what makes him such a kind husband and solicitous father is the confession about his weakness that he has made to himself in his inclosed innermost being.

<hr/>

35. See *The Point of View, KW* XXII.

If it were possible for anyone to share the secret of his inclosing reserve and if one were then to say to him, "It is pride, you are really proud of yourself," he probably would never make the confession to anyone else. Alone with himself, he no doubt would confess that there is something to it, but the passionateness with which his self has interpreted his weakness would soon lead him into believing that it cannot possibly be pride, because it is indeed his very weakness that he despairs over—just as if it were not pride that places such tremendous emphasis on the weakness, just as if it were not because he wants to be proud of his self that he cannot bear this consciousness of weakness.—If someone were to say to him, "This is a curious entanglement, a curious kind of knot, for the whole trouble is really the way your thinking twists around; otherwise it is even normal, in fact, this is precisely the course you have to take: you must go through the despair of the self to the self. You are quite right about the weakness, but that is not what you are to despair over; the self must be broken in order to become itself, but quit despairing over that"—if someone were to speak that way to him, he would understand it in a dispassionate moment, but his passion would soon see mistakenly again, and then once more he would make a wrong turn—into despair.

As stated, this kind of despair is quite rare in the world. If it does not stop there and just mark time on the spot, and if on the other hand the person in despair does not experience an upheaval that puts him on the right road to faith, despair of this kind will either become intensified in a higher form of despair and continue to be inclosing reserve, or it will break through and destroy the outward trappings in which such a despairing person has been living out his life as if in an incognito. In the latter case, a person in this kind of despair will hurl himself into life, perhaps into the diversion of great enterprises; he will become a restless spirit whose life certainly leaves its mark, a restless spirit who wants to forget, and when the internal tumult is too much for him, he has to take strong measures, although of another kind

The Sickness unto Death · 97

than Richard III used in order not to hear his mother's curses.[36] Or he will seek oblivion in sensuality, perhaps in dissolute living; in despair he wants to go back to immediacy, but always with the consciousness of the self he does not want to be. In the first case, if the despair is intensified, it becomes defiance, and it now becomes clear how much untruth there was in this whole matter of weakness—it becomes clear how dialectically correct it is that the first expression for defiance is this very despair over his weakness.

In conclusion, let us take still another little look at the person of inclosing reserve who in his inclosing reserve marks time on the spot. If this inclosing reserve is maintained completely, *omnibus numeris absolute* [completely in every respect], then his greatest danger is suicide. Most men, of course, have no intimation of what such a person of inclosing reserve can endure; if they knew, they would be amazed. The danger, then, for the completely inclosed person is suicide. But if he opens up to one single person, he probably will become so relaxed, or so let down, that suicide will not result from inclosing reserve. Such a person of inclosing reserve with one confidant is moderated by one whole tone in comparison with one who is fully inclosed. Presumably he will avoid suicide. However, it may happen that just because he has opened himself to another person he will despair over having done so; it may seem to him that he might have held out far, far longer in silence rather than to have a confidant. There are examples of persons of inclosing reserve who were thrown into despair by having found a confidant. In this way, suicide may still result. In a poetic treatment, the denouement (assuming *poetice* [poetically] that the person was, for example, a king or an emperor) could be designed so that the confidant is killed. It is possible to imagine a demonic tyrant like that, one who craves to speak with someone about his torment and then successively consumes a considerable number of people, for to

36. *Richard the Third*, IV, 4; *Shakespeare's Werke*, tr. Schlegel and Tieck, III, p. 339.

become his confidant means certain death: as soon as the tyrant has spoken in his presence, he is put to death.—It would be a task for a poet to depict this solution to a demoniac's tormenting self-contradiction: not to be able to do without a confidant and not to be able to have a confidant.

β. *In Despair to Will to Be Oneself: Defiance*

As pointed out, the despair in α could be called feminine; similarly, this despair may be called masculine. It is, therefore, in relation to the foregoing, despair considered within the qualification of spirit. So perceived, however, masculinity essentially belongs within the qualification of spirit, while femininity is a lower synthesis.

The kind of despair described in α(2) was over one's weakness; the despairing individual does not will to be himself. But if the person in despair goes one single dialectical step further, if he realizes why he does not will to be himself, then there is a shift, then there is defiance, and this is the case precisely because in despair he wills to be himself.

First comes despair over the earthly or over something earthly, then despair of the eternal, over oneself. Then comes defiance, which is really despair through the aid of the eternal, the despairing misuse of the eternal within the self to will in despair to be oneself. But just because it is despair through the aid of the eternal, in a certain sense it is very close to the truth; and just because it lies very close to the truth, it is infinitely far away. The despair that is the thoroughfare to faith comes also through the aid of the eternal; through the aid of the eternal the self has the courage to lose itself in order to win itself. Here, however, it is unwilling to begin with losing itself but wills to be itself.

In this form of despair, there is a rise in the consciousness of the self, and therefore a greater consciousness of what despair is and that one's state is despair. Here the despair is conscious of itself as an act; it does not come from the outside as a suffering under the pressure of externalities but comes directly from the self. Therefore defiance, compared with despair over one's weakness, is indeed a new qualification.

In order in despair to will to be oneself, there must be consciousness of an infinite self. This infinite self, however, is really only the most abstract form, the most abstract possibility of the self. And this is the self that a person in despair wills to be, severing the self from any relation to a power that has established it, or severing it from the idea that there is such a power. With the help of this infinite form, the self in despair wants to be master of itself or to create itself, to make his self into the self he wants to be, to determine what he will have or not have in his concrete self. His concrete self or his concretion certainly has necessity and limitations, is this very specific being with these natural capacities, predispositions, etc. in this specific concretion of relations etc. But with the help of the infinite form, the negative self, he wants first of all to take upon himself the transformation of all this in order to fashion out of it a self such as he wants, produced with the help of the infinite form of the negative self—and in this way he wills to be himself. In other words, he wants to begin a little earlier than do other men, not at and with the beginning, but "in the beginning";[37] he does not want to put on his own self, does not want to see his given self as his task—he himself wants to compose his self by means of being the infinite form.

If a generic name for this despair is wanted, it could be called stoicism, but understood as not referring only to that sect. To elucidate this kind of despair more precisely, it is best to distinguish between an acting self and a self acted upon and to show how the self, when it is acting, relates itself to itself, and how the self, when it is acted upon, in being affected, relates itself to itself—and thus to show that the formula always is: in despair to will to be oneself.

If the self in despair is an *acting self,* it constantly relates itself to itself only by way of imaginary constructions, no matter what it undertakes, however vast, however amazing, however perse-

37. Genesis 1:1.

veringly pursued. It recognizes no power over itself; therefore it basically lacks earnestness and can conjure forth only an appearance of earnestness, even when it gives its utmost attention to its imaginary constructions. This is a simulated earnestness. Like Prometheus stealing fire from the gods, this is stealing from God the thought—which is earnestness—that God pays attention to one; instead, the self in despair is satisfied with paying attention to itself, which is supposed to bestow infinite interest and significance upon his enterprises, but it is precisely this that makes them imaginary constructions. For even if this self does not go so far into despair that it becomes an imaginatively constructed god—no derived self can give itself more than it is in itself by paying attention to itself—it remains itself from first to last; in its self-redoubling it becomes neither more nor less than itself. In so far as the self in its despairing striving to be itself works itself into the very opposite, it really becomes no self. In the whole dialectic within which it acts there is nothing steadfast; at no moment is the self steadfast, that is, eternally steadfast. The negative form of the self exercises a loosening power as well as a binding power;[38] at any time it can quite arbitrarily start all over again, and no matter how long one idea is pursued, the entire action is within a hypothesis. The self is so far from successfully becoming more and more itself that the fact merely becomes increasingly obvious that it is a hypothetical self. The self is its own master, absolutely its own master, so-called; and precisely this is the despair, but also what it regards as its pleasure and delight. On closer examination, however, it is easy to see that this absolute ruler is a king without a country, actually ruling over nothing; his position, his sovereignty, is subordinate to the dialectic that rebellion is legitimate at any moment. Ultimately, this is arbitrarily based upon the self itself.

Consequently, the self in despair is always building only castles in the air, is only shadowboxing. All these imaginatively con-

38. See Matthew 16:19.

structed virtues make it look splendid; like oriental poetry, they fascinate for a moment; such self-command, such imperturbability, such ataraxia, etc. practically border on the fabulous. Yes, they really do, and the basis of the whole thing is nothing. In despair the self wants to enjoy the total satisfaction of making itself into itself, of developing itself, of being itself; it wants to have the honor of this poetic, masterly construction, the way it has understood itself. And yet, in the final analysis, what it understands by itself is a riddle; in the very moment when it seems that the self is closest to having the building completed, it can arbitrarily dissolve the whole thing into nothing.[39]

If the self in despair is *acted upon,* the despair is nevertheless: in despair to will to be oneself. Perhaps such an imaginatively constructing self, which in despair wills to be itself, encounters some difficulty or other while provisionally orienting itself to its concrete self, something the Christian would call a cross, a basic defect, whatever it may be. The negative self, the infinite form of the self, will perhaps reject this completely, pretend that it does not exist, will having nothing to do with it. But it does not succeed, its proficiency in imaginative constructing does not stretch that far, even though its proficiency in abstracting does; in a Promethean way, the infinite, negative self feels itself nailed to this servitude. Consequently, it is a self acted upon. What, then, are the manifestations of this despair that is: in despair to will to be oneself?

In the preceding pages, the form of despair that despairs over the earthly or something earthly was understood basically to be—and it also manifests itself as being—despair of the eternal, that is, an unwillingness to be comforted by and healed by the eternal, an overestimation of the things of this world to the extent that the eternal can be no consolation. But this is also a form of the despair, to be unwilling to hope in the possibility that an earthly need, a temporal cross, can come to an end. The despair-

39. See *Either/Or,* II, *KW* IV.

ing person who in despair wills to be himself is unwilling to do that. He has convinced himself that this thorn in the flesh[40] gnaws so deeply that he cannot abstract himself from it (whether this is actually the case or his passion makes it so to him*), and therefore he might as well accept it forever, so to speak. He is offended by it, or, more correctly, he takes it as an occasion to be offended at all existence; he defiantly wills to be himself, to be himself not in spite of it or without it (that would indeed be to abstract himself from it, and that he cannot do, or that would be movement in the direction of resignation)—no, in spite of or in defiance of all existence, he wills to be himself with it, takes it along, almost flouting his agony. Hope in the possibility of help, especially by virtue of the absurd, that for God everything is possible—no, that he does not want. And to seek help from someone else—no, not for all the world does he want that. Rather than to seek help, he prefers, if necessary, to be himself with all the agonies of hell.

That popular notion that "of course, a person who suffers wants to be helped if only someone is able to help him" is not really so, is far from true, even though the contrary instance is not always as deep in despair as the one above. This is how things go. A sufferer usually has one or several ways in which he might want to be helped. If he is helped in these ways, then he is glad to be helped. But when having to be helped becomes a pro-

---

40. See *The Point of View*, *KW* XXII.

* Moreover, lest it be overlooked, from this point of view one will see that much of what in the world is dressed up under the name of resignation is a kind of despair: in despair to will to be one's abstract self, in despair to will to make the eternal suffice, and thereby to be able to defy or ignore suffering in the earthly and the temporal. The dialectic of resignation is essentially this: to will to be one's eternal self and then, when it comes to something specific in which the self suffers, not to will to be oneself, taking consolation in the thought that it may disappear in eternity and therefore feeling justified in not accepting it in time. Although suffering under it, the self will still not make the admission that it is part of the self, that is, the self will not in faith humble itself under it. Resignation viewed as despair is thus essentially different from the despair of not willing in despair to be oneself, for in despair one does will to be oneself, but with the exclusion of something specific in regard to which one in despair does not will to be oneself.

foundly earnest matter, especially when it means being helped by a superior, or by the supreme one, there is the humiliation of being obliged to accept any kind of help unconditionally, of becoming a nothing in the hand of the "Helper" for whom all things are possible, or the humiliation of simply having to yield to another person, of giving up being himself as long as he is seeking help. Yet there is undoubtedly much suffering, even prolonged and agonized suffering, in which the self nevertheless is not pained in this way, and therefore it fundamentally prefers the suffering along with the retention of being itself.

The more consciousness there is in such a sufferer who in despair wills to be himself, the more his despair intensifies and becomes demonic. It usually originates as follows. A self that in despair wills to be itself is pained in some distress or other that does not allow itself to be taken away from or separated from his concrete self. So now he makes precisely this torment the object of all his passion, and finally it becomes a demonic rage. By now, even if God in heaven and all the angels offered to help him out of it—no, he does not want that, now it is too late. Once he would gladly have given everything to be rid of this agony, but he was kept waiting; now it is too late, now he would rather rage against everything and be the wronged victim of the whole world and of all life, and it is of particular significance to him to make sure that he has his torment on hand and that no one takes it away from him—for then he would not be able to demonstrate and prove to himself that he is right. This eventually becomes such a fixation that for an extremely strange reason he is afraid of eternity, afraid that it will separate him from his, demonically understood, infinite superiority over other men, his justification, demonically understood, for being what he is.—Himself is what he wills to be. He began with the infinite abstraction of the self, and now he has finally become so concrete that it would be impossible to become eternal in that sense; nevertheless, he wills in despair to be himself. What demonic madness—the thought that most infuriates him is that eternity could get the notion to deprive him of his misery.

This kind of despair is rarely seen in the world; such characters really appear only in the poets, the real ones, who always lend "demonic" ideality—using the word in its purely Greek sense—to their creations. Nevertheless, at times despair like this does appear in actuality. What, then, is the corresponding externality? Well, there is nothing "corresponding," inasmuch as a corresponding externality—corresponding to inclosing reserve—is a self-contradiction, for if it corresponds, then it does in fact disclose. But externality in this case is of no consequence whatsoever here where inclosing reserve, or what could be called an inwardness with a jammed lock, must be the particular object of attention. The lowest forms of despair—in which there is really no inwardness, or in any case none worth mentioning—the lowest forms may be presented by describing or discussing some external aspect of the person in despair. But the more spiritual the despair becomes and the more the inwardness becomes a peculiar world of its own in inclosing reserve, the more inconsequential are the externalities under which the despair conceals itself. But the more spiritual despair becomes, the more attention it pays with demonic cleverness to keeping despair closed up in inclosing reserve, and the more attention it pays to neutralizing the externalities, making them as insignificant and inconsequential as possible. Just as the troll in the fairy story disappears through a crevice that no one can see,[41] so it is with despair: the more spiritual it is, the more urgent it is to dwell in an externality behind which no one would ordinarily think of looking for it. This secrecy is itself something spiritual and is one of the safeguards to ensure having, as it were, an *in*-closure [*I n d e lukke*] behind actuality, a world *ex*-clusively [*u d e lukkende*] for itself, a world where the self in despair is restlessly and tormentedly engaged in willing to be itself.

We began in α(1) with the lowest form of despair: in despair not to will to be oneself. Demonic despair is the most intensive

41. Probably a reference to the third legend in the story of Rübezahl. I. A. Musäus, *Volksmärchen der Deutschen*, I–V (Gotha: 1826), II, pp. 62–63; *Musæus Folkeæventyr*, I–III, tr. F. Schaldemose (Copenhagen: 1840), II, pp. 65–66.

form of the despair: in despair to will to be oneself. It is not even in stoic self-infatuation and self-apotheosis that this despair wills to be itself; it does not will to be itself as that does which, mendaciously to be sure, yet in a certain sense, wills it according to its perfection. No, in hatred toward existence, it wills to be itself, wills to be itself in accordance with its misery. Not even in defiance or defiantly does it will to be itself, but for spite; not even in defiance does it want to tear itself loose from the power that established it, but for spite wants to force itself upon it, to obtrude defiantly upon it, wants to adhere to it out of malice—and, of course, a spiteful denunciation must above all take care to adhere to what it denounces. Rebelling against all existence, it feels that it has obtained evidence against it, against its goodness. The person in despair believes that he himself is the evidence, and that is what he wants to be, and therefore he wants to be himself, himself in his torment, in order to protest against all existence with this torment. Just as the weak, despairing person is unwilling to hear anything about any consolation eternity has for him, so a person in such despair does not want to hear anything about it, either, but for a different reason: this very consolation would be his undoing—as a denunciation of all existence. Figuratively speaking, it is as if an error slipped into an author's writing and the error became conscious of itself as an error—perhaps it actually was not a mistake but in a much higher sense an essential part of the whole production—and now this error wants to mutiny against the author, out of hatred toward him, forbidding him to correct it and in maniacal defiance saying to him: No, I refuse to be erased; I will stand as a witness against you, a witness that you are a second-rate author.

FRIEDRICH NIETZSCHE

Using different fulcrums, three late-nineteenth-century German thinkers turned the world upside down. They were Karl Marx (1818–83), Sigmund Freud (1856–1939), and our philosopher with a hammer, Friedrich Nietzsche. Nietzsche, the philosopher who announced the death of God, was born in Saxony on October 15, 1844. Like Sartre and Camus, Nietzsche lost his father in early childhood. Ironically enough, given his critique of faith, Nietzsche's father, grandfather, and great-grandfather were all Lutheran pastors.

After his father's death, Nietzsche moved to Naumberg, where he lived with his mother, grandmother, sister, and two aunts. As an elementary school student, he was already troubled with the severe headaches that would plague the man who would make a veritable religion out of health the rest of his life. Quiet and withdrawn as a child, Nietzsche was dubbed "the Little Pastor" by his schoolmates. But the Little Pastor was a very good student. At fourteen, Nietzsche won a scholarship to Schulpforta, the most prestigious private school in Germany at that time.

In 1864, Nietzsche entered the University of Bonn with plans to study theology and philosophy, but a year later he followed his favorite professor, Friedrich Ritschl, to the University of Leipzig. There he began the study of the German philosopher and pessimist Arthur Schopenhauer. Schopenhauer had absolute faith in the nonexistence of God. Further, he believed that human beings had very poor prospects for achieving anything approaching happiness. For Schopenhauer, the aim of life was in effect to renounce the desire for life. Nietzsche found an intellectual soulmate in Schopenhauer, but unlike Schopenhauer, Nietzsche was devoted to finding a way of affirming life even though it was without a master plan and planner.

In 1866, Nietzsche began publishing scholarly essays. In 1867, he was drafted into service in the Prussian army; however, he suffered a severe chest injury while dismounting from a horse and was discharged. While in uniform, Nietzsche became disenchanted with what he termed "the molelike" lifestyle of academics. Like the young Kierkegaard, Nietzsche believed that all thinking ought to be connected with action. But just as Nietzsche was spiritually departing from the hallowed halls of the university, he was also being pursued for his enormous scholarly potential. At the tender age of twenty-four, Nietzsche was appointed professor of classical philology at the University of Basel in Switzerland. At this time, his star burned so brightly that his professors in Leipzig awarded Nietzsche his doctorate without even making him sit for his final exam.

In 1868, Nietzsche met and began an important relationship with the composer Richard Wagner. Nietzsche was himself a musician and composer, and, like Schopenhauer, his teacher at second hand, he gave a great deal of thought to the philosophy of music. For a time, Nietzsche imagined that Wagner and his music provided a way to return to the salutary, life-affirming values of pre-Christian and ultimately pre-Socratic values; however, within a few years of becoming friends with Wagner, he would become disabused of this fantasy. (For more on the Nietzsche-Wagner connection read Nietzsche's *The Birth of Tragedy from the Spirit of Music,* and *Nietzsche Contra Wagner.*)

In 1870, Nietzsche volunteered for service as a medical orderly in the Franco-Prussian War. After seeing action and bloodshed, Nietzsche developed diphtheria and was released from the service. During this time, the Prussian military machine that would roar in the next century was just becoming established. For all his kudos to blond beasts and supermen of action, Nietzsche was highly critical of both Prussian nationalism and the military-cultural ideals that it promulgated.

Nietzsche's *The Birth of Tragedy from the Spirit of Music* appeared in 1872. In this, the first movement of Nietzsche's philosophy, the author focuses on the struggle between the two main currents of life— the Dionysian or ecstatic and the Apollonian or rational. Nietzsche concludes that Western civilization has repressed its Dionysian side at great cost. The book, which was, to say the least, academically unconventional in its style, only received one critical notice, in which the reviewer prophetically remarked, "Anyone who has written a thing like that is finished as a scholar." And sure enough, Nietzsche was soon thereafter finished with the world of academic scholarship. Constantly on sick leave from Basel, Nietzsche resigned his university post in 1879.

For the next ten years, Nietzsche led a nomadic existence, always searching for spots that were conducive to his health and to being able to write. During these years of astounding productivity, Nietzsche wrote his *Untimely Meditations, Thus Spake Zarathustra, Beyond Good and Evil, On the Genealogy of Morals, Twilight of the Idols,* and other works. In these texts, Nietzsche shook the very crossbeams of the Western psyche by pressing probing questions about the origins and ultimate value of ethics and religion.

At one point in his writings, Nietzsche remarks that genius is not a matter of having a superabundance of intelligence but rather of being possessed of the ability to tolerate enormous amounts of stimulation without going mad. Nietzsche clasped the electric current of his ideas for years, but in the late 1880s he was beginning to show signs of madness, which many scholars believe were the effects of syphilis.

In 1889, in Turin, a man was beating his horse. Nietzsche intervened and threw his arms around the animal to protect it. He collapsed and was taken to a hospital where he continued to decline. For the last decade of his life, Nietzsche lived in a childlike mental state under the care of his mother and sister. He died on August 25, 1900.

The selection that follows is from Nietzsche's *On the Genealogy of Morals.* Here he plumbs the origins of morality in the West and formulates his famous notions of the slave revolt and herd morality. For the reader who wants to look more deeply into Nietzsche's evaluation of values, I strongly suggest a perusal of his *Beyond Good and Evil.* For those who might be interested in exploring Nietzsche's concept of the superman, I suggest a reading of his lyrical but somewhat uneven *Thus Spake Zarathustra.*

FROM

ON THE GENEALOGY
OF MORALS

First Essay: "Good and Evil," "Good and Bad"

1

These English psychologists, whom one has also to thank for the
only attempts hitherto to arrive at a history of the origin of
morality—they themselves are no easy riddle; I confess that, as
living riddles, they even possess one essential advantage over
their books—*they are interesting!* These English psychologists—
what do they really want? One always discovers them voluntarily
or involuntarily at the same task, namely at dragging the *partie
honteuse*[1] of our inner world into the foreground and seeking the
truly effective and directing agent, that which has been decisive
in its evolution, in just that place where the intellectual pride of
man would least *desire* to find it (in the *vis inertiae*[2] of habit, for
example, or in forgetfulness, or in a blind and chance mechanistic hooking-together of ideas, or in something purely passive,

1. Shame.
2. Inertia.

Excerpted from Friedrich Nietzsche, *Basic Writings of Nietzsche*, translated by
Walter Kaufmann. 2000 Modern Library Edition. Copyright © 1995 by Mrs.
Hazel Kaufmann. Reprinted by permission of Modern Library.

automatic, reflexive, molecular, and thoroughly stupid)—what is it really that always drives these psychologists in just *this* direction? Is it a secret, malicious, vulgar, perhaps self-deceiving instinct for belittling man? Or possibly a pessimistic suspicion, the mistrustfulness of disappointed idealists grown spiteful and gloomy? Or a petty subterranean hostility and rancor toward Christianity (and Plato) that has perhaps not even crossed the threshold of consciousness? Or even a lascivious taste for the grotesque, the painfully paradoxical, the questionable and absurd in existence? Or finally—something of each of them, a little vulgarity, a little gloominess, a little anti-Christianity, a little itching and need for spice?

But I am told they are simply old, cold, and tedious frogs, creeping around men and into men as if in their own proper element, that is, in a *swamp*. I rebel at that idea; more, I do not believe it; and if one may be allowed to hope where one does not know, then I hope from my heart they may be the reverse of this—that these investigators and microscopists of the soul may be fundamentally brave, proud, and magnanimous animals, who know how to keep their hearts as well as their sufferings in bounds and have trained themselves to sacrifice all desirability to truth, *every* truth, even plain, harsh, ugly, repellent, unchristian, immoral truth.—For such truths do exist.—

2

All respect then for the good spirits that may rule in these historians of morality! But it is, unhappily, certain that the *historical spirit* itself is lacking in them, that precisely all the good spirits of history itself have left them in the lurch! As is the hallowed custom with philosophers, the thinking of all of them is *by nature* unhistorical; there is no doubt about that. The way they have bungled their moral genealogy comes to light at the very beginning, where the task is to investigate the origin of the concept and judgment "good." "Originally"—so they decree—"one approved unegoistic actions and called them good from the point of view of those to whom they were done, that is to say, those to whom they were *useful;* later one *forgot* how this approval originated and, simply because unegoistic actions were always *habitually* praised as good, one also felt them to be good—as if they were something good in themselves." One sees straightaway that this primary derivation already contains all the typical traits of the idiosyncrasy of the English psychologists—we have "utility," "forgetting," "habit," and finally "error," all as the basis of an evaluation of which the higher man has hitherto been proud as though it were a kind of prerogative of man as such. This pride *has* to be humbled, this evaluation disvalued: has that end been achieved?

Now it is plain to me, first of all, that in this theory the source of the concept "good" has been sought and established in the wrong place: the judgment "good" did *not* originate with those to whom "goodness" was shown! Rather it was "the good" themselves, that is to say, the noble, powerful, high-stationed and high-minded, who felt and established themselves and their actions as good, that is, of the first rank, in contradistinction to all the low, low-minded, common and plebeian. It was out of this *pathos of distance*[3] that they first seized the right to create values and to coin names for values: what had they to do with utility! The viewpoint of utility is as remote and inappropriate as it possibly could be in face of such a burning eruption of the highest rank-ordering, rank-defining value judgments: for here feeling has attained the antithesis of that low degree of warmth which any calculating prudence, any calculus of utility, presupposes—and not for once only, not for an exceptional hour, but for good. The pathos of nobility and distance, as aforesaid, the protracted and domineering fundamental total feeling on the part of a higher ruling order in relation to a lower order, to a "below"—*that* is the origin of the antithesis "good" and "bad." (The lordly right of giving names extends so far that one should allow oneself to conceive the origin of language itself as an expression of power on the part of the rulers: they say "this *is* this and this," they seal

3. Cf. *Beyond Good and Evil*, section 257.

every thing and event with a sound and, as it were, take possession of it.) It follows from this origin that the word "good" was
definitely *not* linked from the first and by necessity to "unegoistic" actions, as the superstition of these genealogists of morality
would have it. Rather it was only when aristocratic value judgments *declined* that the whole antithesis "egoistic" "unegoistic"
obtruded itself more and more on the human conscience—it is,
to speak in my own language, the *herd instinct* that through this
antithesis at last gets its word (and its *words*) in. And even then it
was a long time before that instinct attained such dominion that
moral evaluation was actually stuck and halted at this antithesis
(as, for example, is the case in contemporary Europe: the prejudice that takes "moral," "unegoistic," "*désintéressé*" as concepts of
equivalent value already rules today with the force of a "fixed
idea" and brain-sickness).

3

In the second place, however: quite apart from the historical un-
tenability of this hypothesis regarding the origin of the value
judgment "good," it suffers from an inherent psychological absurdity. The utility of the unegoistic action is supposed to be the
source of the approval accorded it, and this source is supposed to
have been *forgotten*—but how is this forgetting *possible*? Has the
utility of such actions come to an end at some time or other?
The opposite is the case: this utility has rather been an everyday
experience at all times, therefore something that has been un-
derlined again and again: consequently, instead of fading from
consciousness, instead of becoming easily forgotten, it must have
been impressed on the consciousness more and more clearly.
How much more reasonable is that opposing theory (it is not for
that reason more true—) which Herbert Spencer,[4] for example,
espoused: that the concept "good" is essentially identical with

4. Herbert Spencer (1820–1903) was probably the most widely read English philosopher of his time. He applied the principle of evolution to many fields, including sociol-
ogy and ethics.

the concept "useful," "practical," so that in the judgments "good" and "bad" mankind has summed up and sanctioned precisely its *unforgotten* and *unforgettable* experiences regarding what is useful-practical and what is harmful-impractical. According to this theory, that which has always proved itself useful is good: therefore it may claim to be "valuable in the highest degree," "valuable in itself." This road to an explanation is, as aforesaid, also a wrong one, but at least the explanation is in itself reasonable and psychologically tenable.

4

The signpost to the *right* road was for me the question: what was the real etymological significance of the designations for "good" coined in the various languages? I found they all led back to the *same conceptual transformation*—that everywhere "noble," "aristocratic" in the social sense, is the basic concept from which "good" in the sense of "with aristocratic soul," "noble," "with a soul of a high order," "with a privileged soul" necessarily developed: a development which always runs parallel with that other in which "common," "plebeian," "low" are finally transformed into the concept "bad." The most convincing example of the latter is the German word *schlecht* [bad] itself: which is identical with *schlicht* [plain, simple]—compare *schlechtweg* [plainly], *schlechterdings* [simply]—and originally designated the plain, the common man, as yet with no inculpatory implication and simply in contradistinction to the nobility. About the time of the Thirty Years' War, late enough therefore, this meaning changed into the one now customary.[5]

With regard to a moral genealogy this seems to me a *fundamental* insight; that it has been arrived at so late is the fault of the retarding influence exercised by the democratic prejudice in the modern world toward all questions of origin. And this is so even in the apparently quite objective domain of natural science and

5. Cf. *Twilight of the Idols*, section 231.

physiology, as I shall merely hint here. But what mischief this prejudice is capable of doing, especially to morality and history, once it has been unbridled to the point of hatred is shown by the notorious case of Buckle;[6] here the *plebeianism* of the modern spirit, which is of English origin, erupted once again on its native soil, as violently as a mud volcano and with that salty, noisy, vulgar eloquence with which all volcanos have spoken hitherto.—

5

With regard to *our* problem, which may on good grounds be called a *quiet* problem and one which fastidiously directs itself to few ears, it is of no small interest to ascertain that through those words and roots which designate "good" there frequently still shines the most important nuance by virtue of which the noble felt themselves to be men of a higher rank. Granted that, in the majority of cases, they designate themselves simply by their superiority in power (as "the powerful," "the masters," "the commanders") or by the most clearly visible signs of this superiority, for example, as "the rich," "the possessors" (this is the meaning of *arya;* and of corresponding words in Iranian and Slavic). But they also do it by a *typical character trait:* and this is the case that concerns us here. They call themselves, for instance, "the truthful"; this is so above all of the Greek nobility, whose mouthpiece is the Megarian poet Theognis.[7] The root of the word coined for this, *esthlos,*[8] signifies one who *is,* who possesses reality, who is ac-

---

6. Henry Thomas Buckle (1821–1862), English historian, is known chiefly for his *History of Civilization* (pp. 1857ff.). The suggestion in the text is developed more fully in section 876 of *The Will to Power.*

7. Nietzsche's first publication, in 1867 when he was still a student at the University of Leipzig, was an article in a leading classical journal, *Rheinisches Museum,* on the history of the collection of the maxims of Theognis ("Zur Geschichte der Theognideischen Spruchsammlung"). Theognis of Megara lived in the sixth century B.C.

8. Greek: good, brave. Readers who are not classical philologists may wonder as they read this section how well taken Nietzsche's points about the Greeks are. In this connection one could obviously cite a vast literature, but in this brief commentary it will be sufficient to quote Professor Gerald F. Else's monumental study *Aristotle's Poetics: The Argument* (Cambridge, Mass., Harvard University Press, 1957), a work equally notable for

tual, who is true; then, with a subjective turn, the true as the truthful: in this phase of conceptual transformation it becomes a slogan and catchword of the nobility and passes over entirely into the sense of "noble," as distinct from the *lying* common man, which is what Theognis takes him to be and how he describes him—until finally, after the decline of the nobility, the word is left to designate nobility of soul and becomes as it were ripe and sweet. In the word *kakos*,[9] as in *deilos*[10] (the plebeian in contradistinction to the *agathos*[11]), cowardice is emphasized: this perhaps gives an indication in which direction one should seek the etymological origin of *agathos*, which is susceptible of several interpretations. The Latin *malus*[12] (beside which I set *melas*[13]) may designate the common man as the dark-colored, above all as the black-haired man ("*hic niger est*[14]—"), as the pre-Aryan occupant of the soil of Italy who was distinguished most obviously from

its patient and thorough scholarship and its spirited defense of some controversial interpretations. On the points at issue here, Else's comments are not, I think, controversial; and that is the reason for citing them here.

"The dichotomy is mostly taken for granted in Homer: there are not many occasions when the heaven-wide gulf between heroes and commoners even has to be mentioned.[30] [Still, one finds 'good' (*esthloi*) and 'bad' (*kakoi*) explicitly contrasted a fair number of times: B366, Z489, I319, . . .] In the . . . seventh and sixth centuries, on the other hand, the antithesis grows common. In Theognis it amounts to an obsession . . . Greek thinking begins with and for a long time holds to the proposition that mankind is divided into 'good' and 'bad,' and these terms are quite as much social, political, and economic as they are moral. . . . The dichotomy is absolute and exclusive for a simple reason: it began as the aristocrats' view of society and reflects their idea of the gulf between themselves and the 'others.' In the minds of a comparatively small and close-knit group like the Greek aristocracy there are only two kinds of people, 'we' and 'they'; and of course 'we' are the good people, the proper, decent, good-looking, right-thinking ones, while 'they' are the rascals, the poltroons, the good-for-nothings . . . Aristotle knew and sympathized with this older aristocratic, 'practical' ideal, not as superior to the contemplative, but at least as next best to it" (p. 75).

9. Greek: bad, ugly, ill-born, mean, craven.

10. Greek: cowardly, worthless, vile, wretched.

11. Greek: good, well-born, gentle, brave, capable.

12. Bad.

13. Greek: black, dark.

14. Quoted from Horace's *Satires,* I.4, line 85: "He that backbites an absent friend . . . and cannot keep secrets, is black, O Roman, beware!" *Niger,* originally "black," also came to mean unlucky and, as in this quotation, wicked. Conversely, *candidus* means white,

the blond, that is Aryan, conqueror race by his color; Gaelic, at any rate, offers us a precisely similar case—*fin* (for example in the name *Fin-Gal*), the distinguishing word for nobility, finally for the good, noble, pure, originally meant the blond-headed, in contradistinction to the dark, black-haired aboriginal inhabitants.

The Celts, by the way, were definitely a blond race; it is wrong to associate traces of an essentially dark-haired people which appear on the more careful ethnographical maps of Germany with any sort of Celtic origin or blood-mixture, as Virchow[15] still does: it is rather the *pre-Aryan* people of Germany who emerge in these places. (The same is true of virtually all Europe: the suppressed race has gradually recovered the upper hand again, in coloring, shortness of skull, perhaps even in the intellectual and social instincts: who can say whether modern democracy, even more modern anarchism and especially that inclination for "*commune*," for the most primitive form of society, which is now shared by all the socialists of Europe, does not signify in the main a tremendous *counterattack*—and that the conqueror and *master race*, the Aryan, is not succumbing physiologically, too?

I believe I may venture to interpret the Latin *bonus*[16] as "the warrior," provided I am right in tracing *bonus* back to an earlier *duonus*[17] (compare *bellum = duellum = duen-lum*, which seems to me to contain *duonus*). Therefore *bonus* as the man of strife, of dissention (*duo*), as the man of war: one sees what constituted the "goodness" of a man in ancient Rome. Our German *gut* [good] even: does it not signify "the godlike," the man of "godlike race"? And is it not identical with the popular (originally noble) name

---

bright, beautiful, pure, guileless, candid, honest, happy, fortunate. And in *Satires,* I.5, 41, Horace speaks of "the whitest souls earth ever bore" (*animae qualis neque candidiores terra tulit*).

15. Rudolf Virchow (1821–1902) was one of the greatest German pathologists, as well as a liberal politician, a member of the German Reichstag (parliament), and an opponent of Bismarck.

16. Good.

17. Listed in Harper's Latin Dictionary as the old form of *bonus,* with the comment: "for *duonus,* cf. *bellum*." And *duellum* is identified as an early and poetic form of *bellum* (war).

of the Goths? The grounds for this conjecture cannot be dealt
with here.—

6

To this rule that a concept denoting political superiority always
resolves itself into a concept denoting superiority of soul it is
not necessarily an exception (although it provides occasions for
exceptions) when the highest caste is at the same time the *priestly*
caste and therefore emphasizes in its total description of itself a
predicate that calls to mind its priestly function. It is then, for
example, that "pure" and "impure" confront one another for the
first time as designations of station; and here too there evolves a
"good" and a "bad" in a sense no longer referring to station. One
should be warned, moreover, against taking these concepts
"pure" and "impure" too ponderously or broadly, not to say symbolically: all the concepts of ancient man were rather at first in-
credibly uncouth, coarse, external, narrow, straightforward, and
altogether *unsymbolical* in meaning to a degree that we can scarcely
conceive. The "pure one" is from the beginning merely a man
who washes himself, who forbids himself certain foods that produce skin ailments, who does not sleep with the dirty women of
the lower strata, who has an aversion to blood—no more, hardly
more! On the other hand, to be sure, it is clear from the whole
nature of an essentially priestly aristocracy why antithetical val-
uations could in precisely this instance soon become danger-
ously deepened, sharpened, and internalized; and indeed they
finally tore chasms between man and man that a very Achilles of
a free spirit would not venture to leap without a shudder. There
is from the first something *unhealthy* in such priestly aristocracies
and in the habits ruling in them which turn them away from action and alternate between brooding and emotional explosions,
habits which seem to have as their almost invariable consequence that intestinal morbidity and neurasthenia which has afflicted priests at all times; but as to that which they themselves
devised as a remedy for this morbidity—must one not assert that

it has ultimately proved itself a hundred times more dangerous in its effects than the sickness it was supposed to cure? Mankind itself is still ill with the effects of this priestly naïveté in medicine! Think, for example, of certain forms of diet (abstinence from meat), of fasting, of sexual continence, of flight "into the wilderness" (the Weir Mitchell isolation cure[18]—without, to be sure, the subsequent fattening and overfeeding which constitute the most effective remedy for the hysteria induced by the ascetic ideal): add to these the entire antisensualistic metaphysic of the priests that makes men indolent and overrefined, their autohypnosis in the manner of fakirs and Brahmins—Brahma used in the shape of a glass knob and a fixed idea—and finally the only-too-comprehensible satiety with all this, together with the radical cure for it, *nothingness* (or God—the desire for a *unio mystica* with God is the desire of the Buddhist for nothingness, Nirvana—and no more!). For with the priests *everything* becomes more dangerous, not only cures and remedies, but also arrogance, revenge, acuteness, profligacy, love, lust to rule, virtue, disease—but it is only fair to add that it was on the soil of this *essentially dangerous* form of human existence, the priestly form, that man first became *an interesting animal,* that only here did the human soul in a higher sense acquire *depth* and become *evil*— and these are the two basic respects in which man has hitherto been superior to other beasts!

7

One will have divined already how easily the priestly mode of valuation can branch off from the knightly-aristocratic and then develop into its opposite; this is particularly likely when the priestly caste and the warrior caste are in jealous opposition to one another and are unwilling to come to terms. The knightly-aristocratic value judgments presupposed a powerful physicality, a flourishing, abundant, even overflowing health, together with

18. The cure developed by Dr. Silas Weir Mitchell (1829–1914, American) consisted primarily in isolation, confinement to bed, dieting, and massage.

that which serves to preserve it: war, adventure, hunting, dancing, war games, and in general all that involves vigorous, free, joyful activity. The priestly-noble mode of valuation presupposes, as we have seen, other things: it is disadvantageous for it when it comes to war! As is well known, the priests are the *most evil enemies*—but why? Because they are the most impotent. It is because of their impotence that in them hatred grows to monstrous and uncanny proportions, to the most spiritual and poisonous kind of hatred. The truly great haters in world history have always been priests; likewise the most ingenious[19] haters: other kinds of spirit[20] hardly come into consideration when compared with the spirit of priestly vengefulness. Human history would be altogether too stupid a thing without the spirit that the impotent have introduced into it—let us take at once the most notable example. All that has been done on earth against "the noble," "the powerful," "the masters," "the rulers," fades into nothing compared with what the *Jews* have done against them; the Jews, that priestly people, who in opposing their enemies and conquerors were ultimately satisfied with nothing less than a radical revaluation of their enemies' values, that is to say, an act of the *most spiritual revenge.* For this alone was appropriate to a priestly people, the people embodying the most deeply repressed[21] priestly vengefulness. It was the Jews who, with awe-inspiring consistency, dared to invert the aristocratic value-equation (good = noble = powerful = beautiful = happy = beloved of God) and to hang on to this inversion with their teeth, the teeth of the most abysmal hatred (the hatred of impotence), saying "the wretched alone are the good; the poor, impotent, lowly alone are the good; the suffering, deprived, sick, ugly alone are pious, alone are blessed by God, blessedness is for them alone—and you, the powerful and noble, are on the contrary the evil, the cruel, the lustful, the insatiable, the godless to all eternity; and you shall be in all eternity the unblessed, ac-

19. *Geistreich.*
20. *Geist.*
21. *Zurückgetretensten.*

cursed, and damned!" . . . One knows *who* inherited this Jewish revaluation . . . In connection with the tremendous and immeasurably fateful initiative provided by the Jews through this most fundamental of all declarations of war, I recall the proposition I arrived at on a previous occasion (*Beyond Good and Evil,* section 195)—that with the Jews there begins *the slave revolt in morality:* that revolt which has a history of two thousand years behind it and which we no longer see because it—has been victorious.

8

But you do not comprehend this? You are incapable of seeing something that required two thousand years to achieve victory?— There is nothing to wonder at in that: all *protracted* things are hard to see, to see whole. *That,* however, is what has happened: from the trunk of that tree of vengefulness and hatred, Jewish hatred—the profoundest and sublimest kind of hatred, capable of creating ideals and reversing values, the like of which has never existed on earth before—there grew something equally incomparable, a *new love,* the profoundest and sublimest kind of love—and from what other trunk could it have grown?

One should not imagine it grew up as the denial of that thirst for revenge, as the opposite of Jewish hatred! No, the reverse is true! That love grew out of it as its crown, as its triumphant crown spreading itself farther and farther into the purest brightness and sunlight, driven as it were into the domain of light and the heights in pursuit of the goals of that hatred—victory, spoil, and seduction—by the same impulse that drove the roots of that hatred deeper and deeper and more and more covetously into all that was profound and evil. This Jesus of Nazareth, the incarnate gospel of love, this "Redeemer" who brought blessedness and victory to the poor, the sick, and the sinners—was he not this seduction in its most uncanny and irresistible form, a seduction and bypath to precisely those *Jewish* values and new ideals? Did Israel not attain the ultimate goal of its sublime vengefulness precisely through the bypath of this "Redeemer," this ostensible opponent and disintegrator of Israel? Was it not part of the secret black art of truly *grand* politics of revenge, of a farseeing, subterranean, slowly advancing, and premeditated revenge, that Israel must itself deny the real instrument of its revenge before all the world as a mortal enemy and nail it to the cross, so that "all the world," namely all the opponents of Israel, could unhesitatingly swallow just this bait? And could spiritual subtlety imagine any *more dangerous* bait than this? Anything to equal the enticing, intoxicating, overwhelming, and undermining power of that symbol of the "holy cross," that ghastly paradox of a "God on the cross," that mystery of an unimaginable ultimate cruelty and self-crucifixion of God *for the salvation of man?*

What is certain, at least, is that *sub hoc signo*[22] Israel, with its vengefulness and revaluation of all values, has hitherto triumphed again and again over all other ideals, over all *nobler* ideals.——

9

"But why are you talking about *nobler* ideals! Let us stick to the facts: the people have won—or 'the slaves' or 'the mob' or 'the herd' or whatever you like to call them—if this has happened through the Jews, very well! in that case no people ever had a more world-historic mission. 'The masters' have been disposed of; the morality of the common man has won. One may conceive of this victory as at the same time a blood-poisoning (it has mixed the races together)—I shan't contradict; but this in-toxication has undoubtedly been *successful.* The 'redemption' of the human race (from 'the masters,' that is) is going forward; everything is visibly becoming Judaized, Christianized, mob-ized (what do the words matter!). The progress of this poison through the entire body of mankind seems irresistible, its pace and tempo may from now on even grow slower, subtler, less audible, more cautious—there is plenty of time.—To this end, does the church today still

22. Under this sign.

have any *necessary* role to play? Does it still have the right to exist? Or could one do without it? *Quaeritur.*[23] It seems to hinder rather than hasten this progress. But perhaps that is its usefulness.—Certainly it has, over the years, become something crude and boorish, something repellent to a more delicate intellect, to a truly modern taste. Ought it not to become at least a little more refined?—Today it alienates rather than seduces.—Which of us would be a free spirit if the church did not exist? It is the church, and not its poison, that repels us.—Apart from the church, we, too, love the poison.—"

This is the epilogue of a "free spirit" to my speech; an honest animal, as he has abundantly revealed, and a democrat, moreover; he had been listening to me till then and could not endure to listen to my silence. For at this point I have much to be silent about.

10

The slave revolt in morality begins when *ressentiment*[24] itself becomes creative and gives birth to values: the *ressentiment* of natures that are denied the true reaction, that of deeds, and compensate themselves with an imaginary revenge. While every noble morality develops from a triumphant affirmation of itself, slave morality from the outset says No to what is "outside," what is "different," what is "not itself"; and *this* No is its creative deed. This inversion of the value-positing eye—this *need* to direct one's view outward instead of back to oneself—is of the essence of *ressentiment:* in order to exist, slave morality always first needs a hostile external world; it needs, physiologically speaking, external stimuli in order to act at all—its action is fundamentally reaction.

The reverse is the case with the noble mode of valuation: it acts and grows spontaneously, it seeks its opposite only so as to affirm itself more gratefully and triumphantly—its negative

23. One asks.
24. Resentment.

concept "low," "common," "bad" is only a subsequently-invented pale, contrasting image in relation to its positive basic concept—filled with life and passion through and through—"we noble ones, we good, beautiful, happy ones!" When the noble mode of valuation blunders and sins against reality, it does so in respect to the sphere with which it is *not* sufficiently familiar, against a real knowledge of which it has indeed inflexibly guarded itself: in some circumstances it misunderstands the sphere it despises, that of the common man, of the lower orders; on the other hand, one should remember that, even supposing that the affect of contempt, of looking down from a superior height, *falsifies* the image of that which it despises, it will at any rate still be a much less serious falsification than that perpetrated on its opponent—*in effigie* of course—by the submerged hatred, the vengefulness of the impotent. There is indeed too much carelessness, too much taking lightly, too much looking away and impatience involved in contempt, even too much joyfulness, for it to be able to transform its object into a real caricature and monster.

One should not overlook the almost benevolent nuances that the Greek nobility, for example, bestows on all the words it employs to distinguish the lower orders from itself; how they are continuously mingled and sweetened with a kind of pity, consideration, and forbearance, so that finally almost all the words referring to the common man have remained as expressions signifying "unhappy," "pitiable" (compare *deilos*,[25] *deilaios*,[26] *ponēros*,[27] *mochthēros*,[28] the last two of which properly designate the common man as work-slave and beast of burden)—and how on the other hand "bad," "low," "unhappy" have never ceased to sound to the Greek ear as one note with a tone-color in which "unhappy" preponderates: this as an inheritance from the ancient

25. All of the footnoted words in this section are Greek. The first four mean *wretched*, but each has a separate note to suggest some of its other connotations. *Deilos:* cowardly, worthless, vile.

26. Paltry.

27. Oppressed by toils, good for nothing, worthless, knavish, base, cowardly.

28. Suffering hardship, knavish.

nobler aristocratic mode of evaluation, which does not belie itself even in its contempt (—philologists should recall the sense in which *oïzyros*,[29] *anolbos*,[30] *tlēmōn*,[31] *dystychein*,[32] *xymphora*[33] are employed). The "well-born" *felt* themselves to be the "happy"; they did not have to establish their happiness artificially by examining their enemies, or to persuade themselves, *deceive* themselves, that they were happy (as all men of *ressentiment* are in the habit of doing); and they likewise knew, as rounded men replete with energy and therefore *necessarily* active, that happiness should not be sundered from action—being active was with them necessarily a part of happiness (whence *eu prattein*[34] takes its origin)—all very much the opposite of "happiness" at the level of the impotent, the oppressed, and those in whom poisonous and inimical feelings are festering, with whom it appears as essentially narcotic, drug, rest, peace, "sabbath," slackening of tension and relaxing of limbs, in short *passively.*

While the noble man lives in trust and openness with himself (*gennaios*[35] "of noble descent" underlines the nuance "upright" and probably also "naïve"), the man of *ressentiment* is neither upright nor naïve nor honest and straightforward with himself. His soul *squints;* his spirit loves hiding places, secret paths and back doors, everything covert entices him as *his* world, *his* security, *his* refreshment; he understands how to keep silent, how not to forget, how to wait, how to be provisionally self-deprecating and humble. A race of such men of *ressentiment* is bound to become eventually *cleverer* than any noble race; it will also honor cleverness to a far greater degree: namely, as a condition of existence of the first importance; while with noble men cleverness can easily acquire a subtle flavor of luxury and subtlety—for here it is far less essential than the perfect functioning of the regulating

29. Woeful, miserable, toilsome; wretch.
30. Unblest, wretched, luckless, poor.
31. Wretched, miserable.
32. To be unlucky, unfortunate.
33. Misfortune.
34. To do well in the sense of faring well.
35. High-born, noble, high-minded.

unconscious instincts or even than a certain imprudence, perhaps a bold recklessness whether in the face of danger or of the enemy, or that enthusiastic impulsiveness in anger, love, reverence, gratitude, and revenge by which noble souls have at all times recognized one another. *Ressentiment* itself, if it should appear in the noble man, consummates and exhausts itself in an immediate reaction, and therefore does not *poison:* on the other hand, it fails to appear at all on countless occasions on which it inevitably appears in the weak and impotent.

To be incapable of taking one's enemies, one's accidents, even one's misdeeds seriously for very long—that is the sign of strong, full natures in whom there is an excess of the power to form, to mold, to recuperate and to forget (a good example of this in modern times is Mirabeau,[36] who had no memory for insults and vile actions done him and was unable to forgive simply because he—forgot). Such a man shakes off with a *single* shrug many vermin that eat deep into others; here alone genuine "love of one's enemies" is possible—supposing it to be possible at all on earth. How much reverence has a noble man for his enemies!—and such reverence is a bridge to love.—For he desires his enemy for himself, as his mark of distinction; he can endure no other enemy than one in whom there is nothing to despise and *very much* to honor! In contrast to this, picture "the enemy" as the man of *ressentiment* conceives him—and here precisely is his deed, his creation: he has conceived "the evil enemy," "*the Evil One*," and this in fact is his basic concept, from which he then evolves, as an afterthought and pendant, a "good one"—himself!

11

This, then, is quite the contrary of what the noble man does, who conceives the basic concept "good" in advance and spontaneously out of himself and only then creates for himself an idea of "bad"! This "bad" of noble origin and that "evil" out of the

36. Honoré Gabriel Riqueti, Comte de Mirabeau (1749–1791), was a celebrated French Revolutionary statesman and writer.

cauldron of unsatisfied hatred—the former an after-production, a side issue, a contrasting shade, the latter on the contrary the original thing, the beginning, the distinctive *deed* in the conception of a slave morality—how different these words "bad" and "evil" are, although they are both apparently the opposite of the same concept "good." But it is *not* the same concept "good": one should ask rather precisely *who* is "evil" in the sense of the morality of *ressentiment*. The answer, in all strictness, is: *precisely* the "good man" of the other morality, precisely the noble, powerful man, the ruler, but dyed in another color, interpreted in another fashion, seen in another way by the venomous eye of *ressentiment*. Here there is one thing we shall be the last to deny: he who knows these "good men" only as enemies knows only *evil enemies*, and the same men who are held so sternly in check *inter pares*[37] by custom, respect, usage, gratitude, and even more by mutual suspicion and jealousy, and who on the other hand in their relations with one another show themselves so resourceful in consideration, self-control delicacy, loyalty, pride, and friendship—once they go outside, where the strange, the *stranger* is found, they are not much better than uncaged beasts of prey. There they savor a freedom from all social constraints, they compensate themselves in the wilderness for the tension engendered by protracted confinement and enclosure within the peace of society, they go *back* to the innocent conscience of the beast of prey, as triumphant monsters who perhaps emerge from a disgusting[38] procession of murder, arson, rape, and torture, exhilarated and undisturbed of soul, as if it were no more than a students' prank, convinced they have provided the poets with a lot more material for song and praise. One cannot fail to see at the bottom of all these noble races the beast of prey, the splendid *blond beast*[39] prowling about

37. Among equals.

38. *Scheusslichen.*

39. This is the first appearance in Nietzsche's writings of the notorious "blond beast." It is encountered twice more in the present section; a variant appears in section 17 of the second essay; and then the *blonde Bestie* appears once more in *Twilight of the Idols,* "The 'Improvers' of Mankind," section 2. That is all. For a detailed discussion of these passages see Kaufmann's *Nietzsche,* Chapter 7, section III: ". . . The 'blond beast' is not a racial con-

avidly in search of spoil and victory; this hidden core needs to erupt from time to time, the animal has to get out again and go back to the wilderness: the Roman, Arabian, Germanic, Japanese nobility, the Homeric heroes, the Scandinavian Vikings—they all shared this need.

It is the noble races that have left behind them the concept "barbarian" wherever they have gone; even their highest culture betrays a consciousness of it and even a pride in it (for example, when Pericles says to his Athenians in his famous funeral oration "our boldness has gained access to every land and sea, everywhere raising imperishable monuments to its goodness *and wickedness*"). This "boldness" of noble races, mad, absurd, and sudden in its expression, the incalculability, even incredibility of their undertakings—Pericles specially commends the *rhathymia*[40] of the Athenians—their indifference to and contempt for security,

---

cept and does not refer to the 'Nordic race' of which the Nazis later made so much. Nietzsche specifically refers to Arabs and Japanese . . .—and the 'blondness' presumably refers to the beast, the lion."

Francis Golffing, in his free translation of the *Genealogy*, deletes the blond beast three times out of four; only where it appears the second time in the original text, he has "the blond Teutonic beast." This helps to corroborate the myth that the blondness refers to the Teutons. Without the image of the lion, however, we lose not only some of Nietzsche's poetry as well as any chance to understand one of his best known coinages; we also lose an echo of the crucial first chapter of *Zarathustra*, where the lion represents the second stage in "The Three Metamorphoses" of the spirit—above the obedient camel but below the creative child (*The Portable Nietzsche*, pp. 138f.).

Arthur Danto has suggested that if lions were black and Nietzsche had written "Black Beast," the expression would "provide support for African instead of German nationalists" (*Nietzsche as Philosopher*, New York, Macmillan, 1965, p. 170). Panthers *are* black and magnificent animals, but anyone calling Negroes black beasts and associating them with "a disgusting procession of murder, arson, rape, and torture," adding that "the animal has to get out again and go back to the wilderness," and then going on to speak of "their hair-raising cheerfulness and profound joy in all destruction," would scarcely be taken to "provide support for . . . nationalists." On the contrary, he would be taken for a highly prejudiced critic of the Negro.

No other German writer of comparable stature has been a more extreme critic of German nationalism than Nietzsche. For all that, it is plain that in this section he sought to describe the behavior of the ancient Greeks and Romans, the Goths and the Vandals, not that of nineteenth-century Germans.

40. Thucydides, 2.39. In *A Historical Commentary on Thucydides*, vol. II (Oxford, Clarendon Press, 1956; corrected imprint of 1966), p. 118, A. W. Gomme comments on this

body, life, comfort, their hair-raising[41] cheerfulness and profound joy in all destruction, in all the voluptuousness of victory and cruelty—all this came together, in the minds of those who suffered from it, in the image of the "barbarian," the "evil enemy," perhaps as the "Goths," the "Vandals." The deep and icy mistrust the German still arouses today whenever he gets into a position of power is an echo of that inextinguishable horror with which Europe observed for centuries that raging of the blond Germanic beast (although between the old Germanic tribes and us Germans there exists hardly a conceptual relationship, let alone one of blood).

I once drew attention to the dilemma in which Hesiod found himself when he concocted his succession of cultural epochs and sought to express them in terms of gold, silver, and bronze: he knew no way of handling the contradiction presented by the glorious but at the same time terrible and violent world of Homer except by dividing one epoch into two epochs, which he then placed one behind the other—first the epoch of the heroes and demigods of Troy and Thebes, the form in which that world had survived in the memory of the noble races who were those heroes' true descendants; then the bronze epoch, the form in which that same world appeared to the descendants of the downtrodden, pillaged, mistreated, abducted, enslaved: an epoch of bronze, as aforesaid, hard, cold, cruel, devoid of feeling or conscience, destructive and bloody.

Supposing that what is at any rate believed to be the "truth" really is true, and the *meaning of all culture* is the reduction of the beast of prey "man" to a tame and civilized animal, a *domestic animal,* then one would undoubtedly have to regard all those instincts of reaction and *ressentiment* through whose aid the noble races and their ideals were finally confounded and overthrown

---

word: "in its original sense, 'ease of mind,' 'without anxiety' . . . But ease of mind can in certain circumstances become carelessness, remissness, frivolity: Demosthenes often accused the Athenians of *rhathymia . . .*"

41. *Entsetzliche.*

as the actual *instruments of culture*; which is not to say that the *bearers* of these instincts themselves represent culture. Rather is the reverse not merely probable—no! today it is *palpable*! These bearers of the oppressive instincts that thirst for reprisal, the descendants of every kind of European and non-European slavery, and especially of the entire pre-Aryan populace—they represent the *regression* of mankind! These "instruments of culture" are a disgrace to man and rather an accusation and counterargument against "culture" in general! One may be quite justified in continuing to fear the blond beast at the core of all noble races and in being on one's guard against it: but who would not a hundred times sooner fear where one can also admire than *not* fear but be permanently condemned to the repellent sight of the ill-constituted, dwarfed, atrophied, and poisoned?[42] And is that not *our* fate? What today constitutes *our* antipathy to "man"?—for we *suffer* from man, beyond doubt.

Not fear; rather that we no longer have anything left to fear in man; that the maggot[43] "man" is swarming in the foreground; that the "tame man," the hopelessly mediocre and insipid[44] man, has already learned to feel himself as the goal and zenith, as the meaning of history, as "higher man"—that he has indeed a certain right to feel thus, insofar as he feels himself elevated above the surfeit of ill-constituted, sickly, weary and exhausted people of which Europe is beginning to stink today, as something at least relatively well-constituted, at least still capable of living, at least affirming life.

42. If the present section is not clear enough to any reader, he might turn to *Zarathustra*'s contrast of the *overman* and the *last man* (Prologue, sections 3–5) and, for good measure, read also the first chapter or two of Part One. Then he will surely see how Aldous Huxley's *Brave New World* and George Orwell's *1984*—but especially the former—are developments of Nietzsche's theme. Huxley, in his novel, uses Shakespeare as a foil; Nietzsche, in the passage above, Homer.

43. *Gewürm* suggests wormlike animals; *wimmelt* can mean swarm or crawl but is particularly associated with maggots—in a cheese, for example.

44. *Unerquicklich*.

12

At this point I cannot suppress a sigh and a last hope. What is it that I especially find utterly unendurable? That I cannot cope with, that makes me choke and faint? Bad air! Bad air! The approach of some ill-constituted thing; that I have to smell the entrails of some ill-constituted soul!

How much one is able to endure: distress, want, bad weather, sickness, toil, solitude. Fundamentally one can cope with everything else, born as one is to a subterranean life of struggle; one emerges again and again into the light, one experiences again and again one's golden hour of victory—and then one stands forth as one was born, unbreakable, tensed, ready for new, even harder, remoter things, like a bow that distress only serves to draw tauter.

But grant me from time to time—if there are divine goddesses in the realm beyond good and evil—grant me the sight, but *one* glance of something perfect, wholly achieved, happy, mighty, triumphant, something still capable of arousing fear! Of a man who justifies *man,* of a complementary and redeeming lucky hit on the part of man for the sake of which one may still *believe in man*!

For this is how things are: the diminution and leveling of European man constitutes *our* greatest danger, for the sight of him makes us weary.—We can see nothing today that wants to grow greater, we suspect that things will continue to go down, down, to become thinner, more good-natured, more prudent, more comfortable, more mediocre, more indifferent, more Chinese, more Christian—there is no doubt that man is getting "better" all the time.

Here precisely is what has become a fatality for Europe—together with the fear of man we have also lost our love of him, our reverence for him, our hopes for him, even the will to him. The sight of man now makes us weary—what is nihilism today if it is not *that?*—We are weary *of man.*

13

But let us return: the problem of the *other* origin of the "good," of the good as conceived by the man of *ressentiment,* demands its solution.

That lambs dislike great birds of prey does not seem strange: only it gives no ground for reproaching these birds of prey for bearing off little lambs. And if the lambs say among themselves: "these birds of prey are evil; and whoever is least like a bird of prey, but rather its opposite, a lamb—would he not be good?" there is no reason to find fault with this institution of an ideal, except perhaps that the birds of prey might view it a little ironically and say: "*we* don't dislike them at all, these good little lambs; we even love them: nothing is more tasty than a tender lamb."

To demand of strength that it should *not* express itself as strength, that it should *not* be a desire to overcome, a desire to throw down, a desire to become master, a thirst for enemies and resistances and triumphs, is just as absurd as to demand of weakness that it should express itself as strength. A quantum of force is equivalent to a quantum of drive, will, effect—more, it is nothing other than precisely this very driving, willing, effecting, and only owing to the seduction of language (and of the fundamental errors of reason that are petrified in it) which conceives and misconceives all effects as conditioned by something that causes effects, by a "subject," can it appear otherwise. For just as the popular mind separates the lightning from its flash and takes the latter for an *action,* for the operation of a subject called lightning, so popular morality also separates strength from expressions of strength, as if there were a neutral substratum behind the strong man, which was *free* to express strength or not to do so. But there is no such substratum; there is no "being" behind doing, effecting, becoming; "the doer" is merely a fiction added to the deed—the deed is everything. The popular mind in fact doubles the deed; when it sees the lightning flash, it is the deed of a deed: it posits the same event first as cause and then a second time as its effect. Scientists do no better when they say "force moves," "force causes," and the like—all its coolness, its freedom from emotion notwithstanding, our entire science still lies under the misleading influence of language and has not disposed of that little changeling, the "subject" (the atom, for example, is such a changeling, as is the Kantian "thing-in-itself"); no wonder if the submerged, darkly glowering emotions of vengefulness and hatred exploit this belief for their own ends and in fact maintain no belief more ardently than the belief that *the strong man is free* to be weak and the bird of prey to be a lamb—for thus they gain the right to make the bird of prey *accountable* for being a bird of prey.

When the oppressed, downtrodden, outraged exhort one another with the vengeful cunning of impotence: "let us be different from the evil, namely good! And he is good who does not outrage, who harms nobody, who does not attack, who does not requite, who leaves revenge to God, who keeps himself hidden as we do, who avoids evil and desires little from life, like us, the patient, humble, and just"—this, listened to calmly and without previous bias, really amounts to no more than: "we weak ones are, after all, weak; it would be good if we did nothing *for which we are not strong enough*"; but this dry matter of fact, this prudence of the lowest order which even insects possess (posing as dead, when in great danger, so as not to do "too much"), has, thanks to the counterfeit and self-deception of impotence, clad itself in the ostentatious garb of the virtue of quiet, calm resignation, just as if the weakness of the weak—that is to say, their *essence,* their effects, their sole ineluctable, irremovable reality— were a voluntary achievement, willed, chosen, a *deed,* a *meritorious* act. This type of man *needs* to believe in a neutral independent "subject," prompted by an instinct for self-preservation and self-affirmation in which every lie is sanctified. The subject (or, to use a more popular expression, the *soul*) has perhaps been believed in hitherto more firmly than anything else on earth because it makes possible to the majority of mortals, the weak and oppressed of every kind, the sublime self-deception that interprets weakness as freedom, and their being thus-and-thus as a *merit*.

14

Would anyone like to take a look into the secret of how *ideals are made* on earth? Who has the courage?—Very well! Here is a point we can see through into this dark workshop. But wait a moment or two, Mr. Rash and Curious: your eyes must first get used to this false iridescent light.—All right! Now speak! What is going on down there? Say what you see, man of the most perilous kind of inquisitiveness—now I am the one who is listening.—

—"I see nothing, but I hear the more. There is a soft, wary, malignant muttering and whispering coming from all the corners and nooks. It seems to me one is lying; a saccharine sweetness clings to every sound. Weakness is being lied into something *meritorious*, no doubt of it—so it is just as you said"—

—Go on!

—"and impotence which does not requite into 'goodness of heart'; anxious lowliness into 'humility'; subjection to those one hates into 'obedience' (that is, to one of whom they say he commands this subjection—they call him God). The inoffensiveness of the weak man, even the cowardice of which he has so much, his lingering at the door, his being ineluctably compelled to wait, here acquire flattering names, such as 'patience,' and are even called virtue itself; his inability for revenge is called unwillingness to revenge, perhaps even forgiveness ('for *they* know not what they do—we alone know what *they* do!'). They also speak of 'loving one's enemies'—and sweat as they do so."

—Go on!

—"They are miserable, no doubt of it, all these mutterers and nook counterfeiters, although they crouch warmly together—but they tell me their misery is a sign of being chosen by God; one beats the dogs one likes best; perhaps this misery is also a preparation, a testing, a schooling, perhaps it is even more—something that will one day be made good and recompensed with interest, with huge payments of gold, no! of happiness. This they call 'bliss.' "

—Go on!

—"Now they give me to understand that they are not merely better than the mighty, the lords of the earth whose spittle they have to lick (*not* from fear, not at all from fear! but because God has commanded them to obey the authorities)[45]—that they are not merely better but are also 'better off,' or at least will be better off someday. But enough! enough! I can't take any more. Bad air! Bad air! This workshop where *ideals are manufactured*—it seems to me it stinks of so many lies."

—No! Wait a moment! You have said nothing yet of the masterpiece of these black magicians, who make whiteness, milk, and innocence of every blackness—haven't you noticed their perfection of refinement, their boldest, subtlest, most ingenious, most mendacious artistic stroke? Attend to them! These cellar rodents full of vengefulness and hatred—what have they made of revenge and hatred? Have you heard these words uttered? If you trusted simply to their words, would you suspect you were among men of *ressentiment*? . . .

—"I understand; I'll open my ears again (oh! oh! oh! and *close* my nose). Now I can really hear what they have been saying all along: 'We good men—*we are the just*'—what they desire they call, not retaliation, but 'the triumph of *justice*'; what they hate is not their enemy, no! they hate 'injustice,' they hate 'godlessness'; what they believe in and hope for is not the hope of revenge, the intoxication of sweet revenge (—'sweeter than honey' Homer called it), but the victory of God, of the *just* God, over the godless; what there is left for them to love on earth is not their brothers in hatred but their 'brothers in love,' as they put it, all the good and just on earth."

—And what do they call that which serves to console them for all the suffering of life—their phantasmagoria of anticipated future bliss?

---

45. Allusion to Romans 13:1–2.

—"What? Do I hear aright? They call that 'the Last Judgment,' the coming of *their* kingdom, of the 'Kingdom of God'—meanwhile, however, they live 'in faith,' 'in love,' 'in hope.' "

—Enough! Enough!

15

In faith in what? In love of what? In hope of what?—These weak people—some day or other *they* too intend to be the strong, there is no doubt of that, some day *their* "kingdom" too shall come—they term it "the kingdom of God," of course, as aforesaid: for one is so very humble in all things! To experience *that* one needs to live a long time, beyond death—indeed one needs eternal life, so as to be eternally indemnified in the "kingdom of God" for this earthly life "in faith, in love, in hope." Indemnified for what? How indemnified?

Dante, I think, committed a crude blunder when, with a terror-inspiring ingenuity, he placed above the gateway of his hell the inscription "I too was created by eternal love"—at any rate, there would be more justification for placing above the gateway to the Christian Paradise and its "eternal bliss" the inscription "I too was created by eternal *hate*"—provided a truth may be placed above the gateway to a lie! For *what* is it that constitutes the bliss of this Paradise?

We might even guess, but it is better to have it expressly described for us by an authority not to be underestimated in such matters, Thomas Aquinas, the great teacher and saint. *"Beati in regno coelesti,"* he says, meek as a lamb, *"videbunt poenas damnatorum,* **ut beatitudo illis magis complaceat."**[46] Or if one would like to hear it in a stronger key, perhaps from the mouth of a tri-

---

46. The blessed in the kingdom of heaven will see the punishments of the damned, *in order that their bliss be more delightful for them.*—To be precise, what we find in *Summa Theologiae,* III, *Supplementum,* Q. 94, Art. 1, is this: "In order that the bliss of the saints may be more delightful for them and that they may render more copious thanks to God for it, it is given to them to see perfectly the punishment of the damned." *Ut beatitudo sanctorum eis magis complaceat, et de ea uberiores gratias Deo agant, datur eis ut poenam impiorum perfecte intueantur.*

umphant Church Father, adjuring his Christians to avoid the cruel pleasures of the public games—but why? "For the faith offers us much more"—he says, *De Spectaculis,* chs. 29f.—"*something much stronger;* thanks to the Redemption, quite other joys are at our command; in place of athletes we have our martyrs; if we crave blood, we have the blood of Christ . . . But think of what awaits us on the day of his return, the day of his triumph!"—and then he goes on, the enraptured visionary.[47] *"At enim supersunt alia spectacula, ille ultimus et perpetuus judicii dies, ille nationibus insperatus, ille derisus, cum tanta saeculi vetustas et tot ejus nativitates uno igne haurientur. Quae tunc spectaculi latitudo!* **Quid admirer! Quid rideam! Ubi gaudeam! Ubi exultem,** *spectans tot et tantos* **reges,** *qui in coelum recepti nuntiabantur, cum ipso Jove et ipsis suis testibus in imis tenebris congemescentes! Item praesides"* (the provincial governors) *"persecutores dominici nominis sacvioribus quam ipsi flammis saevierunt insultantibus contra Christianos liquescentes! Quos praeterea sapientes*

47. Nietzsche quotes Tertullian in the original Latin. This footnote offers, first, an English translation, and then some discussion.

"Yes, and there are other sights: that last day of judgment, with its everlasting issues; that day unlooked for by the nations, the theme of their derision, when the world hoary with age, and all its many products, shall be consumed in one great flame! How vast a spectacle then bursts upon the eye! *What there excites my admiration? what my derision? Which sight gives me joy? which rouses me to exultation?*—as I see so many illustrious monarchs, whose reception into the heavens was publicly announced, groaning now in the lowest darkness with great Jove himself, and those, too, who bore witness of their exultation; governors of provinces, too, who persecuted the Christian name, in fires more fierce than those with which in the days of their pride they raged against the followers of Christ. What world's wise men besides, the very philosophers, in fact, who taught their followers that God had no concern in aught that is sublunary, and were wont to assure them that either they had no souls, or that they would never return to the bodies which at death they had left, now covered with shame before the poor deluded ones, as one fire consumes them! Poets also, trembling not before the judgment-seat of Rhadamanthus or Minos, but of the unexpected Christ! I shall have a better opportunity then of hearing the tragedians, louder-voiced in their own calamity; of viewing the play-actors, much more 'dissolute' [another translation has "much lither of limb"] in the dissolving flame; of looking upon the charioteer, all glowing in his chariot of fire; of beholding the wrestlers, not in their gymnasia, but tossing in the fiery billows; unless even then I shall not care to attend to such ministers of sin, in my eager wish rather to fix a gaze *insatiable* on those whose fury vented itself against the Lord. 'This,' I shall say, 'this is that carpenter's or hireling's son, that Sabbath-breaker, that Samaritan and devil-possessed! This is He whom you purchased from Judas! [*Quaestuaria* means prostitute, not carpenter: see

illos philosophos coram discipulis suis una conflagrantibus erubescentes, quibus nihil ad deum pertinere suadebant, quibus animas aut nullas aut non in pristina corpora redituras affirmabant! Etiam poëtas non ad Rhadamanti nec ad Minois, sed ad inopinati Christi tribunal palpitantes! Tunc magis tragoedi audiendi, magis scilicet vocales" (in better voice, yet worse screamers) *"in sua propria calamitate; tunc histriones cognoscendi, solutiores multo per ignem; tunc spectandus auriga in flammea rota lotus rubens, tunc xystici contemplandi non in gymnasiis, sed in igne jaculati, nisi quod ne tunc quidem illos velim vivos, ut qui malim ad eos potius conspectum* **insatiabilem** *conferre, qui in dominum desaevierunt. 'Hic est ille,' dicam, 'fabri aut quaestuariae filius' "* (what follows, and especially this term for the mother of Jesus, which is found in the Talmud, shows that from here on Tertullian is referring to the Jews), *" 'sabbati destructor, Samarites et daemonium habens. Hic est, quem a Juda redemistis, hic est ille arundine et colaphis diverberatus, sputamentis dedecoratus, felle et aceto potatus. Hic est, quem clam discentes sub-*

Nietzsche's parenthesis above.] This is He whom you struck with reed and fist, whom you contemptuously spat upon, to whom you gave gall and vinegar to drink! This is He whom His disciples secretly stole away, that it might be said He had risen again, or the gardener abstracted, that his lettuces might come to no harm from the crowds of visitants!' What quaestor or priest in his munificence will bestow on you the favour of seeing and *exulting in such things as these*? And yet even now we in a measure have them *by faith* in the picturings of imagination. But what are the things which eye has not seen, ear has not heard, and which have not so much as dimly dawned upon the human heart? Whatever they are, they are nobler, I believe, than circus, and both theatres, and every racecourse." [Translation by the Rev. S. Thelwall.] There are two standard translations of Tertullian's *De Spectaculis*. One is by the Rev. S. Thelwall in *The Ante-Nicene Fathers: Translations of the Writings of the Fathers down to A.D. 325,* edited by the Rev. Alexander Roberts, D.D., and James Donaldson, LL.D., in volume III: *Latin Christianity: Its Founder, Tertullian* (American Reprint of the Edinburgh Edition, Grand Rapids, Mich., Wm. B. Eerdmans Publishing Company, 1957). The other translation is by Rudolph Arbesmann, O.S.A., Ph.D., Fordham University, in *The Fathers of the Church: A New Translation,* in the volume entitled *Tertullian: Disciplinary, Moral and Ascetical Works* (New York, Fathers of the Church, Inc., 1959, Imprimatur Francis Cardinal Spellman).

In the former edition we are told in a footnote to the title that although there has been some dispute as to whether the work was written before or after Tertullian's "lapse" from orthodoxy to Montanism, "a work so colourless that doctors can disagree about even its shading, must be regarded as practically orthodox. Exaggerated expressions are but the characteristics of the author's genius. We find the like in all writers of strongly marked individuality. Neander dates this treatise *circa* A.D. 197." And in a footnote to the last sentence quoted by Nietzsche, which concludes the last chapter of the treatise, we

ripuerunt, ut resurrexisse dicatur vel hortulanus detraxit, ne lactucae suae frequentia commeantium laederentur.' Ut talia spectes, **ut talibus exultes,** *quis tibi praetor aut consul aut guaestor aut sacerdos de sua liberalitate praestabit? Et tamen haec jam habemus quodammodo* **per fidem** *spiritu imaginante repraesentata. Ceterum qualia illa sunt, quae nec oculus vidit nec auris audivit nec in cor hominis ascenderunt?"* (1 Cor. 2,9.) *"Credo circo et utraque cavea"* (first and fourth rank or, according to others, the comic and tragic stage) *"et omni stadio gratiora."*—**Per fidem:** thus is it written.

16

Let us conclude. The two *opposing* values "good and bad," "good and evil" have been engaged in a fearful struggle on earth for thousands of years; and though the latter value has certainly been on top for a long time, there are still places where the struggle is as yet undecided. One might even say that it has risen

---

read: "This concluding chapter, which Gibbon delights to censure, because its fervid rhetoric so fearfully depicts the punishments of Christ's enemies, 'appears to Dr. Neander to contain a beautiful specimen of lively faith and Christian confidence.'"

In the latter edition we are informed that *"De Spectaculis* is one of Tertullian's most interesting and original works" (p. 38). And chapter 30, which Nietzsche quotes almost in its entirety, omitting only the first four lines, is introduced by a footnote that begins (and it continues in the same vein): "Tertullian gives here a colorful description of the millennium, picturing the feverish expectation of an early return of Christ . . ."

It is noteworthy that the Protestant edition finds the work "so colourless," while the Roman Catholic edition considers it "colorful"—and neither of them evinces any sensitivity to what outraged Nietzsche or Gibbon.

Edward Gibbon's comments are found in Chapter XV of *The History of the Decline and Fall of the Roman Empire:* "The condemnation of the wisest and most virtuous of the Pagans, on account of their ignorance or disbelief of the divine truth, seems to offend the reason and the humanity of the present age. But the primitive church, whose faith was of a much firmer consistence, delivered over, without hesitation, to eternal torture the far greater part of the human species. . . . These rigid sentiments, which had been unknown to the ancient world, appear to have infused a spirit of bitterness into a system of love and harmony. . . . The Christians, who, in this world, found themselves oppressed by the power of the Pagans, were sometimes seduced by resentment and spiritual pride to delight in the prospect of their future triumph. 'You are fond of spectacles,' exclaims the stern Tertullian; 'except the greatest of all spectacles, the last and eternal judgment of the universe. How shall I admire, how laugh . . .'"

ever higher and thus become more and more profound and spiritual: so that today there is perhaps no more decisive mark of a "*higher nature*," a more spiritual nature, than that of being divided in this sense and a genuine battleground of these opposed values.[48]

The symbol of this struggle, inscribed in letters legible across all human history, is "Rome against Judea, Judea against Rome":— there has hitherto been no greater event than *this* struggle, *this* question, *this* deadly contradiction. Rome felt the Jew to be something like anti-nature itself, its antipodal monstrosity as it were: in Rome the Jew stood "*convicted* of hatred for the whole human race"; and rightly, provided one has a right to link the salvation and future of the human race with the unconditional dominance of aristocratic values, Roman values.

How, on the other hand, did the Jews feel about Rome? A thousand signs tell us; but it suffices to recall the Apocalypse of John, the most wanton of all literary outbursts that vengefulness has on its conscience. (One should not underestimate the profound consistency of the Christian instinct when it signed this book of hate with the name of the disciple of love, the same disciple to whom it attributed that amorous-enthusiastic Gospel: there is a piece of truth in this, however much literary counterfeiting might have been required to produce it.) For the Romans were the strong and noble, and nobody stronger and nobler has yet existed on earth or even been dreamed of: every remnant of them, every inscription gives delight, if only one divines *what* it was that was there at work. The Jews, on the contrary, were the priestly nation of *ressentiment par excellence*, in whom there dwelt an unequaled popular-moral genius: one only has to compare similarly gifted nations—the Chinese or the Germans, for instance—

48. This remark which recalls *Beyond Good and Evil*, section 200, is entirely in keeping with the way in which the contrast of master and slave morality is introduced in *Beyond Good and Evil*, section 260; and it ought not to be overlooked. It sheds a good deal of light not only on this contrast but also on Nietzsche's *amor fati*, his love of fate. Those who ignore all this material are bound completely to misunderstand Nietzsche's moral philosophy.

with the Jews, to sense which is of the first and which of the fifth rank.[49]

Which of them has won *for the present*, Rome or Judea? But there can be no doubt: consider to whom one bows down in Rome itself today, as if they were the epitome of all the highest values—and not only in Rome but over almost half the earth, everywhere that man has become tame or desires to become tame: *three Jews*, as is known, and *one Jewess* (Jesus of Nazareth, the fisherman Peter, the rug weaver Paul, and the mother of the aforementioned Jesus, named Mary). This is very remarkable: Rome has been defeated beyond all doubt.

There was, to be sure, in the Renaissance an uncanny and glittering reawakening of the classical ideal, of the noble mode of evaluating all things; Rome itself, oppressed by the new superimposed Judaized Rome that presented the aspect of an ecumenical synagogue and was called the "church," stirred like one awakened from seeming death: but Judea immediately triumphed again, thanks to that thoroughly plebeian (German and English) *ressentiment* movement called the Reformation, and to that which was bound to arise from it, the restoration of the church—the restoration too of the ancient sepulchral repose of classical Rome.

With the French Revolution, Judea once again triumphed over the classical ideal, and this time in an even more profound and decisive sense: the last political noblesse in Europe, that of the *French* seventeenth and eighteenth century, collapsed beneath the popular instincts of *ressentiment*—greater rejoicing, more uproarious enthusiasm had never been heard on earth! To be sure, in the midst of it there occurred the most tremendous, the most unexpected thing: the ideal of antiquity itself stepped *incarnate* and in unheard-of splendor before the eyes and conscience of mankind—and once again, in opposition to the men-

49. Having said things that can easily be misconstrued as grist to the mill of the German anti-Semites, Nietzsche goes out of his way, as usual, to express his admiration for the Jews and his disdain for the Germans.

dacious slogan of *ressentiment*, "supreme rights of the majority," in opposition to the will to the lowering, the abasement, the leveling and the decline and twilight of mankind, there sounded stronger, simpler, and more insistently than ever the terrible and rapturous counterslogan "supreme rights of the few"! Like a last signpost to the *other* path, Napoleon appeared, the most isolated and late-born man there has ever been, and in him the problem of the *noble ideal as such* made flesh—one might well ponder *what* kind of problem it is: Napoleon, this synthesis of the *inhuman* and *superhuman*.

17

Was that the end of it? Had that greatest of all conflicts of ideals been placed *ad acta*[50] for all time? Or only adjourned, indefinitely adjourned?

Must the ancient fire not some day flare up much more terribly, after much longer preparation? More: must one not desire it with all one's might? even will it? even promote it?

Whoever begins at this point, like my readers, to reflect and pursue his train of thought will not soon come to the end of it— reason enough for me to come to an end, assuming it has long since been abundantly clear what my *aim* is, what the aim of that dangerous slogan is that is inscribed at the head of my last book *Beyond Good and Evil.*—At least this does *not* mean "Beyond Good and Bad."——

———

Note.[51] I take the opportunity provided by this treatise to express publicly and formally a desire I have previously voiced only in occasional conversation with scholars; namely, that some philosophical faculty might advance *historical* studies *of morality* through a series of academic prize-essays—perhaps this present book will serve to provide a powerful impetus in this direction. In case

50. Disposed of.
51. *Anmerkung.*

this idea should be implemented, I suggest the following question: it deserves the attention of philologists and historians as well as that of professional philosophers:

"What light does linguistics, and especially the study of etymology, throw on the history of the evolution of moral concepts?"

On the other hand, it is equally necessary to engage the interest of physiologists and doctors in these problems (of the *value* of existing evaluations); it may be left to academic philosophers to act as advocates and mediators in this matter too, after they have on the whole succeeded in the past in transforming the originally so reserved and mistrustful relations between philosophy, physiology, and medicine into the most amicable and fruitful exchange. Indeed, every table of values, every "thou shalt" known to history or ethnology, requires first a *physiological* investigation and interpretation, rather than a psychological one; and every one of them needs a critique on the part of medical science. The question: what is the *value* of this or that table of values and "morals"? should be viewed from the most divers perspectives; for the problem "value *for what?*" cannot be examined too subtly. Something, for example, that possessed obvious value in relation to the longest possible survival of a race (or to the enhancement of its power of adaptation to a particular climate or to the preservation of the greatest number) would by no means possess the same value if it were a question, for instance, of producing a stronger type. The well-being of the majority and the well-being of the few are opposite viewpoints of value: to consider the former *a priori* of higher value may be left to the naïveté of English biologists.—*All* the sciences have from now on to prepare the way for the future task of the philosophers: this task understood as the solution of the *problem of value*, the determination of the *order of rank among values*.

SECOND ESSAY:
"GUILT," "BAD CONSCIENCE,"[1]
AND THE LIKE

1

To breed an animal *with the right to make promises*—is not this the paradoxical task that nature has set itself in the case of man? is it not the real problem regarding man?

That this problem has been solved to a large extent must seem all the more remarkable to anyone who appreciates the strength of the opposing force, that of *forgetfulness*. Forgetting is no mere *vis inertiae*[2] as the superficial imagine; it is rather an ac-

---

1. *Schlechtes Gewissen* is no technical term but simply the common German equivalent of "bad conscience." Danto's translation "bad consciousness" (*Nietzsche as Philosopher,* New York, Macmillan, 1965, pp. 164 and 180) is simply wrong: *Gewissen,* like conscience, and unlike the French *conscience,* cannot mean consciousness.

There are many mistranslations in Danto's *Nietzsche.* Another one, though relatively unimportant, is of some interest and relevant to the *Genealogy: Schadenfreude*—a German word for which there is no English equivalent—is not quite "the wicked pleasure in the beholding of suffering" (p. 181) or "in the sheer spectacle of suffering: in fights, executions, . . . bullbaiting, cockfights, and the like" (p. 174). In such contexts the word is utterly out of place: it signifies the petty, mischievous delight felt in the discomfiture of another human being.

2. Inertia.

tive and in the strictest sense positive faculty of repression,[3] that is responsible for the fact that what we experience and absorb enters our consciousness as little while we are digesting it (one might call the process "inpsychation") as does the thousandfold process, involved in physical nourishment—so-called "incorporation." To close the doors and windows of consciousness for a time; to remain undisturbed by the noise and struggle of our underworld of utility organs working with and against one another; a little quietness, a little *tabula rasa*[4] of the consciousness, to make room for new things, above all for the nobler functions and functionaries, for regulation, foresight, premeditation (for our organism is an oligarchy)—that is the purpose of active forgetfulness, which is like a doorkeeper, a preserver of psychic order, repose, and etiquette: so that it will be immediately obvious how there could be no happiness, no cheerfulness, no hope, no pride, no *present*, without forgetfulness. The man in whom this apparatus of repression is damaged and ceases to function properly may be compared (and more than merely compared) with a dyspeptic—he cannot "have done" with anything.

Now this animal which needs to be forgetful, in which forgetting represents a force, a form of *robust* health, has bred in itself an opposing faculty, a memory, with the aid of which forgetfulness is abrogated in certain cases—namely in those cases where promises are made. This involves no mere passive inability to rid oneself of an impression, no mere indigestion through a once-pledged word with which one cannot "have done," but an active *desire* not to rid oneself, a desire for the continuance of something desired once, a real *memory of the will:* so that between the original "I will," "I shall do this" and the actual discharge of the will, its *act*, a world of strange new things, circumstances, even acts of will may be interposed without breaking this long chain of will. But how many things this presupposes! To ordain the future in advance in this way, man must first have learned to distinguish necessary events from chance ones, to think causally, to

3. *Positives Hemmungsvermögen.*
4. Clean slate.

see and anticipate distant eventualities as if they belonged to the present, to decide with certainty what is the goal and what the means to it, and in general be able to calculate and compute. Man himself must first of all have become *calculable, regular, necessary,* even in his own image of himself, if he is to be able to stand security for *his own future,* which is what one who promises does!

2

This precisely is the long story of how *responsibility* originated. The task of breeding an animal with the right to make promises evidently embraces and presupposes as a preparatory task that one first *makes* men to a certain degree necessary, uniform, like among like, regular, and consequently calculable. The tremendous labor of that which I have called "morality of mores" (*Dawn,* sections 9, 14, 16)[5]—the labor performed by man upon himself during the greater part of the existence of the human race, his entire *prehistoric* labor, finds in this its meaning, its great justification, notwithstanding the severity, tyranny, stupidity, and idiocy involved in it: with the aid of the morality of mores and the social straitjacket, man was actually *made* calculable.

If we place ourselves at the end of this tremendous process, where the tree at last brings forth fruit, where society and the morality of custom at last reveal *what* they have simply been the means to: then we discover that the ripest fruit is the *sovereign individual,* like only to himself, liberated again from morality of custom, autonomous and supramoral (for "autonomous" and "moral" are mutually exclusive),[6] in short, the man who has his

5. See also *Human, All-Too-Human,* section 96; *Mixed Opinions and Maxims,* section 89; and *The Dawn,* section 18, all of which are included in the present volume. *Dawn,* section 16, is included in *The Portable Nietzsche,* p. 76. The German phrase is *die Sittlichkeit der Sitte,* the morality of mores.

6. The parenthetical statement is the contrary of Kant's view. When it was written, it must have struck most readers as paradoxical, but in the twentieth century it is apt to seem *less* paradoxical than Kant's view. *The Lonely Crowd* (by David Riesman, with Nathan Glazer and Reuel Denney; New Haven, Conn., Yale University Press, 1950) has popu-

own independent, protracted will and the *right to make promises*—and in him a proud consciousness, quivering in every muscle, of *what* has at length been achieved and become flesh in him, a consciousness of his own power and freedom, a sensation of mankind come to completion. This emancipated individual, with the actual *right* to make promises, this master of a *free* will, this sovereign man—how should he not be aware of his superiority over all those who lack the right to make promises and stand as their own guarantors, of how much trust, how much fear, how much reverence he arouses—he "*deserves*" all three—and of how this mastery over himself also necessarily gives him mastery over circumstances, over nature, and over all more short-willed and unreliable creatures? The "free" man, the possessor of a protracted and unbreakable will, also possesses his *measure of value:* looking out upon others from himself, he honors or he despises; and just as he is bound to honor his peers, the strong and reliable (those with the *right* to make promises)—that is, all those who promise like sovereigns, reluctantly, rarely, slowly, who are chary of trusting, whose trust is a mark of *distinction,* who give their word as something that can be relied on because they know themselves strong enough to maintain it in the face of accidents, even "in the face of fate"—he is bound to reserve a kick for the feeble windbags who promise without the right to do so, and a rod for the liar who breaks his word even at the moment he utters it. The proud awareness of the extraordinary privilege of *responsibility,* the consciousness of this rare freedom, this power over oneself and over fate, has in his case penetrated to the profoundest depths and become instinct, the dominating instinct. What will he call this dominating instinct, supposing he feels the need to give it a name? The answer is beyond doubt: this sovereign man calls it his *conscience.*

---

larized a Nietzschean, non-Kantian conception of the autonomous individual, who is contrasted with the tradition-directed (Nietzsche's morality of mores), the inner-directed (Kant, for example), and the other-directed (Nietzsche's "last man").

3

His conscience?—It is easy to guess that the concept of "conscience" that we here encounter in its highest, almost astonishing, manifestation, has a long history and variety of forms behind it. To possess the right to stand security for oneself and to do so with pride, thus to possess also the *right to affirm oneself*—this, as has been said, is a ripe fruit, but also a *late* fruit: how long must this fruit have hung on the tree, unripe and sour! And for a much longer time nothing whatever was to be seen of any such fruit: no one could have promised its appearance, although everything in the tree was preparing for and growing toward it!

"How can one create a memory for the human animal? How can one impress something upon this partly obtuse, partly flighty mind, attuned only to the passing moment, in such a way that it will stay there?"

One can well believe that the answers and methods for solving this primeval problem were not precisely gentle; perhaps indeed there was nothing more fearful and uncanny in the whole prehistory of man than his *mnemotechnics.* "If something is to stay in the memory it must be burned in: only that which never ceases to *hurt* stays in the memory"—this is a main clause of the oldest (unhappily also the most enduring) psychology on earth. One might even say that wherever on earth solemnity, seriousness, mystery, and gloomy coloring still distinguish the life of man and a people, something of the terror that formerly attended all promises, pledges, and vows on earth is *still effective:* the past, the longest, deepest and sternest past, breathes upon us and rises up in us whenever we become "serious." Man could never do without blood, torture, and sacrifices when he felt the need to create a memory for himself; the most dreadful sacrifices and pledges (sacrifices of the first-born among them), the most repulsive mutilations (castration, for example), the cruelest rites of all the religious cults (and all religions are at the deepest level systems of cruelties)—all this has its origin in the instinct that realized that pain is the most powerful aid to mnemonics.

In a certain sense, the whole of asceticism belongs here: a few ideas are to be rendered inextinguishable, ever-present, unforgettable, "fixed," with the aim of hypnotising the entire nervous and intellectual system with these "fixed ideas"—and ascetic procedures and modes of life are means of freeing these ideas from the competition of all other ideas, so as to make them "unforgettable." The worse man's memory has been, the more fearful has been the appearance of his customs; the severity of the penal code provides an especially significant measure of the degree of effort needed to overcome forgetfulness and to impose a few primitive demands of social existence as *present realities* upon these slaves of momentary affect and desire.

We Germans certainly do not regard ourselves as a particularly cruel and hardhearted people, still less as a particularly frivolous one, living only for the day; but one has only to look at our former codes of punishments to understand what effort it costs on this earth to breed a "nation of thinkers" (which is to say, *the* nation in Europe in which one still finds today the maximum of trust, seriousness, lack of taste, and matter-of-factness—and with these qualities one has the right to breed every kind of European mandarin). These Germans have employed fearful means to acquire a memory, so as to master their basic mob-instinct and its brutal coarseness. Consider the old German punishments; for example, stoning (the sagas already have millstones drop on the head of the guilty), breaking on the wheel (the most characteristic invention and speciality of the German genius in the realm of punishment!), piercing with stakes, tearing apart or trampling by horses ("quartering"), boiling of the criminal in oil or wine (still employed in the fourteenth and fifteenth centuries), the popular flaying alive ("cutting straps"), cutting flesh from the chest, and also the practice of smearing the wrongdoer with honey and leaving him in the blazing sun for the flies. With the aid of such images and procedures one finally remembers five or six "I will not's," in regard to which one had given one's *promise* so as to participate in the advantages of society—and it was indeed with the aid of this kind of memory that one at last came "to reason"! Ah, reason, seriousness, mastery over the affects, the whole somber thing called reflection, all these prerogatives and showpieces of man: how dearly they have been bought! How much blood and cruelty lie at the bottom of all "good things"!

4

But how did the other "somber thing," the consciousness of guilt, the "bad conscience," come into the world?—And at this point we return to the genealogists of morals. To say it again— or haven't I said it yet?—they are worthless. A brief span of experience that is merely one's own, merely modern; no knowledge or will to knowledge of the past; even less of historical instinct, of that "second sight" needed here above all—and yet they undertake history of morality: it stands to reason that their results stay at a more than respectful distance from the truth. Have these genealogists of morals had even the remotest suspicion that, for example, the major moral concept *Schuld* [guilt] has its origin in the very material concept *Schulden* [debts]?[7] Or that punishment, as requital, evolved quite independently of any presupposition concerning freedom or non-freedom of the will?— to such an extent, indeed, that a *high* degree of humanity had to be attained before the animal "man" began even to make the much more primitive distinctions between "intentional," "negligent," "accidental," "accountable," and their opposites and to take them into account when determining punishments. The idea, now so obvious, apparently so natural, even unavoidable, that had to serve as the explanation of how the sense of justice ever appeared on earth—"the criminal deserves punishment *because* he could have acted differently"—is in fact an extremely

7. The German equivalent of "guilt" is *Schuld;* and the German for "debt(s)" is *Schuld(en).* "Innocent" is *unschuldig;* "debtor" is *Schuldner;* and so forth. This obviously poses problems for an English translation of this essay; but once the point has been clearly stated, no misunderstandings need result. Nietzsche's claims obviously do not *depend* on the double meaning of a German word; nor are they weakened by the fact that in English there are two different words, one derived from an Anglo-Saxon root, the other from Latin.

late and subtle form of human judgment and inference: whoever transposes it to the beginning is guilty of a crude misunderstanding of the psychology of more primitive mankind. Throughout the greater part of human history punishment was *not* imposed *because* one held the wrongdoer responsible for his deed, thus *not* on the presupposition that only the guilty one should be punished: rather, as parents still punish their children, from anger at some harm or injury, vented on the one who caused it—but this anger is held in check and modified by the idea that every injury has its *equivalent* and can actually be paid back, even if only through the *pain* of the culprit. And whence did this primeval, deeply rooted, perhaps by now ineradicable idea draw its power— this idea of an equivalence between injury and pain? I have already divulged it: in the contractual relationship between *creditor* and *debtor,* which is as old as the idea of "legal subjects" and in turn points back to the fundamental forms of buying, selling, barter, trade, and traffic.

5

When we contemplate these contractual relationships, to be sure, we feel considerable suspicion and repugnance toward those men of the past who created or permitted them. This was to be expected from what we have previously noted. It was here that *promises* were made; it was here that a memory had to be *made* for those who promised; it is here, one suspects, that we shall find a great deal of severity, cruelty, and pain. To inspire trust in his promise to repay, to provide a guarantee of the seriousness and sanctity of his promise, to impress repayment as a duty, an obligation upon his own conscience, the debtor made a contract with the creditor and pledged that if he should fail to repay he would substitute something else that he "possessed," something he had control over; for example, his body, his wife, his freedom, or even his life (or, given certain religious presuppositions, even his bliss after death, the salvation of his soul, ultimately his peace in the grave: thus it was in Egypt, where the debtor's corpse found no peace from the creditor even in the grave—and among the Egyptians such peace meant a great deal). Above all, however, the creditor could inflict every kind of indignity and torture upon the body of the debtor; for example, cut from it as much as seemed commensurate with the size of the debt—and everywhere and from early times one had exact evaluations, *legal* evaluations, of the individual limbs and parts of the body from this point of view, some of them going into horrible and minute detail. I consider it as an advance, as evidence of a freer, more generous, *more Roman* conception of law when the Twelve Tables of Rome decreed it a matter of indifference how much or how little the creditor cut off in such cases: *"si plus minusve secuerunt, ne fraude esto."*[8]

Let us be clear as to the logic of this form of compensation: it is strange enough. An equivalence is provided by the creditor's receiving, in place of a literal compensation for an injury (thus in place of money, land, possessions of any kind), a recompense in the form of a kind of *pleasure*—the pleasure of being allowed to vent his power freely upon one who is powerless, the voluptuous pleasure *"de faire le mal pour le plaisir de le faire,"*[9] the enjoyment of violation. This enjoyment will be the greater the lower the creditor stands in the social order, and can easily appear to him as a most delicious morsel, indeed as a foretaste of higher rank. In "punishing" the debtor, the creditor participates in a *right of the masters:* at last he, too, may experience for once the exalted sensation of being allowed to despise and mistreat someone as "beneath him"—or at least, if the actual power and administration of punishment has already passed to the "authorities," to *see* him despised and mistreated. The compensation, then, consists in a warrant for and title to cruelty.—

---

8. If they have secured more or less, let that be no crime.
9. Of doing evil for the pleasure of doing it.

6

It was in *this* sphere then, the sphere of legal obligations, that the moral conceptual world of "guilt," "conscience," "duty," "sacredness of duty" had its origin: its beginnings were, like the beginnings of everything great on earth, soaked in blood thoroughly and for a long time. And might one not add that, fundamentally, this world has never since lost a certain odor of blood and torture? (Not even in good old Kant: the categorical imperative smells of cruelty.) It was here, too, that that uncanny intertwining of the ideas "guilt and suffering" was first effected—and by now they may well be inseparable. To ask it again: to what extent can suffering balance debts or guilt?[10] To the extent that to *make* suffer was in the highest degree pleasurable, to the extent that the injured party exchanged for the loss he had sustained, including the displeasure caused by the loss, an extraordinary counterbalancing pleasure: that of *making* suffer—a genuine *festival*, something which, as aforesaid, was prized the more highly the more violently it contrasted with the rank and social standing of the creditor. This is offered only as a conjecture; for the depths of such subterranean things are difficult to fathom, besides being painful; and whoever clumsily interposes the concept of "revenge" does not enhance his insight into the matter but further veils and darkens it (—for revenge merely leads us back to the same problem: "how can making suffer constitute a compensation?").

It seems to me that the delicacy and even more the tartuffery of tame domestic animals (which is to say modern men, which is to say us) resists a really vivid comprehension of the degree to which *cruelty* constituted the great festival pleasure of more primitive men and was indeed an ingredient of almost every one of their pleasures; and how naïvely, how innocently their thirst for cruelty manifested itself, how, as a matter of principle, they

10. "Debts or guilt": *"Schulden."*

posited "disinterested malice" (or, in Spinoza's words, *sympathia malevolens*) as a *normal* quality of man—and thus as something to which the conscience cordially says *Yes!* A more profound eye might perceive enough of this oldest and most fundamental festival pleasure of man even in our time; in *Beyond Good and Evil*, section 229[11] (and earlier in *The Dawn*, sections 18, 77, 113)[12] I pointed cautiously to the ever-increasing spiritualization and "deification" of cruelty which permeates the entire history of higher culture (and in a significant sense actually constitutes it). In any event, it is not long since princely weddings and public festivals of the more magnificent kind were unthinkable without executions, torturings, or perhaps an auto-da-fé, and no noble household was without creatures upon whom one could heedlessly vent one's malice and cruel jokes. (Consider, for instance, Don Quixote at the court of the Duchess. Today we read *Don Quixote* with a bitter taste in our mouths, almost with a feeling of torment, and would thus seem very strange and incomprehensible to its author and his contemporaries: they read it with the clearest conscience in the world as the most cheerful of books, they laughed themselves almost to death over it). To see others suffer does one good, to make others suffer even more: this is a hard saying but an ancient, mighty, human, all-too-human principle to which even the apes might subscribe; for it has been said that in devising bizarre cruelties they anticipate man and are, as it were, his "prelude." Without cruelty there is no festival: thus the longest and most ancient part of human history teaches—and in punishment there is so much that is *festive!*—

11. Nietzsche, as usual, furnishes a page reference to the first edition—in this instance, pp. 117ff., which would take us to the middle of section 194 and the following section(s); and German editors, down to Karl Schlechta, give the equivalent page reference. But 117 is plainly a misprint for 177, which takes us to section 229—beyond a doubt, the passage Nietzsche means.

12. Section 113 is quoted and analyzed in Kaufmann's *Nietzsche,* Chapter 6, section II. Both repay reading in connection with the passage above, to avoid misunderstanding.

7

With this idea, by the way, I am by no means concerned to furnish our pessimists with more grist for their discordant and creaking mills of life-satiety. On the contrary, let me declare expressly that in the days when mankind was not yet ashamed of its cruelty, life on earth was more cheerful than it is now that pessimists exist. The darkening of the sky above mankind has deepened in step with the increase in man's feeling of shame *at man*. The weary pessimistic glance, mistrust of the riddle of life, the icy No of disgust with life—these do not characterize the most *evil* epochs of the human race: rather do they first step into the light of day as the swamp weeds they are when the swamp to which they belong comes into being—I mean the morbid softening and moralization through which the animal "man" finally learns to be ashamed of all his instincts. On his way to becoming an "angel" (to employ no uglier word) man has evolved that queasy stomach and coated tongue through which not only the joy and innocence of the animal but life itself has become repugnant to him—so that he sometimes holds his nose in his own presence and, with Pope Innocent the Third, disapprovingly catalogues his own repellent aspects ("impure begetting, disgusting means of nutrition in his mother's womb, baseness of the matter out of which man evolves, hideous stink, secretion of saliva, urine, and filth").

Today, when suffering is always brought forward as the principal argument *against* existence, as the worst question mark, one does well to recall the ages in which the opposite opinion prevailed because men were unwilling to refrain from *making* suffer and saw in it an enchantment of the first order, a genuine seduction *to* life. Perhaps in those days—the delicate may be comforted by this thought—pain did not hurt as much as it does now; at least that is the conclusion a doctor may arrive at who has treated Negroes (taken as representatives of prehistoric man—) for severe internal inflammations that would drive even the best constituted European to distraction—in the case of Negroes they do *not* do so. (The curve of human susceptibility to pain seems in fact to take an extraordinary and almost sudden drop as soon as one has passed the upper ten thousand or ten million of the top stratum of culture; and for my own part, I have no doubt that the combined suffering of all the animals ever subjected to the knife for scientific ends is utterly negligible compared with *one* painful night of a single hysterical bluestocking.) Perhaps the possibility may even be allowed that this joy in cruelty does not really have to have died out: if pain hurts more today, it simply requires a certain sublimation and subtilization, that is to say it has to appear translated into the imaginative and psychical and adorned with such innocent names that even the tenderest and most hypocritical conscience is not suspicious of them ("tragic pity" is one such name; *"les nostalgies de la croix"*[13] is another).

What really arouses indignation against suffering is not suffering as such but the senselessness of suffering: but neither for the Christian, who has interpreted a whole mysterious machinery of salvation into suffering, nor for the naïve man of more ancient times, who understood all suffering in relation to the spectator of it or the causer of it, was there any such thing as *senseless* suffering. So as to abolish hidden, undetected, unwitnessed suffering from the world and honestly to deny it, one was in the past virtually compelled to invent gods and genii of all the heights and depths, in short something that roams even in secret, hidden places, sees even in the dark, and will not easily let an interesting painful spectacle pass unnoticed. For it was with the aid of such inventions that life then knew how to work the trick which it has always known how to work, that of justifying itself, of justifying its "evil." Nowadays it might require other auxiliary inventions (for example, life as a riddle, life as an epistemological problem). "Every evil the sight of which edifies a god is justified": thus spoke the primitive logic of feeling—and was it, indeed, only primitive? The gods conceived of as the friends of *cruel* spectacles—oh how profoundly this ancient idea still permeates

13. The nostalgia of the cross.

our European humanity! Merely consult Calvin and Luther. It is certain, at any rate, that the *Greeks* still knew of no tastier spice to offer their gods to season their happiness than the pleasures of cruelty. With what eyes do you think Homer made his gods look down upon the destinies of men? What was at bottom the ultimate meaning of Trojan Wars and other such tragic terrors? There can be no doubt whatever: they were intended as *festival plays* for the gods; and, insofar as the poet is in these matters of a more "godlike" disposition than other men, no doubt also as festival plays for the poets.

It was in the same way that the moral philosophers of Greece later imagined the eyes of God looking down upon the moral struggle, upon the heroism and self-torture of the virtuous: the "Herakles of duty" was on a stage and knew himself to be; virtue without a witness was something unthinkable for this nation of actors. Surely, that philosophers' invention, so bold and so fateful, which was then first devised for Europe, the invention of "free will," of the absolute spontaneity of man in good and in evil, was devised above all to furnish a right to the idea that the interest of the gods in man, in human virtue, *could never be exhausted.* There must never be any lack of real novelty, of really unprecedented tensions, complications, and catastrophies on the stage of the earth: the course of a completely deterministic world would have been predictable for the gods and they would have quickly grown weary of it—reason enough for those *friends of the gods,* the philosophers, not to inflict such a deterministic world on their gods! The entire mankind of antiquity is full of tender regard for "the spectator," as an essentially public, essentially visible world which cannot imagine happiness apart from spectacles and festivals.—And, as aforesaid, even in great *punishment* there is so much that is festive!

8

To return to our investigation: the feeling of guilt, of personal obligation, had its origin, as we saw, in the oldest and most primitive personal relationship, that between buyer and seller, creditor and debtor: it was here that one person first encountered another person, that one person first *measured himself* against another. No grade of civilization, however low, has yet been discovered in which something of this relationship has not been noticeable. Setting prices, determining values, contriving equivalences, exchanging—these preoccupied the earliest thinking of man to so great an extent that in a certain sense they constitute thinking *as such:* here it was that the oldest kind of astuteness developed; here likewise, we may suppose, did human pride, the feeling of superiority in relation to other animals, have its first beginnings. Perhaps our word "man" (*manas*) still expresses something of precisely *this* feeling of self-satisfaction: man designated himself as the creature that measures values, evaluates and measures, as the "valuating animal as such."

Buying and selling, together with their psychological appurtenances, are older even than the beginnings of any kind of social forms of organization and alliances: it was rather out of the most rudimentary form of personal legal rights that the budding sense of exchange, contract, guilt, right, obligation, settlement, first *transferred* itself to the coarsest and most elementary social complexes (in their relations with other similar complexes), together with the custom of comparing, measuring, and calculating power against power. The eye was now focused on this perspective; and with that blunt consistency characteristic of the thinking of primitive mankind, which is hard to set in motion but then proceeds inexorably in the same direction, one forthwith arrived at the great generalization, "everything has its price; *all* things can be paid for"—the oldest and naïvest moral canon of *justice,* the beginning of all "good-naturedness," all "fairness," all "good will," all "objectivity" on earth. Justice on this elementary level is the good will among parties of approximately equal power to come to terms with one another, to reach an "understanding" by means of a settlement—and to *compel* parties of lesser power to reach a settlement among themselves.—

9

Still retaining the criteria of prehistory (this prehistory is in any case present in all ages or may always reappear)[14]: the community, too, stands to its members in that same vital basic relation, that of the creditor to his debtors. One lives in a community, one enjoys the advantages of a communality (oh what advantages! we sometimes underrate them today), one dwells protected, cared for, in peace and trustfulness, without fear of certain injuries and hostile acts to which the man *outside,* the "man without peace," is exposed—a German will understand the original connotations of *Elend*[15]—since one has bound and pledged oneself to the community precisely with a view to injuries and hostile acts. What will happen *if this pledge is broken?* The community, the disappointed creditor, will get what repayment it can, one may depend on that. The direct harm caused by the culprit is here a minor matter; quite apart from this, the lawbreaker is above all a "breaker," a breaker of his contract and his word *with the whole* in respect to all the benefits and comforts of communal life of which he has hitherto had a share. The lawbreaker is a debtor who has not merely failed to make good the advantages and advance payments bestowed upon him but has actually attacked his creditor: therefore he is not only deprived henceforth of all these advantages and benefits, as is fair—he is also reminded *what these benefits are really worth.* The wrath of the disappointed creditor, the community, throws him back again into the savage and outlaw state against which he has hitherto been protected: it thrusts him away—and now every kind of hostility may be vented upon him. "Punishment" at this level of civilization is simply a copy, a *mimus,* of the normal attitude toward a hated, disarmed, prostrated enemy, who has lost not only every right and protection, but all hope of quarter as well; it is thus the rights of war and the victory celebration of the *vae victis!*[16] in all

14. A prophetic parenthesis.
15. Misery. Originally, exile.
16. Woe to the losers!

their mercilessness and cruelty—which explains why it is that war itself (including the warlike sacrificial cult) has provided all the *forms* that punishment has assumed throughout history.

10

As its power increases, a community ceases to take the individual's transgressions so seriously, because they can no longer be considered as dangerous and destructive to the whole as they were formerly: the malefactor is no longer "set beyond the pale of peace" and thrust out; universal anger may not be vented upon him as unrestrainedly as before—on the contrary, the whole from now on carefully defends the malefactor against this anger, especially that of those he has directly harmed, and takes him under its protection. A compromise with the anger of those directly injured by the criminal; an effort to localize the affair and to prevent it from causing any further, let alone a general, disturbance; attempts to discover equivalents and to settle the whole matter (*compositio*); above all, the increasingly definite will to treat every crime as in some sense *dischargeable*, and thus at least to a certain extent to *isolate* the criminal and his deed from one another—these traits become more and more clearly visible as the penal law evolves. As the power and self-confidence of a community increase, the penal law always becomes more moderate; every weakening or imperiling of the former brings with it a restoration of the harsher forms of the latter. The "creditor" always becomes more humane to the extent that he has grown richer; finally, how much injury he can endure without suffering from it becomes the actual *measure* of his wealth. It is not unthinkable that a society might attain such a *consciousness of power* that it could allow itself the noblest luxury possible to it—letting those who harm it go *unpunished*. "What are my parasites to me?" it might say. "May they live and prosper: I am strong enough for that!"

The justice which began with, "everything is dischargeable, everything must be discharged," ends by winking and letting those incapable of discharging their debt go free: it ends, as does every good thing on earth, by *overcoming itself.*[17] This self-overcoming of justice: one knows the beautiful name it has given itself—*mercy;* it goes without saying that mercy remains the privilege of the most powerful man, or better, his—beyond the law.[18]

11

Here a word in repudiation of attempts that have lately been made to seek the origin of justice in quite a different sphere—namely in that of *ressentiment.* To the psychologists first of all, presuming they would like to study *ressentiment* close up for once, I would say: this plant blooms best today among anarchists and anti-Semites—where it has always bloomed, in hidden places, like the violet, though with a different odor. And as like must always produce like, it causes us no surprise to see a repetition in such circles of attempts often made before—see above, section

17. *Sich selbst aufhebend.* And in the next sentence *Selbstaufhebung* has been translated as self-overcoming. Similarly, *aufzuheben* in the middle of section 13, below, and *aufgehoben* in section 8 of the third essay have been rendered "overcome." See also III, section 27, with note. *Aufheben* is a very troublesome word, though common in ordinary German. Literally, it means "pick up"; but it has two derivative meanings that are no less common: "cancel" and "preserve" or "keep." Something picked up is no longer there, but the point of picking it up may be to keep it. Hegel made much of this term; his use of it is explained and discussed in Walter Kaufmann, *Hegel* (Garden City, N.Y., Doubleday, 1965; Garden City, N.Y., Doubleday Anchor Books, 1966), section 34—and a comparison of Hegel and Nietzsche on this point may be found in Kaufmann's *Nietzsche,* Chapter 8, section II.

18. The theme sounded here is one of the central motifs of Nietzsche's philosophy. Cf. *Dawn,* section 202: ". . . Let us eliminate the concept of *sin* from the world—and let us soon dispatch the concept of *punishment* after it! May these exiled monsters live somewhere else henceforth and not among men—if they insist on living and will not perish of disgust with themselves! . . . Shouldn't we be mature enough yet for the opposite view? Shouldn't we be able to say yet: every 'guilty' person is sick?—No, the hour for that has not yet come. As yet the physicians are lacking above all . . . As yet no thinker has had the courage of measuring the health of a society and of individuals according to how many parasites they can stand . . ." (See *The Portable Nietzsche,* pp. 85–88.) Cf. also *Zarathustra* II, "On the Tarantulas": *"That man be delivered from revenge,* that is for me the bridge to the highest hope . . ." (*ibid.,* p. 211). Many other pertinent passages are cited in Kaufmann, *Nietzsche,* Chapter 12, sections II and V.

14—to sanctify *revenge*[19] under the name of *justice*[20]—as if justice were at bottom merely a further development of the feeling of being aggrieved—and to rehabilitate not only revenge but all *reactive* affects in general. To the latter as such I would be the last to raise any objection: in respect to the entire biological problem (in relation to which the value of these affects has hitherto been underrated) it even seems to me to constitute a *service*. All I draw attention to is the circumstance that it is the spirit of *ressentiment* itself out of which this new nuance of scientific fairness (for the benefit of hatred, envy, jealousy, mistrust, rancor, and revenge) proceeds. For this "scientific fairness" immediately ceases and gives way to accents of deadly enmity and prejudice once it is a question of dealing with another group of affects, affects that, it seems to me, are of even greater biological value than those reactive affects and consequently deserve even more to be *scientifically* evaluated and esteemed: namely, the truly *active* affects, such as lust for power, avarice, and the like. (E. Dühring:[21] *The Value of Life; A Course in Philosophy;* and, fundamentally, *passim.*)

So much against this tendency in general: as for Dühring's specific proposition that the home of justice is to be sought in the sphere of the reactive feelings, one is obliged for truth's sake to counter it with a blunt antithesis: the *last* sphere to be conquered by the spirit of justice is the sphere of the reactive feelings! When it really happens that the just man remains just even toward those who have harmed him (and not merely cold, temperate, remote, indifferent: being just is always a *positive* attitude), when the exalted, clear objectivity, as penetrating as it is mild, of the eye of justice and *judging* is not dimmed even under the assault of personal injury, derision, and calumny, this is a piece of perfection and supreme mastery on earth—something

19. *Rache.*

20. *Gerechtigkeit.*

21. Eugen Dühring (1833-1901), a prolific German philosopher and political economist, was among other things an impassioned patriot and anti-Semite and hated the cosmopolitan Goethe and the Greeks. He is remembered chiefly as the butt of polemical works by Karl Marx and Friedrich Engels and of scattered hostile remarks in Nietzsche's writings.

it would be prudent not to expect or to *believe* in too readily. On the average, a small dose of aggression, malice, or insinuation certainly suffices to drive the blood into the eyes—and fairness out of the eyes—of even the most upright people. The active, aggressive, arrogant man is still a hundred steps closer to justice than the reactive man; for he has absolutely no need to take a false and prejudiced view of the object before him in the way the reactive man does and is bound to do. For that reason the aggressive man, as the stronger, nobler, more courageous, has in fact also had at all times a *freer* eye, a *better* conscience on his side: conversely, one can see who has the invention of the "bad conscience" on his conscience—the man of *ressentiment*!

Finally, one only has to look at history: in which sphere has the entire administration of law[22] hitherto been at home—also the need for law? In the sphere of reactive men, perhaps? By no means: rather in that of the active, strong, spontaneous, aggressive. From a historical point of view, law represents on earth—let it be said to the dismay of the above-named agitator (who himself once confessed: "the doctrine of revenge is the red thread of justice that runs through all my work and efforts")—the struggle *against* the reactive feelings, the war conducted against them on the part of the active and aggressive powers who employed some of their strength to impose measure and bounds upon the excesses of the reactive pathos and to compel it to come to terms. Wherever justice is practiced and maintained one sees a stronger power seeking a means of putting an end to the senseless raging of *ressentiment* among the weaker powers that stand under it (whether they be groups or individuals)—partly by taking the object of *ressentiment* out of the hands of revenge, partly by substituting for revenge the struggle against the enemies of peace and order, partly by devising and in some cases imposing settlements, partly by elevating certain equivalents for injuries into norms to which from then on *ressentiment* is once and for all directed. The most decisive act, however, that the

22. *Recht.*

supreme power performs and accomplishes against the predom-
inance of grudges and rancor—it always takes this action as soon
as it is in any way strong enough to do so—is the institution of
law,[23] the imperative declaration of what in general counts as
permitted, as just,[24] in its eyes, and what counts as forbidden, as
unjust:[25] once it has instituted the law, it treats violence and
capricious acts on the part of individuals or entire groups as offenses against the law, as rebellion against the supreme power itself, and thus leads the feelings of its subjects away from the
direct injury caused by such offenses; and in the long run it thus
attains the reverse of that which is desired by all revenge that is
fastened exclusively to the viewpoint of the person injured: from
now on the eye is trained to an ever more *impersonal* evaluation of
the deed, and this applies even to the eye of the injured person
himself (although last of all, as remarked above).

"Just" and "unjust" exist, accordingly, only after the institution of the law (and *not*, as Dühring would have it, after the per-
petration of the injury). To speak of just or unjust *in itself* is quite
senseless; *in itself*, of course, no injury, assault, exploitation, destruction can be "unjust," since life operates *essentially*, that is in
its basic functions, through injury, assault, exploitation, destruction and simply cannot be thought of at all without this character. One must indeed grant something even more unpalatable:
that, from the highest biological standpoint, legal conditions can
never be other than *exceptional conditions*, since they constitute a
partial restriction of the will of life, which is bent upon power,
and are subordinate to its total goal as a single means: namely, as
a means of creating *greater* units of power. A legal order thought
of as sovereign and universal, not as a means in the struggle between power-complexes but as a means of *preventing* all struggle
in general—perhaps after the communistic cliché of Dühring,
that every will must consider every other will its equal—would
be a principle *hostile to life*, an agent of the dissolution and de-

23. *Gesetz.*
24. *Recht.*
25. *Unrecht.*

struction of man, an attempt to assassinate the future of man, a sign of weariness, a secret path to nothingness.—

12

Yet a word on the origin and the purpose of punishment—two problems that are separate, or ought to be separate: unfortunately, they are usually confounded. How have previous genealogists of morals set about solving these problems? Naïvely, as has always been their way: they seek out some "purpose" in punishment, for example, revenge or deterrence, then guilelessly place this purpose at the beginning as *causa fiendi*[26] of punishment, and—have done. The "purpose of law," however, is absolutely the last thing to employ in the history of the origin of law: on the contrary, there is for historiography of any kind no more important proposition than the one it took such effort to establish but which really *ought to be* established now: the cause of the origin of a thing and its eventual utility, its actual employment and place in a system of purposes, lie worlds apart; whatever exists, having somehow come into being, is again and again reinterpreted to new ends, taken over, transformed, and redirected by some power superior to it; all events in the organic world are a subduing, a *becoming master*, and all subduing and becoming master involves a fresh interpretation, an adaptation through which any previous "meaning" and "purpose" are necessarily obscured or even obliterated. However well one has understood the *utility* of any physiological organ (or of a legal institution, a social custom, a political usage, a form in art or in a religious cult), this means nothing regarding its origin: however uncomfortable and disagreeable this may sound to older ears—for one has always believed that to understand the demonstrable purpose, the utility of a thing, a form, or an institution, was also to understand the reason why it originated—the eye being made for seeing, the hand being made for grasping.

26. The cause of the origin.

Thus one also imagined that punishment was devised for punishing. But purposes and utilities are only *signs* that a will to power has become master of something less powerful and imposed upon it the character of a function; and the entire history of a "thing," an organ, a custom can in this way be a continuous sign-chain of ever new interpretations and adaptations whose causes do not even have to be related to one another but, on the contrary, in some cases succeed and alternate with one another in a purely chance fashion. The "evolution" of a thing, a custom, an organ is thus by no means its *progressus* toward a goal, even less a logical *progressus* by the shortest route and with the smallest expenditure of force—but a succession of more or less profound, more or less mutually independent processes of subduing, plus the resistances they encounter, the attempts at transformation for the purpose of defense and reaction, and the results of successful counteractions. The form is fluid, but the "meaning" is even more so.

The case is the same even within each individual organism: with every real growth in the whole, the "meaning" of the individual organs also changes; in certain circumstances their partial destruction, a reduction in their numbers (for example, through the disappearance of intermediary members) can be a sign of increasing strength and perfection. It is not too much to say that even a partial *diminution of utility,* an atrophying and degeneration, a loss of meaning and purposiveness—in short, death—is among the conditions of an actual *progressus,* which always appears in the shape of a will and way to *greater power* and is always carried through at the expense of numerous smaller powers. The magnitude of an "advance" can even be measured by the mass of things that had to be sacrificed to it; mankind in the mass sacrificed to the prosperity of a single *stronger* species of man— that *would* be an advance.

I emphasize this major point of historical method all the more because it is in fundamental opposition to the now prevalent instinct and taste which would rather be reconciled even to the absolute fortuitousness, even the mechanistic senselessness of all

events than to the theory that in all events a *will to power* is oper-
ating. The democratic idiosyncrasy which opposes everything
that dominates and wants to dominate, the modern *misarchism*[27]
(to coin an ugly word for an ugly thing) has permeated the realm
of the spirit and disguised itself in the most spiritual forms to
such a degree that today it has forced its way, has acquired the
right to force its way into the strictest, apparently most objective
sciences; indeed, it seems to me to have already taken charge of
all physiology and theory of life—to the detriment of life, as
goes without saying, since it has robbed it of a fundamental concept, that of *activity*. Under the influence of the above-mentioned
idiosyncracy, one places instead "adaptation" in the foreground,
that is to say, an activity of the second rank, a mere reactivity;
indeed, life itself has been defined as a more and more efficient
inner adaptation to external conditions (Herbert Spencer[28]). Thus
the essence of life, its *will to power*, is ignored; one overlooks the
essential priority of the spontaneous, aggressive, expansive, form-
giving forces that give new interpretations and directions, although "adaptation" follows only after this; the dominant role of
the highest functionaries within the organism itself in which the
will to life appears active and form-giving is denied. One should
recall what Huxley[29] reproached Spencer with—his "adminis-
trative nihilism": but it is a question of rather *more* than mere
"administration."

13

To return to our subject, namely *punishment*, one must distinguish two aspects: on the one hand, that in it which is relatively
enduring, the custom, the act, the "drama," a certain strict se-

27. Hatred of rule or government.

28. On Spencer, see the note in section 3 of the first essay, above.

29. Thomas Henry Huxley (1825–95), the English biologist and writer, fought tirelessly for the acceptance of Darwinism. In 1869 he coined the word *agnosticism*, which
Spencer took over from him. Aldous Huxley (1894–1963), the author of *Brave New World*
(1932), and Julian Huxley (born 1897), the biologist, are T. H. Huxley's grandsons.

quence of procedures; on the other, that in it which is *fluid,* the meaning, the purpose, the expectation associated with the performance of such procedures. In accordance with the previously developed major point of historical method, it is assumed without further ado that the procedure itself will be something older, earlier than its employment in punishment, that the latter is *projected* and interpreted *into* the procedure (which has long existed but been employed in another sense), in short, that the case is *not* as has hitherto been assumed by our naïve genealogists of law and morals, who have one and all thought of the procedure as *invented* for the purpose of punishing, just as one formerly thought of the hand as invented for the purpose of grasping.

As for the other element in punishment, the fluid element, its "meaning," in a very late condition of culture (for example, in modern Europe) the concept "punishment" possesses in fact not *one* meaning but a whole synthesis of "meanings": the previous history of punishment in general, the history of its employment for the most various purposes, finally crystallizes into a kind of unity that is hard to disentangle, hard to analyze and, as must be emphasized especially, totally *indefinable.* (Today it is impossible to say for certain *why* people are really punished: all concepts in which an entire process is semiotically concentrated elude definition; only that which has no history is definable.[30]) At an earlier stage, on the contrary, this synthesis of "meanings" can still be disentangled, as well as changed; one can still perceive how in each individual case the elements of the synthesis undergo a shift in value and rearrange themselves accordingly, so that now this, now that element comes to the fore and dominates at the expense of the others; and under certain circumstances one element (the purpose of deterrence perhaps) appears to overcome all the remaining elements.

To give at least an idea of how uncertain, how supplemental, how accidental "the meaning" of punishment is, and how one and the same procedure can be employed, interpreted, adapted

---

30. A superb epigram that expresses a profound insight. Cf. *The Wanderer and His Shadow,* section 33, included in the present volume, pp. 159ff.

to ends that differ fundamentally, I set down here the pattern that has emerged from consideration of relatively few chance instances I have noted. Punishment as a means of rendering harmless, of preventing further harm. Punishment as recompense to the injured party for the harm done, rendered in any form (even in that of a compensating affect). Punishment as the isolation of a disturbance of equilibrium, so as to guard against any further spread of the disturbance. Punishment as a means of inspiring fear of those who determine and execute the punishment. Punishment as a kind of repayment for the advantages the criminal has enjoyed hitherto (for example, when he is employed as a slave in the mines). Punishment as the expulsion of a degenerate element (in some cases, of an entire branch, as in Chinese law: thus as a means of preserving the purity of a race or maintaining a social type). Punishment as a festival, namely as the rape and mockery of a finally defeated enemy. Punishment as the making of a memory, whether for him who suffers the punishment—so-called "improvement"—or for those who witness its execution. Punishment as payment of a fee stipulated by the power that protects the wrongdoer from the excesses of revenge. Punishment as a compromise with revenge in its natural state when the latter is still maintained and claimed as a privilege by powerful clans. Punishment as a declaration of war and a war measure against an enemy of peace, of the law, of order, of the authorities, whom, as a danger to the community, as one who has broken the contract that defines the conditions under which it exists, as a rebel, a traitor, and breaker of the peace, one opposes with the means of war.—

14

This list is certainly not complete; it is clear that punishment is overdetermined[31] by utilities of all kinds. All the more reason, then, for deducting from it a *supposed* utility that, to be sure,

---

31. *Überladen.*

counts in the popular consciousness as the most essential one— belief in punishment, which for several reasons is tottering today, always finds its strongest support in this. Punishment is supposed to possess the value of awakening the *feeling of guilt* in the guilty person; one seeks in it the actual *instrumentum* of that psychical reaction called "bad conscience," "sting of conscience." Thus one misunderstands psychology and the reality of things even as they apply today: how much more as they applied during the greater part of man's history, his prehistory!

It is precisely among criminals and convicts that the sting of conscience is extremely rare; prisons and penitentiaries are *not* the kind of hotbed in which this species of gnawing worm is likely to flourish: all conscientious observers are agreed on that, in many cases unwillingly enough and contrary to their own in- clinations. Generally speaking, punishment makes men hard and cold; it concentrates; it sharpens the feeling of alienation; it strengthens the power of resistance. If it happens that punish- ment destroys the vital energy and brings about a miserable pros- tration and self-abasement, such a result is certainly even less pleasant than the usual effects of punishment—characterized by dry and gloomy seriousness.

If we consider those millennia *before* the history of man, we may unhesitatingly assert that it was precisely through punish- ment that the development of the feeling of guilt was most pow- erfully *hindered*—at least in the victims upon whom the punitive force was vented. For we must not underrate the extent to which the sight of the judicial and executive procedures prevents the criminal from considering his deed, the type of his action *as such,* reprehensible: for he sees exactly the same kind of actions prac- ticed in the service of justice and approved of and practiced with a good conscience: spying, deception, bribery, setting traps, the whole cunning and underhand art of police and prosecution, plus robbery, violence, defamation, imprisonment, torture, mur- der, practiced as a matter of principle and without even emotion to excuse them, which are pronounced characteristics of the various forms of punishment—all of them therefore actions which his judges in no way condemn and repudiate *as such*, but only when they are applied and directed to certain particular ends.

The "bad conscience," this most uncanny and most interesting plant of all our earthly vegetation, did *not* grow on this soil; indeed, during the greater part of the past the judges and punishers themselves were *not at all* conscious of dealing with a "guilty person." But with an instigator of harm, with an irresponsible piece of fate. And the person upon whom punishment subsequently descended, again like a piece of fate, suffered no "inward pain" other than that induced by the sudden appearance of something unforeseen, a dreadful natural event, a plunging, crushing rock that one cannot fight.

15

This fact once came insidiously into the mind of Spinoza (to the vexation of his interpreters, Kuno Fischer,[32] for example, who make a real *effort* to misunderstand him on this point), when one afternoon, teased by who knows what recollection, he mused on the question of what really remained to him of the famous *morsus conscientiae*[33]—he who had banished good and evil to the realm of human imagination and had wrathfully defended the honor of his "free" God against those blasphemers who asserted that God effected all things *sub ratione boni*[34] ("but that would mean making God subject to fate and would surely be the greatest of all absurdities"). The world, for Spinoza, had returned to that state of innocence in which it had lain before the invention of the bad conscience: what then had become of the *morsus conscientiae*?

32. Kuno Fischer (1824–1907), professor at Heidelberg, made a great reputation with a ten-volume history of modern philosophy that consists of imposing monographs on selected modern philosophers. One of the volumes is devoted to Spinoza.

33. Sting of conscience.

34. For a good reason.

"The opposite of *gaudium*,"[35] he finally said to himself—"a sadness accompanied by the recollection of a past event that flouted all of our expectations." *Eth. III, propos. XVIII, schol. I. II.* Mischief-makers overtaken by punishments have for thousands of years felt in respect of their "transgressions" *just as Spinoza did:* "here something has unexpectedly gone wrong," *not:* "I ought not to have done that." They submitted to punishment as one submits to an illness or to a misfortune or to death, with that stout-hearted fatalism without rebellion through which the Russians, for example, still have an advantage over us Westerners in dealing with life.

If there existed any criticism of the deed in those days, it was prudence that criticized the deed: the actual *effect* of punishment must beyond question be sought above all in a heightening of prudence, in an extending of the memory, in a will henceforth to go to work more cautiously, mistrustfully, secretly, in the insight that one is definitely too weak for many things, in a kind of improvement in self-criticism. That which can in general be attained through punishment, in men and in animals, is an increase of fear, a heightening of prudence, mastery of the desires: thus punishment *tames* men, but it does not make them "better"—one might with more justice assert the opposite. ("Injury makes one prudent," says the proverb: insofar as it makes one prudent it also makes one bad. Fortunately, it frequently makes people stupid.)

16

At this point I can no longer avoid giving a first, provisional statement of my own hypothesis concerning the origin of the "bad conscience": it may sound rather strange and needs to be pondered, lived with, and slept on for a long time. I regard the bad conscience as the serious illness that man was bound to con-

35. Joy.

tract under the stress of the most fundamental change he ever experienced—that change which occurred when he found himself finally enclosed within the walls of society and of peace. The situation that faced sea animals when they were compelled to become land animals or perish was the same as that which faced these semi-animals, well adapted to the wilderness, to war, to prowling, to adventure: suddenly all their instincts were disvalued and "suspended." From now on they had to walk on their feet and "bear themselves" whereas hitherto they had been borne by the water: a dreadful heaviness lay upon them. They felt unable to cope with the simplest undertakings; in this new world they no longer possessed their former guides, their regulating, unconscious and infallible drives: they were reduced to thinking, inferring, reckoning, co-ordinating cause and effect, these unfortunate creatures; they were reduced to their "consciousness," their weakest and most fallible organ! I believe there has never been such a feeling of misery on earth, such a leaden discomfort—and at the same time the old instincts had not suddenly ceased to make their usual demands! Only it was hardly or rarely possible to humor them: as a rule they had to seek new and, as it were, subterranean gratifications.

All instincts that do not discharge themselves outwardly *turn inward*—this is what I call the *internalization*[36] of man: thus it was that man first developed what was later called his "soul." The entire inner world, originally as thin as if it were stretched between two membranes, expanded and extended itself, acquired depth, breadth, and height, in the same measure as outward discharge was *inhibited*. Those fearful bulwarks with which the political organization protected itself against the old instincts of freedom—punishments belong among these bulwarks—brought about that all those instincts of wild, free, prowling man turned backward *against man himself*. Hostility, cruelty, joy in persecuting, in attacking, in change, in destruction—all this turned against the

36. *Verinnerlichung.* Cf. Freud.

possessors of such instincts: *that* is the origin of the "bad conscience."

The man who, from lack of external enemies and resistances and forcibly confined to the oppressive narrowness and punctiliousness of custom, impatiently lacerated, persecuted, gnawed at, assaulted, and maltreated himself; this animal that rubbed itself raw against the bars of its cage as one tried to "tame" it; this deprived creature, racked with homesickness for the wild, who had to turn himself into an adventure, a torture chamber, an uncertain and dangerous wilderness—this fool, this yearning and desperate prisoner became the inventor of the "bad conscience." But thus began the gravest and uncanniest illness, from which humanity has not yet recovered, man's suffering *of man, of himself*— the result of a forcible sundering from his animal past, as it were a leap and plunge into new surroundings and conditions of existence, a declaration of war against the old instincts upon which his strength, joy, and terribleness had rested hitherto.

Let us add at once that, on the other hand, the existence on earth of an animal soul turned against itself, taking sides against itself, was something so new, profound, unheard of, enigmatic, contradictory, *and pregnant with a future* that the aspect of the earth was essentially altered. Indeed, divine spectators were needed to do justice to the spectacle that thus began and the end of which is not yet in sight—a spectacle too subtle, too marvelous, too paradoxical to be played senselessly unobserved on some ludicrous planet! From now on, man is *included* among the most unexpected and exciting lucky throws in the dice game of Heraclitus' "great child," be he called Zeus or chance; he gives rise to an interest, a tension, a hope, almost a certainty, as if with him something were announcing and preparing itself, as if man were not a goal but only a way, an episode, a bridge, a great promise.—

17

Among the presuppositions of this hypothesis concerning the origin of the bad conscience is, first, that the change referred to was not a gradual or voluntary one and did not represent an organic adaptation to new conditions but a break, a leap, a compulsion, an ineluctable disaster which precluded all struggle and even all *ressentiment*. Secondly, however, that the welding of a hitherto unchecked and shapeless populace into a firm form was not only instituted by an act of violence but also carried to its conclusion by nothing but acts of violence—that the oldest "state" thus appeared as a fearful tyranny, as an oppressive and remorseless machine, and went on working until this raw material of people and semi-animals was at last not only thoroughly kneaded and pliant but also *formed*.

I employed the word "state": it is obvious what is meant—some pack of blond beasts of prey,[37] a conqueror and master race which, organized for war and with the ability to organize, unhesitatingly lays its terrible claws upon a populace perhaps tremendously superior in numbers but still formless and nomad. That is after all how the "state" began on earth: I think that sentimentalism which would have it begin with a "contract" has been disposed of. He who can command, he who is by nature "master," he who is violent in act and bearing—what has he to do with contracts! One does not reckon with such natures; they come like fate, without reason, consideration, or pretext; they appear as lightning appears, too terrible, too sudden, too convincing, too "different" even to be hated. Their work is an instinctive creation and imposition of forms; they are the most involuntary, unconscious artists there are—wherever they appear something new soon arises, a ruling structure that *lives*, in which parts and

---

37. *Irgendein Rudel blonder Raubtiere, eine Eroberer- und Herren-Rasse:* Francis Golffing, in his translation, spirits away both the blond beasts of prey and the master race by rendering these words "a pack of savages, a race of conquerors." Cf. section 11 of the first essay, above, with its three references to the *blonde Bestie,* and note 3 of section 11. See also Kaufmann's *Nietzsche,* Chapter 10, "The Master-Race."

functions are delimited and coordinated, in which nothing whatever finds a place that has not first been assigned a "meaning" in relation to the whole. They do not know what guilt, responsibility, or consideration are, these born organizers; they exemplify that terrible artists' egoism that has the look of bronze and knows itself justified to all eternity in its "work," like a mother in her child. It is not in *them* that the "bad conscience" developed, that goes without saying—but it would not have developed *without them*, this ugly growth, it would be lacking if a tremendous quantity of freedom had not been expelled from the world, or at least from the visible world, and made as it were *latent* under their hammer blows and artists' violence. This *instinct for freedom* forcibly made latent—we have seen it already—this instinct for freedom pushed back and repressed, incarcerated within and finally able to discharge and vent itself only on itself: that, and that alone, is what the *bad conscience* is in its beginnings.

18

One should guard against thinking lightly of this phenomenon merely on account of its initial painfulness and ugliness. For fundamentally it is the same active force that is at work on a grander scale in those artists of violence and organizers who build states, and that here, internally, on a smaller and pettier scale, directed backward, in the "labyrinth of the breast," to use Goethe's expression, creates for itself a bad conscience and builds negative ideals—namely, the *instinct for freedom* (in my language: the will to power); only here the material upon which the form-giving and ravishing nature of this force vents itself is man himself, his whole ancient animal self—and *not*, as in that greater and more obvious phenomenon, some *other* man, *other* men. This secret self-ravishment, this artists' cruelty, this delight in imposing a form upon oneself as a hard, recalcitrant, suffering material and in burning a will, a critique, a contradiction, a contempt, a No into it, this uncanny, dreadfully joyous labor of a soul voluntarily at odds with itself that makes itself suffer out of joy in

making suffer—eventually this entire *active* "bad conscience"—
you will have guessed it—as the womb of all ideal and imaginative phenomena, also brought to light an abundance of strange
new beauty and affirmation, and perhaps beauty itself.—After
all, what would be "beautiful" if the contradiction had not first
become conscious of itself, if the ugly had not first said to itself:
"I am ugly"?

This hint will at least make less enigmatic the enigma of how
contradictory concepts such as *selflessness, self-denial, self-sacrifice*
can suggest an ideal, a kind of beauty; and one thing we know
henceforth—I have no doubt of it—and that is the nature of the
delight that the selfless man, the self-denier, the self-sacrificer
feels from the first: this delight is tied to cruelty.

So much for the present about the origin of the moral value
of the "unegoistic," about the soil from which this value grew:
only the bad conscience, only the will to self-maltreatment provided the conditions for the *value* of the unegoistic.—

19

The bad conscience is an illness, there is no doubt about that, but
an illness as pregnancy is an illness. Let us seek out the conditions under which this illness has reached its most terrible and
most sublime height; we shall see what it really was that thus entered the world. But for that one needs endurance—and first of
all we must go back again to an earlier point of view.

The civil-law relationship between the debtor and his creditor, discussed above, has been interpreted in an, historically
speaking, exceedingly remarkable and dubious manner into a
relationship in which to us modern men it seems perhaps least to
belong: namely into the relationship between the present generation and its ancestors.

Within the original tribal community—we are speaking of
primeval times—the living generation always recognized a ju-
ridical duty toward earlier generations, and especially toward
the earliest, which founded the tribe (and by no means a merely

sentimental obligation: there are actually reasons for denying the existence of the latter for the greater part of human history). The conviction reigns that it is only through the sacrifices and accomplishments of the ancestors that the tribe *exists*—and that one has to *pay them back* with sacrifices and accomplishments: one thus recognizes a *debt* that constantly grows greater, since these forebears never cease, in their continued existence as powerful spirits, to accord the tribe new advantages and new strength. In vain, perhaps? But there is no "in vain" for these rude and "poor-souled" ages. What can one give them in return? Sacrifices (initially as food in the coarsest sense), feasts, music, honors; above all, obedience—for all customs, as works of the ancestors, are also their statutes and commands: can one ever give them enough? This suspicion remains and increases; from time to time it leads to a wholesale sacrifice, something tremendous in the way of re-payment to the "creditor" (the notorious sacrifice of the first-born, for example; in any case blood, human blood).

The *fear* of the ancestor and his power, the consciousness of indebtedness to him, increases, according to this kind of logic, in exactly the same measure as the power of the tribe itself increases, as the tribe itself grows ever more victorious, independent, honored, and feared. By no means the other way round! Every step toward the decline of a tribe, every misfortune, every sign of degeneration, of coming disintegration always *diminishes* fear of the spirit of its founder and produces a meaner impression of his cunning, foresight, and present power. If one imagines this rude kind of logic carried to its end, then the ancestors of the *most powerful* tribes are bound eventually to grow to monstrous dimensions through the imagination of growing fear and to recede into the darkness of the divinely uncanny and unimaginable: in the end the ancestor must necessarily be transfigured into a *god*. Perhaps this is even the origin of gods, an origin therefore out of *fear*! . . . And whoever should feel obliged to add, "but out of piety also!" would hardly be right for the greater part of the existence of man, his prehistory. To be sure, he would be quite right for the *intermediate* age, in which the noble tribes developed—who indeed paid back their originators, their ancestors (heroes, gods) with interest all the qualities that had become palpable in themselves, the *noble* qualities. We shall take another look later at the ennoblement of the gods (which should not be confused with their becoming "holy"); let us first of all follow to its end the course of this whole development of the consciousness of guilt.

20

History shows that the consciousness of being in debt[38] to the deity did not by any means come to an end together with the organization of communities on the basis of blood relationship. Even as mankind inherited the concepts "good and bad" from the tribal nobility (along with its basic psychological propensity to set up orders of rank), it also inherited, along with the tribal and family divinities, the burden of still unpaid debts and of the desire to be relieved of them. (The transition is provided by those numerous slave and dependent populations who, whether through compulsion or through servility and mimicry, adapted themselves to their masters' cult of the gods: this inheritance then overflows from them in all directions.) The guilty feeling of indebtedness[39] to the divinity continued to grow for several millennia—always in the same measure as the concept of God and the feeling for divinity increased on earth and was carried to the heights. (The entire history of ethnic struggle, victory, reconciliation, fusion, everything that precedes the definitive ordering of rank of the different national elements in every great racial synthesis, is reflected in the confused genealogies of their gods, in the sagas of the gods' struggles, victories, and reconciliations; the advance toward universal empires is always also an advance toward universal divinities; despotism with its triumph over the independent nobility always prepares the way for some kind of monotheism.)

The advent of the Christian God, as the maximum god at-

---

38. *Schulden zu haben.*
39. *Das Schuldgefühl.*

tained so far, was therefore accompanied by the maximum feeling of guilty indebtedness[40] on earth. Presuming we have gradually entered upon the *reverse* course, there is no small probability that with the irresistible decline of faith in the Christian God there is now also a considerable decline in mankind's feeling of guilt;[41] indeed, the prospect cannot be dismissed that the complete and definitive victory of atheism might free mankind of this whole feeling of guilty indebtedness[42] toward its origin, its *causa prima.*[43] Atheism and a kind of *second innocence*[44] belong together.—

21

So much for a first brief preliminary on the connection of the concepts "guilt" and "duty" with religious presuppositions: I have up to now deliberately ignored the moralization of these concepts (their pushing back into the conscience; more precisely, the involvement of the *bad* conscience with the concept of god); and at the end of the last section I even spoke as if this moralization had not taken place at all, and as if these concepts were now necessarily doomed since their presupposition, the faith in our "creditor,"[45] in God, had disappeared. The reality is, to a fearful degree, otherwise.

The moralization of the concepts guilt and duty, their being pushed back into the *bad* conscience, actually involves an attempt to *reverse* the direction of the development described above, or at least to bring it to a halt: the *aim* now is to preclude pessimistically, once and for all, the prospect of a final discharge; the *aim* now is to make the glance recoil disconsolately from an iron impossibility; the *aim* now is to turn back the concepts "guilt" and "duty"—back against whom? There can be no doubt:

40. *Des Schuldgefühls.*
41. *Schuldbewusstseins.*
42. *Gefühl, Schulden . . . zu haben.*
43. First cause.
44. *Unschuld.*
45. *Der Glaube an unsern "Gläubiger":* the creed in our "creditor"—or: that one credits our "creditor."

against the "debtor" first of all, in whom from now on the bad conscience is firmly rooted, eating into him and spreading within him like a polyp, until at last the irredeemable debt gives rise to the conception of irredeemable penance, the idea that it cannot be discharged ("*eternal* punishment"). Finally, however, they are turned back against the "creditor," too: whether we think of the *causa prima* of man, the beginning of the human race, its primal ancestor who is from now on burdened with a curse ("Adam," "original sin," "unfreedom of the will"), or of nature from whose womb mankind arose and into whom the principle of evil is projected from now on ("the diabolizing of nature"), or of existence in general, which is now considered *worthless as such* (nihilistic withdrawal from it, a desire for nothingness or a desire for its antithesis, for a different mode of being, Buddhism and the like)— suddenly we stand before the paradoxical and horrifying expedient that afforded temporary relief for tormented humanity, that stroke of genius on the part of Christianity: God himself sacrifices himself for the guilt of mankind, God himself makes payment to himself, God as the only being who can redeem man from what has become unredeemable for man himself—the creditor sacrifices himself for his debtor, out of *love* (can one credit that?), out of love for his debtor!—

22

You will have guessed *what* has really happened here, *beneath* all this: that will to self-tormenting, that repressed cruelty of the animal-man made inward and scared back into himself, the creature imprisoned in the "state" so as to be tamed, who invented the bad conscience in order to hurt himself after the *more natural* vent for this desire to hurt had been blocked—this man of the bad conscience has seized upon the presupposition of religion so as to drive his self-torture to its most gruesome pitch of severity and rigor. Guilt before *God:* this thought becomes an instrument of torture to him. He apprehends in "God" the ultimate antithesis of his own ineluctable animal instincts; he reinterprets these animal instincts themselves as a form of guilt before God (as hostility, rebellion, insurrection against the "Lord," the "father," the primal ancestor and origin of the world); he stretches himself upon the contradiction "God" and "Devil"; he ejects from himself all his denial of himself, of his nature, naturalness, and actuality, in the form of an affirmation, as something existent, corporeal, real, as God, as the holiness of God, as God the Judge, as God the Hangman, as the beyond, as eternity, as torment without end, as hell, as the immeasurability of punishment and guilt.

In this psychical cruelty there resides a madness of the will which is absolutely unexampled: the *will* of man to find himself guilty and reprehensible to a degree that can never be atoned for; his *will* to think himself punished without any possibility of the punishment becoming equal to the guilt; his *will* to infect and poison the fundamental ground of things with the problem of punishment and guilt so as to cut off once and for all his own exit from this labyrinth of "fixed ideas"; his *will* to erect an ideal— that of the "holy God"—and in the face of it to feel the palpable certainty of his own absolute unworthiness. Oh this insane, pathetic beast—man! What ideas he has, what unnaturalness, what paroxysms of nonsense, what *bestiality of thought* erupts as soon as he is prevented just a little from being a *beast in deed*!

All this is interesting, to excess, but also of a gloomy, black, unnerving sadness, so that one must forcibly forbid oneself to gaze too long into these abysses. Here is *sickness,* beyond any doubt, the most terrible sickness that has ever raged in man; and whoever can still bear to hear (but today one no longer has ears for this!) how in this night of torment and absurdity there has resounded the cry of *love,* the cry of the most nostalgic rapture, of redemption through *love,* will turn away, seized by invincible horror.—There is so much in man that is hideous!—Too long, the earth has been a madhouse!—

23

This should dispose once and for all of the question of how the "holy God" originated.

That the conception of gods *in itself* need not lead to the degradation of the imagination that we had to consider briefly, that there are *nobler* uses for the invention of gods than for the self-crucifixion and self-violation of man in which Europe over the past millennia achieved its distinctive mastery—that is fortunately revealed even by a mere glance at the *Greek gods,* those reflections of noble and autocratic men, in whom *the animal* in man felt deified and did *not* lacerate itself, did *not* rage against itself! For the longest time these Greeks used their gods precisely so as to ward off the "bad conscience," so as to be able to rejoice in their freedom of soul the very opposite of the use to which Christianity put its God. They went *very far* in this direction, these splendid and lionhearted children; and no less an authority than the Homeric Zeus himself occasionally gives them to understand that they are making things too easy for themselves. "Strange!" he says once—the case is that of Aegisthus, a *very* bad case—

> *Strange how these mortals so loudly complain of the gods!*
> We alone produce evil, *they say; yet themselves*
> *Make themselves wretched through folly, even counter to fate.*[46]

Yet one can see and hear how even this Olympian spectator and judge is far from holding a grudge against them or thinking ill of them on that account: "how *foolish* they are!" he thinks when he observes the misdeeds of mortals—and "foolishness," "folly," a little "disturbance in the head," this much even the Greeks of the strongest, bravest age conceded of themselves as the reason for much that was bad and calamitous—foolishness, *not* sin! do you grasp that?

46. *Odyssey,* I, line 32ff.

Even this disturbance in the head, however, presented a problem: "how is it possible? how could it actually have happened to heads such as *we* have, we men of aristocratic descent, of the best society, happy, well-constituted, noble, and virtuous?"—thus noble Greeks asked themselves for centuries in the face of every incomprehensible atrocity or wantonness with which one of their kind had polluted himself. "He must have been deluded by a *god*," they concluded finally, shaking their heads . . . This expedient is *typical* of the Greeks . . . In this way the gods served in those days to justify man to a certain extent even in his wickedness, they served as the originators of evil—in those days they took upon themselves, not the punishment but, what is *nobler,* the guilt.[47]

24

I end up with three question marks; that seems plain. "What are you really doing, erecting an ideal or knocking one down?" I may perhaps be asked.

But have you ever asked yourselves sufficiently how much the erection of *every* ideal on earth has cost? How much reality has had to be misunderstood and slandered, how many lies have had to be sanctified, how many consciences disturbed, how much "God" sacrificed every time? If a temple is to be erected *a temple must be destroyed:* that is the law—let anyone who can show me a case in which it is not fulfilled!

We modern men are the heirs of the conscience-vivisection and self-torture[48] of millennia: this is what we have practiced longest, it is our distinctive art perhaps, and in any case our subtlety in which we have acquired a refined taste. Man has all

---

47. Cf. *Ecce Homo,* Chapter I, section 5, and Sartre's play *The Flies,* which was decisively influenced by Nietzsche, as I have shown in "Nietzsche Between Homer and Sartre: Five Treatments of the Orestes Story" (*Revue Internationale de Philosophie,* LXVII, 1964, pp. 50–73). See also my *Tragedy and Philosophy,* section 51.

48. *Selbsttierquälerei: Tierquälerei* really means cruelty to animals or, literally, animal torture; hence Nietzsche's coinage suggests that this kind of self-torture involves mortification of the animal nature of man.

too long had an "evil eye" for his natural inclinations, so that they have finally become inseparable from his "bad conscience." An attempt at the reverse would *in itself* be possible—but who is strong enough for it?—that is, to wed the bad conscience to all the *unnatural* inclinations, all those aspirations to the beyond, to that which runs counter to sense, instinct, nature, animal, in short all ideals hitherto, which are one and all hostile to life and ideals that slander the world. To whom should one turn today with *such* hopes and demands?

One would have precisely the *good* men against one; and, of course, the comfortable, the reconciled, the vain, the sentimental, the weary.

What gives greater offense, what separates one more fundamentally, than to reveal something of the severity and respect with which one treats oneself? And on the other hand—how accommodating, how friendly all the world is toward us as soon as we act as all the world does and "let ourselves go" like all the world!

The attainment of this goal would require a *different* kind of spirit from that likely to appear in this present age: spirits strengthened by war and victory, for whom conquest, adventure, danger, and even pain have become needs; it would require habituation to the keen air of the heights, to winter journeys, to ice and mountains in every sense; it would require even a kind of sublime wickedness, an ultimate, supremely self-confident mischievousness in knowledge that goes with great health; it would require, in brief and alas, precisely this *great health*!

Is this even possible today?—But some day, in a stronger age than this decaying, self-doubting present, he must yet come to us, the *redeeming* man of great love and contempt, the creative spirit whose compelling strength will not let him rest in any aloofness or any beyond, whose isolation is misunderstood by the people as if it were flight *from* reality—while it is only his absorption, immersion, penetration *into* reality, so that, when he one day emerges again into the light, he may bring home the *redemption* of this reality: its redemption from the curse that the hitherto reigning ideal has laid upon it. This man of the future, who will redeem us not only from the hitherto reigning ideal but also from that which was bound to grow out of it, the great nausea, the will to nothingness, nihilism; this bell-stroke of noon and of the great decision that liberates the will again and restores its goal to the earth and his hope to man; this Antichrist and antinihilist; this victor over God and nothingness—*he must come one day.*—

25

But what am I saying? Enough! Enough! At this point it behooves me only to be silent; or I shall usurp that to which only one younger, "heavier with future," and stronger than I has a right—that to which only *Zarathustra* has a right, *Zarathustra the godless.*—

FYODOR DOSTOEVSKY

Fyodor Dostoevsky was a Russian Orthodox true believer; nevertheless, Friedrich Nietzsche, who was a virtual St. Paul of doubt, praised him as the most profound of all psychologists. Another Galileo of the inner world, Sigmund Freud, held Dostoevsky in like esteem. Nietzsche and Freud were right to bow before Dostoevsky. He had a marksman's eye for the most subtle and deeply hidden perturbations of the human spirit.

The second of seven children, Fyodor Mikhaylovich Dostoevsky was born in Moscow on October 30, 1821 (Old Style). His father was an army doctor. Dostoevsky was educated at home until the age of seventeen, when he enrolled at Military Engineering Academy in St. Petersburg. At the academy he stuck to himself and read voraciously.

In 1839, Dostoevsky's father was mysteriously slain by the serfs on his country estate. Freud hypothesized that the murder was the precipitating cause for the severe epilepsy that Dostoevsky suffered from for the rest of his life. Though Dostoevsky did not say how, it is evident that his father's death marked him, as almost all of his writings reflect a fascination with murder and its connection to poverty.

After graduating in 1843, Dostoevsky was commissioned as a lieutenant in the Engineering Corp of the War Ministry in St. Petersburg. But he quickly lost interest in both engineering and the military and resigned his commission in 1844. In the same year, he translated Honoré de Balzac's *Eugénie Grandet*. The next year saw his own first book, *Poor Folk*, come into print. It was an immediate and immense success, and Dostoevsky was taken under the wing of some of the most powerful of the Russian literati. Unfortunately, his life was soon to change.

Much as in the rest of Europe, the 1840s were a time of great upheaval in Russia. Dostoevsky became involved in a group clamoring for democratic reforms. He was arrested in 1849. After nine months in prison, he and his associates were tried and sentenced to death by a firing squad. In late December 1849, Dostoevsky and his comrades were lined up for execution. The drumrolls reverberated and their sentences were read. The condemned men were told to prepare to die. Dostoevsky whispered a prayer, turned to the man next to him, and said, "Today we will meet in heaven." His friend responded that he did not think that was likely. A moment later, the commander of a military detail galloped up to announce that the death sentences of all of the men had been commuted to prison time. The tsar had planned the charade himself. The memory of this scene would always have a hypnotic hold on Dostoevsky.

Dostoevsky spent several years in a brutal prison camp in Siberia. These hardscrabble times would radically change him. His epilepsy would become much worse. He went from trumpeting democratic values to becoming a Russian nationalist who believed that because of her suffering and the moral purification that such pangs had wrought, Mother Russia had a special moral and political role in world history.

After his prison term came to an end, Dostoevsky was required to serve in the infantry and was stationed in Semipalatinsk, on the Mongolian border. There was not much to do in the remote outpost town, and Dostoevsky read everything he could lay his hands on. In 1857, he married a widow. Two years later, the couple returned to St. Petersburg, where Dostoevsky once again picked up his pen. In 1860, he published his remarkable *House of the Dead*, a chronicle of his prison years in Siberia. This book reestablished his literary reputation.

In 1863, Dostoevsky traveled to western Europe and carried on a wild love affair with a poetess whom he met in Paris. At this time, he also developed an addiction to gambling that often left him and his wife impecunious. A year later, Dostoevsky returned to Russia and published his *Notes from the Underground*, a book that the scholar Walter Kaufmann would tab "the greatest overture to existentialism ever written." However, during the same year he would bury both his wife and his brother.

Soon thereafter, Dostoevsky brought out *Crime and Punishment* (1866), one of the most profound probes of the human psyche ever published. In both *Notes from the Underground* and *Crime and Punishment*, Dostoevsky works with a theme that will leave its signature on all of his writing, namely the redemptive power of suffering.

Often at the razor's edge of deadlines and threats from publishers,

Dostoevsky would dictate his novels while pacing the room. In 1867, he married his stenographer, the twenty-one-year-old Anna Grigorievna Suitkina. A very practical and intelligent woman, she would become her husband's guardian angel and bring a semblance of stability to Dostoevsky's disastrous financial affairs. But not long after their wedding, the couple moved to Germany and then France to dodge creditors. In 1868, Dostoevsky published *The Idiot,* his staggeringly beautiful portrait of Jesus. While acknowledging it as his favorite creation, Dostoevsky reckoned that *The Idiot* was not as structurally sound as some of his other works.

He returned to Russia in 1871 and, in the guise of his novel *The Possessed,* published his biting critique of what he took to be the decadent and nihilistic values of western Europe. With minor books in between, Dostoevsky published, in serial form, *The Brothers Karamazov* in 1880. The case has often been made—and the reader will get no counterargument here—that this book is nothing short of the Platonic form of the novel.

In 1880, Dostoevsky delivered a spellbinding speech at the dedication of the Pushkin Memorial in Moscow. Overnight, he joined the company of Leo Tolstoy and Ivan Turgenev and became a national hero. At last, Dostoevsky was receiving some of the acclaim that he richly deserved, only to die suddenly on January 28, 1881.

One should never forget that Dostoevsky was always writing to keep body and soul together. After his brother died in 1864, he had the immense financial burden of supporting both his immediate family and his brother's. Rapacious publishers would strike crooked deals in which Dostoevsky would sign over the rights to future works for a small but desperately needed sum of money. Not that he would have written differently in other circumstances, but Dostoevsky often wrote his novels in installments in periodicals. He had to be entertaining and was. Like Shakespeare, Dostoevsky was able to alight the deepest and darkest aspects of human nature, while at the same time being flat-out hysterical. There are lines in both *Notes from the Underground* and *The Brothers Karamazov* that will elicit a belly laugh.

In both books, Dostoevsky joins his existentialist brethren in examining the question of what it means to be free. A cultured individual, the Underground Man is a determinist who is subject to mood swings. In certain agitated states of mind, he imagines that he can crack the shackles of determinism by acts of self-destruction and moral degradation.

"The Grand Inquisitor" is a classic chapter from *The Brothers Karamazov*. Here the author seems to be suggesting that for all our slogans, freedom is not necessarily something that we desire to obtain. The priest in Ivan's story exclaims, "I tell Thee that man is tormented by no greater anxiety than to find some one quickly to whom he can hand over that gift of freedom with which the ill-fated creature is born."

The individual who has found a conversation partner in Dostoevsky should continue on and read Part II of *Notes from the Underground*. The last section is a sheet of light on the issue of human willfulness, love, and redemption.

NOTES FROM THE UNDERGROUND

Part I: Underground*

I

I am a sick man. . . . I am a spiteful man. No, I am not a pleasant man at all. I believe there is something wrong with my liver. However, I don't know a damn thing about my liver; neither do I know whether there is anything really wrong with me. I am not under medical treatment, and never have been, though I do respect medicine and doctors. In addition, I am extremely superstitious, at least sufficiently so to respect medicine. (I am well

---

* Both the author of the Notes and the Notes themselves are, of course, fictitious. Nevertheless, such persons as the author of such memoirs not only may, but must, exist in our society, if we take into consideration the circumstances which led to the formation of our society. It was my intention to bring before our reading public, more conspicuously than is usually done, one of the characters of our recent past. He is one of the representatives of a generation that is still with us. In this extract, entitled *Underground,* this person introduces himself and his views and, as it were, tries to explain those causes which have not only led, but also were bound to lead, to his appearance in our midst. —FYODOR DOSTOEVSKY

Excerpted from Fyodor Dostoevsky, *The Best Short Stories of Dostoevsky,* translated by David Magarshack. 1992 Modern Library Edition. Reprinted by permission of Modern Library.

educated enough not to be superstitious, but I am superstitious for all that.) The truth is, I refuse medical treatment out of spite. I don't suppose you will understand that. Well, I do. I don't expect I shall be able to explain to you who it is I am actually trying to annoy in this case by my spite; I realise full well that I can't "hurt" the doctors by refusing to be treated by them; I realise better than anyone that by all this I am only hurting myself and no one else. Still, the fact remains that if I refuse to be medically treated, it is only out of spite. My liver hurts me—well, let it damn well hurt—the more it hurts the better.

I have been living like this a long time—about twenty years, I should think. I am forty now. I used to be in the Civil Service, but I am no longer there now. I was a spiteful civil servant. I was rude and took pleasure in being rude. Mind you, I never accepted any bribes, so that I had at least to find something to compensate myself for that. (A silly joke, but I shan't cross it out. I wrote it thinking it would sound very witty, but now that I have seen myself that I merely wanted to indulge in a bit of contemptible bragging, I shall let it stand on purpose!)

Whenever people used to come to my office on some business, I snarled at them and felt as pleased as Punch when I succeeded in making one of them really unhappy. I nearly always did succeed. They were mostly a timid lot: what else can you expect people who come to a Government office to be? But among the fine gentlemen who used to come to me to make inquiries there was one officer in particular whom I could not bear. He would not submit with a good grace and he had a disgusting habit of rattling his sword. For sixteen months I waged a regular war with him over that sword. In the end, I got the better of him. He stopped rattling. However, all this happened a long time ago when I was still a young man. And do you know, gentlemen, what was the chief point about my spitefulness? Well, the whole point of it, I mean, the whole nasty, disgusting part of it was that all the time I was shamefully conscious—even at the moments of my greatest exasperation—that I was not at all a spiteful or even an exasperated man, but that I was merely frightening sparrows for no reason in the world, and being hugely amused by this pastime. I might foam at the mouth, but just present me with some little toy, give me a cup of tea with sugar in it, and I shouldn't be at all surprised if I calmed down completely, even be deeply touched, though afterwards I should most certainly snarl at myself and be overcome with shame and suffer from insomnia for months. That's the sort of man I am.

Incidentally, I was rather exaggerating just now when I said that I was a spiteful civil servant. All I did, as a matter of fact, was to indulge in a little innocent fun at the expense of the officer and the people who came to my office on business, for actually I never could become a spiteful man. I was always conscious of innumerable elements in me which were absolutely contrary to that. I felt them simply swarming in me all my life and asking to be allowed to come out, but I wouldn't let them. I would not let them! I would deliberately not let them. They tormented me to the point of making me ashamed of myself; they reduced me to a state of nervous exhaustion and, finally, I got fed up with them. Oh, how thoroughly I got fed up with them in the end! But doesn't it seem to you, gentlemen, that I might possibly be apologising to you for something? Asking you to forgive me for something? Yes, I'm sure it does. . . . Well, I assure you I don't care a damn whether it does seem so to you or not. . . .

Not only did I not become spiteful, I did not even know how to become anything, either spiteful or good, either a blackguard or an honest man, either a hero or an insect. And now I've been spending the last four years of my life in my funk-hole, consoling myself with the rather spiteful, though entirely useless, reflection that an intelligent man cannot possibly become anything in particular and that only a fool succeeds in becoming anything. Yes, a man of the nineteenth century must be, and is indeed morally bound to be, above all a characterless person; a man of character, on the other hand, a man of action, is mostly a fellow with a very circumscribed imagination. This is my conviction as a man of forty. I am forty now and, mind you, forty years is a whole lifetime. It is extreme old age. It is positively immoral, indecent, and vulgar to live more than forty years. Who lives longer than forty? Answer me that—sincerely and honestly. I'll tell you who—fools and blackguards—they do! I don't mind telling that to all old men to their face—all those worthy old men, all those silver-haired and ambrosial old men! I'll tell it to the whole world, damned if I won't! I have a right to say so, for I shall live to the age of sixty myself. I'll live to be seventy! I'll live to be eighty! Wait a minute, let me take breath. . . .

I expect you must be thinking, gentlemen, that I want to amuse you. Well, you're mistaken there too. I'm not at all the jolly sort of person you think I am, or may think I am. However, if irritated with all this idle talk (and I feel that you are irritated), you were to ask me who I really am, then I should reply, I'm a retired civil servant of humble rank, a collegiate assessor. I got myself a job in the Civil Service because I had to eat (and only for that reason), and when a distant relative of mine left me six thousand roubles in his will last year, I immediately resigned from the Civil Service and settled in my little corner. I used to live in this corner before, but now I'm settled permanently here. My room is a dreadful, horrible hole, on the very outskirts of the town. My maidservant is an old country woman, bad-tempered from sheer stupidity, and there is, besides, always a bad smell about her. I'm told the Petersburg climate isn't good for me any more and that with my small means it is very expensive to live in Petersburg. I know that perfectly well, much better than all those experienced and wise mentors and counsellors. But I'm staying in Petersburg. I shall never leave Petersburg! I shan't leave it—oh, but it really makes no damned difference whether I leave it or not.

By the way, what does a decent chap talk about with the greatest possible pleasure?

Answer: about himself.

Very well, so I will talk about myself.

II

I should like to tell you now, gentlemen, whether you want to listen to me or not, why I've never been able to become even an insect. I declare to you solemnly that I've wished to become an insect many times. But even that has not been vouchsafed to me. I assure you, gentlemen, that to be too acutely conscious is a disease, a real, honest-to-goodness disease. It would have been quite sufficient for the business of everyday life to possess the ordinary human consciousness, that is to say, half or even a quarter of the share which falls to the lot of an intelligent man of our unhappy nineteenth century who, besides, has the double misfortune of living in Petersburg, the most abstract and premeditated city in the whole world. (There are premeditated and unpremeditated cities.) It would have been quite sufficient, for instance, to possess the sort of consciousness with which all the so-called plain men and men of action are endowed. I bet you think I'm writing all this just out of a desire to show off or to crack a joke at the expense of our men of action, and that if I'm rattling my sword like my army officer it is merely because I want to show off, and in rather bad taste, too. But, gentlemen, who wants to show off his own infirmities, let alone boast about them?

However, what am I talking about? Everyone does it; everyone does show off his infirmities, and I more than anyone else perhaps. But don't let us quibble about it; the point I raised was absurd. Still, I firmly believe that not only too much consciousness, but any sort of consciousness is a disease. I insist upon that. But let us leave that, too, for a moment. Tell me this: why did it invariably happen that just at those moments—yes, at those very moments—when I was acutely conscious of "the sublime and beautiful," as we used to call it in those days, I was not only conscious but also guilty of the most contemptible actions which— well, which, in fact, everybody is guilty of, but which, as though on purpose, I only happened to commit when I was most conscious that they ought not to be committed? The more conscious I became of goodness and all that was "sublime and beautiful," the more deeply did I sink into the mire and the more ready I was to sink into it altogether. And the trouble was that all this did not seem to happen to me by accident, but as though it couldn't possibly have happened otherwise. As though it were my normal condition, and not in the least a disease or a vice, so that at last I no longer even attempted to fight against this vice. It ended by my almost believing (and perhaps I did actually believe) that this was probably my normal condition. At first, at the very outset, I mean, what horrible agonies I used to suffer in that struggle! I did not think others had the same experience, and afterwards I kept it to myself as though it were a secret. I was ashamed (and quite possibly I still am ashamed); it got so far that I felt a sort of secret, abnormal, contemptible delight when, on coming home on one of the foulest nights in Petersburg, I used to realise intensely that again I had been guilty of some particularly dastardly action that day, and that once more it was no earthly use crying over spilt milk; and inwardly, secretly, I used to go on nagging myself, worrying myself, accusing myself, till at last the bitterness I felt turned into a sort of shameful, damnable sweetness, and finally, into real, positive delight! Yes, into delight. Into delight! I'm certain of it. As a matter of fact, I've mentioned this because I should like to know for certain whether other people feel the same sort of delight. Let me explain it to you. The feeling of delight was there just because I was so intensely aware of my own degradation; because I felt myself that I had come up against a blank wall; that no doubt, it was bad, but that it couldn't be helped; that there was no escape, and that I should never become a different man; that even if there still was any time or faith left to make myself into something different, I should most likely have refused to do so; and even if I wanted to I should still have done nothing, because as a matter of fact there was nothing I could change into. And above all—and this is the final point I want to make—whatever happened, happened in accordance with the normal and fundamental laws of intensified consciousness and by a sort of inertia which is a direct consequence of those laws, and that therefore you not only could not change yourself, but you simply couldn't make any attempt to. Hence it follows that as a result of that intensified consciousness you are quite right in being a blackguard, as though it were any consolation to the blackguard that he actually is a blackguard. But enough. . . . Good Lord, I have talked a lot, haven't I? But have I explained anything? How is one to explain this feeling of delight? But I shall explain myself. I shall pursue the matter to the bitter end! That is why I've taken up my pen. . . .

Now, for instance, I'm very vain. I'm as suspicious and as quick to take offence as a hunchback or a dwarf, but as a matter of fact there were moments in my life when, if someone had slapped my face, I should perhaps have been glad even of that. I'm saying this seriously: I should quite certainly have found even there a sort of pleasure, the pleasure of despair, no doubt, but despair too has its moments of intense pleasure, intense delight, especially if you happen to be acutely conscious of the hopelessness of your position. And there, too, I mean, after you'd had your face slapped, you'd be overwhelmed by the consciousness of having been utterly humiliated and snubbed. The trouble is, of course, that however much I tried to find some excuse for what had happened, the conclusion I'd come to would always be that it was my own fault to begin with, and what hurt most of all was that though innocent I was guilty and, as it were, guilty according to the laws of nature. I was guilty, first of all, because I was cleverer than all the people round me. (I have always considered myself cleverer than any one else in the world, and sometimes, I assure you, I've been even ashamed of it. At least, all my life I looked away and I could never look people straight in the face.) I was, finally, guilty because even if I had had a grain of magnanimity in me, I should have suffered a thousand times more from the consciousness of its uselessness. For I should most certainly not have known what to do with my magnanimity— neither to forgive, since the man who would have slapped my face, would most probably have done it in obedience to the laws of nature; nor to forget, since though even if it is the law of nature, it hurts all the same. Finally, even if I had wanted to be utterly ungenerous and, on the contrary, had desired to avenge myself on the man who had offended me, I couldn't have avenged myself on anyone for anything because I should never have had the courage to do anything even if I could. Why shouldn't I have had the courage? Well, I'd like to say a few words about that by itself.

III

You see, people who know how to avenge themselves and, generally, how to stand up for themselves—how do they, do you think, do it? They are, let us assume, so seized by the feeling of revenge that while that feeling lasts there is nothing but that feeling left in them. Such a man goes straight to his goal, like a mad bull, with lowered horns, and only a stone wall perhaps will stop him. (Incidentally, before such a stone wall such people, that is to say, plain men and men of action, as a rule capitulate at once. To them a stone wall is not a challenge as it is, for instance, to us thinking men who, because we are thinking men, do nothing; it is not an excuse for turning aside, an excuse in which one of our sort does not believe himself, but of which he is always very glad. No, they capitulate in all sincerity. A stone wall exerts a sort of calming influence upon them, a sort of final and morally decisive influence, and perhaps even a mystic one.... But of the stone wall later.) Well, that sort of plain man I consider to be the real, normal man, such as his tender mother nature herself wanted to see him when she so lovingly brought him forth upon the earth. I envy such a man with all the forces of my embittered heart. He is stupid—I am not disputing that. But perhaps the normal man should be stupid. How are you to know? Why, perhaps this is even beautiful. And I'm all the more convinced of that—shall we say?—suspicion, since if we take, for instance, the antithesis of the normal man, that is to say, the man of great sensibility, who of course has sprung not out of the lap of nature, but out of a test tube (this is almost mysticism, gentlemen, but I, too, suspect it), then this test-tube-begotten man sometimes capitulates to his antithesis to such an extent that for all his intense sensibility he frankly considers himself a mouse and not a man. I grant you it is an intensely conscious mouse, but it's a mouse all the same, whereas the other is a man, and consequently . . . etc. And, above all, he himself—oh, yes, he in his own person—considers himself a mouse; no one asks him to do so; and this is an important point.

Well, let us now have a look at this mouse in action. Let us suppose, for instance, that its feelings are hurt (and its feelings are almost always hurt), and that it also wants to avenge itself. There will perhaps be a greater accumulation of spite in it than in *l'homme de la nature et de la vérité*. A nasty, mean little desire to repay whoever has offended it in his own coin stirs within it more nastily perhaps than in *l'homme de la nature et de la vérité*; for because of his inborn stupidity *l'homme de la nature et de la vérité* looks upon his revenge merely as a matter of justice whereas because of its intense sensibility the mouse denies that there is any question of justice here. At last we come to the business itself, to the act of revenge. The unhappy mouse has already succeeded in piling up—in the form of questions and doubts—a large number of dirty tricks in addition to its original dirty trick; it has accumulated such a large number of insoluble questions round every one question that it is drowned in a sort of deadly brew, a stinking puddle made up of its doubts, its flurries of emotion, and lastly, the contempt with which the plain men of action cover it from head to foot while they stand solemnly round as judges and dictators and split their sides with laughter at it. Well, of course, all that is left for it to do is to dismiss it with a disdainful wave of its little paw and with a smile of simulated contempt, in which it does not believe itself, and to scurry back ingloriously into its hole. There, in its stinking, disgusting, subterranean hole, our hurt, ridiculed, and beaten mouse plunges into cold, venomous, and, above all, unremitting spite. For forty years it will continuously remember its injury to the last and most shameful detail, and will, besides add to it still more shameful details, worrying and exciting itself spitefully with the aid of its own imagination. It will be ashamed of its own fancies, but it will nevertheless remember everything, go over everything with the utmost care, think up all sorts of imaginary wrongs on the pretext that they, too, might have happened, and will forgive nothing. Quite likely it will start avenging itself, but, as it were, by fits and starts, in all sorts of trivial ways, from behind the stove, incognito, without believing in its right to avenge itself, nor in the success of its vengeance, and knowing beforehand that it will suffer a hundred times more itself from all its attempts at revenge than the person on whom it is revenging itself, who will most probably not care a hang about it. Even on its deathbed it will remember everything with the interest accumulated during all that time, and. . . . And it is just in that cold and loathsome half-despair and half-belief—in that conscious burying oneself alive for grief for forty years—in that intensely perceived, but to some extent uncertain, helplessness of one's position—in all that poison of unsatisfied desires that have turned inwards—in that fever of hesitations, firmly taken decisions, and regrets that follow almost instantaneously upon them—that the essence of that delight I have spoken of lies. It is so subtle and sometimes so difficult to grasp by one's conscious mind that people whose mental horizon is even a little bit circumscribed, or simply people with strong nerves, will not understand anything of it. "Perhaps," you will add with a grin, "those who have never had their faces slapped will not understand it, either," and in that polite way give me a hint that I too have perhaps had my face slapped in my life and that for that reason I'm speaking about it with authority. I bet that's what you are thinking. But don't worry, gentlemen, I've never had my face slapped, and I don't care a damn what you may think about it. Very likely I am sorry not to have boxed the ears of a sufficient number of people in my lifetime. But enough! Not another word about this subject which seems to interest you so much.

Let me continue calmly about the people with strong nerves who do not understand the subtleties of the pleasure I have been speaking of. Though on some occasions these gentlemen may roar at the top of their voices like bulls, and though this, let us assume, does them the greatest credit, yet as I've already said, they at once capitulate in face of the impossible. The impossible is to them equivalent to a stone wall. What stone wall? Why, the laws of nature, of course, the conclusions of natural science, mathematics. When, for instance, it is proved to you that you are descended from a monkey, then it's no use pulling a long face about it: you just have to accept it. When they prove to you that one drop of your own fat must, as a matter of course, be dearer to you than a hundred thousand of your fellow-men and that all the so-called virtues and duties and other vain fancies and prejudices are, as a result of that consideration, of no importance whatever, then you have to accept it whether you like it or not, because twice-two—mathematics. Just try to refute that.

"Good Lord," they'll scream at you, "you can't possibly deny that: twice two *is* four! Never does nature ask you for your opinion; she does not care a damn for your wishes, or whether you like her laws or not. You are obliged to accept her as she is and, consequently, all her results. A stone wall, that is, is a stone wall ... etc., etc." But, goodness gracious me, what do I care for the laws of nature and arithmetic if for some reason or other I don't like those laws of twice-two? No doubt I shall never be able to break through such a stone wall with my forehead, if I really do not possess the strength to do it, but I shall not reconcile myself to it just because I have to deal with a stone wall and haven't the strength to knock it down.

As though such a stone wall were really the same thing as peace of mind, and as though it really contained some word of comfort simply because a stone wall is merely the equivalent of twice-two-makes-four. Oh, what stuff and nonsense this is! Is it not much better to understand everything, to be aware of everything, to be conscious of all the impossibilities and stone walls? Not to be reconciled to any of those impossibilities or stone walls if you hate being reconciled to them? To reach by way of the most irrefutable logical combinations the most hideous conclusions on the eternal theme that it is somehow your own fault if there is a stone wall, though again it is abundantly clear that it is not your fault at all, and therefore to abandon yourself sensuously to doing nothing, silently and gnashing your teeth impotently, hugging the illusion that there isn't really anyone you can be angry with; that there is really no object for your anger and that perhaps there never will be an object for it; that the whole thing is nothing but some imposition, some hocus-pocus, some card-sharping trick, or simply some frightful mess—no one knows what and no one knows who. But in spite of these uncertainties and this hocus-pocus, you have still got a headache, and the less you know the more splitting the headache!

IV

"Ha-ha-ha! After this you'll no doubt be finding some pleasure in toothache too!" you cry with a laugh.

"Well, why not? There's pleasure even in toothache," I reply.

I had toothache for a whole month, and I know there is pleasure in it. For, you see, if you have toothache, you don't lose your temper in silence. You groan. But these groans of yours are not sincere groans. They are groans mixed with malice. And it is the malice here that matters. By these groans the sufferer expresses his pleasure. If he did not feel any pleasure, he would not groan. That is an excellent example, gentlemen, and I'm going to develop it.

In these groans there is expressed, in the first place, the whole purposelessness of your pain which is so humiliating to your consciousness; the crowning stroke of nature, for which you, of course, don't care, but from which you suffer all the same, while she goes scot free. They express the consciousness of the fact that even though you had no enemies, you do have pain; the consciousness that for all the dentists in the world you are entirely at the mercy of your teeth; that if someone should desire it, your teeth would stop aching, and if he does not, they will go on aching another three months; and that, finally, if you are still unconvinced and still keep on protesting, all that is left for your own gratification is to give yourself a thrashing or hit the wall with your fist as hard as you can, and absolutely nothing more.

Well, it is from those mortal injuries, from those gibes that come from goodness knows whom, that pleasure at last arises, pleasure that sometimes reaches the highest degree of voluptuousness. I beg of you, gentlemen, listen sometimes to the groans of an educated man of the nineteenth century who is suffering from toothache on—shall we say?—the second or third day of his indisposition, when he is beginning to groan in quite a different way from the way he groaned on the first day, that is, not simply because he has toothache, not like some coarse peasant, but like a man of culture and European civilisation, like a man "who has divorced himself from the soil and uprooted himself from his people," to use a phrase which is at present in vogue. His groans become nasty and offensively ill-tempered groans, and go on for days and nights. And yet he knows perfectly well that he is doing no good with his groaning; he knows better than anyone that he is merely irritating and worrying himself and others for nothing; he knows that the audience before whom he is performing with such zeal and all his family are listening to him with disgust, that they don't believe him in the least, and that in their hearts they know that, if he wished, he could have groaned differently and more naturally, without such trills and flourishes, and that he is only amusing himself out of spite and malice. Well, all those apprehensions and infamies are merely the expression of sensual pleasure. "I'm worrying you, am I?" he seems to say. "I'm breaking your hearts, I'm not letting anyone in the house sleep, am I? All right, don't sleep. I want you, too, to feel every minute that I have toothache. I'm no longer the same hero to you now as I tried to appear before, but just a loathsome little fellow, a nuisance? Very well then. So be it. I'm very glad you've found me out at last. You hate to listen to my mean little groans, do you? Well, all right. Hate it if you like. Just you listen to my next flourish. It'll be much worse than the one before, I promise you. . . ." You still don't understand, gentlemen? Well, it seems we have to develop still further and more thoroughly, we have to sharpen our consciousness still more, before we can fully appreciate all the twists and turns of this sort of voluptuous pleasure. You are laughing? I'm very glad, I'm sure. I'm afraid, gentlemen, my jokes are in very bad taste, they are lame and a bit confused, and show a lack of self-confidence, too. That is because I have no self-respect. But can a man of acute sensibility respect himself at all?

V

Well, can you expect a man who tries to find pleasure even in the feeling of his own humiliation to have an atom of respect for himself? I'm not saying this now from any hypersensitive feeling of remorse. And, anyway, I never could stand saying, "Sorry, father, I won't do it again,"—not because I'm not capable of saying it; on the contrary, because I'm too capable of saying it. Yes, indeed! I used to get into awful trouble on such occasions though I was not even remotely to be blamed for anything. That was the most horrible part of it. But every time that happened, I used to be touched to the very depth of my soul, I kept on repeating how sorry I was, shedding rivers of tears, and of course deceiving myself, though I was not pretending at all. It was my heart that somehow was responsible for all that nastiness. . . . Here one could not blame even the laws of nature, though the laws of nature have, in fact, always and more than anything else caused me infinite worry and trouble all through my life. It is disgusting to call to mind all this, and as a matter of fact it was a disgusting business even then. For after a minute or so I used to realise bitterly that it was all a lie, a horrible lie, a hypocritical lie, I mean, all those repentances, all those emotional outbursts, all those promises to turn over a new leaf. And if you ask why I tormented myself like that, the answer is because I was awfully bored sitting about and doing nothing, and that is why I started on that sort of song and dance. I assure you it is true. You'd better start watching yourselves more closely, gentlemen, and you will understand that it is so. I used to invent my own adventures, I used to devise my own life for myself, so as to be able to carry on somehow. How many times, for instance, used I to take offence without rhyme or reason, deliberately; and of course I realised very well that I had taken offence at nothing, that the whole thing was just a piece of playacting, but in the end I would work myself up into such a state that I would be offended in good earnest. All my life I felt drawn to play such tricks, so that in the end I simply lost control of myself. Another time I tried hard to fall in love. This happened to me twice, as a matter of fact. And I can assure you, gentlemen, I suffered terribly. In my heart of hearts, of course, I did not believe that I was suffering, I'd even sneer at myself in a vague sort of way, but I suffered agonies none the less, suffered in the most genuine manner imaginable, as though I were really in love. I was jealous. I made scenes. And all because I was so confoundedly bored, gentlemen, all because I was so horribly bored. Crushed by doing nothing. For the direct, the inevitable, and the legitimate result of consciousness is to make all action impossible, or—to put it differently—consciousness leads to thumb-twiddling. I've already said so before, but let me repeat, and repeat most earnestly: all plain men and men of action are active only because they are dull-witted and mentally undeveloped. How is that to be explained? Why, like this: owing to their arrested mental development they mistake the nearest and secondary causes for primary causes and in this way persuade themselves much more easily and quickly than other people that they have found a firm basis for whatever business they have in hand and, as a result, they are no longer worried, and that is really the main thing. For to start being active you must first of all be completely composed in mind and never be in doubt. But how can I, for instance, compose myself? Where am I to find the primary cause to lean against? Where am I to get the basis from? I am constantly exercising my powers of thought and, consequently, every primary cause with me at once draws another one after itself, one still more primary, and so *ad infinitum*. That, in fact, is the basis of every sort of consciousness and analysis. That, too, therefore is a law of nature. What is the result of it then? Why, the same. Remember I was speaking of revenge just now. (I don't suppose you grasped that.) I argued that a man revenges himself because he finds justice in it. This of course means that he has found a primary cause, a basis, namely, justice. It follows therefore that now he is absolutely calm and, consequently, he revenges himself calmly and successfully, being convinced that what he does is both right and just. But I can't for the life of me see any justice here, and therefore if I should start revenging myself, it would be merely out of spite. Now spite, of course, could get the better of anything, of all my doubts, and so could very well take the place of any primary cause just because it is not a cause. But what can I do if I have not even spite (I began with that just now). Besides, my feeling of bitterness, too, is subject to the process of disintegration as a result of those damned laws of consciousness. One look and the object disappears into thin air, your reasons evaporate, there is no guilty man, the injury is no longer an injury but just fate, something in the nature of toothache for which no one can be blamed, and consequently there is only one solution left, namely, knocking your head against the wall as hard as you can. Well, so you just give it up because you've failed to find the primary cause. But try letting yourself be carried away by your emotions blindly, without reasoning, without any primary cause, letting your consciousness go hang at least for a time; hate or love just for the sake of not having to twiddle your thumbs. What will happen, of course, is that the day after tomorrow (and that at the latest) you will begin despising yourself for having knowingly duped yourself. As a result—a soap bubble and doing nothing again. As a matter of fact, gentlemen, the reason why I consider myself a clever man is simply because I could never in my life finish anything I'd started. All right, I am a talker, a harmless, boring talker as we all are. But what can I do if the direct and sole purpose of every intelligent man is to talk, that is to say, to waste his time deliberately?

VI

Oh, if only I had done nothing merely out of laziness! Lord, how I should have respected myself then. I should have respected myself just because I should at least have been able to be lazy; I should at least have possessed one quality which might be mistaken for a positive one and in which I could have believed myself. Question—who is he? Answer—a loafer. I must say it would have been a real pleasure to have heard that said about myself, for it would have meant that a positive definition had been found for me and that there was something one could say about me. "A loafer!"—why, it's a title, a purpose in life. It's a career, gentlemen, a career! Don't joke about it. It is so. I should then be a member of the most exclusive club by right and should have done nothing but gone on respecting myself continually. I knew a gentleman who all through his life was proud of the fact that he was a great connoisseur of Château Lafitte. He considered it a positive virtue and never had any misgivings. He died not only with a clear, but positively with a triumphant conscience, and he was absolutely right. So I, too, should have chosen a career for myself: I should have been a loafer and a glutton, but would, for instance, admire the sublime and beautiful in everything. How do you like that? I've been dreaming about it a long time. The "sublime and beautiful" has been a great worry to me during my forty years, but that was only *during* my forty years, at one time—oh, at one time it would have been different! I should at once have found an appropriate occupation for myself, namely, to drink to the health of the sublime and the beautiful. I should have made use of every opportunity to drop a tear into my glass and then drain it to all that was sublime and beautiful. I should then have turned everything in the world into something sublime and beautiful; I should have found the sublime and beautiful in the foullest and most unmistakable rubbish. I should have oozed tears like a sponge. The artist G., for instance, paints a picture. At once I drink to the health of the artist G. who has painted a picture because I love all that is sublime and beautiful.

An author writes something to please "everybody"; at once I drink to the health of "everybody" because I love all that is sublime and beautiful.

I should demand respect for myself for acting like that, and I should persecute anyone who would not show me respect. I should be at peace with the world and die in the odour of sanctity—why, it's delightful, it's simply delightful! And I should have grown such a monumental belly, I should have propagated such a double chin, I should have acquired such a fiery nose that every man in the street would have said as he looked at me, "Now that's a fine chap! Here's something real, something positive!"

And say what you like, gentlemen, it is very pleasant to hear such tributes in this negative age.

VII

But these are just golden dreams. Oh, tell me who was it first said, who was it first proclaimed that the only reason man behaves dishonourably is because he does not know his own interests, and that if he were enlightened, if his eyes were opened to his real normal interests, he would at once cease behaving dishonourably and would at once become good and honourable because, being enlightened and knowing what is good for him, he would see that his advantage lay in doing good, and of course it is well known that no man ever knowingly acts against his own interests and therefore he would, as it were, willy-nilly start doing good. Oh, the babe! Oh, the pure innocent child! When, to begin with, in the course of all these thousands of years has man ever acted in accordance with his own interests? What is one to do with the millions of facts that bear witness that man *knowingly*, that is, fully understanding his own interests, has left them in the background and rushed along a different path to take a risk, to try his luck, without being in any way compelled to do it by anyone or anything, but just as though he deliberately refused to follow the appointed path, and obstinately, wilfully, opened up a new, a difficult, and an utterly preposterous path, groping for it almost in the dark. Well, what does it mean but that to man this obstinacy and wilfulness is pleasanter than any advantage. . . . Advantage! What is advantage? Can you possibly give an exact definition of the nature of human advantage? And what if *sometimes* a man's ultimate advantage not only may, but even must, in certain cases consist in his desiring something that is immediately harmful and not advantageous to himself? If that is so, if such a case can arise, then the whole rule becomes utterly worthless. What do you think? Are there cases where it is so? You are laughing? Well, laugh away, gentlemen, only tell me this: have men's advantages ever been calculated with absolute precision? Are there not some which have not only not fitted in, but cannot possibly be fitted in any classification? You, gentlemen, have, so far as I know, drawn up your entire list of positive human values by taking the averages of statistical figures and relying on scientific and economic formulae. What are your values? They are peace, freedom, prosperity, wealth, and so on and so forth. So that any man who should, for instance, openly and knowingly act contrary to the whole of that list would, in your opinion, and in mine, too, for that matter, be an obscurantist or a plain madman, wouldn't he? But the remarkable thing surely is this: why does it always happen that when all these statisticians, sages, and lovers of the human race reckon up human values they always overlook one value? They don't even take it into account in the form in which it should be taken into account, and the whole calculation depends on that. What harm would there be if they did take it, that value, I mean, and add it to their list? But the trouble, you see, is that this peculiar good does not fall under any classification and cannot be included in any list. Now, I have a friend, for instance—why, good gracious, gentlemen, he is also a friend of yours, and indeed whose friend is he not? In undertaking any business, this gentleman at once explains to you in high-sounding and clear language how he intends to act in accordance with the laws of truth and reason. And not only that. He will talk to you, passionately and vehemently, all about real and normal human interests; he will scornfully reproach the shortsighted fools for not understanding their own advantages, nor the real meaning of virtue, and—exactly a quarter of an hour later, without any sudden or external cause but just because of some inner impulse which is stronger than any of his interests, he will do something quite different, that is to say, he will do something that is exactly contrary to what he has been saying himself: against the laws of reason and against his own interests, in short, against everything.... I'd better warn you, though, that my friend is a collective entity and that for that reason it is a little difficult to blame him alone. That's the trouble, gentlemen, that there exists something which is dearer to almost every man than his greatest good, or (not to upset the logic of my argument) that there exists one most valuable good (and one, too, that is being constantly overlooked, namely, the one we are talking about) which is greater and more desirable than all other goods, and for the sake of which a man, if need be, is ready to challenge all laws, that is to say, reason, honour, peace, prosperity—in short, all those excellent and useful things, provided he can obtain that primary and most desirable good which is dearer to him than anything in the world.

"Well," you say, "but they are values all the same, aren't they?"

Very well, I believe we shall soon understand each other, and, besides, this isn't a matter for quibbling. What is important is that this good is so remarkable just because it sets at naught all our classifications and shatters all the systems set up by the lovers of the human race for the happiness of the human race. In fact, it plays havoc with everything. But before I tell you what this good is, I should like to compromise myself personally and I therefore bluntly declare that all these fine systems, all these theories which try to explain to man all his normal interests so that, in attempting to obtain them by every possible means, he should at once become good and honourable, are in my opinion nothing but mere exercises in logic. Yes, exercises in logic. For to assert that you believed this theory of the regeneration of the whole human race by means of the system of its own advantages is, in my opinion, almost the same as—well, asserting, for instance, with Buckle, that civilisation softens man, who, consequently becomes less bloodthirsty and less liable to engage in wars. I believe he argues it very logically indeed. But man is so obsessed by systems and abstract deductions that he is ready to distort the truth deliberately, he is ready to deny the evidence of his senses, so long as he justifies his logic. That is why I take this example, for it is a most striking example. Well, just take a good look round you: rivers of blood are being spilt, and in the jolliest imaginable way, like champagne. Take all our nineteenth century in which Buckle lived. Look at Napoleon, the Great and the present one. Look at North America—the everlasting union. Look, finally, at Schleswig-Holstein. . . . And what, pray, does civilisation soften in us? All civilisation does is to develop in man the many-sidedness of his sensations, and nothing, absolutely nothing more. And through the development of his many-sidedness man, for all we know, may reach the stage when he will find pleasure in bloodshed. This has already happened to him. Have you noticed that the most subtle shedders of blood have almost invariably been most civilised men, compared with whom all the Attilas and Stenka Razins were just innocent babes, and if they are not so outstanding as Attila or Stenka Razin it is because we meet them so often, because they are *too* ordinary, and because we have got used to them. At any rate, civilisation has made man, if not more bloodthirsty, then certainly more hideously and more contemptibly bloodthirsty. In the past he looked on bloodshed as an act of justice and exterminated those he thought necessary to exterminate with a clear conscience; but now we consider bloodshed an abomination and we engage in this abomination more than ever. Which is worse? You'd better decide for yourselves. They say that Cleopatra (if I may take an instance from Roman history) loved to stick golden pins into the breasts of her slave-girls and enjoyed their screams and contortions. You will say that this happened in relatively speaking barbarous times; but today, too, we live in barbarous times because (again relatively speaking) today, too, we stick pins into people; today, too, though man has learnt to see things more clearly than in barbarous times, he is still very far from having learnt to act in accordance with the dictates of reason and science. But I daresay you are firmly convinced that he will most certainly learn to do so as soon as his so-called bad old habits completely disappear and as soon as common sense and science have completely re-educated human nature and directed it along the road of normal behaviour. You are convinced that, when this happens, man will stop making *deliberate* mistakes and perforce refuse to allow his will to act contrary to his normal interests. And that is not all. You say that science itself will then teach man (though in my opinion it is an unnecessary luxury) that as a matter of fact he possesses neither will nor uncontrollable desires, and never has done, and that he himself is nothing more than a sort of piano-key or organ-stop, and that, in addition, there are the laws of nature in the world; so that whatever he does is not done of his own will at all, but of itself, according to the laws of nature. Consequently, as soon as these laws of nature are discovered, man will no longer have to answer for his actions and will find life exceedingly easy. All human actions will then, no doubt, be computed according to these laws, mathematically, something like the tables of logarithms, up to 108,000, and indexed accordingly. Or, better still, certain well-intentioned words will be published, something like our present encyclopaedic dictionaries, in which everything will be calculated and specified with such an exactness that there will be no more independent actions or adventures in the world.

Then—it is still you who are saying this—new economic relations will be established, relations all ready for use and calculated with mathematical exactitude, so that all sorts of problems will vanish in a twinkling simply because ready-made solutions will be provided for all of them. It is then that the Crystal Palace will be built. Then—why, in fact, the Golden Age will have dawned again. Of course, it is quite impossible to guarantee (it is I who am speaking now) that even then people will not be bored to tears (for what will they have to do when everything is calculated and tabulated), though, on the other hand, everything will be so splendidly rational. Of course, when you are bored, you are liable to get all sorts of ideas into your head. Golden pins, too, are after all stuck into people out of boredom. But all that would not matter. What is bad (and it is again I who am saying this) is that I'm afraid they will be glad even of golden pins then. For man is stupid, phenomenally stupid; I mean, he may not be really stupid, but on the other hand he is so ungrateful that you won't find anything like him in the whole wide world. I would not be at all surprised, for instance, if suddenly and without the slightest possible reason a gentleman of an ignoble or rather a reactionary and sardonic countenance were to arise amid all that future reign of universal common sense and, gripping his sides firmly with his hands, were to say to us all, "Well, gentlemen, what about giving all this common sense a mighty kick and letting it scatter in the dust before our feet simply to send all these logarithms to the devil so that we can again live according to our foolish will?" That wouldn't matter, either, but for the regrettable fact that he would certainly find followers: for man is made like that. And all, mind you, for the most stupid of reasons which seems hardly worth mentioning, namely, because man has always and everywhere— whoever he may be—preferred to do as he chose, and not in the least as his reason or advantage dictated; and one may choose to do something even if it is against one's own advantage, and sometimes one *positively should* (that is my idea). One's own free and unfettered choice, one's own whims, however wild, one's own fancy, overwrought though it sometimes may be to the point of madness—that is that same most desirable good which we overlooked and which does not fit into any classification, and against which all theories and systems are continually wrecked. And why on earth do all those sages assume that man must needs strive after some normal, after some rationally desirable good? All man wants is an absolutely *free* choice, however dear that freedom may cost him and wherever it may lead him to. Well, of course, if it is a matter of choice, then the devil only knows . . .

VIII

"Ha-ha-ha! But there's really no such thing as choice, as a matter of fact, whatever you may say," you interrupt me with a laugh. "Today science has succeeded in so far dissecting man that at least we now know that desire and the so-called free will are nothing but—"

One moment, gentlemen. I am coming to that myself, and I don't mind telling you that I was even feeling a little nervous. I was just about to say that choice depended on the devil only knows what and that that was all to the good, but I suddenly remembered science and—the words died on my lips. And you took advantage of it and began to speak. It is, of course, quite true that if one day they really discover some formula of all our desires and whims, that is to say, if they discover what they all depend on, by what laws they are governed, how they are disseminated, what they are aiming at in one case and another, and so on, that is, a real mathematical formula, man may perhaps at once stop feeling any desire and, I suppose, most certainly will. For who would want to desire according to a mathematical formula? And that is not all. He will at once be transformed from a man into an organ-stop, or something of the sort. For what is man without desires, without free will, and without the power of choice but a stop in an organ pipe? What do you think? Let us calculate the probabilities: is it or is it not likely to happen?

"Well," you decide, "in the majority of cases our desires are mistaken from a mistaken idea of what is to our advantage. Sometimes we desire absolute nonsense because in our stupidity we see in this nonsense the easiest way of attaining some conjectural good."

Very well, and when all that is explained and worked out on paper (which is quite possible, for it would be absurd and unreasonable to assume that man will never discover other laws of nature), the so-called desires will of course no longer exist. For when one day desire comes completely to terms with reason we shall of course reason and not desire, for it is obviously quite impossible to *desire* nonsense while retaining our reason and in that way knowingly go against our reason and wish to harm ourselves. And when all desires and reasons can be actually calculated (for one day the laws of our so-called free will are bound to be discovered) something in the nature of a mathematical table may in good earnest be compiled so that all our desires will in effect arise in accordance with this table. For if it is one day calculated and proved to me, for instance, that if I thumb my nose at a certain person it is because I cannot help thumbing my nose at him, and that I have to thumb my nose at him with that particular thumb, what *freedom* will there be left to me, especially if I happen to be a scholar and have taken my degree at a university? In that case, of course, I should be able to calculate my life for thirty years ahead. In short, if this were really to take place, there would be nothing left for us to do: we should have to understand everything whether we wanted to or not. And, generally speaking, we must go on repeating to ourselves incessantly that at a certain moment and in certain circumstances nature on no account asks us for our permission to do anything; that we have got to take her as she is, and not as we imagine her to be; and that if we are really tending towards mathematical tables and rules of thumb and—well—even towards test tubes, then what else is there left for us to do but to accept everything, test tube and all. Or else the test tube will come by itself and will be accepted whether you like it or not. . . .

Quite right, but there's the rub! I'm sorry, gentlemen, to have gone on philosophising like this: remember my forty years in the dark cellar! Do let me indulge my fancy for a moment. You see, gentlemen, reason is an excellent thing. There is no doubt about it. But reason is only reason, and it can only satisfy the reasoning ability of man, whereas volition is a manifestation of the whole of life, I mean, of the whole of human life, including reason with all its concomitant head-scratchings. And although our life, thus manifested, very often turns out to be a sorry business, it is life none the less and not merely extractions of square roots. For my part, I quite naturally want to live in order to satisfy all my faculties and not my reasoning faculty alone, that is to say, only some twentieth part of my capacity for living. What does reason know? Reason only knows what it has succeeded in getting to know (certain things, I suppose, it will never know; this may be poor comfort, but why not admit it frankly?), whereas human nature acts as a whole, with everything that is in it, consciously, and unconsciously, and though it may commit all sorts of absurdities, it persists. I cannot help thinking, gentlemen, that you look upon me with pity; you go on telling me over and over again that an enlightened and mentally developed man, such a man, in short, as the future man can be expected to be, cannot possibly desire deliberately something which is not a real "good," and that, you say, is mathematics. I quite agree. It is mathematics. But I repeat for the hundredth time that here is one case, one case only, when man can deliberately and consciously desire something that is injurious, stupid, even outrageously stupid, just because he wants *to have the right* to desire for himself even what is very stupid and not to be bound by an obligation to desire only what is sensible. For this outrageously stupid thing, gentlemen, this whim of ours, may really be more accounted by us than anything else on earth, especially in certain cases. And in particular it may be more valuable than any good even when it is quite obviously bad for us and contradicts the soundest conclusions of our reason about what is to our advantage, for at all events it preserves what is most precious and most important to us, namely, our personality and our individuality. Indeed some people maintain that this is more precious than anything else to man. Desire, of course, can, if it chooses, come to terms with reason, especially if people do not abuse it and make use of it in moderation; this is useful and sometimes even praiseworthy. But very often and indeed mostly desire is utterly and obstinately at loggerheads with reason and—and, do you know, that, too, is useful and occasionally even praiseworthy. Let us suppose, gentlemen, that man is not stupid. (As a matter of fact, it cannot possibly be said that man is stupid, if only from the one consideration that if he is, then who is wise?) But if he is not stupid, he is monstrously ungrateful. Phenome-

nally ungrateful. I'm even inclined to believe that the best definition of man is—a creature who walks on two legs and is ungrateful. But that is not all, that is not his principal failing; his
greatest failing is his constant lack of moral sense, constant from
the days of the Flood to the Schleswig-Holstein period of human history. Lack of moral sense and, consequently, lack of good
sense; for it has long been known that lack of good sense is really
the result of lack of moral sense. Well, try and cast your eye
upon the history of mankind and what will you see? Grandeur?
Yes, perhaps even grandeur. The Colossus of Rhodes, for instance, is worth something, isn't it? Well may Mr. Anayevsky bear
witness to the fact that some people maintain that it is the work
of human hands, while others assert that it was wrought by nature herself. Gaiety? Well, yes. Perhaps gaiety, too. One has only
to think of the dress uniforms, military and civilian, of all peoples in all ages—that alone is worth something, and if we throw
in the undress uniforms as well, we can only gasp in astonish-
ment at the gaiety of it all; no historian, I am sure, will be able to
resist it. Monotonous? Well, I suppose it is monotonous: they
fight and fight, they are fighting now, they fought before, and
they will fight again—you must admit this is rather monotonous.
In short, you can say anything you like about world history, anything that might enter the head of a man with the most disordered imagination. One thing, though, you cannot possibly say
about it: you cannot say that it is sensible. If you did, you would
choke at the first word. And, moreover, this is the sort of curious
thing you come across almost every minute: continually there
crop up in life such sensible and moral people, such sages and
lovers of humanity whose only object seems to be to live all their
lives as sensibly and morally as possible, to be, as it were, a shin-
ing light to their neighbours for the sole purpose of proving to
them that it is really possible to live morally and sensibly in the
world. And what happens? We know that many of these altruists,
sooner or later, towards the end of their lives, were untrue to
themselves, committing some folly, sometimes indeed of almost
indecent nature. Now let me ask you this question: what can you

expect of man seeing that he is a being endowed with such strange qualities? Why, shower all the earthly blessings upon him, drown him in happiness, head over ears, so that only bubbles should be visible on its surface, as on the surface of water; bestow such economic prosperity upon him as would leave him with nothing else to do but sleep, eat cakes, and only worry about keeping world history going—and even then he will, man will, out of sheer ingratitude, out of sheer desire to injure you personally, play a dirty trick on you. He would even risk his cakes and ale and deliberately set his heart on the most deadly trash, the most uneconomic absurdity, and do it, if you please, for the sole purpose of infusing into this positive good sense his deadly fantastic element. It is just his fantastic dreams, his most patent absurdities, that he will desire above all else for the sole purpose of proving to himself (as though that were so necessary) that men are still men and not keys of a piano on which the laws of nature are indeed playing any tune they like, but are in danger of going on playing until no one is able to desire anything except a mathematical table. And that is not all: even if he really were nothing but a piano-key, even if this were proved to him by natural science and mathematically, even then he would refuse to come to his senses, but would on purpose, just in spite of everything, do something out of sheer ingratitude; actually, to carry his point. And if he has no other remedy, he will plan destruction and chaos, he will devise all sorts of sufferings, and in the end he will carry his point! He will send a curse over the world, and as only man can curse (this is his privilege which distinguishes him from other animals), he may by his curse alone attain his object, that is, really convince himself that he is a man and not a piano-key! If you say that this, too, can be calculated by the mathematical table—chaos, and darkness, and curses—so that the mere possibility of calculating it all beforehand would stop it all and reason would triumph in the end—well, if that were to happen man would go purposely mad in order to rid himself of reason and carry his point! I believe this is so, I give you my word for it; for it seems to me that the whole meaning of human life can be summed up in the one statement that man only exists for the purpose of proving to himself every minute that he is a man and not an organ-stop! Even if it means physical suffering, even if it means turning his back on civilisation, he will prove it. And how is one after that to resist the temptation to rejoice that all this has not happened yet and that so far desire depends on the devil alone knows what.

You shout at me (if, that is, you will deign to favour me with raising voices) that no one wants to deprive me of my free will, that all they are concerned with is to arrange things in such a way that my will should of itself, of its own will, coincide with my normal interests, with the laws of nature and arithmetic.

But, good Lord, gentlemen, what sort of a free will can it be once it is all a matter of mathematical tables and arithmetic, when the only thing to be taken into account will be that twice-two-makes-four? Twice-two will make four even without my will. Surely, free will does not mean that!

IX

Gentlemen, I am joking of course, and I'm afraid my jokes are rather poor, but you can't after all take everything as a joke. How do you know I'm not joking with a heavy heart? Gentlemen, I'm worried by all sorts of questions; please, answer them for me. For instance, you want to cure man of his old habits and reform his will in accordance with the demands of science and common sense. But how do you know that man not only could but *should* be remade like that? And what leads you to conclude that human desires must *necessarily* be reformed? In short, how do you know that such a reformation will be a gain to man? And, if one is to put all one's cards on the table, why are you so *utterly* convinced that not to go counter to the real normal gains guaranteed by the conclusions of reason and arithmetic is always so certainly right for man and is a universal law so far as mankind is concerned? For at present it is only a supposition on your part. Let us assume it is a law of logic, but how do you know that it is also a human law? You don't by any chance think I'm mad, do you? Let me explain myself. I agree that man is above all a creative animal, condemned consciously to strive towards a goal and to occupy himself with the art of engineering, that is, always and incessantly clear with a path for himself *wherever it may lead.* And I should not be at all surprised if that were not the reason why he sometimes cannot help wishing to turn aside from the path just because he is condemned to clear it, and perhaps, too, because, however stupid the plain man of action may be as a rule, the thought will sometimes occur to him that the path almost always seems to lead *nowhere in particular,* and that the important point is not where it leads but that it should lead somewhere, and that a well-behaved child, disdaining the art of engineering, should not indulge in the fatal idleness which, as we all know, is the mother of all vices. Man likes to create and to clear paths—that is undeniable. But why is he also so passionately fond of destruction and chaos? Tell me that. But, if you don't mind, I'd like to say a few words about that myself. Is he not perhaps so fond of destruction and chaos (and it cannot be denied that he is sometimes very fond of it—that is a fact) because he is instinctively afraid of reaching the goal and completing the building he is erecting? How do you know, perhaps he only loves the building from a distance and not by any means at close quarters; perhaps he only loves building it and not living in it, preferring to leave it later *aux animaux domestiques,* such as ants, sheep, etc., etc. Now, ants are quite a different matter. They have one marvellous building of this kind, a building that is for ever indestructible—the ant-hill.

The excellent ants began with the ant-hill and with the ant-hill they will most certainly end, which does great credit to their steadfastness and perseverance. But man is a frivolous and unaccountable creature, and perhaps, like a chess-player, he is only fond of the process of achieving his aim, but not of the aim itself. And who knows (it is impossible to be absolutely sure about it), perhaps the whole aim mankind is striving to achieve on earth merely lies in this incessant process of achievement, or (to put it differently) in life itself, and not really in the attainment of any goal, which, needless to say, can be nothing else but twice-two-makes-four, that is to say, a formula; but twice-two-makes-four is not life, gentlemen. It is the beginning of death. At least, man seems always to have been afraid of this twice-two-makes-four, and I am afraid of it now. Let us assume that man does nothing but search for this twice-two-makes-four, sails across oceans and sacrifices his life in this search; but to succeed in his quest, really to find what he is looking for, he is afraid—yes, he really seems to be afraid of it. For he feels that when he has found it there will be nothing more for him to look for. When workmen have finished their work they at least receive their wages, and they go to a pub and later find themselves in a police cell—well, there's an occupation for a week. But where can man go? At all events, one observes a certain awkwardness about him every time he achieves one of these aims. He loves the process of achievement but not achievement itself, which, I'm sure you will agree, is very absurd. In a word, man is a comical creature; I expect there must be some sort of jest hidden in it all. But twice-two-makes-four is for all that a most insupportable thing. Twice-two-makes-four is, in my humble opinion, nothing but a piece of impudence. Twice-two-makes-four is a farcical, dressed-up fellow who stands across your path with arms akimbo and spits at you. Mind you, I quite agree that twice-two-makes-four is a most excellent thing; but if we are to give everything its due, then twice-two-makes-five is sometimes a most charming little thing, too.

And why are you so firmly, so solemnly, convinced that only the normal and positive, in short, only prosperity, is of benefit to man? Does not reason make mistakes about benefits? Is it not possible that man loves something besides prosperity? Perhaps he is just as fond of suffering? Perhaps suffering is just as good for him as prosperity? And man does love suffering very much sometimes. He loves it passionately. That is an undeniable fact. You need not even look up world history to prove that; ask yourself, if you are a man and have lived at all. As for my own personal opinion, I believe that to be fond of prosperity is, somehow, indecent even. Whether it is good or bad, it is sometimes very pleasant to smash things, too. Not that I'm particularly anxious to plead the cause of suffering, or of happiness, for that matter. All I plead for is that I should be allowed my whims, and that they should be guaranteed to me whenever I want them. In light comedies, for instance, suffering is not permitted, and I accept that. In the Crystal Palace it is unthinkable: suffering is doubt, it is negation, and what sort of Crystal Palace would it be if one were to have any doubts about it? And yet I am convinced that man will never renounce real suffering, that is to say, destruction and chaos. Suffering! Why, it's the sole cause of consciousness! And though at the beginning I did argue that consciousness was the greatest misfortune to man, yet I know that man loves it and will not exchange it for any satisfaction. Consciousness, for instance, is infinitely superior to twice-two. After twice-two there is nothing left for you to do, or even to learn. All you could do then would be to stop up your five senses and sink into contemplation. While if you hang on to your consciousness you may achieve the same result, that is to say, there will be nothing for you to do, either, you could at least administer a good thrashing to yourself from time to time, and that at any rate livens you up a bit. It may be a reactionary step, but it is better than nothing, isn't it?

XI[1]

You believe in the Crystal Palace, forever indestructible, that is to say, in one at which you won't be able to stick out your tongue even by stealth or cock a snook even in your pocket. Well, perhaps I am afraid of this palace just because it is made of crystal and is forever indestructible, and just because I shan't be able to poke my tongue out at it even by stealth.

You see, if it were not a palace but a hencoop, and if it should rain, I might crawl into it to avoid getting wet, but I would never

---

1. The censor so mangled this chapter that Dostoevsky later complained that he was made to contradict himself several times. (D.M.)

pretend that the hencoop was a palace out of gratitude to it for sheltering me from the rain. You laugh and you tell me that in such circumstances even a hencoop is as good as a palace. Yes, I reply, it certainly is if the only purpose in life is not to get wet.

But what is to be done if I've got it into my head that that is not the only purpose in life, and that if one has to live, one had better live in a palace? That is my choice; that is my desire. You can only force me to give it up when you change my desire. All right, do it. Show me something more attractive. Give me another ideal. For the time being, however, I refuse to accept a hencoop for a palace. The Crystal Palace may be just an idle dream, it may be against all laws of nature, I may have invented it because of my own stupidity, because of certain old and irrational habits of my generation. But what do I care whether it is against the laws of nature? What does it matter so long as it exists in my desires, or rather exists while my desires exist? You are not laughing again, are you? Laugh by all means; I am quite ready to put up with any jeers, but I will still refuse to say that I'm satisfied when I'm hungry. At all events I know that I shall never be content with a compromise, with an everlasting and recurring zero because it exists according to the laws of nature and *actually* exists. I will not accept as the crown of all my desires a big house with model flats for the poor on a lease of ninety-nine hundred and ninety-nine years and, in case of emergency, with the dental surgeon Wagenheim on a signboard. Destroy my desires, eradicate my ideals, show me something better, and I will follow you. I daresay you will probably declare that it isn't worth your while having anything to do with me; but in that case I, too, can say the same to you. We are discussing this seriously; and if you are too proud to give me your attention, I shall have to do without it.

But while I'm still alive and have desires, I'd rather my right hand withered than let it bring even one small brick to such a house of model flats! I know that a short time ago I rejected the Crystal Palace myself for the sole reason that one would not be allowed to stick one's tongue out at it. But I did not say that because I am so fond of sticking out my tongue. Perhaps what I resented was that among all our buildings there has never been one at which one could not stick out one's tongue. On the contrary, I'd gladly have let my tongue be cut off out of gratitude if things could be so arranged that I should have no wish to stick it out at all. It is not my business if things cannot be arranged like that and if one has to be satisfied with model flats. Why then am I made with such desires? Surely, I have not been made for the sole purpose of drawing the conclusion that the way I am made is a piece of rank deceit? Can this be the sole purpose? I don't believe it.

However, do you know what? I am convinced that fellows like me who live in dark cellars must be kept under restraint. They may be able to live in their dark cellars for forty years and never open their mouths, but the moment they get into the light of day and break out they talk and talk and talk. . . .

XI

And, finally, gentlemen, it is much better to do nothing at all! Better passive awareness! And so three cheers for the dark cellar! Though I have said that I envy the normal man to the point of exasperation, I wouldn't care to be in his place in the circumstances in which I find him (though I shall never cease envying him. No, no, the dark cellar is, at any rate, of much greater advantage to me!). In the dark cellar one can at least. . . . Sorry, I'm afraid I am exaggerating. I am exaggerating because I know, as well as twice-two, that it is not the dark cellar that is better, but something else, something else altogether, something I long for but cannot find. To hell with the dark cellar!

Do you know what would be better? It would be better if I myself believed in anything I had just written. I assure you most solemnly, gentlemen, that there is not a word I've just written I believe in! What I mean is that perhaps I do believe, but at the same time I cannot help feeling and suspecting for some unknown reason that I'm lying like a cobbler.

"Then why have you written all this?" you ask me.

"Well, suppose I put you in a dark cellar for forty years without anything to do and then came to see you in your dark cellar after the forty years to find out what had become of you. Can a man be left for forty years with nothing to do?"

"But aren't you ashamed? Don't you feel humiliated?" you will perhaps say, shaking your head contemptuously. "You long for life, yet you try to solve the problems of life by a logical tangle! And how tiresome, how insolent your tricks are, and, at the same time, how awfully frightened you are! You talk a lot of nonsense and you seem to be very pleased with it; you say a lot of impudent things, and you are yourself always afraid and apologising for them. You assure us that you are afraid of nothing, and at the same time you try to earn our good opinion. You assure us that you are gnashing your teeth, but at the same time you crack jokes to make us laugh. You know your jokes are not amusing, but you seem to be highly pleased with their literary merit. You may perhaps have really suffered, but you don't seem to have the slightest respect for your suffering. There may be some truth in you, but there is no humility. You carry your truth to the market place out of the pettiest vanity to make a public show of it and to discredit it. No doubt you mean to say something, but you conceal your last word out of fear, because you haven't the courage to say it, but only craven insolence. You boast about your sensibility, but you merely don't know your own mind. For though your mind is active enough, your heart is darkened with corruption, and without a pure heart there can be no full or genuine sensibility. And how tiresome you are! How you impose yourself on people! The airs you give yourself! Lies, lies, lies!"

Now, of course, I've made up all this speech of yours myself. It, too, comes from the dark cellar. I've been listening to your words for forty years through a crack in the ceiling. I have invented them myself. It is the only thing I did invent. No wonder I got it pat and dressed it up in a literary form.

But are you really so credulous as to imagine that I would

print all this, and let you read it into the bargain? And there is another puzzle I'd like to solve: why on earth do I address you as "gentlemen," as though you really were my readers? Such confessions which I am now about to make are not printed, nor given to other people to read. At least I have not enough pluck for that, nor do I consider it necessary to have it. But, you see, a strange fancy has come into my head and I want to realise it, cost what may. It's like this:—

There are certain things in a man's past which he does not divulge to everybody but, perhaps, only to his friends. Again there are certain things he will not divulge even to his friends; he will divulge them perhaps only to himself, and that, too, as a secret. But, finally, there are things which he is afraid to divulge even to himself, and every decent man has quite an accumulation of such things in his mind. I can put it even this way: the more decent a man is, the larger will the number of such things be. At least I have allowed myself only recently to remember some of my early adventures, having till now avoided them rather uneasily. I'm afraid. Now, however, when I have not only remembered them, but have also made up my mind to write them down, I particularly want to put the whole thing to the test to see whether I can be absolutely frank with myself and not be afraid of the whole truth. Let me add, by the way: Heine says that true biographies are almost impossible, and that a man will most certainly tell a lot of lies about himself. In his view, Rousseau told a lot of lies about himself in his Confessions, and told them deliberately, out of vanity. I am sure Heine is right; I can understand perfectly how sometimes one tells all sorts of lies about oneself out of sheer vanity, even going so far as to confess to all sorts of crimes, and I can perfectly understand that sort of vanity. But Heine had in mind a man who made his confessions to the public. I, however, am writing for myself, and I should like to make it clear once and for all that if I address myself in my writings to a reader, I'm doing it simply as a matter of form, because I find it much easier to write like that. It is only a form, an empty show, for I know that I shall never have any readers. I have already intimated as much....

I don't want to be hampered by any considerations in the editing of my Memoirs. I shan't bother about order or system. I shall put down whatever I remember.

Now, of course, I might, for instance, be taken at my word and asked if I really do not count on any readers, why do I now put down all sorts of conditions, and on paper, too, such as not to pay any attention to order or system, to write down what I remember, etc., etc. Why all these explanations? Why all these apologies?

"Ah," I reply, "now you're asking!"

There is, incidentally, a whole psychology in all this. Perhaps it's simply that I am a coward. Again, perhaps it is simply that I'm imagining an audience on purpose so as to observe the proprieties while I write. There are thousands of reasons, no doubt.

Then again there is this further puzzle: what do I want to write it down for? What is the object of it all? If I'm not writing for the reading public, why not simply recall these things in my mind without putting them down on paper?

Well, I suppose I could do that, but it will look more dignified on paper. There is something imposing about that. There will be a greater sense of passing judgment on myself. The whole style, I'm sure, will be better. Moreover, I really may feel easier in my mind if I write it down. I have, for instance, been latterly greatly oppressed by the memory of some incident that happened to me a long time ago. I remembered it very vividly the other day, as a matter of fact, and it has since been haunting me like some annoying tune you can't get out of your head. And yet I simply must get rid of it. I have hundreds of such memories, but at times one of them stands out from the rest and oppresses me. So why shouldn't I try?

And, lastly, I'm awfully bored, and I have nothing to do. Writing down things is, in fact, a sort of work. People say work makes man better and more honest. Well, here's a chance for me at any rate.

Snow is falling today, almost wet snow, yellow, dirty. It was snowing yesterday, too, and the other day. I think it is because of the wet snow that I remembered the incident which gives me no rest now. So let it be a story apropos of the wet snow.

THE BROTHERS KARAMAZOV

The Grand Inquisitor

"Even this must have a preface—that is, a literary preface," laughed Ivan, "and I am a poor hand at making one. You see, my action takes place in the sixteenth century, and at that time, as you probably learnt at school, it was customary in poetry to bring down heavenly powers on earth. Not to speak of Dante, in France, clerks, as well as the monks in the monasteries, used to give regular performances in which the Madonna, the saints, the angels, Christ, and God Himself were brought on the stage. In those days it was done in all simplicity. In Victor Hugo's 'Notre Dame de Paris' an edifying and gratuitous spectacle was provided for the people in the Hotel de Ville of Paris in the reign of Louis XI, in honour of the birth of the dauphin. It was called *Le bon jugement de la très sainte et gracieuse Vierge Marie,* and she appears herself on the stage and pronounces her *bon jugement.* Similar plays, chiefly from the Old Testament, were occasionally performed in Moscow too, up to the times of Peter the Great. But besides plays there were all sorts of legends and ballads scat-

Excerpted from Fyodor Dostoevsky, *The Brothers Karamazov,* translated by Constance Garnett. 1996 Modern Library Edition. Reprinted by permission of Modern Library.

tered about the world, in which the saints and angels and all the powers of Heaven took part when required. In our monasteries the monks busied themselves in translating, copying, and even composing such poems—and even under the Tatars. There is, for instance, one such poem (of course, from the Greek), 'The Wanderings of Our Lady through Hell,' with descriptions as bold as Dante's. Our Lady visits Hell, and the Archangel Michael leads her through the torments. She sees the sinners and their punishment. There she sees among others one noteworthy set of sinners in a burning lake; some of them sink to the bottom of the lake so that they can't swim out, and 'these God forgets'— an expression of extraordinary depth and force. And so Our Lady, shocked and weeping, falls before the throne of God and begs for mercy for all in Hell—for all she has seen there, and indiscriminately. Her conversation with God is immensely interesting. She beseeches Him, she will not desist, and when God points to the hands and feet of her Son, nailed to the Cross, and asks, 'How can I forgive His tormentors?' she bids all the saints, all the martyrs, all the angels and archangels to fall down with her and pray for mercy on all without distinction. It ends by her winning from God a respite of suffering every year from Good Friday till Trinity day, and the sinners at once raise a cry of thankfulness from Hell, chanting, 'Thou art just, O Lord, in this judgment.' Well, my poem would have been of that kind if it had appeared at that time. He comes on the scene in my poem, but He says nothing, only appears and passes on. Fifteen centuries have passed since He promised to come in His glory, fifteen centuries since His prophet wrote, 'Behold, I come quickly'; 'Of that day and that hour knoweth no man, neither the Son, but the Father,' as He Himself predicted on earth. But humanity awaits him with the same faith and with the same love. Oh, with greater faith, for it is fifteen centuries since man has ceased to see signs from Heaven.

> *No signs from Heaven come to-day*
> *To add to what the heart doth say.*

There was nothing left but faith in what the heart doth say. It is true there were many miracles in those days. There were saints who performed miraculous cures; some holy people, according to their biographies, were visited by the Queen of Heaven herself. But the devil did not slumber, and doubts were already arising among men of the truth of these miracles. And just then there appeared in the north of Germany a terrible new heresy. 'A huge star like to a torch' (that is, to a church) 'fell on the sources of the waters and they became bitter.' These heretics began blasphemously denying miracles. But those who remained faithful were all the more ardent in their faith. The tears of humanity rose up to Him as before, awaiting His coming, loved Him, hoped for Him, yearned to suffer and die for Him as before. And so many ages mankind had prayed with faith and fervour, 'O Lord our God, hasten Thy coming,' so many ages called upon Him, that in His infinite mercy He deigned to come down to His servants. Before that day He had come down, He had visited some holy men, martyrs and hermits, as is written in their 'Lives.' Among us, Tyutchev, with absolute faith in the truth of his words, bore witness that

> *Bearing the Cross, in slavish dress*
> *Weary and worn, the Heavenly King*
> *Our mother, Russia, came to bless,*
> *And through our land went wandering.*

And that certainly was so, I assure you.

"And behold, He deigned to appear for a moment to the people, to the tortured, suffering people, sunk in iniquity, but loving Him like children. My story is laid in Spain, in Seville, in the most terrible time of the Inquisition, when fires were lighted every day to the glory of God, and 'in the splendid *auto da fé* the wicked heretics were burnt.' Oh, of course, this was not the coming in which He will appear according to His promise at the end of time in all His heavenly glory, and which will be sudden 'as lightning flashing from east to west.' No, He visited His children only for a moment, and there where the flames were crackling round the heretics. In His infinite mercy He came once more among men in that human shape in which He walked among men for three years fifteen centuries ago. He came down to the 'ho pavement' of the southern town in which on the day before almost a hundred heretics had, *ad majorem gloriam Dei,* been burnt by the cardinal, the Grand Inquisitor, in a magnificent *auto da fé,* in the presence of the king, the court, the knights, the cardinals, the most charming ladies of the court, and the whole population of Seville.

"He came softly, unobserved, and yet, strange to say, every one recognised Him. That might be one of the best passages in the poem. I mean, why they recognised Him. The people are irresistibly drawn to Him, they surround Him, they flock about Him, follow Him. He moves silently in their midst with a gentle smile of infinite compassion. The sun of love burns in His heart, light and power shine from His eyes, and their radiance, shed on the people, stirs their hearts with responsive love. He holds out His hands to them, blesses them, and a healing virtue comes from contact with Him, even with His garments. An old man in the crowd, blind from childhood, cries out, 'O Lord, heal me and I shall see Thee!' and, as it were, scales fall from his eyes and the blind man sees Him. The crowd weeps and kisses the earth under His feet. Children throw flowers before Him, sing, and cry hosannah. 'It is He—it is He!' all repeat. 'It must be He, it can be no one but Him!' He stops at the steps of the Seville cathedral at the moment when the weeping mourners are bringing in a little open white coffin. In it lies a child of seven, the only daughter of a prominent citizen. The dead child lies hidden in flowers. 'He will raise your child,' the crowd shouts to the weeping mother. The priest, coming to meet the coffin, looks perplexed, and frowns, but the mother of the dead child throws herself at His feet with a wail. 'If it is Thou, raise my child!' she cries, holding out her hands to Him. The procession halts, the coffin is laid on the steps at His feet. He looks with compassion, and His lips once more softly pronounce, 'Maiden, arise!' and the maiden arises. The little girl sits up in the coffin and looks round, smiling with wide-open wondering eyes, holding a bunch of white roses they had put in her hand.

"There are cries, sobs, confusion among the people, and at that moment the cardinal himself, the Grand Inquisitor, passes by the cathedral. He is an old man, almost ninety, tall and erect, with a withered face and sunken eyes, in which there is still a gleam of light. He is not dressed in his gorgeous cardinal's robes, as he was the day before, when he was burning the enemies of the Roman Church—at that moment he was wearing his coarse, old, monk's cassock. At a distance behind him come his gloomy assistants and slaves and the 'holy guard.' He stops at the sight of the crowd and watches it from a distance. He sees everything; he sees them set the coffin down at His feet, sees the child rise up, and his face darkens. He knits his thick grey brows and his eyes gleam with a sinister fire. He holds out his finger and bids the guards take Him. And such is his power, so completely are the people cowed into submission and trembling obedience to him, that the crowd immediately make way for the guards, and in the midst of deathlike silence they lay hands on Him and lead Him away. The crowd instantly bows down to the earth, like one man, before the old inquisitor. He blesses the people in silence and passes on. The guards lead their prisoner to the close, gloomy vaulted prison in the ancient palace of the Holy Inquisition and shut Him in it. The day passes and is followed by the dark, burning 'breathless' night of Seville. The air is 'fragrant with laurel and lemon.' In the pitch darkness the iron door of the prison is suddenly opened and the Grand Inquisitor himself comes in with a light in his hand. He is alone; the door is closed at once behind him. He stands in the doorway and for a minute or two gazes into His face. At last he goes up slowly, sets the light on the table and speaks.

" 'Is it Thou? Thou?' but receiving no answer, he adds at once, 'Don't answer, be silent. What canst Thou say, indeed? I know too well what Thou wouldst say. And Thou hast no right to add anything to what Thou hadst said of old. Why, then, art Thou come to hinder us? For Thou hast come to hinder us, and Thou knowest that. But dost Thou know what will be to-morrow? I know not who Thou art and care not to know whether it is Thou or only a semblance of Him, but to-morrow I shall condemn Thee and burn Thee at the stake as the worst of heretics. And the very people who have to-day kissed Thy feet, to-morrow at the faintest sign from me will rush to heap up the embers of Thy fire. Knowest Thou that? Yes, maybe Thou knowest it,' he added with thoughtful penetration, never for a moment taking his eyes off the Prisoner."

"I don't quite understand, Ivan. What does it mean?" Alyosha, who had been listening in silence, said with a smile. "Is it simply a wild fantasy, or a mistake on the part of the old man—some impossible *quid pro quo?*"

"Take it as the last," said Ivan, laughing, "if you are so corrupted by modern realism and can't stand anything fantastic. If you like it to be a case of mistaken identity, let it be so. It is true," he went on, laughing, "the old man was ninety, and he might well be crazy over his set idea. He might have been struck by the appearance of the Prisoner. It might, in fact, be simply his ravings, the delusion of an old man of ninety, overexcited by the *auto da fé* of a hundred heretics the day before. But does it matter to us after all whether it was a mistake of identity or a wild fantasy? All that matters is that the old man should speak out, should speak openly of what he has thought in silence for ninety years."

"And the Prisoner too is silent? Does He look at him and not say a word?"

"That's inevitable in any case," Ivan laughed again. "The old man has told Him He hasn't the right to add anything to what He has said of old. One may say it is the most fundamental feature of Roman Catholicism, in my opinion at least. 'All has been given by Thee to the Pope,' they say, 'and all, therefore, is still in the Pope's hands, and there is no need for Thee to come now at all. Thou must not meddle for the time, at least.' That's how they speak and write too—the Jesuits, at any rate. I have read it myself in the works of their theologians. 'Hast Thou the right to reveal to us one of the mysteries of that world from which Thou hast come?' my old man asks Him, and answers the question for Him. 'No, Thou hast not; that Thou mayest not add to what has been said of old, and mayest not take from men the freedom which Thou didst exalt when Thou wast on earth. Whatsoever Thou revealest anew will encroach on men's freedom of faith; for it will be manifest as a miracle, and the freedom of their faith was dearer to Thee than anything in those days fifteen hundred years ago. Didst Thou not often say then, "I will make you free"? But now Thou has seen these "free" men,' the old man adds suddenly, with a pensive smile. 'Yes, we've paid dearly for it,' he goes on, looking sternly at Him, 'but at last we have completed that work in Thy name. For fifteen centuries we have been wrestling with Thy freedom, but now it is ended and over for good. Dost Thou not believe that it's over for good? Thou lookest meekly at me and deignest not even to be wroth with me. But let me tell Thee that now, to-day, people are more persuaded than ever that they have perfect freedom, yet they have brought their freedom to us and laid it humbly at our feet. But that has been our doing. Was this what Thou didst? Was this Thy freedom?' "

"I don't understand again," Alyosha broke in. "Is he ironical, is he jesting?"

"Not a bit of it! He claims it as a merit for himself and his Church that at last they have vanquished freedom and have done so to make men happy. 'For now' (he is speaking of the Inquisition, of course) 'for the first time it has become possible to think of the happiness of men. Man was created a rebel; and how can rebels be happy? Thou wast warned,' he says to Him. 'Thou hast had no lack of admonitions and warnings, but Thou didst not listen to those warnings; Thou didst reject the only way by which men might be made happy. But, fortunately, departing Thou didst hand on the work to us. Thou has promised, Thou hast established by Thy word, Thou has given to us the right to bind and to unbind, and now, of course, Thou canst not think of taking it away. Why, then, hast Thou come to hinder us?' "

"And what's the meaning of 'no lack of admonitions and warnings'?" asked Alyosha.

"Why, that's the chief part of what the old man must say.

" 'The wise and dread Spirit, the spirit of self-destruction and non-existence,' the old man goes on, 'the great spirit talked with Thee in the wilderness, and we are told in the books that he "tempted" Thee. Is that so? And could anything truer be said than what he revealed to Thee in three questions and what Thou didst reject, and what in the books is called "the temptation"? And yet if there has ever been on earth a real stupendous miracle, it took place on that day, on the day of the three temptations. The statement of those three questions was itself the miracle. If it were possible to imagine simply for the sake of argument that those three questions of the dread spirit had perished utterly from the books, and that we had to restore them and to invent them anew, and to do so had gathered together all the wise men of the earth—rulers, chief priests, learned men, philosophers, poets—and had set them the task to invent three questions, such as would not only fit the occasion, but express in three words, three human phrases, the whole future history of the world and of humanity—dost Thou believe that all the wisdom of the earth united could have invented anything in depth and force equal to the three questions which were actually put to Thee then by the wise and mighty spirit in the wilderness? From those questions alone, from the miracle of their statement, we can see that we have here to do not with the fleeting human intelligence, but with the absolute and eternal. For in those three questions the whole subsequent history of mankind is, as it were, brought together into one whole, and foretold, and in them are united all the unsolved historical contradictions of human nature. At the time it could not be so clear, since the future was unknown; but now that fifteen hundred years have passed, we see that everything in those three questions was so justly divined and foretold, and has been so truly fulfilled, that nothing can be added to them or taken from them.

" 'Judge Thyself who was right—Thou or he who questioned Thee then? Remember the first question; its meaning, in other words, was this: "Thou wouldst go into the world, and art going with empty hands, with some promise of freedom which men in their simplicity and their natural unruliness cannot even understand, which they fear and dread—for nothing has ever been more insupportable for a man and a human society than freedom. But seest Thou these stones in this parched and barren wilderness? Turn them into bread, and mankind will run after Thee like a flock of sheep, grateful and obedient, though for ever trembling, lest Thou withdraw Thy hand and deny them Thy bread." But Thou wouldst not deprive man of freedom and didst reject the offer, thinking, what is that freedom worth, if obedience is bought with bread? Thou didst reply that man lives not by bread alone. But dost Thou know that for the sake of that earthly bread the spirit of the earth will rise up against Thee and will strive with Thee and overcome Thee, and all will follow him, crying, "Who can compare with this beast? He has given us fire from heaven!" Dost Thou know that the ages will pass, and humanity will proclaim by the lips of their sages that there is no crime, and therefore no sin; there is only hunger? "Feed men, and then ask of them virtue!" that's what they'll write on the banner, which they will raise against Thee, and with which they will destroy Thy temple. Where Thy temple stood will rise a new building; the terrible tower of Babel will be built again, and though, like the one of old, it will not be finished, yet Thou mightest have prevented that new tower and have cut short the sufferings of men for a thousand years; for they will come back to us after a thousand years of agony with their tower. They will seek us again, hidden underground in the catacombs, for we shall be again persecuted and tortured. They will find us and cry to us, "Feed us, for those who have promised us fire from heaven haven't given it!" And then we shall finish building their tower, for he finishes the building who feeds them. And we alone shall feed them in Thy name, declaring falsely that it is in Thy name. Oh, never, never can they feed themselves without us! No science will give them bread so long as they remain free. In the end they will lay their freedom at our feet, and say to us, "Make us your slaves, but feed us." They will understand themselves, at last, that freedom and bread enough for all are inconceivable together, for never, never will they be able to share between them! They will be convinced, too, that they can never be free, for they are weak, vicious, worthless and rebellious. Thou didst promise them the bread of Heaven, but, I repeat again, can it compare with earthly bread in the eyes of the weak, ever sinful and ignoble race of man? And if for the sake of the bread of Heaven thousands and tens of thousands shall follow Thee, what is to become of the millions and tens of thousands of millions of creatures who will not have the strength to forego the earthly bread for the sake of the heavenly? Or dost Thou care only for the tens of thousands of the great and strong, while the millions, numerous as the sands of the sea, who are weak but love Thee, must exist only for the sake of the great and strong? No, we care for the weak too. They are sinful and rebellious, but in the end they too will become obedient. They will marvel at us and look on us as gods, because we are ready to endure the freedom which they have found so dreadful and to rule over them—so awful it will seem to them to be free. But we shall tell them that we are Thy servants and rule them in Thy name. We shall deceive them again, for we will not let Thee come to us again. That deception will be our suffering, for we shall be forced to lie.

" 'This is the significance of the first question in the wilderness, and this is what Thou hast rejected for the sake of that freedom which Thou hast exalted above everything. Yet in this question lies hid the great secret of this world. Choosing "bread," Thou wouldst have satisfied the universal and everlasting craving of humanity—to find some one to worship. So long as man remains free he strives for nothing so incessantly and so painfully as to find some one to worship. But man seeks to worship what is established beyond dispute, so that all men would agree at once to worship it. For these pitiful creatures are concerned not only to find what one or the other can worship, but to find something that all would believe in and worship; what is essential is that all may be *together* in it. This craving for *community* of worship is the chief misery of every man individually and of all humanity from the beginning of time. For the sake of common worship they've slain each other with the sword. They have set up gods and challenged one another, "Put away your gods and come and worship ours, or we will kill you and your gods!" And so it will be to the end of the world, even when gods disappear from the earth; they will fall down before idols just the same. Thou didst know, Thou couldst not but have known, this fundamental secret of human nature, but Thou didst reject the one infallible banner which was offered Thee to make all men bow down to Thee alone—the banner of earthly bread; and Thou hast rejected it for the sake of freedom and the bread of Heaven. Behold what Thou didst further. And all again in the name of freedom! I tell Thee that man is tormented by no greater anxiety than to find some one quickly to whom he can hand over that gift of freedom with which the ill-fated creature is born. But only one who can appease their conscience can take over their freedom. In bread there was offered Thee an invincible banner; give bread, and man will worship Thee, for nothing is more certain than bread. But if some one else gains possession of his conscience—oh! Then he will cast away Thy bread and follow after him who has ensnared his conscience. In that Thou wast right. For the secret of man's being is not only to live but to have something to live for. Without a stable conception of the object of life, man would not consent to go on living, and would rather destroy himself than remain on earth, though he had bread in abundance. That is true. But what happened? Instead of taking men's freedom from them, Thou didst make it greater than ever! Didst Thou forget that man prefers peace, and even death, to freedom of choice in the knowledge of good and evil? Nothing is more seductive for man than his freedom of conscience, but nothing is a greater cause of suffering. And behold, instead of giving a firm foundation for setting the conscience of man at rest for ever, Thou didst choose all that is exceptional, vague and enigmatic; Thou didst choose what was utterly beyond the strength of men, acting as though Thou didst not love them at all—Thou who didst come to give Thy life for them! Instead of taking possession of men's freedom, Thou didst increase it, and burdened the spiritual kingdom of mankind with its sufferings for ever. Thou didst desire man's free love, that he should follow Thee freely, enticed and taken captive by Thee. In place of the rigid ancient law, man must hereafter with free heart decide for himself what is good and what is evil, having only Thy image before him as his guide. But didst Thou not know he would at last reject even Thy image and Thy truth, if he is weighed down with the fearful burden of free choice? They will cry aloud at last that the truth is not in Thee, for they could not have been left in greater confusion and suffering than Thou hast caused, laying upon them so many cares and unanswerable problems.

" 'So that, in truth, Thou didst Thyself lay the foundation for the destruction of Thy kingdom, and no one is more to blame for it. Yet what was offered Thee? There are three powers, three powers alone, able to conquer and to hold captive for ever the conscience of these impotent rebels for their happiness—those forces are miracle, mystery and authority. Thou hast rejected all three and hast set the example for doing so. When the wise and dread spirit set Thee on the pinnacle of the temple and said to Thee, "If Thou wouldst know whether Thou art the Son of God then cast Thyself down, for it is written: the angels shall hold him up lest he fall and bruise himself, and Thou shalt know then whether Thou art the Son of God and shalt prove then how great is Thy faith in Thy Father." But Thou didst refuse and wouldst not cast Thyself down. Oh! Of course, Thou didst proudly and well like God; but the weak, unruly race of men, are they gods? Oh, Thou didst know then that in taking one step, in making one movement to cast Thyself down, Thou wouldst be tempting God and have lost all Thy faith in Him, and wouldst have been dashed to pieces against that earth which Thou didst come to save. And the wise spirit that tempted Thee would have rejoiced. But I ask again, are there many like Thee? And couldst Thou believe for one moment that men, too, could face such a temptation? Is the nature of men such, that they can reject miracle, and at the great moments of their life, the moments of their deepest, most agonising spiritual difficulties, cling only to the free verdict of the heart? Oh, Thou didst know that Thy deed would be recorded in books, would be handed down to remote times and the utmost ends of the earth, and Thou didst hope that man, following Thee, would cling to God and not ask for a miracle. But Thou didst not know that when man rejects miracle he rejects God too; for man seeks not so much God as the miraculous. And as man cannot bear to be without the miraculous, he will create new miracles of his own for himself, and will worship deeds of sorcery and witchcraft, though he might be a hundred times over a rebel, heretic and infidel. Thou didst not come down from the Cross when they shouted to Thee, mocking and reviling Thee, "Come down from the cross and we will believe that Thou art He." Thou didst not come down, for again Thou wouldst not enslave man by a miracle, and didst crave faith given freely, not based on miracle. Thou didst crave for free love and not the base raptures of the slave before the might that has overawed him for ever. But Thou didst think too highly of men therein, for they are slaves, of course, though rebellious by nature. Look round and judge; fifteen centuries have passed, look upon them. Whom hast Thou raised up to Thyself? I swear, man is weaker and baser by nature than Thou hast believed him! Can he, can he do what Thou didst? By showing him so much respect, Thou didst, as it were, cease to feel for him, for Thou didst ask far too much from him—Thou who hast loved him more than Thyself! Respecting him less, Thou wouldst have asked less of him. That would have been more like love, for his burden would have been lighter. He is weak and vile. What though he is everywhere now rebelling against our power, and proud of his rebellion? It is the pride of a child and a schoolboy. They are little children rioting and barring out the teacher at school. But their childish delight will end; it will cost them dear. They will cast down temples and drench the earth with blood. But they will see at last, the foolish children, that, though they are rebels, they are impotent rebels, unable to keep up their own rebellion. Bathed in their foolish tears, they will recognise at last that He who created them rebels must have meant to mock at them. They will say this in despair, and their utterance will be a blasphemy which will make them more unhappy still, for man's nature cannot bear blasphemy, and in the end always avenges it on itself. And so unrest, confusion and unhappiness—that is the present lot of man after Thou didst bear so much for their freedom! Thy great prophet tells in vision and in image, that he saw all those who took part in the first resurrection and that there were of each tribe twelve thousand. But if there were so many of them, they must have been not men but gods. They had borne Thy cross, they had endured scores of years in the barren, hungry wilderness, living upon locusts and roots—and Thou mayest indeed point with pride at those children of freedom, of free love, of free and splendid sacrifice for Thy name. But remember that they were only some thousands; and what of the rest? And how are the other weak ones to blame, because they could not endure what the strong have endured? How is the weak soul to blame that it is unable to receive such terrible gifts? Canst Thou have simply come to the elect and for the elect? But if so, it is a mystery and we cannot understand it. And if it is a mystery, we too have a right to preach a mystery, and to teach them that it's not the free judgment of their hearts, not love that matters, but a mystery which they must follow blindly, even against their conscience. So we have done. We have corrected Thy work and have founded it upon *miracle, mystery* and *authority.* And men rejoiced that they were again led like sheep, and that the terrible gift that had brought them such suffering, was, at last, lifted from their hearts. Were we right teaching them this? Speak! Did we not love mankind, so meekly acknowledging their feebleness, lovingly lightening their burden, and permitting their weak nature even sin with our sanction? Why hast Thou come now to hinder us?

And why dost Thou look silently and searchingly at me with Thy mild eyes? Be angry. I don't want Thy love, for I love Thee not. And what use is it for me to hide anything from Thee? Don't I know to Whom I am speaking? All that I can say is known to Thee already. And is it for me to conceal from Thee our mystery? Perhaps it is Thy will to hear it from my lips. Listen, then. We are not working with Thee, but with *him*—that is our mystery. It's long—eight centuries—since we have been on *his* side and not on Thine. Just eight centuries ago, we took from him what Thou didst reject with scorn, that last gift he offered Thee, showing Thee all the kingdoms of the earth. We took from him Rome and the sword of Cæsar, and proclaimed ourselves sole rulers of the earth, though hitherto we have not been able to complete our work. But whose fault is that? Oh, the work is only beginning, but it has begun. It has long to await completion and the earth has yet much to suffer, but we shall triumph and shall be Cæsars, and then we shall plan the universal happiness of man. But Thou mightest have taken even then the sword of Cæsar. Why didst Thou reject that last gift? Hadst Thou accepted that last counsel of the mighty spirit, Thou wouldst have accomplished all that man seeks on earth—that is, some one to worship, some one to keep his conscience, and some means of uniting all in one unanimous and harmonious ant-heap, for the craving for universal unity is the third and last anguish of men. Mankind as a whole has always striven to organise a universal state. There have been many great nations with great histories, but the more highly they were developed the more unhappy they were, for they felt more acutely than other people the craving for worldwide union. The great conquerors, Timours and Ghenghis-Khans, whirled like hurricanes over the face of the earth striving to subdue its people, and they too were but the unconscious expression of the same craving for universal unity. Hadst Thou taken the world and Cæsar's purple, Thou wouldst have founded the universal state and have given universal peace. For who can rule men if not he who holds their conscience and their bread in his hands. We have taken the sword of Cæsar, and in taking it, of course, have rejected Thee and followed *him*. Oh, ages are yet to come of the confusion of free thought, of their science and cannibalism. For having begun to build their tower of Babel without us, they will end, of course, with cannibalism. But then the beast will crawl to us and lick our feet and spatter them with tears of blood. And we shall sit upon the beast and raise the cup, and on it will be written, "Mystery." But then, and only then, the reign of peace and happiness will come for men. Thou art proud of Thine elect, but Thou hast only the elect, while we give rest to all. And besides, how many of those elect, those mighty ones who could become elect, have grown weary waiting for Thee, and have transferred and will transfer the powers of their spirit and the warmth of their heart to the other camp, and end by raising their *free* banner against Thee. Thou didst Thyself lift up that banner. But with us all will be happy and will no more rebel nor destroy one another as under Thy freedom. Oh, we shall persuade them that they will only become free when they renounce their freedom to us and submit to us. And shall we be right or shall we be lying? They will be convinced that we are right, for they will remember the horrors of slavery and confusion to which Thy freedom brought them. Freedom, free thought and science, will lead them into such straits and will bring them face to face with such marvels and insoluble mysteries, that some of them, the fierce and rebellious, will destroy themselves, others, rebellious but weak, will destroy one another, while the rest, weak and unhappy, will crawl fawning to our feet and whine to us: "Yes, you were right, you alone possess His mystery, and we come back to you, save us from ourselves!"

" 'Receiving bread from us, they will see clearly that we take the bread made by their hands from them, to give it to them, without any miracle. They will see that we do not change the stones to bread, but in truth they will be more thankful for taking it from our hands than for the bread itself! For they will remember only too well that in old days, without our help, even the bread they made turned to stones in their hands, while since they have come back to us, the very stones have turned to bread in their hands. Too, too well they know the value of complete submission! And until men know that, they will be unhappy. Who is most to blame for their not knowing it, speak? Who scattered the flock and sent it astray on unknown paths? But the flock will come together again and will submit once more, and then it will be once for all. Then we shall give them the quiet humble happiness of weak creatures such as they are by nature. Oh, we shall persuade them at last not to be proud, for Thou didst lift them up and thereby taught them to be proud. We shall show them that they are weak, that they are only pitiful children, but that childlike happiness is the sweetest of all. They will become timid and will look to us and huddle close to us in fear, as chicks to the hen. They will marvel at us and will be awe-stricken before us, and will be proud at our being so powerful and clever, that we have been able to subdue such a turbulent flock of thousands of millions. They will tremble impotently before our wrath, their minds will grow fearful, they will be quick to shed tears like women and children, but they will be just as ready at a sign from us to pass to laughter and rejoicing, to happy mirth and childish song. Yes, we shall set them to work, but in their leisure hours we shall make their life like a child's game, with children's songs and innocent dance. Oh, we shall allow them even sin, they are weak and helpless, and they will love us like children because we allow them to sin. We shall tell them that every sin will be expiated, if it is done with our permission, that we allow them to sin because we love them, and the punishment for these sins we take upon ourselves. And we shall take it upon ourselves, and they will adore us as their saviour who have taken on themselves their sins before God. And they will have no secrets from us. We shall allow or forbid them to live with their wives and mistresses, to have or not to have children—according to whether they have been obedient or disobedient—and they will submit to us gladly and cheerfully. The most painful secrets of their conscience, all, all they will bring to us, and we shall have an answer for all. And they will be glad to believe our answer, for it will save them from the great anxiety and terrible agony they endure at present in making a free decision for them-selves. And all will be happy, all the millions of creatures except the hundred thousand who rule over them. For only we, we who guard the mystery, shall be unhappy. There will be thousands of millions of happy babes, and a hundred thousand sufferers who have taken upon themselves the curse of the knowledge of good and evil. Peacefully they will die, peacefully they will expire in Thy name, and beyond the grave they will find nothing but death. But we shall keep the secret, and for their happiness we shall allure them with the reward of heaven and eternity. Though if there were anything in the other world, it certainly would not be for such as they. It is prophesied that Thou wilt come again in victory, Thou wilt come with Thy chosen, the proud and strong, but we will say that they have only saved themselves, but we have saved all. We are told that the harlot who sits upon the beast, and holds in her hands the *mystery,* shall be put to shame, that the weak will rise up again, and will rend her royal purple and will strip naked her loathsome body. But then I will stand up and point out to Thee the thousand millions of happy children who have known no sin. And we who have taken their sins upon us for their happiness will stand up before Thee and say: "Judge us if Thou canst and darest." Know that I fear Thee not. Know that I too have been in the wilderness, I too have lived on roots and locusts, I too prized the freedom with which Thou hast blessed men, and I too was striving to stand among Thy elect, among the strong and powerful, thirsting "to make up the number." But I awakened and would not serve mad-ness. I turned back and joined the ranks of those *who have cor-rected Thy work.* I left the proud and went back to the humble, for the happiness of the humble. What I say to Thee will come to pass, and our dominion will be built up. I repeat, to-morrow Thou shalt see that obedient flock who at a sign from me will hasten to heap up the hot cinders about the pile on which I shall burn Thee for coming to hinder us. For if any one has ever de-served our fires, it is Thou. To-morrow I shall burn Thee. Dixi.' "

Ivan stopped. He was carried away as he talked and spoke with excitement; when he had finished, he suddenly smiled.

Alyosha had listened in silence; towards the end he was greatly moved and seemed several times on the point of interrupting, but restrained himself. Now his words came with a rush.

"But . . . that's absurd!" he cried, flushing. "Your poem is in praise of Jesus, not in blame of Him—as you meant it to be. And who will believe you about freedom? Is that the way to understand it? That's not the idea of it in the Orthodox Church . . . That's Rome, and not even the whole of Rome, it's false—those are the worst of the Catholics, the Inquisitors, the Jesuits! . . . And there could not be such a fantastic creature as your Inquisitor. What are these sins of mankind they take on themselves? Who are these keepers of the mystery who have taken some curse upon themselves for the happiness of mankind? When have they been seen? We know the Jesuits, they are spoken ill of, but surely they are not what you describe? They are not that at all, not at all. . . . They are simply the Romish army for the earthly sovereignty of the world in the future, with the Pontiff of Rome for Emperor . . . that's their ideal, but there's no sort of mystery or lofty melancholy about it. . . . It's simple lust of power, of filthy earthly gain, of domination—something like a universal serfdom with them as masters—that's all they stand for. They don't even believe in God perhaps. Your suffering inquisitor is a mere fantasy."

"Stay, stay," laughed Ivan, "how hot you are! A fantasy you say, let it be so! Of course it's a fantasy. But allow me to say: do you really think that the Roman Catholic movement of the last centuries is actually nothing but the lust of power, of filthy earthly gain? Is that Father Païssy's teaching?"

"No, no, on the contrary, Father Païssy did once say something rather the same as you . . . but of course it's not the same, not a bit the same," Alyosha hastily corrected himself.

"A precious admission, in spite of your 'not a bit the same.' I ask you why your Jesuits and Inquisitors have united simply for vile material gain? Why can there not be among them one martyr oppressed by great sorrow and loving humanity? You see, only suppose that there was one such man among all those who desire nothing but filthy material gain—if there's only one like my old inquisitor, who had himself eaten roots in the desert and made frenzied efforts to subdue his flesh to make himself free and perfect. But yet all his life he loved humanity, and suddenly his eyes were opened, and he saw that it is no great moral blessedness to attain perfection and freedom, if at the same time one gains the conviction that millions of God's creatures have been created as a mockery, that they will never be capable of using their freedom, that these poor rebels can never turn into giants to complete the tower, that it was not for such geese that the great idealist dreamt his dream of harmony. Seeing all that he turned back and joined—the clever people. Surely that could have happened?"

"Joined whom, what clever people?" cried Alyosha, completely carried away. "They have no such great cleverness and no mysteries and secrets. . . . Perhaps nothing but Atheism, that's all their secret. Your inquisitor does not believe in God, that's his secret!"

"What if it is so! At last you have guessed it. It's perfectly true that that's the whole secret, but isn't that suffering, at least for a man like that, who has wasted his whole life in the desert and yet could not shake off his incurable love of humanity? In his old age he reached the clear conviction that nothing but the advice of the great dread spirit could build up any tolerable sort of life for the feeble, unruly 'incomplete, empirical creatures created in jest.' And so, convinced of this, he sees that he must follow the council of the wise spirit, the dread spirit of death and destruction, and therefore accept lying and deception, and lead men consciously to death and destruction, and yet deceive them all the way so that they may not notice where they are being led, that the poor blind creatures may at least on the way think themselves happy. And note, the deception is in the name of Him in

Whose ideal the old man had so fervently believed all his life long. Is not that tragic? And if only one such stood at the head of the whole army 'filled with the lust of power only for the sake of filthy gain'—would not one such be enough to make a tragedy? More than that, one such standing at the head is enough to create the actual leading idea of the Roman Church with all its armies and Jesuits, its highest idea. I tell you frankly that I firmly believe that there has always been such a man among those who stood at the head of the movement. Who knows, there may have been some such even among the Roman Popes. Who knows, perhaps the spirit of that accursed old man who loves mankind so obstinately in his own way, is to be found even now in a whole multitude of such old men, existing not by chance but by agreement, as a secret league formed long ago for the guarding of the mystery, to guard it from the weak and the unhappy, so as to make them happy. No doubt it is so, and so it must be indeed. I fancy that even among the Masons there's something of the same mystery at the bottom, and that that's why the Catholics so detest the Masons as their rivals breaking up the unity of the idea, while it is so essential that there should be one flock and one shepherd. . . . But from the way I defend my idea I might be an author impatient of your criticism. Enough of it."

"You are perhaps a Mason yourself!" broke suddenly from Alyosha. "You don't believe in God," he added, speaking this time very sorrowfully. He fancied besides that his brother was looking at him ironically. "How does your poem end?" he asked, suddenly looking down. "Or was it the end?"

"I meant to end it like this. When the Inquisitor ceased speaking he waited some time for his Prisoner to answer him. His silence weighed down upon him. He saw that the Prisoner had listened intently all the time, looking gently in his face and evidently not wishing to reply. The old man longed for Him to say something, however bitter and terrible. But He suddenly approached the old man in silence and softly kissed him on his bloodless aged lips. That was all his answer. The old man shuddered. His lips moved.

He went to the door, opened it, and said to Him: 'Go, and come no more. . . . Come not at all, never, never!' And he let Him out into the dark alleys of the town. The Prisoner went away."

"And the old man?"

"The kiss glows in his heart, but the old man adheres to his idea."

"And you with him, you too?" cried Alyosha, mournfully.

Ivan laughed.

"Why, it's all nonsense, Alyosha. It's only a senseless poem of a senseless student, who could never write two lines of verse. Why do you take it so seriously? Surely you don't suppose I am going straight off to the Jesuits, to join the men who are correcting His work? Good Lord, it's no business of mine. I told you, all I want is to live on to thirty, and then . . . dash the cup to the ground!"

"But the little sticky leaves, and the precious tombs, and the blue sky, and the woman you love! How will you live, how will you love them?" Alyosha cried sorrowfully. "With such a hell in your heart and your head, how can you? No, that's just what you are going away for, to join them . . . if not, you will kill yourself, you can't endure it!"

"There is a strength to endure everything," Ivan said with a cold smile.

"What strength?"

"The strength of the Karamazovs—the strength of the Karamazov baseness."

"To sink into debauchery, to stifle your soul with corruption, yes?"

"Possibly even that . . . only perhaps till I am thirty I shall escape it, and then."

"How will you escape it? By what will you escape it? That's impossible with your ideas."

"In the Karamazov way, again."

" 'Everything is lawful,' you mean? Everything is lawful, is that it?"

Ivan scowled, and all at once turned strangely pale.

"Ah, you've caught up yesterday's phrase, which so offended Miüsov—and which Dmitri pounced upon so naïvely and paraphrased!" he smiled queerly. "Yes, if you like, 'everything is lawful' since the word has been said. I won't deny it. And Mitya's version isn't bad."

Alyosha looked at him in silence.

"I thought that going away from here I have you at least," Ivan said suddenly, with unexpected feeling; "but now I see that there is no place for me even in your heart, my dear hermit. The formula, 'all is lawful,' I won't renounce—will you renounce me for that, yes?"

Alyosha got up, went to him and softly kissed him on the lips.

"That's plagiarism," cried Ivan, highly delighted. "You stole that from my poem. Thank you though. Get up, Alyosha, it's time we were going, both of us."

They went out, but stopped when they reached the entrance of the restaurant.

"Listen, Alyosha," Ivan began in a resolute voice, "if I am really able to care for the sticky little leaves I shall only love them, remembering you. It's enough for me that you are somewhere here, and I shan't lose my desire for life yet. Is that enough for you? Take it as a declaration of love if you like. And now you go to the right and I to the left. And it's enough, do you hear, enough. I mean even if I don't go away to-morrow (I think I certainly shall go) and we meet again, don't say a word more on these subjects. I beg that particularly. And about Dmitri too, I ask you specially never to speak to me again," he added, with sudden irritation; "it's all exhausted, it has all been said over and over again, hasn't it? And I'll make you one promise in return for it. When at thirty, I want to 'dash the cup to the ground,' wherever I may be I'll come to have one more talk with you, even though it were from America, you may be sure of that. I'll come on purpose. It will be very interesting to have a look at you, to see what you'll be by that time. It's rather a solemn promise, you see. And we really may be parting for seven years or ten. Come, go now to your Pater Seraphicus, he is dying. If he dies without you, you will be angry with me for having kept you. Good-bye, kiss me once more; that's right, now go."

Ivan turned suddenly and went his way without looking back. It was just as Dmitri had left Alyosha the day before, though the parting had been very different. The strange resemblance flashed like an arrow through Alyosha's mind in the distress and dejection of that moment. He waited a little, looking after his brother. He suddenly noticed that Ivan swayed as he walked and that his right shoulder looked lower than his left. He had never noticed it before. But all at once he turned too, and almost ran to the monastery. It was nearly dark, and he felt almost frightened; something new was growing up in him for which he could not account. The wind had risen again as on the previous evening, and the ancient pines murmured gloomily about him when he entered the hermitage copse. He almost ran. "Pater Seraphicus—he got that name from somewhere—where from?" Alyosha wondered. "Ivan, poor Ivan, and when shall I see you again? . . . Here is the hermitage. Yes, yes, that he is, Pater Seraphicus, he will save me—from him and for ever!"

Several times afterwards he wondered how he could on leaving Ivan so completely forget his brother Dmitri, though he had that morning, only a few hours before, so firmly resolved to find him and not to give up doing so, even should he be unable to return to the monastery that night.

MIGUEL DE
UNAMUNO Y JUGO

Miguel de Unamuno y Jugo was a divided soul. Like every Nicodemus, he could not bring himself to believe that death was the end. And yet, Unamuno confesses, "The vital longing for human immortality finds no consolation in human reason." The Basque philosopher knew fourteen languages. One of those languages was Danish. Unamuno learned it simply because he wanted to read Kierkegaard in the original. And he follows Kierkegaard in his conviction that faith involves a collision with the understanding. Indeed, Unamuno, more than Kierkegaard, is often classified as antirationalist. He held that it is absurd to believe in God and a hereafter; nevertheless, almost on the basis of our unquenchable thirst for life, the same learned man tells us that we ought to believe just the same. Not surprisingly, Don Quixote was one of Unamuno's heroes and the subject of one of his best books, *The Life of Don Quixote.*

The third of six children, Unamuno was born in Bilbao, Spain, on September 29, 1864. His father died when he was only a child and he was raised by his uncle. When he was ten he witnessed the bloody siege of Bilbao in which traditionalists and progressive forces were pitted against one another.

Unamuno took his doctorate from the University of Madrid in 1884. In 1891, he was appointed professor of Greek at the University of Salamanca. The same year, Unamuno married. He and his wife had nine children. One of his sons came into the world with terrible birth defects and died at age six. The boy's death precipitated a spiritual earthquake in his father. Though the philosopher, dramatist, and novelist would always come back to the fold, Unamuno felt the absence of faith at a number of points in the maelstrom of his life.

From the 1890s on, Unamuno had the Muse, and despite all his academic duties and his huge family, he published a shelf of philosophical treatises, plays, and poems. In 1913, he was elected rector of the University of Salamanca, but a year later he was removed from this office because of his opposition to the king. In 1924, he was sent into exile for opposing the military dictator, General Primo de Rivera. The general died in 1930, and Unamuno made a triumphant return to Salamanca and was once again installed as rector in 1931. However, the philosopher took silence in a political crisis to be equivalent to deceit. A few years after being reappointed, Unamuno denounced Francisco Franco's Falangists, and in 1936 he was driven from his office and placed under house arrest. Unamuno was heartbroken by the dark turn of political events. He died on December 31, 1936, a few months after the first shots were fired in the Spanish Civil War.

Apropos of our text, "Saint Manuel Bueno, Martyr," St. Paul said that faith without love is empty. But is true Christian love of neighbor in and of itself enough for faith? Saint Manuel, the main character in this novella, is as good a Samaritan as he could be, but he does not believe that his bottomless love for his neighbor makes him a faithful servant of Christ. For that, he would have to believe Jesus' promise that death is only the beginning. And though he is a priest, he cannot imagine that there is anything beyond the grave. But perhaps Saint Manuel's authorial creator thinks that the priest should not be so hard in his self-assessment. Perhaps Unamuno is suggesting that some believers are unaware that they are believers. I am not sure. Readers who enjoy this story should proceed to Unamuno's philosophical magnum opus, *On the Tragic Sense of Life*.

SAINT MANUEL BUENO, MARTYR

> If in this life only we have hope in Christ, we are of all
> men most miserable.
> —SAINT PAUL: 1 COR. 15:19

Now that the bishop of the diocese of Renada, to which this my
beloved village of Valverde de Lucerna belongs, is said to be
urging the process of beatification of our Don Manuel, or rather,
Saint Manuel Bueno, who was parish priest here, I want to put in
writing, by way of confession (although to what end only God,
and not I can say), all that I know and remember about that matriarchal man who pervaded the most secret life of my soul, who
was my true spiritual father, the father of my spirit, the spirit of
myself, Angela Carballino.

The other, my flesh-and-blood temporal father, I scarcely
knew, for he died when I was still very young. I know he came to
Valverde de Lucerna from elsewhere—he was a stranger to the
place—and that he settled here when he married my mother. He
had brought a number of books with him: *Don Quixote,* some classical plays, some novels, a few histories, the *Bertoldo,* a veritable
grab bag. These books (practically the only ones in the entire
village), set me daydreaming, and I was devoured by my day-

dreams. My dear mother told me very little about the words or the deeds of my father. For the words and deeds of Don Manuel, whom she worshiped, of whom she was enamored, in common with all the rest of the village—in an exquisitely chaste manner, of course—had obliterated all memory of the words and deeds of her husband whom she fervently commended to God, as she said her daily rosary.

I remember Don Manuel as if it were yesterday, from the time when I was a girl of ten, just before I was taken to the convent school in the cathedral city of Renada. At that time Don Manuel, our saint, must have been about thirty-seven years old. He was tall, slim; he carried himself erect, his head the way our Buitre Peak carries its crest, and his eyes had all the blue depth of our lake. As he walked he commanded all eyes, and not only the eyes but the hearts of all; gazing round at us he seemed to look through our flesh as through glass and penetrate our hearts. We all loved him, especially the children. And the things he said to us! The villagers could scent the odor of sanctity, they were intoxicated with it.

It was at this time that my brother Lázaro, who was in America, from where he regularly sent us money with which we lived in decent comfort, had my mother send me to the convent school, so that my education might be completed outside the village; he suggested this move despite the fact that he had no special fondness for the nuns. "But, since, as far as I know," he wrote us, "there are no lay schools there yet—especially not for young ladies—we will have to make use of the ones that do exist. The important thing is for Angelita to receive some polish and not be forced to continue among village girls." And so I entered the convent school. At one point I even thought of becoming a teacher; but pedagogy soon palled.

———

At school I met girls from the city and I made friends with some of them. But I still kept in touch with people in our village, and I received frequent news from them and sometimes a visit. And the fame of the parish priest even reached the school, for he was beginning to be talked of in the cathedral city. And the nuns never tired of asking me about him.

Ever since I was a child I had been endowed, I don't really know why, with a large degree of curiosity and uneasiness, due in part at least to that jumble of books which my father had collected, and at school these qualities were stimulated, especially in the course of a friendship I developed with a girl who grew excessively attached to me. At times she suggested that we enter the same convent together, swearing to an everlasting "sisterhood"— and even that we seal the oath in blood. At other times she talked to me, with half-closed eyes, of sweethearts and marriage adventures. Strangely enough, I have never heard anything of her since, nor of what became of her, despite the fact that whenever our Don Manuel was mentioned, or when my mother wrote me something about him in her letters—which happened in almost every letter—and I read it to her, the girl would cry out ecstatically: "What a lucky girl you are to be able to live near a saint like that, a living saint, of flesh and blood, and to be able to kiss his hand; when you go back to your village write to me a lot and tell me lots of things about him."

I spent five years at school, five years which have now evanesced in memory like a dream at dawn, and when I was fifteen I returned to my own Valverde de Lucerna. By now everything there revolved around Don Manuel: Don Manuel, the lake, and the mountain. I arrived home anxious to know him, to place myself in his care, and hopeful that he would set me on my path in life.

It was rumored that he had entered the seminary to become a priest so that he might thus look after the children of a recently widowed sister and provide for them in place of their father; that in the seminary his keen mind and his talents had distinguished him and that he had subsequently turned down opportunities of a brilliant career in the Church because he wanted to remain exclusively a part of his Valverde de Lucerna, of his remote village which lay like a brooch between the lake and the mountain reflected in it.

How he loved his people! He spent his life salvaging wrecked marriages, forcing unruly children to submit to their parents, or reconciling parents to their children, and, above all, he consoled the embittered and weary in spirit and helped everyone to die well.

I recall, among other incidents, the occasion when the unfortunate daughter of old Aunt Rabona returned to our town. She had been living in the city and lost her virtue there; now she returned unmarried and abandoned, and she brought back a little son. Don Manuel did not rest until he had persuaded an old sweetheart, Perote by name, to marry the poor girl and, moreover, to legitimize the infant with his own name. Don Manuel told Perote:

"Come now, give this poor waif a father, for he hasn't got one except in heaven."

"But, Don Manuel, it's not my fault . . . !"

"Who knows, my son, who knows . . . ! And in any case, it's not a question of guilt."

And today, poor old Perote, inspired on that occasion to saintliness by Don Manuel, and now a paralytic and invalid, has the support and consolation of his life in the son he accepted as his own when the boy was not his at all.

On Midsummer's Night, the shortest night of the year, it was, and still is, a local custom here for all the old crones, and a lot of old men, who thought they were possessed or bewitched—they were, in fact, hysterical for the most part, and in some cases epileptics—to flock to the lake. Don Manuel undertook to fulfill the same function as the lake, to serve as a pool of healing, to treat his people and even, if possible, to cure them. And such was the effect of his presence, of his gaze, and above all of his voice—his miraculous voice!—and the infinitely sweet authority of his words, that he actually did achieve some remarkable cures. Whereupon his fame increased, drawing all the sick of the environs to our lake and our priest. And yet, once, when a mother came to ask for a miracle on behalf of her son, he answered her with a sad smile:

"Ah, but I don't have my bishop's permission to perform miracles."

He was particularly interested in seeing that all the villagers kept themselves clean. If he chanced upon someone with a torn garment he would say: "Go and see the sacristan, and let him mend that tear." The sacristan was a tailor. And when, on the first day of the year, everyone went to congratulate the priest on his saint's day—his holy patron was Our Lord Jesus Himself—it was Don Manuel's wish that everyone should appear in a new shirt, and those that had none received the present of a new one from Don Manuel himself.

He treated everyone with the greatest kindness; if he favored anyone, it was the most unfortunate, and especially those who rebelled. There was a congenital idiot in the village, the fool Blasillo, and it was toward him that Don Manuel chose to show the greatest love and concern; as a consequence he succeeded in miraculously teaching him things which had appeared beyond the idiot's comprehension. The fact was that the embers of understanding feebly glowing in the idiot were kindled whenever, like a pitiable monkey, he imitated his Don Manuel.

The marvel of the man was his voice; a divine voice which brought one close to weeping. Whenever he officiated at Solemn High Mass and intoned the Preface, a tremor ran through the congregation and all who heard his voice were moved to the depths of their being. The sound of his chanting, overflowing the church, went on to float over the lake and settle at the foot of the mountain. And when on Good Friday he chanted, "My God, my God, why hast Thou forsaken me?" a profound shudder swept through the multitude, like the lash of the northeast wind across the waters of the lake. It was as if these people heard Our Lord Jesus Christ Himself, as if the voice sprang from the ancient crucifix, at the foot of which generations of mothers had offered up their sorrows. And it happened that on one occasion when his mother heard him, she was unable to contain herself, and cried out to him right in the church, "My son!" And the entire congregation was visibly affected, tears pouring down every cheek. It was as if the mother's cry had issued from the half-open lips of the Mater Dolorosa—her heart transfixed by seven swords—which stood in one of the side chapels. Afterwards, the fool Blasillo went about piteously repeating, like an echo, "My God, my God, why hast Thou forsaken me?" with such effect that everyone who heard him was moved to tears, to the great satisfaction of the fool, who prided himself on this triumph of imitation.

The priest's effect on people was such that no one ever dared to tell him a lie, and everyone confessed to him without need of a confessional. So true was this that one day, after a revolting crime had been committed in a neighboring village, the judge—a dull fellow who badly misunderstood Don Manuel—called on the priest and said:

"Let's see if *you*, Don Manuel, can get this bandit to admit the truth."

"So that *you* may punish him afterwards?" asked the saintly man. "No, Judge, no; I will not extract from any man a truth which could be the death of him. That is a matter between him and his God. . . . Human justice is none of my affair. 'Judge not that ye be not judged,' said Our Lord."

"But the fact is, Father, that I, a judge . . ."

"I understand. You, Judge, must render unto Caesar that which is Caesar's, while I shall render unto God that which is God's."

And, as Don Manuel departed, he gazed at the suspected criminal and said:

"Make sure, only, that God forgives you, for that is all that matters."

———

Everyone in the village went to Mass, even if it were only to hear him and see him at the altar, where he appeared to be transfigured, his countenance lit from within. He introduced one holy practice into popular worship; it consisted in assembling the whole town inside the church, men and women, old and young, about a thousand souls; there we recited the Creed, in unison, so that it sounded like a single voice: "I believe in God, the Father almighty, creator of heaven and earth . . ." and all the rest. It was not a chorus, but a single voice, all the voices blending into one forming a kind of mountain, whose peak, lost at times in the clouds, was Don Manuel. As we reached the section "I believe in the resurrection of the flesh and eternal life," Don Manuel's voice was submerged, drowned in the voice of the populace as in a lake. In truth, he was silent. And I could hear the bells of the city which is said hereabouts to be at the bottom of the lake—bells which are said also to be audible on Midsummer's Night—the bells of the city which is submerged in the spiritual lake of our people. I was hearing the voice of our dead, resurrected in us by the communion of saints. Later, when I had learned the secret of our saint, I understood that it was as if a caravan crossing the desert lost its leader as they approached the goal of their trek, whereupon his people lifted him up on their shoulders to bring his lifeless body into the promised land.

When it came to dying themselves, most of the villagers refused to die unless they were holding onto Don Manuel's hand, as if to an anchor chain.

In his sermons he never inveighed against unbelievers, Free-masons, liberals, or heretics. What for, when there were none in the village? Nor did it occur to him to speak out against the wickedness of the press. On the other hand, one of his most frequent themes was the sinfulness of gossip. As he himself forgave everything and everyone, he would not accept the existence of forked tongues.

"Envy," he liked to repeat, "is nurtured by those who prefer to think they are envied, and most persecutions are the result of a persecution complex rather than of an impulse to persecute."

"But Don Manuel, just listen to what that fellow was trying to tell me. . . ."

"We should concern ourselves less with what people are trying to tell us than with what they tell us without trying. . . ."

His life was active rather than contemplative, and he constantly fled from idleness, even from leisure. Whenever he heard it said that idleness was the mother of all vices, he added: "And also of the greatest vice of them all, which is to think idly." Once I asked him what he meant and he answered: "Thinking idly is thinking as a substitute for doing, or thinking too much about what is already done instead of about what must be done. What's done is done and over with, and one must go on to something else, for there is nothing worse than remorse without possible solution." Action! Action! Even in those early days I had already begun to realize that Don Manuel fled from being left to think in solitude, and I sensed that some obsession haunted him.

And so it was that he was always busy, sometimes even busy looking for things to do. He wrote very little on his own, so that he scarcely left us anything in writing, not even notes; on the other hand, he acted as scribe for everyone else, especially composing letters for mothers to their absent children.

He also worked with his hands, pitching in to help with some of the village tasks. At threshing time he reported to the threshing floor to flail and winnow, meanwhile teaching and entertaining the workers by turn. Sometimes he took the place of a worker who had fallen sick. One bitter winter's day he came upon a child half-dead with cold. The child's father had sent him into the woods to bring back a calf that had strayed.

"Listen," he said to the child, "you go home and get warm, and tell your father that I am bringing back the calf." On the way back with the animal he ran into the father, who had come out to meet him, thoroughly ashamed of himself.

In winter he chopped wood for the poor. When a certain magnificent walnut tree died—"that matriarchal walnut," he called it, a tree under whose shade he had played as a boy and whose nuts he had eaten for so many years—he asked for the trunk, carried it to his house and, after he had cut six planks from it, which he kept at the foot of his bed, he made firewood of the rest to warm the poor. He also was in the habit of making handballs for the boys and many toys for the younger children.

—

Often he used to accompany the doctor on his rounds, and stressed the importance of following the doctor's orders. Most of all he was interested in maternity cases and the care of children; it was his opinion that the old wives' sayings "from the cradle to heaven" and the other one about "little angels belong in heaven" were nothing short of blasphemy. The death of a child moved him deeply.

"A stillborn child, or one who dies soon after birth are, like suicides, the most terrible mystery to me," I once heard him say. "Like a child crucified!"

And once, when a man had taken his own life and the father of the suicide, an outsider, asked Don Manuel if his son could be buried in consecrated ground, the priest answered:

"Most certainly, for at the last moment, in the very last throes, he must surely have repented. There is no doubt of it whatsoever in my mind."

Often he would visit the local school too, to help the teacher, to teach alongside him—and not only the catechism. The simple truth was that he fled relentlessly from idleness and from solitude. He went so far in this desire of his to mingle with the villagers, especially the young people and the children, that he even attended the village dances. And more than once he played the drum to keep time for the boys and girls dancing; this kind of activity, which in another priest would have seemed like a grotesque mockery of his calling, in him somehow took on the appearance of a divine office. When the Angelus rang out, he would put down the drum and sticks, take off his hat (all the others doing the same) and pray: "The angel of the Lord declared unto Mary: Hail Mary . . ." And afterwards: "Now let us rest until tomorrow."

———

"The most important thing," he would say, "is for the people to be happy; everyone must be happy just to be alive. To be satisfied with life is of first importance. No one should want to die until it is God's will."

"I want to die now," a recently widowed woman once told him, "I want to follow my husband. . . ."

"But why?" he asked. "Stay here and pray God for his soul."

Once he commented at a wedding: "Ah, if I could only change all the water in our lake into wine, into a gentle little wine which, no matter how much of it one drank, would always make one joyful without making one drunk . . . or, if it made one drunk, would make one joyfully tipsy."

One day a band of poor circus people came through the village. Their leader—who arrived with a gravely ill and pregnant wife and three children to help him—played the clown. While he was in the village square making all the children, and even some of the adults, laugh with glee, his wife suddenly fell desperately ill and had to leave; she went off accompanied by a look of anguish from the clown and a howl of laughter from the children. Don Manuel hurried after her, and a little later, in a corner of the inn's stable, he helped her give up her soul in a state of grace. When the performance was over and the villagers and the clown learned of the tragedy, they came to the inn, and there the poor, bereaved clown, in a voice overcome with tears, said to Don Manuel, as he took his hand and kissed it: "They are quite right, Father, when they say you are a saint." Don Manuel took the clown's hand in his and replied in front of everyone:

"It is you who are the saint, good clown. I watched you at your work and understood that you do it not only to provide bread for your own children, but also to give joy to the children of others. And I tell you now that your wife, the mother of your children, whom I sent to God while you worked to give joy, is at rest in the Lord, and that you will join her there, and that the angels, whom you will make laugh with happiness in heaven, will reward you with their laughter."

And everyone present wept, children and adults alike, as much from sorrow as from a mysterious joy in which all sorrow was drowned. Later, recalling that solemn hour, I came to realize that the imperturbable happiness of Don Manuel was merely the temporal, earthly form of an infinite, eternal sadness which the priest concealed from the eyes and ears of the world with heroic saintliness.

His constant activity, his ceaseless intervention in the tasks and diversions of his flock, had the appearance of a flight from himself, a flight from solitude. He confirmed this suspicion: "I have a fear of solitude," he would say. And still, from time to time he would go off by himself, along the shores of the lake, to the ruins of the abbey where the souls of pious Cistercians seem still to repose, although history has long since buried them in oblivion. There, the cell of the so-called Father-Captain can still be found, and it is said that the drops of blood spattered on the walls as he flagellated himself can still be seen. What thoughts occupied our Don Manuel as he walked there? I remember a conversation we held once when I asked him, as he was speaking of the abbey, why it had never occurred to him to enter a monastery, and he answered me:

"It is not at all because my sister is a widow and I have her children and herself to support—for God looks after the poor—but rather because I simply was not born to be a hermit, an anchorite; the solitude would crush my soul; and, as far as a monastery is concerned, my monastery is Valverde de Lucerna. I was not meant to live alone, or die alone. I was meant to live for my village, and die for it too. How should I save my soul if I were not to save the soul of my village as well?"

"But there have been saints who were hermits, solitaries . . . ," I said.

"Yes, the Lord gave them the grace of solitude which He has denied me, and I must resign myself. I must not throw away my village to win my soul. God made me that way. I would not be able, alone, to carry the cross of birth. . . ."

I trust that these recollections, which keep my faith alive, will portray our Don Manuel as he was when I, a young girl of almost sixteen, returned from the convent of Renada to our "monastery of Valverde de Lucerna," to kneel once more at the feet of our "abbot."

"Well, here is Simona's daughter," he said as soon as he saw me, "quite a young woman, and knowing French, and how to play the piano, and embroider, and heaven knows what else besides! Now you must get ready to give us a family. And your brother Lázaro, when is he coming back? Is he still in the New World?"

"Yes, Father, he is still in America."

"The New World! And we in the Old. Well, then, when you write to him, tell him from me, on behalf of the parish priest, that I should like to know when he is returning from the New World to the Old, to bring us the latest from over there. And tell him that he will find the lake and the mountain as he left them."

When I first went to him for confession, I became so confused that I could not enunciate a word. I recited the "Forgive me, Father, for I have sinned," in a stammer, almost sobbing. And he, observing this, said:

"Good heavens, my dear, what are you afraid of, or of whom are you afraid? Certainly you're not trembling under the weight of your sins, nor in fear of God. No, you're trembling because of me, isn't that so?"

At this point I burst into tears.

"What have they been telling you about me? What fairy tales? Was it your mother, perhaps? Come, come, please be calm: you must imagine you are talking to your brother...."

At this I plucked up courage and began to tell him of my anxieties, doubts, and sorrows.

"Bah! Where did you read all this, Miss Bluestocking? All this is literary nonsense. Don't believe everything you read just yet, not even Saint Teresa. If you want to amuse yourself, read the *Bertoldo*, as your father before you did."

I came away from my first confession to that holy man deeply consoled. The initial fear—simple fright more than respect— with which I had approached him, turned into a profound pity. I was at that time a very young woman, almost a girl still; and yet, I was beginning to be a woman, in my innermost being I felt the maternal instinct, and when I found myself in the confessional at the side of the saintly priest, I sensed a kind of unspoken confession on his part in the soft murmur of his voice. And I remembered how when he had chanted in the church the words of Jesus Christ: "My God, my God, why hast Thou forsaken me?" his own mother had cried out in the congregation: "My son!"; and I could hear the cry that had rent the silence of the temple. And I went to him again for confession—and to comfort him.

Another time in the confessional I told him of a doubt which assailed me, and he responded:

"As to that, you know what the catechism says. Don't question me about it, for I am ignorant; in Holy Mother Church there are learned doctors of theology who will know how to answer you."

"But you are the learned doctor here."

"Me? A learned doctor? Not even in my dreams! I, my little theologian, am only a poor country priest. And those questions, . . . do you know who whispers them into your ear? Well . . . the Devil does!"

Then, making bold, I asked him point-blank:

"And suppose he were to whisper these questions to you?"

"Who? To me? The Devil? No, we don't even know each other, my child, we haven't even met."

"But if he did whisper them? . . ."

"I wouldn't pay any attention. And that's enough of that; let's get on, for there are some sick people, some really sick people, waiting for me."

I went away thinking, I don't know why, that our Don Manuel, so famous for curing the bedeviled, didn't really believe in the Devil. As I started home, I ran into the fool Blasillo, who had probably been hovering around outside; as soon as he saw me, and by way of treating me to a display of his virtuosity, he began repeating—and in what a manner!—"My God, my God, why hast Thou forsaken me?" I arrived home utterly saddened and locked myself in my room to cry, until finally my mother arrived.

"With all these confessions, Angelita, you will end up going off to a nunnery."

"Don't worry, Mother," I answered her. "I have plenty to do here; the village is my convent."

"Until you marry."

"I don't intend to," I rejoined.

The next time I saw Don Manuel I asked him, looking him straight in the eye:

"Is there really a Hell, Don Manuel?"

And he, without altering his expression, answered:

"For you, my child, no."

"For others, then?"

"Does it matter to you, if you are not to go there?"

"It matters to me for the others. Is there a Hell?"

"Believe in Heaven, the Heaven we can see. Look at it there"—and he pointed to the heavens above the mountain, and then down into the lake, to the reflection.

"But we are supposed to believe in Hell as well as in Heaven," I said.

"Yes, that's true. We must believe everything that our Holy Mother Church believes and teaches, our Holy Mother Church, Catholic, Apostolic, and Roman. And now, that's enough of that!"

I thought I read a deep sadness in his eyes, eyes as blue as the waters of the lake.

———

Those years went by as if in a dream. Within me, a reflected image of Don Manuel was unconsciously taking form. He was an ordinary enough man in many ways, as everyday as the daily bread we asked for in our Paternoster. I helped him whenever I could with his tasks, visiting his sick, our sick, the girls at school, and helping, too, with the church linen and the vestments; I served in the role, as he said, of his deaconess. Once I was invited to the city for a few days by an old schoolfriend, but I had to hurry back home, for the city stifled me—something was missing, I was thirsty for a sight of the waters of the lake, hungry for a sight of the peaks of the mountain; and even more, I missed my Don Manuel, as if he were calling me, as if he were endangered by my being so far away, as if he were in need of me. I began to feel a kind of maternal affection for my spiritual father; I longed to help him bear the cross of birth.

My twenty-fourth birthday was approaching when my brother Lázaro came back from America with the small fortune he had saved up. He came back to Valverde de Lucerna with the intention of taking me and my mother to live in a city, perhaps even in Madrid.

"In the country," he said, "in these villages, a person becomes dull, brutalized, and spiritually impoverished." And he added: "Civilization is the very opposite of everything countrified. The idiocy of country life! No, that's not for us; I didn't have you sent away to school so that afterwards you might go to waste here, among these ignorant peasants."

I said nothing, though I was ready to oppose any idea of moving. But our mother, already past sixty, took a firm stand from the start: "Change pastures at my age?" she demurred at once. A little later she made it quite clear that she could not live away from her lake, her mountain, and above all, her Don Manuel.

"You are both of you like those cats that get attached to houses," my brother kept saying.

When he realized the extent of the sway exercised over the entire village—especially over my mother and myself—by the saintly priest, my brother began to resent him. He saw in this situation an example of the obscurantist theocracy which, according to him, smothered Spain. And he began to spout the old anticlerical commonplaces, to which he added antireligious and "progressive" propaganda brought back from the New World.

"In this Spain of useless, easy-going men, the priests manipulate the women, and the women manipulate the men. Not to mention the idiocy of the country, and this feudal backwater!"

"Feudal," to him, meant something frightful. "Feudal" and "medieval" were the epithets he employed to condemn something out of hand.

The absolute failure of his diatribes to move us and their lack of effect upon the village—where they were listened to with respectful indifference—disconcerted him no end. "The man does not exist who could move these clods." But he soon began to understand—for he was an intelligent man, and therefore a good one—the kind of influence exercised over the village by Don Manuel, and he came to appreciate the effect of the priest's work in the village.

"This priest is not like the rest of them," he announced. "He is, in fact, a saint."

"How do you know what the rest of them are like?" I asked him, and he replied:

"I can imagine."

Even so, he did not set foot inside the church nor did he miss an opportunity to parade his lack of belief—though he always exempted Don Manuel from his scornful accusations. In the village, an unconscious expectancy began to build up, the anticipation of a kind of duel between my brother Lázaro and Don Manuel—in short, it was expected that Don Manuel would convert my brother. No one doubted but that in the end the priest would bring him into the fold. On his side, Lázaro was eager (he told me so himself, later) to go and hear Don Manuel, to see and hear him in the church, to get to know him and to talk with him, so that he might learn the secret of his spiritual sway over our souls. And he let himself be coaxed to this end, so that finally— "out of curiosity," as he said—he went to hear the preacher.

"Now, this is something else again," he told me as soon as he came back from hearing Don Manuel for the first time. "He's not like the others; still, he doesn't fool me, he's too intelligent to believe everything he has to teach."

"You mean you think he's a hypocrite?"

"A hypocrite . . . no! But he has to live by his job."

As for me, my brother was determined I should read the books he brought me, and others which he urged me to buy.

"So your brother Lázaro wants you to read," Don Manuel declared. "Well, read, my child, read and make him happy. I know you will only read worthy books. Read, even if you only read novels; they are as good as histories which claim to be 'true.' You are better off reading than concerning yourself with village gossip and old wives' tales. Above all, though, you will do well to read some devotional books which will bring you contentment in life, a quiet, gentle contentment, and peace."

And he, did he enjoy such contentment?

———

It was about this time that our mother fell mortally sick and died. In her last days her one wish was that Don Manuel should convert Lázaro, whom she hoped to see again in heaven, in some little corner among the stars from where they could see the lake and the mountain of Valverde de Lucerna. She felt she was going there now, to see God.

"You are not going anywhere," Don Manuel kept telling her; "you are staying right here. Your body will remain here, in this earth, and your soul also, in this house, watching and listening to your children though they will not see or hear you."

"But, Father," she said, "I am going to see God."

"God, my daughter, is all around us, and you will see Him from here, right from here. And all of us see in Him, and He in all of us."

"God bless you," I whispered to him.

"The peace in which your mother dies will be her eternal life," he told me.

And, turning to my brother Lázaro: "Her heaven is to go on seeing you, and it is at this moment that she must be saved. Tell her you will pray for her."

"But . . ."

"But what? . . . Tell her you will pray for her, to whom you owe your life. And I know that once you promise her, you *will* pray, and I know that once you pray . . ."

My brother, with tears in his eyes, went up to our dying mother and gave her his solemn promise to pray for her.

"And I, in heaven will pray for you, for all of you," my mother replied. And then, kissing the crucifix and fixing her eyes on Don Manuel, she gave up her soul to God.

"Into Thy hands I commend my spirit," prayed the priest.

—

My brother and I stayed on in the house alone. What had happened at the time of my mother's death had established a bond between Lázaro and Don Manuel. The latter seemed even to neglect some of his charges, his patients, and his other needy to look after my brother. In the afternoons, they would go for a walk together, beside the lake or toward the ivy-covered ruins of the old Cistercian abbey.

"He's an extraordinary man," Lázaro told me. "You know the story they tell of how there is a city at the bottom of the lake, submerged beneath the water, and that on Midsummer's Night at midnight the sound of its church bells can be heard. . . ."

"Yes, a city 'feudal and medieval' . . ."

"And I believe," he went on, "that at the bottom of Don Manuel's soul there is a city, submerged and drowned, and that sometimes the sound of its bells can be heard. . . ."

"Yes. . . . And this city submerged in Don Manuel's soul, and perhaps—why not?—in yours as well, is certainly the cemetery of the souls of our ancestors, the ancestors of our Valverde de Lucerna . . . 'feudal and medieval'!"

—

Eventually my brother began going to Mass. He went regularly to hear Don Manuel. When it became known that he was prepared to comply with his annual duty of receiving Communion, that he would receive Communion when the others did, an inner joy ran through the town, which felt that by this act he was restored to his people. The rejoicing was so simple and honest, that Lázaro never did feel that he had been "vanquished" or "overcome."

The day of his Communion arrived; of Communion before and with the entire village. When my brother's turn came, I saw Don Manuel—white as the January snow on the mountain, and moving like the surface of the lake when it is stirred by the northeast wind—come up to him with the holy wafer in his hand, trembling violently as he reached out to Lázaro's mouth; at that moment the priest shook so that the wafer dropped to the ground. My brother himself recovered it and placed it in his mouth. The people saw the tears on Don Manuel's cheeks, and everyone wept, saying: "How he loves him!" And then, because it was dawn, a cock crowed.

On returning home I shut myself in with my brother; alone with him I put my arms around his neck and kissed him.

"Lázaro, Lázaro, what joy you have given us all today; the entire village, the living and the dead, especially our mother. Did you see how Don Manuel wept for joy? What joy you have given us all!"

"That's why I did it," he answered me.

"Is that why? Just to give us pleasure? Surely you did it for your own sake, because you were converted."

And then Lázaro, my brother, grew as pale and tremulous as Don Manuel when he was giving Communion, and bade me sit down, in the chair where our mother used to sit. He took a deep breath, and, in the intimate tone of a family confession, he told me:

"Angelita, it is time for me to tell you the truth, the absolute truth, and I shall tell it, because I must, because I cannot and ought not to conceal it from you, and because sooner or later, you are bound to find it out anyway, if only halfway—which would be worse."

Thereupon, serenely and tranquilly, in a subdued voice, he recounted a tale that cast me into a lake of sorrow. He told me how Don Manuel had begged him, particularly during the walks to the ruins of the old Cistercian abbey, to set a good example, to avoid scandalizing the townspeople, to take part in the religious life of the community, to feign belief even if he did not feel any, to conceal his own ideas—all this without attempting in any way to catechize him, to instruct him in religion, or to effect a true conversion.

"But is it possible?" I asked in consternation.

"Very possible and absolutely true. When I said to him: 'Is it really you, the priest, who suggests that I pretend?' he replied, hesitatingly: 'Pretend? Not at all! It would not be pretending.

"Dip your fingers in holy water, and you will end by believing," as someone said.' And I, gazing into his eyes, asked him: 'And you, by celebrating the Mass, have you ended up by believing?' He looked away and stared out at the lake, until his eyes filled with tears. And it was in this way that I came to understand his secret."

"Lázaro!" I moaned.

At that moment the fool Blasillo came along our street, crying out his: "My God, my God, why hast Thou forsaken me?" And Lázaro shuddered, as if he had heard the voice of Don Manuel, or even that of Christ.

"It was then," my brother at length continued, "that I really understood his motives and his saintliness; for a saint he is, Sister, a true saint. In trying to convert me to his holy cause—for it is a holy cause, a most holy cause—he was not attempting to score a triumph, but rather was doing it to protect the peace, the happiness, the illusions, perhaps, of his flock. I understood that if he thus deceives them—if it *is* deceit—it is not for his own advantage. I submitted to his logic—and that was my conversion. And I shall never forget the day on which I said to him: 'But, Don Manuel, the truth, the truth, above all!'; and he, all a-tremble, whispered in my ear—though we were all alone in the middle of the countryside—'The truth? The truth, Lázaro, is perhaps something so unbearable, so terrible, something so deadly, that simple people could not live with it!'

" 'And why do you allow me a glimpse of it now, here, as if we were in the confessional?' I asked. And he said: 'Because if I did not, I would be so tormented by it, so tormented that I would finally shout it in the middle of the Plaza, which I must never, never, never do. . . . I am put here to give life to the souls of my charges, to make them happy, to make them dream they are immortal—and not to destroy them. The important thing is that they live undisturbed, in concord with one another—and with the truth, with my truth, they could not live at all. Let them live. That is what the Church does, it lets them live. As for true religion, all religions are true insofar as they give spiritual life to the people who profess them, insofar as they console them for having been born only to die. And for each race the truest religion is their own, the religion that made them. . . . And mine? Mine consists in consoling myself by consoling others, even though the consolation I give them is not ever mine.' I shall never forget his words."

"But then this Communion of yours has been a sacrilege," I dared interrupt, regretting my words as soon as I said them.

"Sacrilege? What about the priest who gave it to me? And his Masses?"

"What martyrdom!" I exclaimed.

"And now," said my brother, "there is one more person to console the people."

"To deceive them, you mean?" I said.

"Not at all," he replied, "but rather to confirm them in their faith."

"And they, the people, do you think they really believe?"

"As to that, I know nothing! . . . They probably believe without trying, from force of habit, tradition. The important thing is not to stir them up. To let them live on the thin diet of their emotions rather than acquiring the torments of luxury. Blessed are the poor in spirit!"

"So that is what you have learned from Don Manuel. . . . And tell me, do you feel you have carried out your promise to our mother on her deathbed, when you promised to pray for her?"

"Do you think I could fail her? What do you take me for, Sister? Do you think I would go back on my word, my solemn promise made at the hour of death to a mother?"

"I don't know. . . . You might have wanted to deceive her so she could die in peace."

"The fact is, though, that if I had not lived up to my promise, I would be totally miserable."

"And . . ."

"I have carried out my promise and I have never neglected for a single day to pray for her."

"Only for her?"

"Well, for whom else?"

"For yourself! And now, for Don Manuel."

We parted and each went to his room, I to weep through the night, praying for the conversion of my brother and of Don Manuel. And Lázaro, to what purpose, I know not.

———

From that day on I was nervous about finding myself alone with Don Manuel, whom I continued to help in his pious works. And he seemed to sense my inner state and to guess at its cause. When at last I approached him in the confessional's penitential tribunal (who was the judge, and who the offender?) the two of us, he and I, bowed our heads in silence and began to weep. It was Don Manuel who finally broke the silence, with a voice that seemed to issue from a tomb:

"Angelita, you have the same faith you had when you were ten, don't you? You believe, don't you?"

"Yes, I believe, Father."

"Then go on believing. And if doubts come to torment you, suppress them utterly, even to yourself. The main thing is to live. . . ."

I summoned up my courage, and dared to ask, trembling:

"But, Father, do you believe?"

For a brief moment he hesitated, and then, taking hold of himself, he said:

"I believe!"

"In what, Father, in what? Do you believe in the life hereafter? Do you believe that when we die, we do not die altogether? Do you believe that we will see each other again, that we will love each other in the next world? Do you believe in the next life?"

The poor saint was sobbing.

"My child, leave off, leave off!"

Now, as I write this memoir, I ask myself: Why did he not deceive me? Why did he not deceive me as he deceived the others? Why did he torture himself? Why could he not deceive himself, or why could he not deceive me? And I prefer to think that he was tormented because he could not deceive himself into deceiving me.

"And now," he said, "pray for me, for your brother, and for yourself—for all of us. We must go on living. And giving life."

And, after a pause:

"Angelita, why don't you marry?"

"You know why."

"No, no; you must marry. Lázaro and I will find you a suitor. For it would be good for you to marry, and rid yourself of these obsessions."

"Obsessions, Don Manuel?"

"I know what I am saying. You should not torment yourself for the sake of others, for each of us has more than enough to do answering for himself."

"That it should be you, Don Manuel, saying this! That you should advise me to marry and answer for myself alone and not suffer over others! That it should be you!"

"Yes, you are right, Angelita. I am no longer sure of what I am saying since I began to confess to you. Only, one must go on living. Yes! One must live!"

And when I rose to leave the church, he asked me:

"Now, Angelita, in the name of the people, do you absolve me?"

I felt pierced by a mysterious and priestly prompting and said:

"In the name of the Father, the Son, and the Holy Ghost, I absolve you, Father."

We left the church, and as I went out I felt the quickening of maternal feelings within me.

———

My brother, now totally devoted to the work of Don Manuel, had become his closest and most zealous collaborator and companion. They were bound together, moreover, by their common secret. Lázaro accompanied the priest on his visits to the sick, and to schools, and he placed his fortune at the disposition of the saintly man. And he nearly learned to help celebrate Mass. All the while he was sounding deeper the unfathomable soul of the priest.

"What an incredible man!" he exclaimed to me once. "Yesterday, as we were walking along beside the lake he said: 'There lies my greatest temptation.' When I interrogated him with my eyes, he went on: 'My poor father, who was close to ninety when he died, was tormented all his life, as he himself confessed to me, by a temptation to commit suicide, by an instinct toward self-destruction, which had come to him from a time before memory—from birth, from his *nation*, as he said—and he was forced to fight against it always. And this struggle grew to be his life. So as not to succumb to this temptation he was forced to take precautions, to guard his life. He told me of terrible episodes. His urge was a form of madness—and I have inherited it. How that water beckons me with its deep quiet! . . . an apparent serenity reflecting the sky like a mirror—and beneath it the hidden current! My life, Lázaro, is a kind of continual suicide, or a struggle against suicide, which is the same thing. . . . Just so long as our people go on living!' And then he added: 'Here the river eddies to form a lake, so that later, flowing down the plateau, it may form cascades, waterfalls, and torrents, hurling itself through gorges and chasms. Thus life eddies in the village; and the temptation to commit suicide is greater beside the still waters which at night reflect the stars, than it is beside the crashing falls which drive one back in fear. Listen, Lázaro, I have helped poor villagers to die well, ignorant, illiterate villagers who had scarcely ever been out of their village, and I have learned from their own lips, or sensed it when they were silent, the real cause of their sickness unto death, and there at their deathbed I have been able to see into the black abyss of their life-weariness. A weariness a thousand times worse than hunger! For our part, Lázaro, let us go on with our kind of suicide working for the people, and let them dream their lives as the lake dreams the heavens.'

"Another time," said my brother, "as we were coming back, we caught sight of a country girl, a goatherd, standing tall, on the crest of the mountain slope overlooking the lake and she was singing in a voice fresher than the waters. Don Manuel stopped me, and pointing to her said: 'Look, it's as though time had stopped, as though this country girl had always been there just as she is, singing the way she is, and it's as though she would always be there, as she was before my consciousness began, as she will be when it is past. That girl is a part of nature—not of history—along with the rocks, the clouds, the trees, and the water.' He has such a subtle feeling for nature, he infuses it with feeling! I shall never forget the day when snow was falling and he asked me: 'Have you ever seen a greater mystery, Lázaro, than the snow falling, and dying, in the lake, while a headdress is laid upon the mountain?'"

———

Don Manuel had to moderate and temper my brother's zeal and his neophyte's rawness. As soon as he heard that Lázaro was going about inveighing against some of the popular superstitions he told him firmly:

"Leave them alone! It's difficult enough making them understand where orthodox belief leaves off and where superstition begins. And it's even harder for us. Leave them alone, then, as long as they get some comfort. . . . It's better for them to believe everything, even things that contradict one another, than to believe nothing. The idea that someone who believes too much ends up not believing anything is a Protestant notion. Let us not protest! Protestation destroys contentment and peace."

My brother told me, too, about one moonlit night when they were returning to the village along the lake, whose surface was being stirred by a mountain breeze, so that the moonbeams topped the white-crested waves, and Don Manuel turned to him and said:

"Look, the water is reciting the litany and saying: *ianua caeli, ora pro nobis;* gate of heaven, pray for us."

And two tears fell from his lashes to the grass, where the light of the full moon shone upon them like dew.

And time sped by, and my brother and I began to notice that Don Manuel's spirits were failing, that he could no longer control completely the deep-rooted sadness which consumed him;

perhaps some treacherous illness was undermining his body and soul. In an effort to arouse his interest, Lázaro spoke to him of the good effect the organization of something like a Catholic agrarian syndicate in the Church would have.

"A syndicate?" Don Manuel replied sadly. "A syndicate? And what is that? The Church is the only syndicate I know of. And you have certainly heard 'My kingdom is not of this world.' Our kingdom, Lázaro, is not of this world. . . ."

"And of the other?"

Don Manuel bowed his head:

"The other is here. Two kingdoms exist in this world. Or rather, the other world. . . . Ah, I don't really know what I am saying. But as for the syndicate, that's a carry-over from your radical days. No, Lázaro, no; religion does not exist to resolve the economic or political conflicts of this world, which God handed over to men for their disputes. Let men think and act as they will, let them console themselves for having been born, let them live as happily as possible in the illusion that all this has a purpose. I don't propose to advise the poor to submit to the rich, nor to suggest to the rich that they submit to the poor; but rather to preach resignation in everyone, and charity toward everyone. For even the rich man must resign himself—to his riches, and to life; and the poor man must show charity—even to the rich. The Social Question? Ignore it, for it is none of our business. So, a new society is on the way, in which there will be neither rich nor poor, in which wealth will be justly divided, in which everything will belong to everyone—and so, what then? Won't this general well-being and comfort lead to even greater tedium and weariness of life? I know well enough that one of those leaders of what they call the Social Revolution said that religion is the opium of the people. Opium . . . Opium . . . Yes, opium it is. We should give them opium, and help them sleep, and dream. I, myself, with my mad activity am giving myself opium. And still I don't manage to sleep well, let alone dream well. . . . What a fearful nightmare! . . . I, too, can say, with the Divine Master: 'My soul is exceedingly sorrowful, even unto death.' No, Lázaro, no;

no syndicates for us. If *they* organize them, well and good—they would be distracting themselves in that way. Let them play at syndicates, if that makes them happy."

———

The entire village began to realize that Don Manuel's spirit was weakening, that his strength was waning. His very voice—that miracle of a voice—acquired a kind of tremor. Tears came into his eyes at the slightest provocation—or without provocation. Whenever he spoke to people about the next world, about the next life, he was forced to pause at frequent intervals, and he would close his eyes. "It is a vision," people would say, "he has a vision of what lies ahead." At such moments the fool Blasillo was the first to burst into tears. He wept copiously these days, crying now more than he laughed, and even his laughter had the sound of tears.

The last Easter Week which Don Manuel was to celebrate among us, in this world, in this village of ours, arrived, and all the village sensed that the tragedy was coming to an end. And how those words struck home when for the last time Don Manuel cried out before us: "My God, my God, why hast Thou forsaken me?" And when he repeated the words of the Lord to the Good Thief—"all thieves are good," Don Manuel used to tell us—: "Today shalt thou be with me in paradise." And then, the last general Communion which our saint was to give! When he came to my brother to give him the Host—his hand steady this time— just after the liturgical "... *in vitam aeternam,*" he bent down and whispered to him: "There is no other life but this, no life more eternal ... let them dream it eternal ... let it be eternal for a few years. . . ." And when he came to me, he said: "Pray, my child, pray for us all." And then, something so extraordinary happened that I carry it now in my heart as the greatest of mysteries: he leant over and said, in a voice which seemed to belong to the other world: "... and pray, too, for our Lord Jesus Christ."

I stood up weakly like a sleepwalker. Everything around me seemed dreamlike. And I thought: "Am I to pray, too, for the lake and the mountain?" And next: "Am I bedeviled, then?" Home at last, I took up the crucifix my mother had held in her hands when she had given up her soul to God, and, gazing at it through my tears and recalling the "My God, my God, why hast Thou forsaken me?" of our two Christs, the one of this earth and the other of this village, I prayed: "Thy will be done on earth as it is in heaven," and then, "And lead us not into temptation. Amen." After this I turned to the statue of the Mater Dolorosa—her heart transfixed by seven swords—which had been my poor mother's most sorrowful comfort, and I prayed again: "Holy Mary, Mother of God, pray for us sinners, now and at the hour of our death. Amen." I had scarcely finished the prayer, when I asked myself: "Sinners? Us, sinners? And what is our sin, what is it?" And all day I brooded over the question.

The next day I went to see Don Manuel—now in the full sunset of his magnificent religiosity—and I said to him:

"Do you remember, my Father, years ago when I asked you a certain question you answered: 'That is a question you must not ask me; for I am ignorant; there are learned doctors of the Holy Mother Church who will know how to answer you'?"

"Do I remember? . . . Of course, I do. And I remember I told you those were questions put to you by the Devil."

"Well, then, Father, I have come again, bedeviled, to ask you another question put to me by my Guardian Devil."

"Ask it."

"Yesterday, when you gave me Communion, you asked me to pray for all of us, and even for . . ."

"That's enough! . . . Go on."

"I arrived home and began to pray; when I came to the part 'Pray for us sinners, now and at the hour of our death,' a voice inside me asked: 'Sinners? Us, sinners? And what is our sin?' What is our sin, Father?"

"Our sin?" he replied. "A great doctor of the Spanish Catholic Apostolic Church has already explained it; the great doctor of *Life Is a Dream* has written 'The greatest sin of man is to have been born.' That, my child, is our sin: to have been born."

"Can it be atoned, Father?"

"Go away and pray again. Pray once more for us sinners, now and at the hour of our death. . . . Yes, at length the dream is atoned . . . at length life is atoned . . . at length the cross of birth is expiated and atoned, and the dogma comes to an end. . . . And as Calderón said, to have done good, to have feigned good, even in dreams, is something which is not lost."

———

The hour of his death arrived at last. The entire village saw it come. And he made it his finest lesson. For he did not want to die alone or at rest. He died preaching to his people in the church. But first, before being carried to the church—his paralysis made it impossible for him to move—he summoned Lázaro and me to his bedside. Alone there, the three of us together, he said:

"Listen to me: watch over my poor flock; find some comfort for them in living, and let them believe what I could not. And Lázaro, when your hour comes, die as I die, as Angela will die, in the arms of the Holy Mother Church, Catholic, Apostolic, and Roman; that is to say, the Holy Mother Church of Valverde de Lucerna. And now farewell; until we never meet again, for this dream of life is coming to an end. . . ."

"Father, Father," I cried out.

"Do not grieve, Angela, only go on praying for all sinners, for all who have been born. Let them dream, let them dream. . . . Oh, how I long to sleep, to sleep, to sleep without end, to sleep for all eternity, and never dream! Forgetting this dream! . . . When they bury me, let it be in a box made from the six planks I cut from the old walnut tree—poor old tree!—in whose shade I played as a child, when I began the dream. . . . In those days, I really did believe in life everlasting. That is to say, it seems to me now that I believed. For a child, to believe is the same as to dream. And for a people too . . . You'll find those six planks I cut at the foot of the bed."

He was seized by a sudden fit of choking, and then, feeling better, he went on:

"You will recall that when we prayed together, animated by a common sentiment, a community of spirit, and we came to the final verse of the Creed, you will remember that I would fall silent. . . . When the Israelites were coming to the end of their wandering in the desert, the Lord told Aaron and Moses that because they had not believed in Him they would not set foot in the Promised Land with their people; and he bade them climb the heights of Mount Hor, where Moses ordered Aaron to be stripped of his garments, so that Aaron died there, and then Moses went up from the plains of Moab to Mount Nebo, to the top of Pisgah, looking into Jericho, and the Lord showed him all of the land promised to His people, but He said to him: 'Thou shalt not go over thither.' And there Moses died, and no one knew his grave. And he left Joshua to be chief in his place. You, Lázaro, must be my Joshua, and if you can make the sun stand still, make it stop, and never mind progress. Like Moses, I have seen the face of God—our supreme dream—face to face, and as you already know, and as the Scriptures say, he who sees God's face, he who sees the eyes of the dream, the eyes with which He looks at us, will die inexorably and forever. And therefore, do not let our people, so long as they live, look into the face of God. Once dead, it will no longer matter, for then they will see nothing. . . ."

"Father, Father, Father," I cried again.

And he said:

"Angela, you must pray always, so that all sinners may go on dreaming, until they die, of the resurrection of the flesh and life everlasting. . . ."

I was expecting "and who knows it might be . . ." but instead, Don Manuel had another choking fit.

"And now," he finally went on, "and now, at the hour of my death, it is high time to have me taken, in this very chair, to the church, so that I may take leave there of my people, who are waiting for me."

He was carried to the church and taken, in his armchair, into the chancel, to the foot of the altar. In his hand he held a crucifix. My brother and I stood close to him, but the fool Blasillo wanted to stand even closer. He wanted to grasp Don Manuel by the hand, so that he could kiss it. When some of the people nearby tried to stop him, Don Manuel rebuked them and said:

"Let him come closer.... Come, Blasillo, give me your hand."

The fool cried for joy. And then Don Manuel spoke:

"I shall say very few words, my children; I scarcely have strength except to die. And I have nothing new to tell you either. I have already said everything I have to say. Live together in peace and happiness, in the hope that we will all see each other again some day, in that other Valverde de Lucerna up there among the stars of the night, the stars which the lake reflects over the image of the reflected mountain. And pray, pray to the Most Blessed Virgin, and to our Lord. Be good ... that is enough. Forgive me whatever wrong I may have done you inadvertently or unknowingly. After I give you my blessing, let us pray together, let us say the Paternoster, the Ave Maria, the Salve, and the Creed."

Then he gave his blessing to the whole village, with the crucifix held in his hand, while the women and children cried and even some of the men wept softly. Almost at once the prayers were begun. Don Manuel listened to them in silence, his hand in the hand of Blasillo the fool, who was falling asleep to the sound of the praying. First the Paternoster, with its "Thy will be done on earth as it is in heaven," then the Ave Maria, with its "Pray for us sinners, now and at the hour of our death"; followed by the Salve, with its "mourning and weeping in this vale of tears"; and finally, the Creed. On reaching "The resurrection of the flesh and life everlasting" the people sensed that their saint had yielded up his soul to God. It was not necessary to close his eyes even, for he died with them closed. When we tried to wake up Blasillo, we found that he, too, had fallen asleep in the Lord forever. So that later there were two bodies to be buried.

The whole village immediately went to the saint's house to carry away holy relics, to divide up pieces of his garments among themselves, to carry off whatever they could find as a memento of the blessed martyr. My brother kept his breviary, between the pages of which he discovered a carnation, dried as in a herbarium and mounted on a piece of paper, and upon the paper a cross and a certain date.

No one in the village seemed willing to believe that Don Manuel was dead; everyone expected to see him—perhaps some of them did—taking his daily walk along the shore of the lake, his figure mirrored in the water, or silhouetted against the background of the mountain. They continued to hear his voice, and they all visited his grave, around which a veritable cult grew up; old women "possessed by devils" came to touch the walnut cross, made with his own hands from the tree which had given the six planks of his coffin. And the ones least willing to believe in his death were my brother and I.

Lázaro carried on the tradition of the saint, and he began to compile a record of the priest's work. Some of the conversations in this account of mine were made possible by his notes.

"It was he," said my brother, "who made me into a new man. I was a true Lazarus whom he raised from the dead. He gave me faith."

"Faith? . . ." I interrupted.

"Yes, faith, faith in life itself, faith in life's consolations. It was he who cured me of my delusion of 'progress,' of my belief in its political implications. For there are, Angela, two types of dangerous and harmful men: those who, convinced of life beyond the grave, of the resurrection of the flesh, torment other people—like the inquisitors they are—so that they will despise this life as a transitory thing and work for the other life; and then, there are those who, believing only in this life . . ."

"Like you, perhaps . . ."

"Yes, and like Don Manuel. Believing only in this world, this second group looks forward to some vague future society and exerts every effort to prevent the populace from finding consolation in the belief in another world. . . ."

"And so . . ."

"The people should be allowed to live with their illusion."

The poor priest who came to replace Don Manuel found himself overwhelmed in Valverde de Lucerna by the memory of the saint, and he put himself in the hands of my brother and myself for guidance. He wanted only to follow in the footsteps of the saint. And my brother told him: "Very little theology, Father, very little theology. Religion, religion, religion." Listening to him, I smiled to myself, wondering if this were not a kind of theology, too.

And at this time I began to fear for my poor brother. From the time of Don Manuel's death it could scarcely be said that he lived. He went to the priest's tomb daily; he stood gazing into the lake for hours on end. He was filled with nostalgia for deep, abiding peace.

"Don't stare into the lake so much," I begged him.

"Don't worry. It's not this lake which draws me, nor the mountain. Only, I cannot live without his help."

"And the joy of living, Lázaro, what about the joy of living?"

"That's for others. Not for those of us who have seen God's face, those of us on whom the Dream of Life has gazed with His eyes."

"What; are you preparing to go and see Don Manuel?"

"No, Sister, no. Here at home now, between the two of us, the whole truth—bitter as it may be, bitter as the sea into which the sweet waters of our lake flow—the whole truth for you, who are so set against it. . . ."

"No, no, Lázaro. You are wrong. Your truth is not the truth."

"It's my truth."

"Yours, perhaps, but surely not . . ."

"His, too."

"No, Lázaro. Not now, it isn't. Now, he must believe otherwise; now he must believe . . ."

"Listen, Angela, once Don Manuel told me that there are truths which, though one reveals them to oneself, must be kept from others; and I told him that telling me was the same as telling himself. And then he said, he confessed to me, that he thought that more than one of the great saints, perhaps the very greatest himself, had died without believing in the other life."

"It's not possible!"

"All too possible! And now, Sister, you must be careful that here, among the people, no one even suspects our secret. . . ."

"Suspect it!" I cried out in amazement. "Why, even if I were to try, in a fit of madness, to explain it to them, they wouldn't understand it. The people do not understand your words, they have only understood your actions. To try and explain all this to them would be like reading some pages from Saint Thomas Aquinas to eight-year-old children, in Latin!"

"All the better. In any case when I am gone, pray for me and for him and for all of us."

At length, his own hour came. A sickness which had been eating away at his robust constitution seemed to flare up with the death of Don Manuel.

"I don't so much mind dying," he said to me in his last days, "as the fact that with me another piece of Don Manuel dies, too. The remainder of him must live on with you. Until, one day, even we dead will die forever."

When he lay in the throes of death, the people, as is customary in our villages, came to bid him farewell and they commended his soul to the care of Don Manuel—Saint Manuel the Good, Martyr. My brother said nothing to them; he had nothing more to say. He had already said everything there was to say. He had become a link between the two Valverdes de Lucerna—the one at the bottom of the lake and the one reflected on its surface. He was already one more of us who had died of life, and, in his way, one more of our saints.

———

I was disconsolate, more than disconsolate; but I was, at least, among my own people, in my own village. Now, having lost my Saint Manuel, the father of my soul, and my own Lázaro, my more than flesh and blood brother, my spiritual brother, it is now that I realize that I have aged. But have I really lost them then? Have I grown old? Is my death approaching?

Life must go on! And he taught me to live, he taught us to live, to feel life, to feel the meaning of life, to merge with the soul of the mountain, with the soul of the lake, with the soul of the village, to lose ourselves in them so as to remain in them forever. He taught me by his life to lose myself in the life of the people of my village, and I no longer felt the passing of the hours, and the days, and the years, any more than I felt the passage of the water in the lake. It began to seem that my life would always be like this. I no longer felt myself growing old. I no longer lived in myself, but in my people, and my people lived in me. I tried to speak as they spoke, as they spoke without trying. I went into the street—it was the one highway—and, since I knew everyone, I lived in them and forgot myself (while, on the other hand, in Madrid, where I went once with my brother, I had felt a terrible loneliness, since I knew no one, and had been tortured by the sight of so many unknown people).

Now, as I write this memoir, this confession of my experience with saintliness, with a saint, I am of the opinion that Don Manuel the Good, my Don Manuel, and my brother, too, died, believing they did not believe, but that, without believing in their belief, they actually believed, in active, resigned desolation.

But why, I have asked myself repeatedly, did not Don Manuel attempt to convert my brother through deception, pretending to be a believer himself without being one? And I have finally come to the conclusion that Don Manuel realized he would not be able to delude him, that with him a fraud would not do, that only through the truth, with his truth, would he be able to convert him; that he knew he would accomplish nothing if he attempted to enact the comedy—the tragedy, rather—which he played out for the benefit of the people. And so, he won him over to his pious fraud; he won him over to the cause of life with the truth of death. And thus did he win me, and I never permitted anyone to see through his divine, his most saintly, game. For I believed then, and I believe now, that God—as part of I know not what sacred and inscrutable purpose—caused them to believe they were unbelievers. And that at the moment of their passing, perhaps, the blindfold was removed.

And I, do I believe?

——

As I write this—here in my mother's old house, and I past my fiftieth year and with my memories growing as dim and faded as my hair—outside it is snowing, snowing upon the lake, snowing upon the mountain, upon the memory of my father, the stranger, upon the memory of my mother, my brother Lázaro, my people, upon the memory of my Saint Manuel, and even on the memory of the poor fool Blasillo, my Saint Blasillo—and may he help me in heaven! The snow effaces corners and blots out shadows, for even in the night it shines and illuminates. Truly, I do not know what is true and what is false, nor what I saw and what I merely dreamt—or rather, what I dreamt and what I merely saw—nor what I really knew or what I merely believed to be true. Neither do I know whether or not I am transferring to this paper, white as the snow outside, my awareness, for it to remain in writing, leaving me without it. But why cling to it any longer?

Do I really understand any of it? Do I really believe in any of it? What I am writing about here, did it actually take place, and did it take place in just the way I am telling it? Can such things really happen? Can all this be more than a dream dreamed within another dream? Can it be that I, Angela Carballino, a woman in her fifties, am the only one in this village to be assailed by these far-fetched thoughts, thoughts unknown to everyone else? And the others, those around me, do they believe? At least they go on living. And now they believe in Saint Manuel the Good, Martyr, who, with no hope of immortality for himself, preserved that hope in them.

It appears that our most illustrious bishop, who set in motion the process of beatifying our saint from Valverde de Lucerna, is intent on writing an account of Don Manuel's life, something which would serve as a guide for the perfect parish priest, and with this end in mind he is gathering information of every sort. He has repeatedly solicited information from me; he has come to see me more than once; and I have supplied him with all sorts of facts and details. But I have never revealed the tragic secret of Don Manuel and my brother. And it is curious that he has never suspected anything. I trust that what I have set down here will never come to his knowledge. For, all temporal authorities are to be feared; I distrust all authorities on this earth—even when they are Church authorities.

And here I end this memoir. Let its fate be what it will. . . .

———

How, you may ask, did this document, this memoir of Angela Carballino, fall into my hands? That, dear reader, is something I must keep secret. I have transcribed it for you just as it was written, with only a few, a very few editorial emendations. Does it remind you of other things I have written? This fact does not gainsay its objectivity nor its reality. Moreover, for all I know, perhaps I created real, actual beings, independent of me, beyond my control, characters with immortal souls. For all I know, Augusto Pérez in my novel *Mist* was right when he claimed to be more real, more objective than I am, I who thought I had invented him. As for the reality of this Saint Manuel the Good, Martyr—as he is revealed to me by his disciple and spiritual daughter, Angela Carballino—it has not occurred to me to doubt his reality. I believe in it more than the saint himself did. I believe in it more than I do in my own reality.

And now, before I bring this epilogue to a close, I wish to remind you, patient reader, of the ninth verse of the Epistle of the forgotten Apostle, Saint Jude—what power in a name!—where we are told how my heavenly patron, Saint Michael Archangel (Michael means "Who such as God?" and archangel means arch-messenger) disputed with the Devil (Devil means accuser, prosecutor) over the body of Moses, and would not allow him to carry it off as a prize, to damnation. Instead, he told the Devil: "May the Lord rebuke thee." And may he who wishes to understand, understand!

I should like also, since Angela Carballino introduced her own feelings into the story—I don't know how it could have been otherwise—to comment on her statement to the effect that if Don Manuel and his disciple Lázaro had confessed their convictions to the people, they, the people, would not have understood. Nor, I should like to add, would they have believed the two of them. They would have believed in their works and not in their words. And works stand by themselves, and need no words to back them up. In a village like Valverde de Lucerna one makes one's confession by one's conduct.

And as for faith, the people scarcely know what it is, and care less.

I am well aware of the fact that no action takes place in this narrative, this *novelistic* narrative, if you will—the novel is, after all, the most intimate, the truest history, so that I scarcely understand why some people are outraged to have the Gospels called a novel, when such a designation actually sets it above some mere chronicle or other. In short, nothing happens. But I hope that this is because everything in it remains, remains forever like the lakes and the mountains and the blessed simple souls, who, beyond faith and despair, the blessed souls who, in the lakes and the mountains, outside history, took refuge in a divine novel.

MARTIN HEIDEGGER

Ask two different philosophers about Martin Heidegger and you are likely to get very different assessments. Many believe that he was one of the greatest philosophers of the twentieth century, many others that he was an intellectual charlatan who used the incantations of obscure language and neologisms to conjure up the impression of profundity. Genius or poseur, Heidegger has exercised an enormous influence over contemporary continental philosophy.

Heidegger was born on September 26, 1889, in Messkirch, in southwest Germany. He was the firstborn in a devout Catholic family. His father worked as a sacristan in the local church. From an early age, Martin was being prepared for the priesthood. The Church supported the young Heidegger's primary and secondary school studies. When he was seventeen, the pastor of his school in Constance gave Heidegger a book that the older man could not fathom. It was Franz Brentano's *On the Manifold Meaning of Being According to Aristotle,* a text in which the author parses out Aristotle's answer to the question, What is being? This question would become the leitmotif of Heidegger's life and works. Many years later, Heidegger acknowledged that the Brentano volume had been "the chief help and guide of my first awkward attempts to penetrate into philosophy."

Heidegger took his baccalaureate in 1909 and became a novitiate in the Jesuit order. However, after two weeks, he was dismissed from the order, apparently because of poor health. He continued studying for the priesthood at Albert-Ludwig University in Freiburg. In his first semester there, he read Edmund Husserl's *Logic* and began dipping into the works of Wilhelm Dilthey. Clearly smitten with philosophy, Heidegger soon abandoned his plans for the priesthood and became a formal student in mathematics and philosophy. In July 1913, he defended his dissertation on "The Doctrine of Judgment in Psychologism." A year later, upon the outbreak of World War I, he volunteered for military service but was released after a couple of months because of troubles with his heart.

In 1915, the faculty at Freiburg approved Heidgger's second dissertation, "The Doctrine of Categories and Signification in Duns Scotus," and Heidegger was granted a license to teach in the university. A year later, Heidegger had a meeting with his future in the form of an encounter with Edmund Husserl, the father of phenomenology. Phenomenology is a philosophical movement that traces itself back to Descartes. In the phenomenological approach to the search for truth, priority is given to the close analysis of the content and structure of consciousness itself. Husserl was to a large extent the inventor of this method, and though Heidegger would eventually part ways with him on other issues, Husserl taught him the ascetic discipline of bracketing out the rest of the world and paying scrupulous attention to the content of experience.

For the next few years, Heidegger studied with Husserl. With the war still smoldering, Heidegger married Elfride Petri, a Protestant student who attended his courses. Toward the end of the war, Heidegger was called back into service for three months. After he returned to the university, he announced that he had broken with Catholicism. In 1919, he was assigned to work as Husserl's teaching assistant and he offered lectures on phenomenology, Descartes, and psychology. In 1923, Heidegger was appointed associate professor at Marburg, where he would come to know Karl Jaspers, Max Scheler, and Paul Tillich. One of his students was the philosopher-to-be Hannah Arendt. She and Heidegger became lovers and decades later, after Heidegger's involvement with the Nazis, Arendt would step forward as Heidegger's intellectual apologist. Heidegger was a scintillating lecturer, and his courses on time, logic, and the history of philosophy were some of the most popular at the university.

In 1926, Heidegger presented his monumental *Being and Time* to Edmund Husserl at Husserl's sixty-seventh birthday celebration. The book, which was published in 1927 and dedicated to Husserl, quickly established Heidegger's reputation, and he was almost immediately appointed full professor at Marburg. When Husserl retired a year later from his post at Freiburg, Heidegger was appointed to his chair. Soon thereafter Heidegger published his important *Kant and the Problem of Metaphysics,* in which he took issue with the well-established interpreter of Kant, Ernst Cassirer. This public disputation increased Heidegger's intellectual prestige.

The next chapter of Heidegger's life is painful to open. In 1933, Hitler became chancellor of Germany, and in April of that year Heidegger was elected rector of the University of Freiburg. He joined the Nazi Party. Heidegger scholar David Krell explains that Heidegger was "weary of the political divisiveness, economic crisis, and general demoralization that plagued postwar Germany" and, like many German academicians, supported "the Nazi Party's call for a German resurgence. On the eve of the Reichstag elections of November 12 Heidegger spoke out in support of Hitlerian policies that had culminated in Germany's withdrawal from the League of Nations." Some say that within a few months, Heidegger was having his doubts about the monster movement; whether or not it was because of those doubts, Heidegger resigned as rector.

After the war Heidegger, as a former Nazi, was prohibited from teaching. But thanks in part to the efforts of Karl Jaspers, the ban was lifted in 1949. In a 1966 interview given to *Der Spiegel* ("Only God Can Save Us Now") and published after his death, Heidegger made a vague and unsatisfying attempt to explain his involvement with the Nazis. Heidegger was deeply attached to the life and soil of southwest Germany. He spent a great deal of his time in a Black Forest cottage that his wife had built for him in the early twenties. But in the years before his death on May 26, 1976, Heidegger gave many lectures abroad.

Heidegger was consumed with the question, What is the being of Being? It was his deep conviction that from the pre-Socratics on, philosophers in the West, including Husserl, had fallen asleep to this vital mystery. According to Heidegger, Husserl's method was aimed at understanding particular beings instead of Being itself. So far as Heidegger was concerned, the language of philosophy contributes to our metaphysical stupor in that it encourages us to see things in means-ends terms, as a world of objects or tools. Far from helping us to wonder, Why is there something rather than nothing?, traditional philosophical discourse is a vehicle for the repression of the great mystery of Being. Indeed, in the analytic tradition, metaphysics or the question of Being has long been an object of ridicule and most especially at the time that Heidegger wrote, that is, at the height of the popularity of logical positivism.

Because he believed that language hid the very issue he wanted to investigate, Heidegger virtually invented a new vocabulary. He uses the term "Da-sein," which in German means "being there," for human existence. In his *Being and Time,* Heidegger reasons that in order to investigate Being itself, we need to understand the being of Da-sein, for it is only in Da-sein that the being of Being reveals itself. Da-sein is a being that relates itself to being in care or concern. It is also a being that is perpetually ahead of itself in possibilities. Following Kierkegaard's lead, Heidegger argues that one of these possibilities is the certainty of Da-sein's coming to the end of all of its possibilities. As Heidegger will claim in the selections before you, anyone who wishes to grasp the being of Da-sein must understand that our being is a being toward death.

Aspiring students of Heidegger should work through the labyrinth of the fecund but often maddening full text of *Being and Time.* Readers who would like a different, more accessible Heidegger should consider reading his percipient "What is Technology" and "The Origin of the Work of Art." Also, for his response to Sartre's apology for existentialism, read Heidegger's "Letter on Humanism."

FROM

BEING AND TIME

The Possible Being-a-Whole of Da-sein and Being-Toward-Death

46. THE SEEMING IMPOSSIBILITY OF ONTOLOGICALLY GRASPING AND DETERMINING DA-SEIN AS A WHOLE

The inadequacy of the hermeneutical situation from which the foregoing analysis originated must be overcome. With regard to the fore-having, which must necessarily be obtained, of the whole of Da-sein, we must ask whether this being, as something existing, can become accessible at all in its being. There seem to be important reasons that speak against the possibility of our required task, reasons that lie in the constitution of Da-sein itself.

Care, which forms the totality of the structural whole of Da-sein, obviously contradicts a possible being whole of this being according to its ontological sense. The primary factor of care, "being ahead of itself," however, means that Da-sein always exists for the sake of itself. "As long as it is," up until its end, it is related to its potentiality-of-being. Even when it, still existing, has nothing further "ahead of it," and has "settled its accounts," its being is still influenced by "being ahead of itself." Hopelessness, for example, does not tear Da-sein away from its possibilities, but is only an independent mode of *being toward* these possibilities. Even when one is without illusions and "is ready *for* anything," the "ahead of itself" is there. This structural factor of care tells us unambiguously that something is always still *outstanding* in Da-sein which has not yet become "real" as a potentiality-of-its-being. A *constant unfinished quality* thus lies in the essence of the constitution of Da-sein. This lack of totality means that there is still something outstanding in one's potentiality-for-being.

However, if Da-sein "exists" in such a way that there is absolutely nothing more outstanding for it, it has also already thus become no-longer-being-there. Eliminating what is outstanding in its being is equivalent to annihilating its being. As long as Da-sein *is* as a being, it has never attained its "wholeness." But if it does, this gain becomes the absolute loss of being-in-the-world. It is then never again to be experienced *as a being*.

The reason for the impossibility of experiencing Da-sein ontically as an existing whole and thus of defining it ontologically in its wholeness does not lie in any imperfection of our *cognitive faculties*. The hindrance lies on the side of the *being* of this being. What cannot even *be* in *such a way* that an experience of Da-sein could pretend to grasp it, fundamentally eludes being experienced. But is it not then a hopeless undertaking to try to discern the ontological wholeness of being of Da-sein?

As an essential structural factor of care, "being ahead of itself" cannot be eliminated. But is what we concluded from this tenable? Did we not conclude in a merely formal argumentation that it is impossible to grasp the whole of Da-sein? Or did we not at bottom inadvertently posit Da-sein as something objectively present ahead of which something not yet objectively present constantly moves along? Did our argumentation grasp not-yet-

being and the "ahead-of-itself" in a genuinely *existential* sense?
Did we speak about "end" and "totality" in a way phenomenally
appropriate to Da-sein? Did the expression "death" have a biological significance or one that is existential and ontological, or
indeed was it sufficiently and securely defined at all? And have
we actually exhausted all the possibilities of making Da-sein accessible in its totality?

We have to answer these questions before the problem of the
wholeness of Da-sein can be dismissed as nothing. The question
of the wholeness of Da-sein, both the existentiell question about
a possible potentiality-for-being-a-whole, as well as the existential question about the constitution of being of "end" and "wholeness," contain the task of a positive analysis of the phenomena of
existence set aside up to now. In the center of these considerations we have the task of characterizing ontologically the being-
toward-the-end of Da-sein and of achieving an existential concept
of death. Our inquiry related to these topics is structured in the
following way: The possibility of experiencing the death of others, and the possibility of grasping the whole of Da-sein (section 47); what is outstanding, end and wholeness (section 48);
how the existential analysis of death is distinguished from other
possible interpretations of this phenomenon (section 49); preliminary sketch of the existential and ontological structure of
death (section 50); being toward death and the everydayness of
Da-sein (section 51); everyday being toward death and the complete existential concept of death (section 52); the existential
project of an authentic being toward death (section 53).

47. THE POSSIBILITY OF EXPERIENCING THE DEATH OF OTHERS AND THE POSSIBILITY OF GRASPING DA-SEIN AS A WHOLE

When Da-sein reaches its wholeness in death, it simultaneously
loses the being of the there. The transition to no-longer-being-
there lifts Da-sein right out of the possibility of experiencing
this transition and of understanding it as something experi-

enced. This kind of thing is denied to actual Da-sein in relation to itself. The death of others, then, is all the more penetrating. In this way, an end of Da-sein becomes "objectively" accessible. Da-sein can gain an experience of death, all the more because it is essentially being-with with others. This "objective" givenness of death must then make possible an ontological analysis of the totality of Da-sein.

Thus from the kind of being that Da-sein possesses as being-with-one-another, we might glean the fairly obvious information that when the Da-sein of others has come to an end, it might be chosen as a substitute theme for our analysis of the totality of Da-sein. But does this lead us to our intended goal?

Even the Da-sein of others, when it has reached its wholeness in death, is a no-longer-being-there in the sense of no-longer-being-in-the-world. Does not dying mean going-out-of-the-world and losing being-in-the-world? Yet, the no-longer-being-in-the-world of the deceased (understood in an extreme sense) is still a being* in the sense of the mere objective presence of a corporeal thing encountered. In the dying of others that remarkable phenomenon of being can be experienced that can be defined as the transition of a being from the kind of being of Da-sein (or of life) to no-longer-being-there. The *end* of the being qua Da-sein is the *beginning* of this being qua something objectively present.

This interpretation of the transition from Da-sein to something merely objectively present, however, misses the phenomenal content in that the being still remaining does not represent a mere corporeal thing. Even the objectively present corpse is, viewed theoretically, still a possible object for pathological anatomy whose understanding is oriented toward the idea of life. Merely-being-objectively-present is "more" than a *lifeless,* material thing. In it we encounter something *unliving* which has lost its life.

But even this way of characterizing what still remains does not exhaust the complete phenomenal findings with regard to Da-sein.

* *ein Sein*—Tʀ.

The "deceased," as distinct from the dead body, has been torn away from "those remaining behind," and is the object of "being taken care of" in funeral rites, the burial, and the cult of graves. And that is so because he is "still more" in his kind of being than an innerworldly thing at hand to be taken care of. In lingering together with him in mourning and commemorating, those remaining behind *are with* him, in a mode of concern which honors him. Thus the relation of being to the dead must not be grasped as a being together with something at hand which *takes care of it.*

In such being-with with the dead, the deceased *himself* is no longer factically "there." However, being-with always means being-with-one-another in the same world. The deceased has abandoned our "*world*" and left it behind. It is *in terms of this world* that those remaining can still *be with him.*

The more appropriately the no-longer-being-there of the deceased is grasped phenomenally, the more clearly it can be seen that in such being-with with the dead, the real having-come-to-an-end of the deceased is precisely *not* experienced. Death does reveal itself as a loss, but as a loss experienced by those remaining behind. However, in suffering the loss, the loss of being as such which the dying person "suffers" does not become accessible. We do not experience the dying of others in a genuine sense; we are at best always just "there" too.

And even if it were possible and feasible to clarify "psychologically" the dying of others, this would by no means let us grasp the way of being we have in mind, namely, coming-to-an-end. We are asking about the ontological meaning of the dying of the person who dies, as a potentiality-of-being of *his being,* and not about the way of being-with and the still-being-there of the deceased with those left behind. If death as experienced in others is to be the theme of our analysis of the end of Da-sein and its totality, this cannot give us what it presumes to give, either ontically or ontologically.

After all, taking the dying of others as a substitute theme for the ontological analysis of the finished character of Da-sein and its totality rests on an assumption that demonstrably fails altogether to recognize the kind of being of Da-sein. That is what one presupposes when one is of the opinion that any Da-sein could arbitrarily be replaced by another, so that what cannot be experienced in one's own Da-sein is accessible in another Da-sein. But is this assumption really so groundless?

Indubitably, the fact that one Da-sein *can be represented* by another belongs to the possibilities-of-being of being-with-one-another in the world. In the everydayness of taking care of things, constant use of such representability is made in many ways. Any going to . . . , any fetching of . . . , is representable in the scope of the "surrounding world" initially taken care of. The broad multiplicity of ways of being-in-the-world in which one person can be represented by another extends not only to the used-up modes of public being with one another, but concerns as well the possibilities of taking care of things limited to definite circles, tailored to professions, social classes, and stages of life. But the very meaning of such representation is such that it is always a representation "in" and "together with" something, that is, in taking care of something. Everyday Da-sein understands itself initially and for the most part, however, in terms of *what* it is accustomed to take care of. "One *is*" what one does. With regard to this being (the everyday being-absorbed-with-one-another in the "world" taken care of), representability is not only possible in general, but is even constitutive for being-with-one-another. *Here* one Da-sein can and must, within certain limits, "*be*" another Da-sein.

However, this possibility of representation gets completely stranded when it is a matter of representing the possibility of being that constitutes the coming-to-an-end of Da-sein and gives it its totality as such. *No one can take the other's dying away from him.* Someone can go "to his death for an other." However, that always means to sacrifice oneself for the other "*in a definite matter.*" Such dying for . . . can never, however, mean that the other has thus had his death in the least taken away. Every Da-sein must itself actually take dying upon itself. Insofar as it "is," death is always essentially my own. And it indeed signifies a peculiar possibility of being in which it is absolutely a matter of the being of my own Da-sein. In dying, it becomes evident that death* is ontologically constituted by mineness and existence. Dying is not an event, but a phenomenon to be understood existentially in an eminent sense still to be delineated more closely.

But if "ending," as dying, constitutes the totality of Da-sein, the being of the totality itself must be conceived as an existential phenomenon of my own Da-sein. In "ending," and in the totality thus constituted of Da-sein, there is essentially no representation. The way out suggested fails to recognize this existential fact when it proposes the dying of others as a substitute theme for the analysis of totality.

Thus the attempt to make the totality of Da-sein phenomenally accessible in an appropriate way gets stranded again. But the result of these considerations is not just negative. They were oriented toward the phenomena, even if rather crudely. We have indicated that death is an existential phenomenon. Our inquiry is thus forced into a purely existential orientation toward my own Da-sein. For the analysis of death as dying, there remains only the possibility of bringing this phenomenon either to a purely *existential* concept or, on the other hand, of renouncing any ontological understanding of it.

Furthermore, it was evident in our characterization of the transition from Da-sein to no-longer-being-there as no-longer-being-in-the-world that the going-out-of-the-world of Da-sein in the sense of dying must be distinguished from a going-out-of-the-world of what is only alive. The ending of what is only alive we formulate terminologically as perishing. The distinction can become visible only by distinguishing the ending characteristic of Da-sein from the ending of a living thing. Dying can, of course, also be conceived physiologically and biologically. But the medical concept of "*exitus*" does not coincide with that of perishing.

From the previous discussion of the ontological possibility of

---

* The relation of Da-sein to death; death itself—its arrival—entrance, dying.

conceiving of death, it becomes clear at the same time that sub-structures of beings of a different kind of being (objective presence or life) thrust themselves to the fore unnoticeably and threaten to confuse the interpretation of the phenomenon, even the *first* appropriate *presentation* of it. We can cope with this problem only by looking for an ontologically adequate way of defining constitutive phenomena for our further analysis, such as end and totality.

48. WHAT IS OUTSTANDING, END, AND TOTALITY

Our ontological characterization of end and totality can only be preliminary in the scope of this inquiry. To perform this task adequately we must not only set forth the *formal* structure of end in general and totality in general. At the same time, we must disentangle the structural variations possible for them in different realms, that is, deformalized variations which are related to definite beings with content and structurally determined in terms of their being. This task again presupposes a sufficiently unequivocal and positive interpretation of the kinds of being that require a regional separation of the whole of beings. The understanding of these ways of being, however, requires a clarified idea of being in general. The task of adequately carrying out the ontological analysis of end and totality gets stranded not only because the theme is so far-reaching, but because there is a difficulty in principle: in order to master this task, we must presuppose that precisely what we are seeking in this inquiry (the meaning of being in general) is something that we have found already and with which we are quite familiar.

In the following considerations, the "variations" in which we are chiefly interested are those of end and totality; these are ontological determinations of Da-sein which are to lead to a primordial interpretation of this being. With constant reference to the existential constitution of Da-sein already developed, we must initially try to decide how ontologically inappropriate to Da-sein are the concepts of end and totality initially forcing

themselves upon us, no matter how indefinite they are categori-
cally. The rejection of such concepts must be further developed
to a positive *directive* to their specific realms. Thus our understanding of end and totality in their variant forms as existentials
will be strengthened, and this guarantees the possibility of an
ontological interpretation of death.

But if the analysis of the end and totality of Da-sein takes an
orientation of such broad scope, this nevertheless cannot mean
that the existential concepts of end and totality are to be gained
by way of a deduction. On the contrary, it is a matter of taking
the existential meaning of the coming-to-an-end of Da-sein
from Da-sein itself and of showing how this "ending" can constitute a *being whole* of that being that *exists.*

What has been discussed up to now about death can be formulated in three theses:

1. As long as Da-sein is, a not-yet belongs to it, which it will be—what
   is constantly outstanding.
2. The coming-to-its-end of what is not-yet-at-an-end (in which what
   is outstanding is liquidated with regard to its being) has the character of no-longer-being-there.
3. Coming-to-an-end implies a mode of being in which the actual Da-
   sein absolutely cannot be represented by someone else.

In Da-sein there is inevitably a constant "fragmentariness"
which finds its end in death. But may we interpret the phenomenal fact that this not-yet "belongs" to Da-sein as long as it is to
mean that it is something *outstanding?* With regard to what kind
of beings do we speak of something outstanding? The expression means indeed what "belongs" to a being, but is still lacking.
Outstanding, as lacking, is based on a belongingness. For example, the remainder of a debt still to be paid is outstanding. What
is outstanding is not yet available. Liquidating the "debt" as paying off what is outstanding means that the money "comes in,"
that is, the remainder is paid in sequence, whereby the not-yet is,
so to speak, filled out until the sum owed is "all together." Thus,

to be outstanding means that what belongs together is not yet together. Ontologically, this implies the unhandiness of portions to be brought in which have the same kind of being of those already at hand. The latter in their turn do not have their kind of being modified by having the remainder come in. The existing untogetherness is liquidated by a cumulative placing together. *The being for which something is outstanding has the kind of being of something at hand.* We characterize the together, or the untogether based on it, as a *sum.*

The untogether belonging to such a mode of the together, lacking as something outstanding, can, however, by no means ontologically define the not-yet that belongs to Da-sein as its possible death. Da-sein does not have the kind of being of a thing at hand in the world at all. The together of the being that Da-sein is "in running its course" until it has completed "its course" is not constituted by a "progressive" piecing-on of beings that, somehow and somewhere, are already at hand in their own right. That Da-sein should *be* together only when its not-yet has been filled out is so far from being the case that precisely then it no longer is. Da-sein always already exists in such a way that its not-yet *belongs* to it. But are there not beings which are as they are and to which a not-yet can belong, without these beings necessarily having the kind of being of Da-sein?

For example, one can say that the last quarter of the moon is outstanding until it is full. The not-yet decreases with the disappearance of the shadow covering it. And yet the moon is, after all, always already objectively present as a whole. Apart from the fact that the moon is never *wholly* to be grasped even when it is full, the not-yet by no means signifies a not-yet-*being*-together of parts belonging together, but rather pertains only to the way we *grasp* it perceptually. The not-yet that belongs to Da-sein, however, not only remains preliminarily and at times inaccessible to one's own or to others' experience, it "is" not yet "real" at all. The problem does not pertain to the *grasp* of the not-yet of the character of Da-sein, but rather its possible *being* or *nonbeing.* Da-sein, as itself, has to *become,* that is, *be,* what it is not yet. In order to thus be able, by comparison, to define the *being of the not-yet of the character of Da-sein,* we must reflect on beings to whose kind of being becoming belongs.

For example, the unripe fruit moves toward its ripeness. In ripening, what it not yet is is by no means pieced together as something not-yet-objectively-present. The fruit ripens itself, and this ripening characterizes its being as fruit. Nothing we can think of which could be added on could remove the unripeness of the fruit, if this being did not ripen *of itself.* The not-yet of un-ripeness does not mean something other which is outstanding that could be objectively present in and with it in a way indiffer-ent to the fruit. It means the fruit itself in its specific kind of being. The sum that is not yet complete is, as something at hand, "indifferent" to the unhandy remainder that is lacking. Strictly speaking, it can be neither indifferent to it nor not indifferent. The ripening fruit, however, is not only not indifferent to its un-ripeness as an other to itself, but, ripening, it *is* the unripeness. The not-yet is already included in its own being, by no means as an arbitrary determination, but as a constituent. Correspond-ingly, Da-sein, too, *is always already its not-yet*[1] as long as it is.

What constitutes the "unwholeness" in Da-sein, the constant being-ahead-of-itself, is neither a summative together which is outstanding, nor even a not-yet-having-become-accessible, but rather a not-yet that any Da-sein always has to be, given the being that it is. Still, the comparison with the unripeness of the fruit does show essential differences despite some similarities. To reflect on these differences means that we shall recognize how indefinite our previous discussion of end and ending has hitherto been.

Ripening is the specific being of the fruit. It is also a kind of being of the not-yet (unripeness), and is formally analogous to

1. The difference between whole and sum, *holon* and *pan, totum* and *compositum* is fa-miliar to us ever since Plato and Aristotle. Of course, the systematics of the categorial transformation already contained in this division is not yet *recognized* and conceptualized. For the beginning of a detailed analysis, cf. E. Husserl, *Logische Untersuchungen,* vol. 2, third investigation: "On the Doctrine of Wholes and Parts."

Da-sein in that the latter, as well as the former, always already *is* its not-yet in a sense yet to be defined. But even then, this does not mean that ripeness as "end" and death as "end" coincide with regard to their ontological structure as ends. With ripeness, the fruit *fulfills* itself. But is the death at which Da-sein arrives a fulfillment in this sense? It is true that Da-sein has "completed its course" with its death. Has it thus necessarily exhausted its specific possibilities? Rather, are these not precisely what gets taken from it? Even "unfulfilled" Da-sein ends. On the other hand, Da-sein so little needs to ripen only with its death that it can already have gone beyond that ripeness before the end. For the most part, it ends in unfulfillment, or else disintegrated and used up.

Ending does not necessarily mean fulfilling oneself. It thus becomes more urgent to ask *in what sense, if any, death must be grasped as the ending of Da-sein.*

Initially, ending means *stopping,* and it means this in senses that are ontologically different. The rain stops. It is no longer objectively present. The road stops. This ending does not cause the road to disappear, but this stopping rather determines the road as this objectively present one. Hence ending, as stopping, can mean either to change into the absence of objective presence or, however, to be objectively present only when the end comes. The latter kind of ending can again be determinative for an *unfinished* thing objectively present, as a road under construction breaks off, or it may rather constitute the "finishedness" of something objectively present—the painting is finished with the last stroke of the brush.

But ending as getting finished does not include fulfillment. On the other hand, whatever has got to be fulfilled must reach its possible finishedness. Fulfillment is the mode of "finishedness," and is founded upon it. Finishedness is itself possible only as a determination of something objectively present or at hand.

Even ending in the sense of disappearing can still be modified according to the kind of being of the being. The rain is at an end, that is, it has disappeared. The bread is at an end, that is, used up, no longer available as something at hand.

None of these modes of ending are able to characterize death appropriately as the end of Da-sein. If dying were understood as being-at-an-end in the sense of an ending of the kind discussed, Da-sein would be posited as something objectively present or at hand. In death, Da-sein is neither fulfilled nor does it simply disappear; it has not become finished or completely available as something at hand.

Rather, just as Da-sein constantly already *is* its not-yet as long as it is, it also always already *is* its end. The ending that we have in view when we speak of death, does not signify a being-at-an-end of Da-sein, but* rather a *being toward the end* of this being. Death is a way to be that Da-sein takes over as soon as it is. "As soon as a human being is born, he is old enough to die right away."[2]

Ending, as being toward the end, must be clarified ontologically in terms of the kind of being of Da-sein. And supposedly the possibility of an existing being of the not-yet that lies "before" the "end" will become intelligible only if the character of ending has been determined existentially. The existential clarification of being toward the end first provides the adequate basis for defining the possible meaning of our discussion of a totality of Da-sein, if indeed this totality is to be constituted by death as an "end."

The attempt to reach an understanding of the totality of Da-sein by starting with a clarification of the not-yet and proceeding to a characterization of ending has not yet attained its goal. It showed only *negatively* that the not-yet which Da-sein always *is* resists an interpretation as something outstanding. The end *toward* which Da-sein *is,* as existing, remains inappropriately defined by being-at-an-end. At the same time, however, our reflec-

---

* death as dying.

2. *Der Ackermann aus Böhmen,* ed. A. Bernt and K. Burdach, in *Vom Mittelalter zur Reformation: Forschungen zur Geschichte der deutschen Bildung,* ed. K. Burdach, vol. 3, part 2 (1917), chap. 20, p. 46.

tions should make it clear that their course must be reversed. A positive characterization of the phenomena in question (not-yet-being, ending, totality) can be successful only when it is unequivocally oriented toward the constitution of being of Da-sein. This unequivocal character, however, is protected in a negative way from being sidetracked when we have an insight into the regional belonging together of the structures of end and totality which belong to Da-sein ontologically.

The positive, existential, and ontological interpretation of death and its character of end are to be developed following the guideline of the fundamental constitution of Da-sein, attained up to now—the phenomenon of care.

49. HOW THE EXISTENTIAL ANALYSIS OF DEATH DIFFERS FROM OTHER POSSIBLE INTERPRETATIONS OF THIS PHENOMENON

The unequivocal character of the ontological interpretation* of death should be made more secure by explicitly bringing to mind what this interpretation can *not* ask about and where it would be useless to expect information and instructions.

In the broadest sense, death is a phenomenon of life.† Life must be understood as a kind of being to which belongs a being-in-the-world. It can only be defined in a privative orientation to Da-sein. Da-sein, too, can be considered as pure life. For the biological and physiological line of questioning, it then moves into the sphere of being which we know as the world of animals and plants. In this field, dates and statistics about the life-span of plants, animals, and human beings can be ontically ascertained. Connections between the life-span, reproduction, and growth can be known. The "kinds" of death, the causes, "arrangements," and ways of its occurrence can be investigated.[3]

---

* That is, the interpretation of fundamental ontology.

† If we are talking about human life, otherwise not—"world."

3. Cf. E. Korschelt's comprehensive portrayal, *Lebensdauer, Altern und Tod*, 3rd edition, 1924, especially the rich bibliography, pp. 414ff.

An ontological problematic underlies this biological and ontic investigation of death. We must still ask how the essence of death is defined in terms of the essence of life. The ontic inquiry into death has always already decided about this. More or less clarified preconceptions of life and death are operative in it. These preliminary concepts need to be sketched out in the ontology of Da-sein. Within the ontology of Da-sein, which has priority over an ontology of life, the existential analytic of death is subordinate to the fundamental constitution of Da-sein. We called the ending of what is alive *perishing*. Da-sein, too, "has" its physiological death of the kind appropriate to anything that lives and has it not ontically in isolation, but as also determined by its primordial kind of being. Da-sein, too, can end without authentically dying, though on the other hand, qua Da-sein, it does not simply perish. We call this intermediate phenomenon its *demise*. Let the term *dying* stand for the *way of being* in which Da-sein *is toward* its death. Thus we can say that Da-sein never perishes. Da-sein can only demise as long as it dies. The medical and biological inquiry into demising can attain results which can also become significant ontologically if the fundamental orientation is ensured for an existential interpretation of death. Or must sickness and death in general—even from a medical point of view—be conceived primarily as existential phenomena?

The existential interpretation of death is prior to any biology and ontology of life. But it also is the foundation for any biographico-historical or ethnologico-psychological inquiry into death. A "typology" of "dying" characterizing the states and ways in which a demise is "experienced," already presupposes the concept of death. Moreover, a psychology of "dying" rather gives information about the "life" of the "dying person" than about dying itself. That is only a reflection of the fact that when Da-sein dies—and even when it dies authentically—it does not have to do so with an experience of its factical demise, or in such an experience. Similarly, the interpretations of death in primitive peoples, of their behavior toward death in magic and cult, throw light primarily on the understanding of *Da-sein*; but the interpretation of this understanding already requires an existential analytic and a corresponding concept of death.

The ontological analysis of being-toward-the-end, on the other hand, does not anticipate any existentiell stance toward death. If death is defined as the "end" of Da-sein, that is, of being-in-the-world, no ontic decision has been made as to whether "after death" another being is still possible, either higher or lower, whether Da-sein "lives on" or even, "outliving itself," is "immortal." Nor is anything decided ontically about the "otherworldly" and its possibility any more than about the "this-worldly"; as if norms and rules for behavior toward death should be proposed for "edification." But our analysis of death remains purely "this-worldly" in that it interprets the phenomenon solely with respect to the question of how it *enters into* actual Da-sein as its possibility-of-being. We cannot even *ask* with any methodological assurance about what "*is after death*" until death is understood in its full ontological essence. Whether such a question presents a possible *theoretical* question at all is not to be decided here. The this-worldly, ontological interpretation of death comes before any ontic, other-worldly speculation.

Finally, an existential analysis of death lies outside the scope of what might be discussed under the rubric of a "metaphysics of death." The questions of how and when death "came into the world," what "meaning" it can and should have as an evil and suffering in the whole of beings—these are questions that necessarily presuppose an understanding not only of the character of being of death, but the ontology of the whole of beings as a whole and the ontological clarification of evil and negativity in particular.

The existential analysis is methodically prior to the questions of a biology, psychology theodicy, and theology of death. Taken ontically, the results of the analysis show the peculiar *formality* and emptiness of any ontological characterization. However, that must not make us blind to the rich and complex structure of the phenomenon. Since Da-sein never becomes accessible at all as something objectively present, because being possible belongs in its own way to its kind of being, even less may we expect to simply read off the ontological structure of death, if indeed death is an eminent possibility of Da-sein.

On the other hand, our analysis cannot be supported by an idea of death that has been devised arbitrarily and at random. We can restrain this arbitrariness only by giving beforehand an ontological characterization of the kind of being in which the "end" enters into the average everydayness of Da-sein. For this we need to envisage fully the structures of everydayness worked out earlier. The fact that existentiell possibilities of being toward death have their resonance in an existential analysis of death, is implied by the essence of any ontological inquiry. All the more explicitly, then, must an existentiell neutrality go together with the existential conceptual definition, especially with regard to death, where the character of possibility of Da-sein can be revealed most clearly of all. The existential problematic aims solely at developing the ontological structure of the being-*toward*-the-end of Da-sein.[4]

---

4. The anthropology developed in Christian theology—from Paul to Calvin's *meditatio futurae vitae*—has always already viewed death together with its interpretation of "life." Dilthey, whose true philosophical tendencies aimed at an ontology of "life," could not fail to recognize its connection with death. "And finally, the relation which most deeply and universally defines the feeling of our Da-sein—that of life toward death, for the limitation of our existence by death is always decisive for our understanding and our estimation of life." *Das Erlebnis und die Dichtung*, 5th edition, p. 230. Recently G. Simmel has also explicitly related the phenomenon of death to the definition of "life," however without a clear separation of the biological and ontic from the ontological and existential problematic. Cf. *Lebensanschauung: Vier metaphysische Kapitel*, 1918, pp. 99–153. For the present inquiry, compare *especially* K. Jaspers, *Psychologie der Weltanschauungen*, 3rd edition, 1925, pp. 299ff. and especially 259–70. Jaspers understands death by following the guidelines of the phenomenon of the "borderline situation" developed by him, whose fundamental significance lies beyond any typology of "attitudes" and "worldviews."

R. Unger took up Dilthey's suggestions in his work *Herder, Novalis und Kleist: Studien über die Entwicklung des Todesproblems im Denken und Dichten von Sturm und Drang Zur Romantik*, 1922. Unger offers a major reflection on Dilthey's questions in the lecture: *Literaturgeschichte als Problemgeschichte: Zur Frage geisteshistorischer Synthese, mit besonderer Beziehung auf W. Dilthey* (*Schriften der Königsberger Gelehrten Gesellschaft*, Geisteswiss. Klass I.1, 1924). Unger (pp. 17ff.) sees clearly the significance of phenomenological investigation for a more radical foundation of the "problems of life."

50. A PRELIMINARY SKETCH OF THE EXISTENTIAL
AND ONTOLOGICAL STRUCTURE OF DEATH

From our considerations of something outstanding, end, and totality there has resulted the necessity of interpreting the phenomenon of death as being-toward-the-end in terms of the
fundamental constitution of Da-sein. Only in this way can it become clear how a wholeness constituted by being-toward-the-
end is possible in Da-sein itself, in accordance with its structure
of being. We have seen that care is the fundamental constitution of Da-sein. The ontological significance of this expression
was expressed in the "definition": being-ahead-of-itself-already-
being-in (the world) as being-together-with beings encountered
(within the world). Thus the fundamental characteristics of
the being of Da-sein are expressed: in being-ahead-of-itself,
existence, in already-being-in . . . , facticity, in being-together-
with . . . , falling prey. Provided that death belongs to the being of
Da-sein in an eminent sense, it (or being-toward-the-end) must
be able to be defined in terms of these characteristics.

We must, in the first instance, make it clear in a preliminary
sketch how the existence, facticity, and falling prey of Da-sein
are revealed in the phenomenon of death.

The interpretation of the not-yet, and thus also of the most
extreme not-yet, of the end of Da-sein in the sense of something
outstanding was rejected as inappropriate. For it included the
ontological distortion of Da-sein as something objectively present. Being-at-an-end means existentially being-toward-the-end.
The most extreme not-yet has the character of something *to
which Da-sein relates*. The end is imminent for Da-sein. Death is
not something not yet objectively present, nor the last outstanding
element reduced to a minimum, but rather an *imminence*.

However, many things can be imminent for Da-sein as being-
in-the-world. The character of imminence is not in itself distinctive for death. On the contrary, this interpretation could
even make us suspect that death would have to be understood in
the sense of an imminent event to be encountered in the sur-

rounding world. For example, a thunderstorm can be imminent, remodeling a house, the arrival of a friend, accordingly, being which are objectively present, at hand or Da-sein-with. Imminent death does not have this kind of being.

But a journey, for example, can also be imminent for Da-sein, or a discussion with others, or a renouncing something which Da-sein itself can be—its own possibilities-of-being which are founded in being-with others.

Death is a possibility of being that Da-sein always has to take upon itself. With death, Da-sein stands before itself in its ownmost potentiality-of-being. In this possibility, Da-sein is concerned about its being-in-the-world absolutely. Its death is the possibility of no-longer-being-able-to-be-there. When Da-sein is imminent to itself as this possibility, it is *completely* thrown back upon its ownmost potentiality-of-being. Thus imminent to itself, all relations to other Da-sein are dissolved in it. This nonrelational ownmost possibility is at the same time the most extreme one. As a potentiality of being, Da-sein is unable to bypass the possibility of death. Death is the possibility of the absolute impossibility of Da-sein. Thus *death* reveals itself as the *ownmost nonrelational possibility not to be bypassed*. As such, it is *an eminent* imminence. Its existential possibility is grounded in the fact that Da-sein is essentially disclosed to itself, in the way of being-ahead-of-itself. This structural factor of care has its most primordial concretion in being-toward-death. Being-toward-the-end becomes phenomenally clearer as being toward the eminent possibility of Da-sein which we have characterized.

The ownmost nonrelational possibility not to be bypassed is not created by Da-sein subsequently and occasionally in the course of its being. Rather, when Da-sein exists, it is already *thrown* into this possibility. Initially and for the most part, Da-sein does not have any explicit or even theoretical knowledge of the fact that it is delivered over to its death, and that death thus belongs to being-in-the-world. Thrownness into death reveals itself to it more primordially and penetratingly in the attunement of *Angst*. *Angst* in the face of death is *Angst* "in the face of" the ownmost nonrelational potentiality-of-being not to be by-passed. What *Angst* is about is being-in-the-world itself. What *Angst* is about is the potentiality-of-being of Da-sein absolutely. *Angst* about death must not be confused with a fear of one's demise. It is not an arbitrary and chance "weak" mood of the individual, but, as a fundamental attunement of Da-sein, the disclosedness of the fact that Da-sein exists as thrown being-*toward*-its-end. Thus the existential concept of dying is clarified as thrown being toward the ownmost nonrelational potentiality-of-being not to be bypassed. Precision is gained by distinguishing this from pure disappearance, and also from merely perishing, and finally from the "experience" of a demise.

Being-toward-the-end does not first arise through some attitude which occasionally turns up, rather it belongs essentially to the thrownness of Da-sein which reveals itself in attunement (mood) in various ways. The factical "knowledge" or "lack of knowledge" prevalent in Da-sein as to its ownmost being-toward-the-end is only the expression of the existentiell possibility of maintaining itself in this being in different ways. The fact that factically many people initially and for the most part do not know about death must not be used to prove that being-toward-death does not "generally" belong to Da-sein, but only proves that Da-sein, fleeing *from* it, initially and for the most part covers over its ownmost being-toward-death. Da-sein dies factically as long as it exists, but initially and for the most part in the mode of *falling prey.* For factical existing is not only generally and without further differentiation a thrown potentiality-for-being-in-the-world, but it is always already absorbed in the "world" taken care of. In this entangled being together with . . . , the flight from uncanniness makes itself known, that is, the flight *from* its ownmost being-toward-death. Existence, facticity, falling prey characterize being-toward-the-end, and are accordingly constitutive for the existential concept of death. *With regard to its ontological possibility, dying is grounded in care.**

---

* But care presences out of the truth of being.

But if being toward death belongs primordially and essentially to the being of Da-sein, it must also be demonstrated in everydayness, although initially in an inauthentic way. And if being-toward-the-end is even supposed to offer the existential possibility for an existentiell wholeness of Da-sein, this would give the phenomenal confirmation for the thesis that care is the ontological term for the wholeness of the structural totality of Da-sein. However, for the complete phenomenal justification of this statement, a *preliminary sketch* of the connection between being-toward-death and care is not sufficient. Above all, we must be able to see this connection in the *concretion* nearest to Da-sein, its everydayness.

51. BEING-TOWARD-DEATH AND THE EVERYDAYNESS OF DA-SEIN

The exposition of everyday, average being-toward-death was oriented toward the structures of everydayness developed earlier. In being-toward-death, Da-sein is related *to itself* as an eminent potentiality-of-being. But the self of everydayness is the they which is constituted in public interpretedness which expresses itself in idle talk. Thus, idle talk must make manifest in what way everyday Da-sein interprets its being-toward-death. Understanding, which is also always attuned, that is, mooded, always forms the basis of this interpretation. Thus we must ask how the attuned understanding lying in the idle talk of the they has disclosed being-toward-death. How is the they related in an understanding way to its ownmost nonrelational possibility not-to-be-bypassed of Da-sein? What attunement discloses to the they that it has been delivered over to death, and in what way?

The publicness of everyday being-with-one-another "knows" death as a constantly occurring event, as a "case of death." Someone or another "dies," be it a neighbor or a stranger. People unknown to us "die" daily and hourly. "Death" is encountered as a familiar event occurring within the world. As such, it remains in the inconspicuousness characteristic of everyday encounters.

The they has also already secured an interpretation for this event. The "fleeting" talk about this which is either expressed or else mostly kept back says: One also dies at the end, but for now one is not involved.

The analysis of "one dies" reveals unambiguously the kind of being of everyday being toward death. In such talk, death is understood as an indeterminate something which first has to show up from somewhere, but which right now is *not yet objectively present* for oneself, and is thus no threat. "One dies" spreads the opinion that death, so to speak, strikes the they. The public interpretation of Da-sein says that "one dies" because in this way everybody can convince him/herself that in no case is it I myself, for this one is *no one*. "Dying" is levelled down to an event which does concern Da-sein, but which belongs to no one in particular. If idle talk is always ambiguous, so is this way of talking about death. Dying, which is essentially and irreplaceably mine, is distorted into a publicly occurring event which the they encounters. Characteristic talk speaks about death as a constantly occurring "case." It treats it as something always already "real," and veils its character of possibility and concomitantly the two factors belonging to it, that it is nonrelational and cannot-be-bypassed. With such ambiguity, Da-sein puts itself in the position of losing itself in the they with regard to an eminent potentiality-of-being that belongs to its own self. The they justifies and aggravates the *temptation* of covering over for itself its ownmost being-toward-death.

The evasion of death which covers over, dominates everydayness so stubbornly that, in being-with-one-another, the "neighbors" often try to convince the "dying person" that he will escape death and soon return again to the tranquillized everydayness of his world taken care of. This "concern" has the intention of thus "comforting" the "dying person." It wants to bring him back to Da-sein by helping him to veil completely his ownmost nonrelational possibility. Thus, the they makes sure of a *constant tranquillization about death*. But, basically, this tranquillization is not only for the "dying person," but just as much for "those who are comforting him." And even in the case of a demise, publicness is still not to be disturbed and made uneasy by the event in the carefreeness it has made sure of. Indeed, the dying of others is seen often as a social inconvenience, if not a downright tactlessness, from which publicness should be spared.[5]

But along with this tranquillization, which keeps Da-sein away from its death, the they at the same time justifies itself and makes itself respectable by silently ordering the way in which *one* is supposed to behave toward death in general. Even "thinking about death" is regarded publicly as cowardly fear, a sigh of insecurity on the part of Da-sein and a dark flight from the world. *The they does not permit the courage to have* Angst *about death.* The dominance of the public interpretedness of the they has already decided what attunement is to determine our stance toward death. In *Angst* about death, Da-sein is brought before itself as delivered over to its possibility not-to-be-bypassed. The they is careful to distort this *Angst* into the fear of a future event. Angst, made ambiguous as fear, is, moreover, taken as a weakness which no self-assured Da-sein is permitted to know. What is "proper" according to the silent decree of the they is the indifferent calm as to the "fact" that one dies. The cultivation of such a "superior" indifference *estranges* Da-sein from its ownmost nonrelational potentiality-of-being.

Temptation, tranquillization, and estrangement, however, characterize the kind of being of *falling prey*. Entangled, everyday being-toward-death is a constant *flight from death*. Being *toward* the end has the mode of *evading that end*—reinterpreting it, understanding it inauthentically, and veiling it. Factically one's own Da-sein is always already dying, that is, it is in a being-toward-its-end. And it conceals this fact from itself by reinterpreting death as a case of death occurring every day with others, a case which always assures us still more clearly that "one oneself" is still "alive." But in the entangled flight *from* death, the everydayness of Da-sein bears witness to the fact that the they

---

5. L. N. Tolstoi in his story "The Death of Ivan Ilyitch" has portrayed the phenomenon of the disruption and collapse of this "one dies."

itself is always already determined *as being toward death,* even when it is not explicitly engaged in "thinking about death." *Even in average everydayness, Da-sein is constantly concerned with its own-most nonrelational potentiality-of-being not-to-be-bypassed, if only in the mode of taking care of things in a mode of untroubled indifference* toward *the most extreme possibility of its existence.*

The exposition of everyday being-toward-death, however, gives us at the same time a directive to attempt to secure a complete existential concept of being-toward-the-end, by a more penetrating interpretation in which entangled being-toward-death is taken as an evasion *of death. That from which* one flees has been made visible in a phenomenally adequate way. We should now be able to project phenomenologically how evasive Da-sein itself understands its death.

52. EVERYDAY BEING-TOWARD-DEATH AND THE COMPLETE EXISTENTIAL CONCEPT OF DEATH

Being-toward-the-end was determined in a preliminary existential sketch as being toward one's ownmost nonrelational potentiality-of-being not-to-be-bypassed. Existing being toward this possibility, brings itself before the absolute impossibility of existence. Beyond this seemingly empty characteristic of being-toward-death, the concretion of this being revealed itself in the mode of everydayness. In accordance with the tendency toward falling prey essential to everydayness, being-toward-death proved to be an evasion of it, an evasion that covers over. Whereas previously our inquiry made the transition from the formal preliminary sketch of the ontological structure of death to the concrete analysis of everyday being-toward-the-end, we now wish to reverse the direction and attain the complete existential concept of death with a supplementary interpretation of everyday being-toward-the-end.

The explication of everyday being-toward-death stayed with the idle talk of the they: one also dies sometime, but for the time being not yet. Up to now we solely interpreted the "one dies" as such. In the "also sometime, but for the time being not yet," everydayness acknowledges something like a *certainty* of death. Nobody doubts that one dies. But this "not doubting" need not already imply that kind of being-certain that corresponds to the way death—in the sense of the eminent possibility characterized above—enters into Da-sein. Everydayness gets stuck in this ambiguous acknowledgment of the "certainty" of death—in order to weaken the certainty by covering dying over still more and alleviating its own thrownness into death.

By its very meaning, this evasive covering over of death can *not* be authentically "certain" of death, and yet it *is*. How does it stand with this "certainty of death"?

To be certain of a being means to *hold* it for true as something true. But truth means discoveredness of beings. All discoveredness, however, is ontologically based in the most primordial truth, in the disclosedness of Da-sein. As a being that is disclosed and disclosing, and one that discovers, Da-sein is essentially "in the truth." *But certainty is based in truth or belongs to it equiprimordially.* The expression "certainty," like the expression "truth," has a double meaning. Primordially, truth means the same as being-disclosive as a mode of behavior of Da-sein. From this comes the derivative meaning: disclosedness of beings. Accordingly, certainty is primordially tantamount to being-certain as a kind of being of Da-sein. However, in a derivative significance, any being of which Da-sein can be certain is also called "certain."

One mode of certainty is *conviction*. In conviction, Da-sein lets the testimony of the thing itself that has been discovered (the true thing itself) be the sole determinant for its being toward that thing understandingly. Holding-something-for-true is adequate as a way of keeping oneself in the truth, if it is based on the discovered beings themselves, and as a being toward the beings thus discovered, has become transparent to itself with regard to its appropriateness to them. Something like this is lacking in any arbitrary invention or in the mere "opinion" about a being.

The adequacy of holding-for-true is measured by the truth claim to which it belongs. This claim gets its justification from the kind of being of the beings to be disclosed, and from the direction of the disclosure. The kind of truth and, along with it, the certainty, changes with the various kinds of beings, and accords with the leading tendency and scope of the disclosure. Our present considerations are limited to an analysis of being-certain with regard to death; and this being-certain will, in the end, present us with an eminent *certainty of Da-sein*.

For the most part, everyday Da-sein covers over its ownmost nonrelational possibility of being not-to-be-bypassed. This factical tendency to cover over confirms our thesis that Da-sein, as factical, is in "untruth." Thus the certainty which belongs to such a covering over of being-toward-death must be an inappropriate way of holding-for-true, and not an uncertainty in the sense of doubting. Inappropriate certainty keeps that of which it is certain covered over. If "one" understands death as an event encountered in the surrounding world, the certainty related to this does not get at being-toward-the-end.

They say that it is certain that "death" comes. *They* say it and overlook the fact that, in order to be able to be certain of death, Da-sein itself must always be certain of its ownmost nonrelational potentiality-of-being not-to-be-bypassed. They say that death is certain, and thus entrench in Da-sein the illusion that it is *itself* certain of its own death. And what is the ground of everyday being-certain? Evidently it is not just mutual persuasion. Yet one experiences daily the "dying" of others. Death is an undeniable "fact of experience."

The way in which everyday being-toward-death understands the certainty thus grounded, betrays itself when it tries to "think" about death, even when it does so with critical foresight—that is to say, in an appropriate way. So far as one knows, all human beings "die." Death is probable to the highest degree for every human being, yet it is not "unconditionally" certain. Strictly speaking, "only" an *empirical* certainty may be attributed to death. Such certainty falls short of the highest certainty, the apodictical one, which we attain in certain areas of theoretical knowledge.

In this "critical" determination of the certainty of death and its imminence, what is manifested in the first instance is, once again, the failure to recognize the kind of being of Da-sein and the being-toward-death belonging to it, a failure characteristic of everydayness. *The fact that demise, as an event that occurs, is "only" empirically certain, in no way decides about the certainty of death.* Cases of death may be the factical occasion for the fact that Da-sein initially notices death at all. But, remaining within the empirical certainty which we characterized, Da-sein cannot become certain at all of death as it "is." Although in the publicness of the they Da-sein seemingly "talks" only of this "empirical" certainty of death, *basically* it does *not* keep exclusively and primarily to those cases of death that merely occur. *Evading its death,* everyday being-toward-the-end is indeed certain of death in another way than it itself would like to realize in purely theoretical considerations. For the most part, everydayness veils this from itself "in another way." It does not dare to become transparent to itself in this way. We have already characterized the everyday attunement that consists in an air of superiority with regard to the certain "fact" of death—a superiority that is "anxiously" concerned while seemingly free of *Angst.* In this attunement, everydayness acknowledges a "higher" certainty than the merely empirical one. One *knows* about the certainty of death, and yet "*is*" not really certain about it. The entangled everydayness of Da-sein knows about the certainty of death, and yet avoids *being*-certain. But in the light of what it evades, this evasion bears witness phenomenally to the fact that death must be grasped as the ownmost non-relational, *certain* possibility not-to-be-bypassed.

One says that death certainly comes, but not right away. With this "but . . . ," the they denies that death is certain. "Not right away" is not a purely negative statement, but a self-interpretation of the they with which it refers itself to what is initially accessible to Da-sein to take care of. Everydayness penetrates to the urgency of taking care of things, and divests itself of the fetters of a weary, "inactive thinking about death." Death is postponed to "sometime later," by relying on the so-called "general opinion." Thus the they covers over what is peculiar to the certainty of death, *that it is possible in every moment.* Together with the certainty of death goes the *indefiniteness* of its when. Everyday being-toward-death evades this indefiniteness by making it something definite. But this procedure cannot mean calculating when the demise is due to arrive. Da-sein rather flees from such definiteness. Everyday taking care of things makes definite for itself the indefiniteness of certain death by interposing before it those manageable urgencies and possibilities of the everyday matters nearest to us.

But covering over this indefiniteness also covers over certainty. Thus the ownmost character of the possibility of death gets covered over: a possibility that is certain, and yet indefinite, that is, possible at any moment.

Now that we have completed our interpretation of the everyday talk of the they about death and the way death enters Da-sein, we have been led to the characteristics of certainty and indefiniteness. The full existential and ontological concept of death can now be defined as follows: *As the end of Da-sein, death is the ownmost nonrelational, certain, and, as such, indefinite and not to be bypassed possibility of Da-sein.* As the end of Da-sein, *death is* in the being of this being-*toward*-its-end.

The delineation of the existential structure of being-toward-the-end helps us to develop a kind of being of Da-sein in which it can be *wholly as Da-sein.* The fact that even everyday Da-sein *is* always already *toward* its end, that is, is constantly coming to grips with its own death, even though "fleetingly," shows that this end, which concludes and defines being-whole, is not something which Da-sein ultimately arrives at only in its demise. In Da-sein, existing toward its death, its most extreme not-yet which everything else precedes is always already included. So if one has given an ontologically inappropriate interpretation of the not-yet of Da-sein as something outstanding, any formal inference from this to the lack of totality of Da-sein will be incorrect. *The phenomenon of the not-yet has been taken from the ahead-of-itself; no more than the structure of care in general, can it serve as a higher court that would rule against a possible, existent wholeness; indeed, this ahead-of-itself first makes possible such a being-toward-the-end.* The problem of the possible wholeness of the being which we ourselves actually are exists justifiably if care, as the fundamental constitution of Da-sein, "is connected" with death as the most extreme possibility of this being.

Yet it remains questionable whether this problem has been as yet adequately developed. Being-toward-death is grounded in care. As thrown being-in-the-world, Da-sein is always already delivered over to its death. Being toward its death, it dies factically and constantly as long as it has not reached its demise. That Da-sein dies factically means at the same time that it has always already decided in this or that way in its being-toward-death. Everyday, entangled evasion *of* death is an *inauthentic* being *toward* it. Inauthenticity has possible authenticity as its basis. Inauthenticity characterizes the kind of being in which Da-sein diverts itself and for the most part has always diverted itself, too, but it does not have to do this necessarily and constantly. Because Da-sein exists, it determines itself as the kind of being it is, and it does so always in terms of a possibility which it itself *is* and understands.

Can Da-sein *authentically understand* its ownmost, nonrelational, certain possibility not-to-be-bypassed that is, as such, indefinite? That is, can it maintain itself in an authentic being-toward-its-end? As long as this authentic being-toward-death has not been set forth and ontologically determined, there is something essentially lacking in our existential interpretation of being-toward-the-end.

Authentic being-toward-death signifies an existentiell possibility of Da-sein. This ontic potentiality-of-being must in its turn be ontologically possible. What are the existential conditions of this possibility? How are they themselves to become accessible?

53. EXISTENTIAL PROJECT OF AN AUTHENTIC BEING-TOWARD-DEATH

Factically, Da-sein maintains itself initially and for the most part in an inauthentic being-toward-death. How is the ontological possibility of an *authentic* being-toward-death to be characterized "objectively," if, in the end, Da-sein is never authentically related to its end, or if this authentic being must remain concealed from others in accordance with its meaning? Is not the project of the existential possibility of such a questionable existentiell potentiality-of-being a fantastical undertaking? What is needed for such a project to get beyond a merely poetizing, arbitrary construction? Does Da-sein itself provide directives for this project? Can the grounds for its phenomenal justification be taken from Da-sein itself? Can our analysis of Da-sein up to now give us any prescriptions for the ontological task we have now formulated, so that what we have before us can be kept on a secure path?

The existential concept of death has been established, and thus we have also established that to which an authentic being-toward-the-end should be able to relate itself. Furthermore, we have also characterized inauthentic being-toward-death and thus we have prescribed how authentic being-toward-death cannot be in a negative way. The existential structure of an authentic being-toward-death must let itself be projected with these positive and prohibitive instructions.

Da-sein is constituted by disclosedness, that is, by attuned understanding. *Authentic* being-toward-death can*not evade* its ownmost nonrelational possibility or *cover* it *over* in this flight and *reinterpret* it for the common sense of the they. The existential project of an authentic being-toward-death must thus set forth the factors of such a being which are constitutive for it as an understanding of death—in the sense of being toward this possibility without fleeing it or covering it over.

First of all, we must characterize being-toward-death as a being *toward a possibility*, toward an eminent possibility of Da-sein itself. Being toward a possibility, that is, toward something possible, can mean to be out for something possible, as in taking care of its actualization. In the field of things at hand and objectively present, we constantly encounter such possibilities: what is attainable, manageable, viable, and so forth. Being out for something possible and taking care of it has the tendency of *annihilating* the *possibility* of the possible by making it available. The actualization of useful things at hand in taking care of them (producing them, getting them ready, readjusting them, etc.), is, however, always merely relative, in that what has been actualized still has the character of being relevant. Even when actualized, as something actual it remains possible for . . . , it is characterized by an in-order-to. Our present analysis should simply make clear how being out for something and taking care of it, is related to the possible. It does so not in a thematic and theoretical reflection on the possible as possible, or even with regard to its possibility as such, but rather in such a way that it *circum*spectly looks *away* from the possible to what it is possible for.

Evidently being-toward-death, which is now in question, cannot have the character of being out for something and taking care of it with a view toward its actualization. For one thing, death as something possible is not a possible thing at hand or objectively present, but a possibility-of-being of *Da-sein*. Then, however, taking care of the actualization of what is thus possible would have to mean bringing about one's own demise. Thus Dasein would precisely deprive itself of the very ground for an existing being-toward-death.

Thus if being-toward-death is not meant as an "actualization" of death, neither can it mean to dwell near the end in its possibility. This kind of behavior would amount to "thinking about death," thinking about this possibility, how and when it might be actualized. Brooding over death does not completely take away from it its character of possibility. It is always brooded over as something coming, but we weaken it by calculating how to have it at our disposal. As something possible, death is supposed to show as little as possible of its possibility. On the contrary, if being-toward-death has to disclose understandingly the possibility which we have characterized as *such*, then in such being-toward-death this possibility must not be weakened, it must be understood *as possibility*, cultivated *as possibility*, and *endured as possibility* in our relation to it.

However, Da-sein relates to something possible in its possibility, by *expecting* it. Anyone who is intent on something possible, may encounter it unimpeded and undiminished in its "whether it comes or not, or whether it comes after all." But with this phenomenon of expecting has our analysis not reached the same kind of being toward the possible which we already characterized as being out for something and taking care of it? To expect something possible is always to understand and "have" it with regard to whether and when and how it will really be objectively present. Expecting is not only an occasional looking away from the possible to its possible actualization, but essentially a *waiting for that actualization*. Even in expecting, one leaps away from the possible and gets a footing in the real. It is for its reality that what is expected is expected. By the very nature of expecting, the possible is drawn into the real, arising from it and returning to it.

But being toward this possibility, as being-toward-death, should relate itself to that *death* so that it reveals itself, in this being and for it, *as possibility*. Terminologically, we shall formulate this being toward possibility as *anticipation of this possibility*. But does not this mode of behavior contain an approach to the possible, and does not its actualization emerge with its nearness? In this kind of coming near, however, one does not tend toward making something real available and taking care of it, but as one comes nearer understandingly, the possibility of the possible only becomes "greater." *The nearest nearness of being-toward-death as possibility is as far removed as possible from anything real.* The more clearly this possibility is understood, the more purely does understanding penetrate to it *as the possibility of the impossibility of existence in general.* As possibility, death gives Da-sein nothing to "be actualized" and nothing which it itself could *be* as something real. It is the possibility of the impossibility of every mode of behavior toward . . . , of every way of existing. In running ahead to this possibility, it becomes "greater and greater," that is, it reveals itself as something which knows no measure at all, no more or less, but means the possibility of the measureless impossibility of existence. Essentially, this possibility offers no support for becoming intent on something, for "spelling out" the real thing that is possible and so forgetting its possibility. As anticipation of possibility, being-toward-death first *makes* this possibility *possible* and sets it free as possibility.

Being-toward-death is the anticipation of a potentiality-of-being of *that* being whose kind of being is anticipation itself. In the anticipatory revealing of this potentiality-of-being, Da-sein discloses itself to itself with regard to its most extreme possibility. But to project oneself upon one's ownmost potentiality of being means to be able to understand oneself in the being of the being thus revealed: to exist. Anticipation shows itself as the possibility of understanding one's *ownmost* and extreme potentiality-of-being, that is, as the possibility of *authentic existence*. Its ontological constitution must be made visible by setting forth the concrete structure of anticipation of death. How is the phenomenal definition of this structure to be accomplished? Evidently by defining the characteristics of anticipatory disclosure which must belong to it so that it can become the pure understanding of the ownmost nonrelational possibility not-to-be-bypassed which is certain and, as such, indefinite. We must remember that understanding does not primarily mean staring at a meaning, but understanding oneself in the potentiality-of-being that reveals itself in the project.

Death is the *ownmost* possibility of Da-sein. Being toward it discloses to Da-sein its *ownmost* potentiality-of-being in which it is concerned about the being of Da-sein absolutely. Here the fact can become evident to Da-sein that in the eminent possibility of itself it is torn away from the they, that is, anticipation can always already have torn itself away from the they. The understanding of this "ability," however, first reveals its factical lostness in the everydayness of the they-self.

The ownmost possibility is *nonrelational.* Anticipation lets Da-sein understand that it has to take over solely from itself the potentiality-of-being in which it is concerned absolutely about its ownmost being. Death does not just "belong" in an undifferentiated way to one's own Da-sein, but it *lays claim* on it as something *individual.* The nonrelational character of death understood in anticipation individualizes Da-sein down to itself. This individualizing is a way in which the "there" is disclosed for existence. It reveals the fact that any being-together-with what is taken care of and any being-with the others fails when one's ownmost potentiality-of-being is at stake. Da-sein can *authentically* be *itself* only when it makes that possible of its own accord. But if taking care of things and being concerned fail us, this does not, however, mean at all that these modes of Da-sein have been cut off from its authentic being a self. As essential structures of the constitution of Da-sein they also belong to the condition of the possibility of existence in general. Da-sein is authentically itself only if it projects itself, *as* being-together with things taken care of and concernful being-with . . . , primarily upon its own-most potentiality-of-being, rather than upon the possibility of the they-self. Anticipation of its nonrelational possibility forces the being that anticipates into the possibility of taking over its ownmost being of its own accord.

The ownmost nonrelational possibility is *not to be bypassed.* Being toward this possibility lets Da-sein understand that the most extreme possibility of existence is imminent, that of giving itself up. But anticipation does not evade the impossibility of by-passing death, as does inauthentic being-toward-death, but *frees* itself *for* it. Becoming free *for* one's own death in anticipation frees one from one's lostness in chance possibilities urging themselves upon us, so that the factical possibilities lying before the possibility not-to-be-bypassed can first be authentically understood and chosen. Anticipation discloses to existence that its extreme inmost possibility lies in giving itself up and thus shatters all one's clinging to whatever existence one has reached. In anticipation, Da-sein guards itself against falling back behind itself, or behind the potentiality-for-being that it has understood. It guards against "becoming too old for its victories" (Nietzsche). Free for its ownmost possibilities, that are determined by the *end*, and so understood as *finite*, Da-sein prevents the danger that it may, by its own finite understanding of existence, fail to recognize that it is getting overtaken by the existence-possibilities of others, or that it may misinterpret these possibilities, thus divesting itself of its ownmost factical existence. As the non-relational possibility, death individualizes, but only, as the possibility not-to-be-bypassed, in order to make Da-sein as being-with understand the potentialities-of-being of the others. Because anticipation of the possibility not-to-be-bypassed also disclosed all the possibilities lying before it, this anticipation includes the possibility of taking the *whole* of Da-sein in advance in an existentiell way, that is, the possibility of existing as a *whole potentiality-of-being*.

The ownmost nonrelational possibility not-to-be-bypassed is *certain*. The mode *of being* certain of it is determined by the truth (disclosedness) corresponding to it. But Da-sein discloses the certain possibility of death as possibility only by making this possibility as its ownmost potentiality-of-being *possible* in anticipating it. The disclosedness of this possibility is grounded in a making possible that anticipates. Holding oneself in this truth, that is, being certain of what has been disclosed, lays claim all the more upon anticipation. The certainty of death cannot be calculated in terms of ascertaining cases of death encountered. This certainty by no means holds itself in the truth of something objectively present. When something objectively present has been discovered, it is encountered most purely by just looking at it and letting it be encountered in itself. Da-sein must first have lost itself in the factual circumstances (this can be one of care's own tasks and possibilities) if it is to gain the pure objectivity, that is, the indifference of apodictic evidence. If being-certain in relation to death does not have this character, that does not mean it is of a lower grade, but that *it does not belong at all to the order of degrees of evidence about things objectively present*.

Holding death for true (death *is* always just one's own) shows a different kind of certainty, and is more primordial than any certainty related to beings encountered in the world or to formal objects, for it is certain of being-in-the-world. As such, it claims not only *one* definite kind of behavior of Da-sein, but claims Da-sein in the complete authenticity of its existence. In anticipation, Da-sein can first make certain of its ownmost being in its totality not-to-be-bypassed. Thus, the evidence of the immediate givenness of experiences, of the ego or of consciousness, necessarily has to lag behind the certainty contained in anticipation. And yet this is not because the kind of apprehension belonging to it is not strict enough, but because at bottom it cannot hold *for true* (disclosed) something that it basically insists upon "having there" as true: namely, the Da-sein which I myself *am* and can be as potentiality-of-being authentically only in anticipation.

The ownmost nonrelational possibility not-to-be-bypassed is *indefinite* with regard to its certainty. How does anticipation disclose this character of the eminent possibility of Da-sein? How does understanding, anticipating, project itself upon a definite potentiality-of-being which is constantly possible in such a way that the when in which the absolute impossibility of existence becomes possible remains constantly indefinite? In anticipating the indefinite certainty of death, Da-sein opens itself to a constant *threat* arising from its own there. Being-toward-the-end must hold itself in this very threat; and can so little phase it out that it rather has to cultivate the indefiniteness of the certainty. How is the genuine disclosing of this constant threat existentially possible? All understanding is attuned. Mood brings Da-sein before the thrownness of its "that-it-is-there." *But the attunement which is able to hold open the constant and absolute threat to itself arising from the ownmost individualized being of Da-sein is* Angst. In *Angst,* Da-sein finds itself *faced* with the nothingness of the possible impossibility of its existence. *Angst* is anxious *about* the potentiality-of-being of the being thus determined, and thus discloses the most extreme possibility. Because the anticipation of Da-sein absolutely individualizes and lets it, in this individualizing of itself, become certain of the wholeness of its potentiality-of-being, the fundamental attunement of *Angst* belongs to this self-understanding of Da-sein in terms of its ground. Being-toward-death is essentially *Angst.** This is attested unmistakably, although "only" indirectly, by being-toward-death as we characterized it, when it distorts *Angst* into cowardly fear and, in overcoming that fear, only makes known its own cowardliness in the face of *Angst*.

What is characteristic about authentic, existentially projected being-toward-death can be summarized as follows: *Anticipation reveals to Da-sein its lostness in the they-self, and brings it face to face with the possibility to be itself, primarily unsupported by concern taking care of things, but to be itself in passionate anxious **freedom toward death** which is free of the illusions of the they, factical, and certain of itself.*

All relations, belonging to being-toward-death, to the complete content of the most extreme possibility of Da-sein, constitute an anticipation that they combine in revealing, unfolding, and holding fast, as that which makes this possibility possible. The existential project in which anticipation has been delimited, has made visible the *ontological* possibility of an existentiell, authentic being-toward-death. But with this, the possibility then appears of an authentic potentiality-for-being-a-whole—*but only as an ontological possibility*. Of course, our existential project of anticipation stayed with those structures of Da-sein gained earlier and let Da-sein itself, so to speak, project itself upon this possibility, without proffering to Da-sein the "content" of an ideal of existence forced upon it "from the outside." And yet this existentially "possible" being-toward-death remains, after all, existentielly a fantastical demand. The ontological possibility of an authentic potentiality-for-being-a-whole of Da-sein means nothing as long as the corresponding ontic potentiality-of-being has not been shown in terms of Da-sein

---

* I.e., but not only *Angst* and certainly not *Angst* as a mere emotion.

itself. Does Da-sein ever project itself factically into such a being-toward-death? Does it even *demand*, on the basis of its ownmost being, an authentic potentiality of being which is determined by anticipation?

Before answering these questions, we must investigate to what extent *at all* and in what way Da-sein *bears witness* to a possible *authenticity* of its existence from its ownmost potentiality-of-being, in such a way that it not only makes this known as *existentielly* possible, but *demands* it of itself.

The question hovering over us of an authentic wholeness of Da-sein and its existential constitution can be placed on a viable, phenomenal basis only if that question can hold fast to a possible authenticity of its being attested by Da-sein itself. If we succeed in discovering phenomenologically such an attestation and what is attested to in it, the problem arises again of *whether the anticipation of death projected up to now only in its **ontological** possibility has an essential connection with that authentic potentiality-of-being **attested** to.*

JEAN-PAUL SARTRE

Jean-Paul Sartre was born in Paris on June 21, 1905. His father, Jean-Baptiste, died in 1905 after contracting a fatal disease while serving as a naval officer in Indochina. Sartre's mother, Anne-Marie (Schweitzer) Sartre, was a cousin of the famed missionary Albert Schweitzer. After his father's death the young boy, affectionately called Paulou, and his mother moved in with her parents. His grandfather was a very stern and controlling individual. Anne-Marie remarried when Sartre was twelve, and the only child felt displaced. Later, the philosopher would claim that he was forever in a state of rebellion against both his grandfather and stepfather.

Sartre was a precocious young boy with an esurient appetite for books and a passion for writing. Short of stature (five foot three), sickly, and far from handsome, Sartre tried to develop a rough exterior to deal with the taunts of bullies, and a rich fantasy life to escape the pangs of a difficult childhood. Sartre enjoyed considerable success as a young student and in 1924 entered the famous Ecole Normale Supérieure, where he was classmates with Simone Weil, Maurice Merleau-Ponty, and Claude Lévi-Strauss. In 1928, he surprisingly failed his aggregate exam, but the next year he took the test again and finished first in the class. Simone de Beauvoir, who was to become his lifelong friend and lover, was second.

Sartre was drafted into the service in 1929. Two years later, after he fulfilled his military obligations, he took up teaching posts in philosophy at high schools in Le Havre, Lyon, and then Paris. While teaching in Le Havre, he began work on his novel *Nausea*. In 1933, Sartre received a grant to study at the French Institute in Berlin. His friend Raymond Aron introduced him to Edmund Husserl's phenomenology, and in 1937, Sartre published his important *Transcendence of the Ego*, in which he argues against the Husserlian idea that we can, as it were, examine consciousness in isolation from the world.

After his study tour in Germany, Sartre accepted a teaching position in Paris, but in 1939, when war broke out between France and Germany, he was once again in military uniform. Sartre, who did meteorological work in the service, was captured in June 1940. While a prisoner, he steeped himself in Kierkegaard and began writing his monumental *Being and Nothingness: An Essay on Phenomenological Ontology*, which was published in 1943.

After nine months in prison, Sartre was released and returned to Paris, where he became active in the Resistance as a journalist and playwright. During the war years, Sartre supported himself by teaching school and writing. While in Paris, he wrote the Resistance pieces *The Flies* and *No Exit*. Sartre convinced his friend Albert Camus to direct *No Exit*. Sartre did most of his writing in cafés, where he claimed that he could concentrate best. There he enjoyed the companionship of the likes of de Beauvoir, Camus, Jean Genet, and Pablo Picasso.

After the war ended, Sartre made his living as a writer and dramatist. While Sartre's plays were usually strident pieces of social criticism, he also had comedic talent, which is evident in his *The Respectful Prostitute* and *Nekrassov*. Like Camus but even more so, Sartre became world-famous following the war. During this highly productive period, Sartre wrote the philosophical trilogy *The Roads to Freedom* and a number of literary studies. He was also editor of the important French literary and political periodical *Les Temps Modernes*.

In 1946, Sartre published the creedal statement, "Existentialism is humanism." As Sartre's renown as an existentialist spread, he was becoming baptized as a Marxist. Over the years, he tried and ultimately failed to integrate the existentialist notion of freedom with the dialectical determinism of Marxism. There was, however, even more to the mix. By Sartre's own account, Sigmund Freud was one of the greatest influences in his life and in his self-understanding. In his autobiography, *The Words*, for example, Sartre confided that his constant writing and publishing may have been driven by the desire to please his grandfather, who both doted on him and tried to dissuade him from becoming a writer. Evidence of Freud's influence on his work is especially pronounced in Sartre's massive three-volume biography of Gustave Flaubert, *The Idiot of the Family*.

Though he never joined the French Communist Party, and after the Russian invasion of Czechoslovakia officially deconverted from Marxism, Sartre remained a staunch leftist. Both conscience and impulse combined to make Sartre politically hyperactive. He was always demonstrating, distributing leftist literature, and writing petitions. He vigorously supported the Algerians in their war for independence from France. In 1966, he joined Bertrand Russell in the War Crimes Commission investigating the United States' involvement in Vietnam. The conservatives accused Sartre of being one of the instigators of the student riots of 1968.

In 1964, Sartre was awarded the Nobel Prize for literature; however, he declined it, explaining that the prize had the unhealthy effect of transforming intellectuals into institutions. In the mid-sixties, existentialism was eclipsed by structuralism. While Sartre would remain the most famous intellectual in France, his work was no longer the rage. Sartre died from a tumor in his lungs on April 15, 1980. It has been reported that there were fifty thousand people at the philosopher's funeral procession.

To cram Sartre's existentialism into a nutshell: Sartre held that consciousness brings nothingness into being by questioning being. For a mundane example: When I go to the café and look for my friend and he is not there, his absence (nothingness) becomes a kind of positive presence. According to Sartre, consciousness is something that erupts spontaneously and threatens to overwhelm us with possibilities which are, in a sense, another face of the nothingness that Sartre claims haunts being. And so, the individual retreats into what Sartre terms "bad faith," that is, into pretending he is an object without freedom and possibility. Sartre, of course, works out these complicated themes in some of our selections from *Being and Nothingness,* but for the reader who would prefer what amounts to the same book in literary guise, I would recommend Sartre's early and best novel, *Nausea.*

EXISTENTIALISM

I should like on this occasion to defend existentialism against some charges which have been brought against it.

First, it has been charged with inviting people to remain in a kind of desperate quietism because, since no solutions are possible, we should have to consider action in this world as quite impossible. We should then end up in a philosophy of contemplation; and since contemplation is a luxury, we come in the end to a bourgeois philosophy. The communists in particular have made these charges.

On the other hand, we have been charged with dwelling on human degradation, with pointing up everywhere the sordid, shady, and slimy, and neglecting the gracious and beautiful, the bright side of human nature; for example, according to Mlle. Mercier, a Catholic critic, with forgetting the smile of the child. Both sides charge us with having ignored human solidarity, with considering man as an isolated being. The communists say that the main reason for this is that we take pure subjectivity, the *Cartesian I think,* as our starting point; in other words, the moment in which man becomes fully aware of what it means to him to be an isolated being; as a result, we are unable to return to a state of solidarity with the men who are not ourselves, a state which we can never reach in the *cogito.*

From the Christian standpoint, we are charged with denying the reality and seriousness of human undertakings, since, if we reject God's commandments and the eternal verities, there no longer remains anything but pure caprice, with everyone permitted to do as he pleases and incapable, from his own point of view, of condemning the points of view and acts of others.

I shall try today to answer these different charges. Many people are going to be surprised at what is said here about humanism. We shall try to see in what sense it is to be understood. In any case, what can be said from the very beginning is that by existentialism we mean a doctrine which makes human life possible and, in addition, declares that every truth and every action implies a human setting and a human subjectivity.

As is generally known, the basic charge against us is that we put the emphasis on the dark side of human life. Someone recently told me of a lady who, when she let slip a vulgar word in a moment of irritation, excused herself by saying, "I guess I'm becoming an existentialist." Consequently, existentialism is regarded as something ugly; that is why we are said to be naturalists; and if we are, it is rather surprising that in this day and age we cause so much more alarm and scandal than does naturalism, properly so called. The kind of person who can take in his stride such a novel as Zola's *The Earth* is disgusted as soon as he starts reading an existentialist novel; the kind of person who is resigned to the wisdom of the ages—which is pretty sad—finds us even sadder. Yet, what can be more disillusioning than saying "true charity begins at home" or "a scoundrel will always return evil for good"?

We know the commonplace remarks made when this subject

comes up, remarks which always add up to the same thing: we shouldn't struggle against the powers-that-be; we shouldn't resist authority; we shouldn't try to rise above our station; any action which doesn't conform to authority is romantic; any effort not based on past experience is doomed to failure; experience shows that man's bent is always toward trouble, that there must be a strong hand to hold him in check, if not, there will be anarchy. There are still people who go on mumbling these melancholy old saws, the people who say, "It's only human!" whenever a more or less repugnant act is pointed out to them, the people who glut themselves on *chansons réalistes;* these are the people who accuse existentialism of being too gloomy, and to such an extent that I wonder whether they are complaining about it, not for its pessimism, but much rather its optimism. Can it be that what really scares them in the doctrine I shall try to present here is that it leaves to man a possibility of choice? To answer this question, we must re-examine it on a strictly philosophical plane. What is meant by the term *existentialism?*

Most people who use the word would be rather embarrassed if they had to explain it, since, now that the word is all the rage, even the work of a musician or painter is being called existentialist. A gossip columnist in *Clartés* signs himself *The Existentialist,* so that by this time the word has been so stretched and has taken on so broad a meaning, that it no longer means anything at all. It seems that for want of an advance-guard doctrine analogous to surrealism, the kind of people who are eager for scandal and flurry turn to this philosophy which in other respects does not at all serve their purposes in this sphere.

Actually, it is the least scandalous, the most austere of doctrines. It is intended strictly for specialists and philosophers. Yet it can be defined easily. What complicates matters is that there are two kinds of existentialist; first, those who are Christian, among whom I would include Jaspers and Gabriel Marcel, both Catholic; and on the other hand the atheistic existentialists, among whom I class Heidegger, and then the French existentialists and myself. What they have in common is that they think that existence precedes essence, or, if you prefer, that subjectivity must be the starting point.

Just what does that mean? Let us consider some object that is manufactured, for example, a book or a paper-cutter: here is an object which has been made by an artisan whose inspiration came from a concept. He referred to the concept of what a paper-cutter is and likewise to a known method of production, which is part of the concept, something which is, by and large, a routine. Thus, the paper-cutter is at once an object produced in a certain way and, on the other hand, one having a specific use; and one can not postulate a man who produces a paper-cutter but does not know what it is used for. Therefore, let us say that, for the paper-cutter, essence—that is, the ensemble of both the production routines and the properties which enable it to be both produced and defined—precedes existence. Thus, the presence of the paper-cutter or book in front of me is determined. Therefore, we have here a technical view of the world whereby it can be said that production precedes existence.

When we conceive God as the Creator, He is generally thought of as a superior sort of artisan. Whatever doctrine we may be considering, whether one like that of Descartes or that of Leibnitz, we always grant that will more or less follows understanding or, at the very least, accompanies it, and that when God creates He knows exactly what He is creating. Thus, the concept of man in the mind of God is comparable to the concept of paper-cutter in the mind of the manufacturer, and, following certain techniques and a conception, God produces man, just as the artisan, following a definition and a technique, makes a paper-cutter. Thus, the individual man is the realization of a certain concept in the divine intelligence.

In the eighteenth century, the atheism of the *philosophes* discarded the idea of God, but not so much for the notion that essence precedes existence. To a certain extent, this idea is found everywhere; we find it in Diderot, in Voltaire, and even in Kant. Man has a human nature; this human nature, which is the concept of the human, is found in all men, which means that each man is a particular example of a universal concept, man. In Kant, the result of this universality is that the wild-man, the natural man, as well as the bourgeois, are circumscribed by the same definition and have the same basic qualities. Thus, here too the essence of man precedes the historical existence that we find in nature.

Atheistic existentialism, which I represent, is more coherent. It states that if God does not exist, there is at least one being in whom existence precedes essence, a being who exists before he can be defined by any concept, and that this being is man, or, as Heidegger says, human reality. What is meant here by saying that existence precedes essence? It means that, first of all, man exists, turns up, appears on the scene, and, only afterwards, defines himself. If man, as the existentialist conceives him, is indefinable, it is because at first he is nothing. Only afterward will he be something, and he himself will have made what he will be. Thus, there is no human nature, since there is no God to conceive it. Not only is man what he conceives himself to be, but he is also only what he wills himself to be after this thrust toward existence.

Man is nothing else but what he makes of himself. Such is the first principle of existentialism. It is also what is called subjectivity, the name we are labeled with when charges are brought against us. But what do we mean by this, if not that man has a greater dignity than a stone or table? For we mean that man first exists, that is, that man first of all is the being who hurls himself toward a future and who is conscious of imagining himself as being in the future. Man is at the start a plan which is aware of itself, rather than a patch of moss, a piece of garbage, or a cauliflower; nothing exists prior to this plan; there is nothing in heaven; man will be what he will have planned to be. Not what he will want to be. Because by the word "will" we generally mean a conscious decision, which is subsequent to what we have already made of ourselves. I may want to belong to a political party, write a book, get married; but all that is only a manifestation of an earlier, more spontaneous choice that is called "will." But if existence really does precede essence, man is responsible for what he is. Thus, existentialism's first move is to make every man aware of what he is and to make the full responsibility of his existence rest on him. And when we say that a man is responsible for himself, we do not only mean that he is responsible for his own individuality, but that he is responsible for all men.

The word subjectivism has two meanings, and our opponents play on the two. Subjectivism means, on the one hand, that an individual chooses and makes himself; and, on the other that it is impossible for man to transcend human subjectivity. The second of these is the essential meaning of existentialism. When we say that man chooses his own self, we mean that every one of us does likewise; but we also mean by that that in making this choice he also chooses all men. In fact, in creating the man that we want to be, there is not a single one of our acts which does not at the same time create an image of man as we think he ought to be. To choose to be this or that is to affirm at the same time the value of what we choose, because we can never choose evil. We always choose the good, and nothing can be good for us without being good for all.

If, on the other hand, existence precedes essence, and if we grant that we exist and fashion our image at one and the same time, the image is valid for everybody and for our whole age. Thus, our responsibility is much greater than we might have supposed, because it involves all mankind. If I am a workingman and choose to join a Christian trade-union rather than be a communist, and if by being a member I want to show that the best thing for man is resignation, that the kingdom of man is not of this world, I am not only involving my own case—I want to be resigned for everyone. As a result, my action has involved all humanity. To take a more individual matter, if I want to marry, to have children; even if this marriage depends solely on my own circumstances or passion or wish, I am involving all humanity in monogamy and not merely myself. Therefore, I am responsible for myself and for everyone else. I am creating a certain image of man of my own choosing. In choosing myself, I choose man.

This helps us understand what the actual content is of such rather grandiloquent words as anguish, forlornness, despair. As you will see, it's all quite simple.

First, what is meant by anguish? The existentialists say at once that man is anguish. What that means is this: the man who involves himself and who realizes that he is not only the person he chooses to be, but also a lawmaker who is, at the same time, choosing all mankind as well as himself, can not help escape the feeling of his total and deep responsibility. Of course, there are many people who are not anxious; but we claim that they are hiding their anxiety, that they are fleeing from it. Certainly, many people believe that when they do something, they themselves are the only ones involved, and when someone says to them, "What if everyone acted that way?" they shrug their shoulders and answer, "Everyone doesn't act that way." But really, one should always ask himself, "What would happen if everybody looked at things that way?" There is no escaping this disturbing thought except by a kind of double-dealing. A man who lies and makes excuses for himself by saying "not everybody does that," is someone with an uneasy conscience, because the act of lying implies that a universal value is conferred upon the lie.

Anguish is evident even when it conceals itself. This is the anguish that Kierkegaard called the anguish of Abraham. You know the story: an angel has ordered Abraham to sacrifice his son; if it really were an angel who has come and said, "You are Abraham, you shall sacrifice your son," everything would be all right. But everyone might first wonder, "Is it really an angel, and am I really Abraham? What proof do I have?"

There was a madwoman who had hallucinations; someone used to speak to her on the telephone and give her orders. Her doctor asked her, "Who is it who talks to you?" She answered, "He says it's God." What proof did she really have that it was God? If an angel comes to me, what proof is there that it's an angel? And if I hear voices, what proof is there that they come from heaven and not from hell, or from the subconscious, or a pathological condition? What proves that they are addressed to me? What proof is there that I have been appointed to impose my choice and my conception of man on humanity? I'll never find any proof or sign to convince me of that. If a voice addresses me, it is always for me to decide that this is the angel's voice; if I consider that such an act is a good one, it is I who will choose to say that it is good rather than bad.

Now, I'm not being singled out as an Abraham, and yet at every moment I'm obliged to perform exemplary acts. For every man, everything happens as if all mankind had its eyes fixed on him and were guiding itself by what he does. And every man ought to say to himself, "Am I really the kind of man who has the right to act in such a way that humanity might guide itself by my actions?" And if he does not say that to himself, he is masking his anguish.

There is no question here of the kind of anguish which would lead to quietism, to inaction. It is a matter of a simple sort of anguish that anybody who has had responsibilities is familiar with. For example, when a military officer takes the responsibility for an attack and sends a certain number of men to death, he chooses to do so, and in the main he alone makes the choice. Doubtless, orders come from above, but they are too broad; he interprets them, and on this interpretation depend the lives of ten or fourteen or twenty men. In making a decision he can not help having a certain anguish. All leaders know this anguish. That doesn't keep them from acting; on the contrary, it is the very condition of their action. For it implies that they envisage a number of possibilities, and when they choose one, they realize that it has value only because it is chosen. We shall see that this kind of anguish, which is the kind that existentialism describes, is explained, in addition, by a direct responsibility to the other men whom it involves. It is not a curtain separating us from action, but is part of action itself.

When we speak of forlornness, a term Heidegger was fond of,

we mean only that God does not exist and that we have to face all the consequences of this. The existentialist is strongly opposed to a certain kind of secular ethics which would like to abolish God with the least possible expense. About 1880, some French teachers tried to set up a secular ethics which went something like this: God is a useless and costly hypothesis; we are discarding it; but, meanwhile, in order for there to be an ethics, a society, a civilization, it is essential that certain values be taken seriously and that they be considered as having an *a priori* existence. It must be obligatory, *a priori*, to be honest, not to lie, not to beat your wife, to have children, etc., etc. So we're going to try a little device which will make it possible to show that values exist all the same, inscribed in a heaven of ideas, though otherwise God does not exist. In other words—and this, I believe, is the tendency of everything called reformism in France—nothing will be changed if God does not exist. We shall find ourselves with the same norms of honesty, progress, and humanism, and we shall have made of God an outdated hypothesis which will peacefully die off by itself.

The existentialist, on the contrary, thinks it very distressing that God does not exist, because all possibility of finding values in a heaven of ideas disappears along with Him; there can no longer be an *a priori* Good, since there is no infinite and perfect consciousness to think it. Nowhere is it written that the Good exists, that we must be honest, that we must not lie; because the fact is we are on a plane where there are only men. Dostoievsky said, "If God didn't exist, everything would be possible." That is the very starting point of existentialism. Indeed, everything is permissible if God does not exist, and as a result man is forlorn, because neither within him nor without does he find anything to cling to. He can't start making excuses for himself.

If existence really does precede essence, there is no explaining things away by reference to a fixed and given human nature. In other words, there is no determinism, man is free, man is freedom. On the other hand, if God does not exist, we find no values or commands to turn to which legitimize our conduct. So, in the bright realm of values, we have no excuse behind us, nor justification before us. We are alone, with no excuses.

That is the idea I shall try to convey when I say that man is condemned to be free. Condemned, because he did not create himself, yet, in other respects is free; because, once thrown into the world, he is responsible for everything he does. The existentialist does not believe in the power of passion. He will never agree that a sweeping passion is a ravaging torrent which fatally leads a man to certain acts and is therefore an excuse. He thinks that man is responsible for his passion.

The existentialist does not think that man is going to help himself by finding in the world some omen by which to orient himself. Because he thinks that man will interpret the omen to suit himself. Therefore, he thinks that man, with no support and no aid, is condemned every moment to invent man. Ponge, in a very fine article, has said, "Man is the future of man." That's exactly it. But if it is taken to mean that this future is recorded in heaven, that God sees it, then it is false, because it would really no longer be a future. If it is taken to mean that, whatever a man may be, there is a future to be forged, a virgin future before him, then this remark is sound. But then we are forlorn.

To give you an example which will enable you to understand forlornness better, I shall cite the case of one of my students who came to see me under the following circumstances: his father was on bad terms with his mother, and, moreover, was inclined to be a collaborationist; his older brother had been killed in the German offensive of 1940, and the young man, with somewhat immature but generous feelings, wanted to avenge him. His mother lived alone with him, very much upset by the half-treason of her husband and the death of her older son; the boy was her only consolation.

The boy was faced with the choice of leaving for England and joining the Free French Forces—that is, leaving his mother behind—or remaining with his mother and helping her to carry on. He was fully aware that the woman lived only for him and that his going-off—and perhaps his death—would plunge her into despair. He was also aware that every act that he did for his mother's sake was a sure thing, in the sense that it was helping her to carry on, whereas every effort he made toward going off and fighting was an uncertain move which might run aground and prove completely useless; for example, on his way to England he might, while passing through Spain, be detained indefinitely in a Spanish camp; he might reach England or Algiers and be stuck in an office at a desk job. As a result, he was faced with two very different kinds of action: one, concrete, immediate, but concerning only one individual; the other concerned an incomparably vaster group, a national collectivity, but for that very reason was dubious, and might be interrupted en route. And, at the same time, he was wavering between two kinds of ethics. On the one hand, an ethics of sympathy, of personal devotion; on the other, a broader ethics, but one whose efficacy was more dubious. He had to choose between the two.

Who could help him choose? Christian doctrine? No. Christian doctrine says, "Be charitable, love your neighbor, take the more rugged path, etc., etc." But which is the more rugged path? Whom should he love as a brother? The fighting man or his mother? Which does the greater good, the vague act of fighting in a group, or the concrete one of helping a particular human being to go on living? Who can decide *a priori*? Nobody. No book of ethics can tell him. The Kantian ethics says, "Never treat any person as a means, but as an end." Very well, if I stay with my mother, I'll treat her as an end and not as a means; but by virtue of this very fact, I'm running the risk of treating the people around me who are fighting, as means; and, conversely, if I go to join those who are fighting, I'll be treating them as an end, and, by doing that, I run the risk of treating my mother as a means.

If values are vague, and if they are always too broad for the concrete and specific case that we are considering, the only thing left for us is to trust our instincts. That's what this young man tried to do; and when I saw him, he said, "In the end, feeling is what counts. I ought to choose whichever pushes me in one direction. If I feel that I love my mother enough to sacrifice everything else for her—my desire for vengeance, for action, for adventure—then I'll stay with her. If, on the contrary, I feel that my love for my mother isn't enough, I'll leave."

But how is the value of a feeling determined? What gives his feeling for his mother value? Precisely the fact that he remained with her. I may say that I like so-and-so well enough to sacrifice a certain amount of money for him, but I may say so only if I've done it. I may say "I love my mother well enough to remain with her" if I have remained with her. The only way to determine the value of this affection is, precisely, to perform an act which confirms and defines it. But, since I require this affection to justify my act, I find myself caught in a vicious circle.

On the other hand, Gide has well said that a mock feeling and a true feeling are almost indistinguishable; to decide that I love my mother and will remain with her, or to remain with her by putting on an act, amount somewhat to the same thing. In other words, the feeling is formed by the acts one performs; so, I can not refer to it in order to act upon it. Which means that I can neither seek within myself the true condition which will impel me to act, nor apply to a system of ethics for concepts which will permit me to act. You will say, "At least, he did go to a teacher for advice." But if you seek advice from a priest, for example, you have chosen this priest; you already knew, more or less, just about what advice he was going to give you. In other words, choosing your adviser is involving yourself. The proof of this is that if you are a Christian, you will say, "Consult a priest." But some priests are collaborating, some are just marking time, some are resisting. Which to choose? If the young man chooses a priest who is resisting or collaborating, he has already decided on the kind of advice he's going to get. Therefore, in coming to see me he knew the answer I was going to give him, and I had only one answer to give: "You're free, choose, that is, invent." No general ethics can show you what is to be done; there are no omens in the world. The Catholics will reply, "But there are." Granted—but, in any case, I myself choose the meaning they have.

When I was a prisoner, I knew a rather remarkable young man

who was a Jesuit. He had entered the Jesuit order in the following way: he had had a number of very bad breaks; in childhood,
his father died, leaving him in poverty, and he was a scholarship
student at a religious institution where he was constantly made
to feel that he was being kept out of charity; then, he failed to get
any of the honors and distinctions that children like; later on, at
about eighteen, he bungled a love affair; finally, at twenty-two,
he failed in military training, a childish enough matter, but it was
the last straw.

This young fellow might well have felt that he had botched
everything. It was a sign of something, but of what? He might
have taken refuge in bitterness or despair. But he very wisely
looked upon all this as a sign that he was not made for secular
triumphs, and that only the triumphs of religion, holiness, and
faith were open to him. He saw the hand of God in all this, and
so he entered the order. Who can help seeing that he alone decided what the sign meant?

Some other interpretation might have been drawn from this
series of setbacks; for example, that he might have done better to
turn carpenter or revolutionist. Therefore, he is fully responsible for the interpretation. Forlornness implies that we ourselves
choose our being. Forlornness and anguish go together.

As for despair, the term has a very simple meaning. It means
that we shall confine ourselves to reckoning only with what depends upon our will, or on the ensemble of probabilities which
make our action possible. When we want something, we always
have to reckon with probabilities. I may be counting on the arrival of a friend. The friend is coming by rail or street-car; this
supposes that the train will arrive on schedule, or that the street-
car will not jump the track. I am left in the realm of possibility;
but possibilities are to be reckoned with only to the point where
my action comports with the ensemble of these possibilities, and
no further. The moment the possibilities I am considering are
not rigorously involved by my action, I ought to disengage myself from them, because no God, no scheme, can adapt the world
and its possibilities to my will. When Descartes said, "Conquer

yourself rather than the world," he meant essentially the same thing.

The Marxists to whom I have spoken reply, "You can rely on the support of others in your action, which obviously has certain limits because you're not going to live forever. That means: rely on both what others are doing elsewhere to help you, in China, in Russia, and what they will do later on, after your death, to carry on the action and lead it to its fulfillment, which will be the revolution. You even *have* to rely upon that, otherwise you're immoral." I reply at once that I will always rely on fellow-fighters insofar as these comrades are involved with me in a common struggle, in the unity of a party or a group in which I can more or less make my weight felt; that is, one whose ranks I am in as a fighter and whose movements I am aware of at every moment. In such a situation, relying on the unity and will of the party is exactly like counting on the fact that the train will arrive on time or that the car won't jump the track. But, given that man is free and that there is no human nature for me to depend on, I can not count on men whom I do not know by relying on human goodness or man's concern for the good of society. I don't know what will become of the Russian revolution; I may make an example of it to the extent that at the present time it is apparent that the proletariat plays a part in Russia that it plays in no other nation. But I can't swear that this will inevitably lead to a triumph of the proletariat. I've got to limit myself to what I see.

Given that men are free and that tomorrow they will freely decide what man will be, I can not be sure that, after my death, fellow-fighters will carry on my work to bring it to its maximum perfection. Tomorrow, after my death, some men may decide to set up Fascism, and the others may be cowardly and muddled enough to let them do it. Fascism will then be the human reality, so much the worse for us.

Actually, things will be as man will have decided they are to be. Does that mean that I should abandon myself to quietism? No. First, I should involve myself; then, act on the old saw, "Nothing ventured, nothing gained." Nor does it mean that I shouldn't belong to a party, but rather that I shall have no illusions and shall do what I can. For example, suppose I ask myself, "Will socialization, as such, ever come about?" I know nothing about it. All I know is that I'm going to do everything in my power to bring it about. Beyond that, I can't count on anything. Quietism is the attitude of people who say, "Let others do what I can't do." The doctrine I am presenting is the very opposite of quietism, since it declares, "There is no reality except in action." Moreover, it goes further, since it adds, "Man is nothing else than his plan; he exists only to the extent that he fulfills himself; he is therefore nothing else than the ensemble of his acts, nothing else than his life."

According to this, we can understand why our doctrine horrifies certain people. Because often the only way they can bear their wretchedness is to think, "Circumstances have been against me. What I've been and done doesn't show my true worth. To be sure, I've had no great love, no great friendship, but that's because I haven't met a man or woman who was worthy. The books I've written haven't been very good because I haven't had the proper leisure. I haven't had children to devote myself to because I didn't find a man with whom I could have spent my life. So there remains within me, unused and quite viable, a host of propensities, inclinations, possibilities, that one wouldn't guess from the mere series of things I've done."

Now, for the existentialist there is really no love other than one which manifests itself in a person's being in love. There is no genius other than one which is expressed in works of art; the genius of Proust is the sum of Proust's works; the genius of Racine is his series of tragedies. Outside of that, there is nothing. Why say that Racine could have written another tragedy, when he didn't write it? A man is involved in life, leaves his impress on it, and outside of that there is nothing. To be sure, this may seem a harsh thought to someone whose life hasn't been a success. But, on the other hand, it prompts people to understand that reality alone is what counts, that dreams, expectations, and hopes warrant no more than to define a man as a disappointed dream, as miscarried hopes, as vain expectations. In other words, to define him negatively and not positively. However, when we say, "You are nothing else than your life," that does not imply that the artist will be judged solely on the basis of his works of art; a thousand other things will contribute toward summing him up. What we mean is that a man is nothing else than a series of undertakings, that he is the sum, the organization, the ensemble of the relationships which make up these undertakings.

When all is said and done, what we are accused of, at bottom, is not our pessimism, but an optimistic toughness. If people throw up to us our works of fiction in which we write about people who are soft, weak, cowardly, and sometimes even downright bad, it's not because these people are soft, weak, cowardly, or bad; because if we were to say, as Zola did, that they are that way because of heredity, the workings of environment, society, because of biological or psychological determinism, people would be reassured. They would say, "Well, that's what we're like, no one can do anything about it." But when the existentialist writes about a coward, he says that this coward is responsible for his cowardice. He's not like that because he has a cowardly heart or lung or brain; he's not like that on account of his physiological make-up; but he's like that because he has made himself a coward by his acts. There's no such thing as a cowardly constitution; there are nervous constitutions; there is poor blood, as the common people say, or strong constitutions. But the man whose blood is poor is not a coward on that account, for what makes cowardice is the act of renouncing or yielding. A constitution is not an act; the coward is defined on the basis of the acts he performs. People feel, in a vague sort of way, that this coward we're talking about is guilty of being a coward, and the thought frightens them. What people would like is that a coward or a hero be born that way.

One of the complaints most frequently made about *The Ways of Freedom*[1] can be summed up as follows: "After all, these people

---

1. *Les Chemins de la Liberté*, M. Sartre's projected trilogy of novels, two of which, *L'Age de Raison* (*The Age of Reason*) and *Le Sursis* (*The Reprieve*) have already appeared.—Translator's note.

are so spineless, how are you going to make heroes out of them?" This objection almost makes me laugh, for it assumes that people are born heroes. That's what people really want to think. If you're born cowardly, you may set your mind perfectly at rest; there's nothing you can do about it; you'll be cowardly all your life, whatever you may do. If you're born a hero, you may set your mind just as much at rest; you'll be a hero all your life; you'll drink like a hero and eat like a hero. What the existentialist says is that the coward makes himself cowardly, that the hero makes himself heroic. There's always a possibility for the coward not to be cowardly any more and for the hero to stop being heroic. What counts is total involvement; some one particular action or set of circumstances is not total involvement.

Thus, I think we have answered a number of the charges concerning existentialism. You see that it can not be taken for a philosophy of quietism, since it defines man in terms of action; nor for a pessimistic description of man—there is no doctrine more optimistic, since man's destiny is within himself; nor for an attempt to discourage man from acting, since it tells him that the only hope is in his acting and that action is the only thing that enables a man to live. Consequently, we are dealing here with an ethics of action and involvement.

Nevertheless, on the basis of a few notions like these, we are still charged with immuring man in his private subjectivity. There again we're very much misunderstood. Subjectivity of the individual is indeed our point of departure, and this for strictly philosophic reasons. Not because we are bourgeois, but because we want a doctrine based on truth and not a lot of fine theories, full of hope but with no real basis. There can be no other truth to take off from than this: *I think; therefore, I exist.* There we have the absolute truth of consciousness becoming aware of itself. Every theory which takes man out of the moment in which he becomes aware of himself is, at its very beginning, a theory which confounds truth, for outside the Cartesian *cogito,* all views are only probable, and a doctrine of probability which is not bound to a truth dissolves into thin air. In order to describe the probable, you must have a firm hold on the true. Therefore, before there can be any truth whatsoever, there must be an absolute truth; and this one is simple and easily arrived at; it's on everyone's doorstep; it's a matter of grasping it directly.

Secondly, this theory is the only one which gives man dignity, the only one which does not reduce him to an object. The effect of all materialism is to treat all men, including the one philosophizing, as objects, that is, as an ensemble of determined reactions in no way distinguished from the ensemble of qualities and phenomena which constitute a table or a chair or a stone. We definitely wish to establish the human realm as an ensemble of values distinct from the material realm. But the subjectivity that we have thus arrived at, and which we have claimed to be truth, is not a strictly individual subjectivity, for we have demonstrated that one discovers in the *cogito* not only himself, but others as well.

The philosophies of Descartes and Kant to the contrary, through the *I think* we reach our own self in the presence of others, and the others are just as real to us as our own self. Thus, the man who becomes aware of himself through the *cogito* also perceives all others, and he perceives them as the condition of his own existence. He realizes that he can not be anything (in the sense that we say that someone is witty or nasty or jealous) unless others recognize it as such. In order to get any truth about myself, I must have contact with another person. The other is indispensable to my own existence, as well as to my knowledge about myself. This being so, in discovering my inner being I discover the other person at the same time, like a freedom placed in front of me which thinks and wills only for or against me. Hence, let us at once announce the discovery of a world which we shall call intersubjectivity; this is the world in which man decides what he is and what others are.

Besides, if it is impossible to find in every man some universal essence which would be human nature, yet there does exist a universal human condition. It's not by chance that today's thinkers speak more readily of man's condition than of his nature. By condition they mean, more or less definitely, the *a priori* limits which outline man's fundamental situation in the universe. Historical situations vary; a man may be born a slave in a pagan society or a feudal lord or a proletarian. What does not vary is the necessity for him to exist in the world, to be at work there, to be there in the midst of other people, and to be mortal there. The limits are neither subjective nor objective, or, rather, they have an objective and a subjective side. Objective because they are to be found everywhere and are recognizable everywhere; subjective because they are *lived* and are nothing if man does not live them, that is, freely determine his existence with reference to them. And though the configurations may differ, at least none of them are completely strange to me, because they all appear as attempts either to pass beyond these limits or recede from them or deny them or adapt to them. Consequently, every configuration, however individual it may be, has a universal value.

Every configuration, even the Chinese, the Indian, or the Negro, can be understood by a Westerner. "Can be understood" means that by virtue of a situation that he can imagine, a European of 1945 can, in like manner, push himself to his limits and reconstitute within himself the configuration of the Chinese, the Indian, or the African. Every configuration has universality in the sense that every configuration can be understood by every man. This does not at all mean that this configuration defines man forever, but that it can be met with again. There is always a way to understand the idiot, the child, the savage, the foreigner, provided one has the necessary information.

In this sense we may say that there is a universality of man; but it is not given, it is perpetually being made. I build the universal in choosing myself; I build it in understanding the configuration of every other man, whatever age he might have lived in. This absoluteness of choice does not do away with the relativeness of each epoch. At heart, what existentialism shows is the connection between the absolute character of free involvement, by virtue of which every man realizes himself in realizing a type of mankind, an involvement always comprehensible in any age whatsoever and by any person whosoever, and the relativeness of the cultural ensemble which may result from such a choice; it must be stressed that the relativity of Cartesianism and the absolute character of Cartesian involvement go together. In this sense, you may, if you like, say that each of us performs an absolute act in breathing, eating, sleeping, or behaving in any way whatever. There is no difference between being free, like a configuration, like an existence which chooses its essence, and being absolute. There is no difference between being an absolute temporarily localized, that is, localized in history, and being universally comprehensible.

This does not entirely settle the objection to subjectivism. In fact, the objection still takes several forms. First, there is the following: we are told, "So you're able to do anything, no matter what!" This is expressed in various ways. First we are accused of anarchy; then they say, "You're unable to pass judgment on others, because there's no reason to prefer one configuration to another"; finally they tell us, "Everything is arbitrary in this choosing of yours. You take something from one pocket and pretend you're putting it into the other."

These three objections aren't very serious. Take the first objection. "You're able to do anything, no matter what" is not to the point. In one sense choice is possible, but what is not possible is not to choose. I can always choose, but I ought to know that if I do not choose, I am still choosing. Though this may seem purely formal, it is highly important for keeping fantasy and caprice within bounds. If it is true that in facing a situation, for example, one in which, as a person capable of having sexual relations, of having children, I am obliged to choose an attitude, and if I in any way assume responsibility for a choice which, in involving myself, also involves all mankind, this has nothing to do with caprice, even if no *a priori* value determines my choice.

If anybody thinks that he recognizes here Gide's theory of the arbitrary act, he fails to see the enormous difference between this doctrine and Gide's. Gide does not know what a situation is. He acts out of pure caprice. For us, on the contrary, man is in an organized situation in which he himself is involved. Through his choice, he involves all mankind, and he can not avoid making a choice: either he will remain chaste, or he will marry without having children, or he will marry and have children; anyhow, whatever he may do, it is impossible for him not to take full responsibility for the way he handles this problem. Doubtless, he chooses without referring to pre-established values, but it is unfair to accuse him of caprice. Instead, let us say that moral choice is to be compared to the making of a work of art. And before going any further, let it be said at once that we are not dealing here with an aesthetic ethics, because our opponents are so dishonest that they even accuse us of that. The example I've chosen is a comparison only.

Having said that, may I ask whether anyone has ever accused an artist who has painted a picture of not having drawn his inspiration from rules set up *a priori*? Has anyone ever asked, "What painting ought he to make?" It is clearly understood that there is no definite painting to be made, that the artist is engaged in the making of his painting, and that the painting to be made is precisely the painting he will have made. It is clearly understood that there are no *a priori* aesthetic values, but that there are values which appear subsequently in the coherence of the painting, in the correspondence between what the artist intended and the result. Nobody can tell what the painting of tomorrow will be like. Painting can be judged only after it has once been made. What connection does that have with ethics? We are in the same creative situation. We never say that a work of art is arbitrary. When we speak of a canvas of Picasso, we never say that it is arbitrary; we understand quite well that he was making himself what he is at the very time he was painting, that the ensemble of his work is embodied in his life.

The same holds on the ethical plane. What art and ethics have in common is that we have creation and invention in both cases. We can not decide *a priori* what there is to be done. I think that I pointed that out quite sufficiently when I mentioned the case of the student who came to see me, and who might have applied to all the ethical systems, Kantian or otherwise, without getting any sort of guidance. He was obliged to devise his law himself. Never let it be said by us that this man—who, taking affection, individual action, and kind-heartedness toward a specific person as his ethical first principle, chooses to remain with his mother, or who, preferring to make a sacrifice, chooses to go to England— has made an arbitrary choice. Man makes himself. He isn't ready made at the start. In choosing his ethics, he makes himself, and force of circumstances is such that he can not abstain from choosing one. We define man only in relationship to involvement. It is therefore absurd to charge us with arbitrariness of choice.

In the second place, it is said that we are unable to pass judgment on others. In a way this is true, and in another way, false. It is true in this sense, that, whenever a man sanely and sincerely involves himself and chooses his configuration, it is impossible for him to prefer another configuration, regardless of what his own may be in other respects. It is true in this sense, that we do not believe in progress. Progress is betterment. Man is always the same. The situation confronting him varies. Choice always remains a choice in a situation. The problem has not changed since the time one could choose between those for and those against slavery, for example, at the time of the Civil War, and the present time, when one can side with the Maquis Resistance Party, or with the Communists.

But, nevertheless, one can still pass judgment, for, as I have said, one makes a choice in relationship to others. First, one can judge (and this is perhaps not a judgment of value, but a logical judgment) that certain choices are based on error and others on truth. If we have defined man's situation as a free choice, with no excuses and no recourse, every man who takes refuge behind the excuse of his passions, every man who sets up a determinism, is a dishonest man.

The objection may be raised, "But why mayn't he choose himself dishonestly?" I reply that I am not obliged to pass moral judgment on him, but that I do define his dishonesty as an error. One can not help considering the truth of the matter. Dishonesty is obviously a falsehood because it belies the complete freedom of involvement. On the same grounds, I maintain that there is also dishonesty if I choose to state that certain values exist prior to me; it is self-contradictory for me to want them and at the same state that they are imposed on me. Suppose someone says to me, "What if I want to be dishonest?" I'll answer, "There's no reason for you not to be, but I'm saying that that's what you are, and that the strictly coherent attitude is that of honesty."

Besides, I can bring moral judgment to bear. When I declare that freedom in every concrete circumstance can have no other aim than to want itself, if man has once become aware that in his forlornness he imposes values, he can no longer want but one thing, and that is freedom, as the basis of all values. That doesn't mean that he wants it in the abstract. It means simply that the ultimate meaning of the acts of honest men is the quest for freedom as such. A man who belongs to a communist or revolutionary union wants concrete goals; these goals imply an abstract desire for freedom; but this freedom is wanted in something concrete. We want freedom for freedom's sake and in every particular circumstance. And in wanting freedom we discover that it depends entirely on the freedom of others, and that the freedom of others depends on ours. Of course, freedom as the definition of man does not depend on others, but as soon as there is involvement, I am obliged to want others to have freedom at the same time that I want my own freedom. I can take freedom as my goal only if I take that of others as a goal as well. Consequently, when, in all honesty, I've recognized that man is a being in whom existence precedes essence, that he is a free being who, in various circumstances, can want only his freedom, I have at the same time recognized that I can want only the freedom of others.

Therefore, in the name of this will for freedom, which freedom itself implies, I may pass judgment on those who seek to hide from themselves the complete arbitrariness and the complete freedom of their existence. Those who hide their complete freedom from themselves out of a spirit of seriousness or by means of deterministic excuses, I shall call cowards; those who try to show that their existence was necessary, when it is the very contingency of man's appearance on earth, I shall call stinkers. But cowards or stinkers can be judged only from a strictly unbiased point of view.

Therefore though the content of ethics is variable, a certain form of it is universal. Kant says that freedom desires both itself and the freedom of others. Granted. But he believes that the formal and the universal are enough to constitute an ethics. We, on the other hand, think that principles which are too abstract run aground in trying to decide action. Once again, take the case of the student. In the name of what, in the name of what great moral maxim do you think he could have decided, in perfect peace of mind, to abandon his mother or to stay with her? There is no way of judging. The content is always concrete and thereby unforeseeable; there is always the element of invention. The one thing that counts is knowing whether the inventing that has been done, has been done in the name of freedom.

For example, let us look at the following two cases. You will see to what extent they correspond, yet differ. Take *The Mill on the Floss*. We find a certain young girl, Maggie Tulliver, who is an embodiment of the value of passion and who is aware of it. She is in love with a young man, Stephen, who is engaged to an insignificant young girl. This Maggie Tulliver, instead of heedlessly preferring her own happiness, chooses, in the name of human solidarity, to sacrifice herself and give up the man she loves. On the other hand, Sanseverina, in *The Charterhouse of Parma*, believing that passion is man's true value, would say that a great love deserves sacrifices; that it is to be preferred to the banality of the conjugal love that would tie Stephen to the young ninny he had to marry. She would choose to sacrifice the girl and fulfill her happiness; and, as Stendhal shows, she is even ready to sacrifice herself for the sake of passion, if this life demands it. Here we are in the presence of two strictly opposed moralities. I claim that they are much the same thing; in both cases what has been set up as the goal is freedom.

You can imagine two highly similar attitudes: one girl prefers to renounce her love out of resignation; another prefers to disregard the prior attachment of the man she loves out of sexual desire. On the surface these two actions resemble those we've just described. However, they are completely different. Sanseverina's attitude is much nearer that of Maggie Tulliver, one of heedless rapacity.

Thus, you see that the second charge is true and, at the same time, false. One may choose anything if it is on the grounds of free involvement.

The third objection is the following: "You take something from one pocket and put it into the other. That is, fundamentally, values aren't serious, since you choose them." My answer to this is that I'm quite vexed that that's the way it is; but if I've discarded God the Father, there has to be someone to invent values. You've got to take things as they are. Moreover, to say that we invent values means nothing else but this: life has no meaning *a priori*. Before you come alive, life is nothing; it's up to you to give it a meaning, and value is nothing else but the meaning that you choose. In that way, you see, there is a possibility of creating a human community.

I've been reproached for asking whether existentialism is humanistic. It's been said, "But you said in *Nausea* that the humanists were all wrong. You made fun of a certain kind of humanist. Why come back to it now?" Actually, the word humanism has two very different meanings. By humanism one can mean a theory which takes man as an end and as a higher value. Humanism in this sense can be found in Cocteau's tale *Around the World in Eighty Hours* when a character, because he is flying over some mountains in an airplane, declares, "Man is simply amazing." That means that I, who did not build the airplanes, shall personally benefit from these particular inventions, and that I, as man, shall personally consider myself responsible for, and honored by, acts of a few particular men. This would imply that we ascribe a value to man on the basis of the highest deeds of certain men. This humanism is absurd, because only the dog or the horse would be able to make such an over-all judgment about man, which they are careful not to do, at least to my knowledge.

But it can not be granted that a man may make a judgment about man. Existentialism spares him from any such judgment. The existentialist will never consider man as an end because he is always in the making. Nor should we believe that there is a mankind to which we might set up a cult in the manner of Auguste Comte. The cult of mankind ends in the self-enclosed humanism of Comte, and, let it be said, of fascism. This kind of humanism we can do without.

But there is another meaning of humanism. Fundamentally it is this: man is constantly outside of himself; in projecting himself, in losing himself outside of himself, he makes for man's existing; and, on the other hand, it is by pursuing transcendent goals that he is able to exist; man, being this state of passing-beyond, and seizing upon things only as they bear upon this passing-beyond, is at the heart, at the center of this passing-beyond. There is no universe other than a human universe, the universe of human subjectivity. This connection between transcendency, as a constituent element of man—not in the sense that God is transcendent, but in the sense of passing beyond—and subjectivity, in the sense that man is not closed in on himself but is always present in a human universe, is what we call existentialism humanism. Humanism, because we remind man that there is no law-maker other than himself, and that in his forlornness he will decide by himself; because we point out that man will fulfill himself as man, not in turning toward himself, but in seeking outside of himself a goal which is just this liberation, just this particular fulfillment.

From these few reflections it is evident that nothing is more unjust than the objections that have been raised against us. Existentialism is nothing else than an attempt to draw all the consequences of a coherent atheistic position. It isn't trying to plunge man into despair at all. But if one calls every attitude of unbelief despair, like the Christians, then the word is not being used in its original sense. Existentialism isn't so atheistic that it wears itself out showing that God doesn't exist. Rather, it declares that even if God did exist, that would change nothing. There you've got our point of view. Not that we believe that God exists, but we think that the problem of His existence is not the issue. In this sense existentialism is optimistic, a doctrine of action, and it is plain dishonesty for Christians to make no distinction between their own despair and ours and then to call us despairing.

BEING AND NOTHINGNESS

SELF-NEGATION

1. BAD FAITH

The human being is not only the being by whom negations are disclosed in the world; he is also the being who can take negative attitudes toward himself. In our introduction we defined consciousness as "a being such that in its being, its being is in question insofar as this being implies a being other than itself." But now that we have examined questioning behavior we can also write the formula thus: "Consciousness is a being, the nature of which is to be conscious of the nothingness of its being." In a prohibition or a veto, for example, the human being denies a future transcendence. But this negation is not a matter of observation. My consciousness is not restricted to envisaging a negation. It constitutes itself in its own flesh as the nihilation of a possibility which another human reality projects as its possibility. For that reason it must arise in the world as a *No:* it is as a No that the slave first apprehends the master, or that the prisoner who is try-

---

ing to escape sees the guard who is watching him. There are even men (*e.g.,* caretakers, overseers, jailers), whose social reality is entirely that of the No, who will live and die, having forever been only a No upon the earth. Others so as to make the No a part of their very subjectivity, establish their human personality as a perpetual negation. This is the meaning and function of what Scheler calls "the man of resentment"—the man who is a No. But there are subtler modes of behavior, the description of which will lead us further into the inwardness of consciousness. Irony is one of these. In irony a man nihilates what he posits within one and the same act; he leads us to believe in order not to be believed; he affirms to deny and denies to affirm; he creates a positive object but it has no being other than its nothingness. Thus attitudes of negation toward the self permit us to raise a new question: What are we to say is the being of man who has the possibility of denying himself? But it is out of the question to discuss the attitude of "self-negation" generally. The kinds of behavior which can be ranked under this heading are too diverse, we risk retaining only the abstract form of them. It is best to choose and to examine one specific attitude which is essential to human reality and which is such that consciousness instead of directing its negation outward turns it toward itself. This attitude, it seems to me, is *bad faith* [*mauvaise foi*].

Frequently this is identified with falsehood. We say indifferently of a person that he is guilty of bad faith or that he lies to himself. We shall willingly grant that bad faith is a lie to oneself, on condition that we distinguish the lie to oneself from lying in general. Lying is a negative attitude, anyone will agree. But this negation does not bear on consciousness itself; it aims only at the transcendent. The essence of the lie implies in fact that the liar actually is in complete possession of the truth which he is hiding. A man does not lie about what he is ignorant of; he does not lie when he spreads an error of which he himself is the dupe; he does not lie when he is mistaken. The ideal case of the liar would be a cynical consciousness, affirming truth within himself, denying it in his words, and denying the denial to himself. Now this doubly negative attitude refers to the transcendent; the fact expressed is transcendent since it does not exist, and the original negation refers to a *truth;* that is, to a particular type of transcendence. As for the inner negation which I effect correlatively with the affirmation for myself of the truth, this refers to words; that is, to an event in the world. Furthermore the inner disposition of the liar is positive; it could be the object of an affirmative judgment. The liar intends to deceive and he does not seek to hide this intention from himself nor to disguise the translucency of consciousness; on the contrary, he has recourse to it when there is a question of deciding secondary behavior. It explicitly exercises a regulatory control over all attitudes. As for his flaunted intention of telling the truth ("I'd never want to deceive you! This it true! I swear it!")—all this, of course, is the object of an inner negation, but also it is not recognized by the liar as his intention. It is played, impersonated, it is the intention of the character which he plays in the eyes of his questioner, but this character, precisely because he *does not exist,* is a transcendent. Thus the lie does not involve the inner structure of present consciousness; all the negations which constitute it refer to objects which as such are removed from consciousness. The lie then does not require special ontological foundation, and the explanations which the existence of negation in general requires hold without alteration in the case of deceit. Of course we have described the ideal lie; doubtless it happens often enough that the liar is more or less the victim of his lie, that he half persuades himself of it. But these common popular forms of the lie are also degenerate aspects of it; they represent intermediaries between falsehood and bad faith. The lie is a behavior of transcendence.

The lie is also a normal phenomenon of what Heidegger calls the "*Mit-sein.*" [1] It presupposes my existence, the existence of the *Other,* my existence *for* the Other, and the existence of the Other *for* me. Thus there is no difficulty in holding that the liar must make the project of the lie in entire clarity and that he must pos-

---

1. A "being-with" others in the world.—Trans.

sess a complete comprehension of the lie and of the truth which he is altering. It is sufficient that an overall opacity hide his intentions from the *Other*; it is sufficient that the Other can take the lie for truth. By the lie consciousness affirms that it exists by nature as *hidden from the Other*; it utilizes for its own profit the ontological duality of myself and myself in the eyes of the Other.

The situation cannot be the same for bad faith if this, as we have said, is indeed a lie to oneself. To be sure, the one who practices bad faith is hiding a displeasing truth or presenting as truth a pleasing untruth. Bad faith then has in appearance the structure of falsehood. Only what changes everything is the fact that in bad faith it is from myself that I am hiding the truth. Thus the duality of the deceiver and the deceived does not exist here. Bad faith on the contrary implies in essence the unity of a *single* consciousness. This does not mean that it cannot be conditioned by the *Mit-sein* like all other phenomena of human reality, but the *Mit-sein* can only solicit bad faith by presenting itself as a *situation* which bad faith permits transcending; bad faith does not come from outside to human reality. One does not undergo his bad faith; one is not infected with it; it is not a *state*. But consciousness affects itself with bad faith. There must be an original intention and a project of bad faith; this project implies a comprehension of bad faith as such and a pre-reflective apprehension (of) consciousness as affecting itself with bad faith. It follows first that the one to whom the lie is told and the one who lies are one and the same person, which means that I must know in my capacity as deceiver the truth which is hidden from me in my capacity as the one deceived. Or rather, I must know what the truth is exactly *in order* to conceal it more carefully—and this not at two different moments, which at a pinch would allow us to re-establish a semblance of duality—but in the unitary structure of a single project. How then can the lie subsist if the duality which conditions it is suppressed?

To this difficulty is added another which is derived from the total translucency of consciousness. That which affects itself with bad faith must be conscious (of) its bad faith since the being of consciousness is consciousness of being. It appears then that I must be in good faith, at least to the extent that I am conscious of my bad faith. But then this whole psychic system is annihilated. We must agree in fact that if I deliberately and cynically attempt to lie to myself, I fail completely in this undertaking; the lie falls back and collapses under my look; it is ruined *from behind* by the very consciousness of lying to myself which pitilessly constitutes itself well within my project as its very condition. We have here an *evanescent* phenomenon which exists only in and through its own differentiation. To be sure, these phenomena are frequent and we shall see that there is in fact an "evanescence" of bad faith, which, it is obvious, vacillates continually between good faith and cynicism: Even though the existence of bad faith is very precarious, and though it belongs to the kind of psychic structures which we might call "metastable,"[2] it presents nonetheless an autonomous and durable form. It can even be the normal aspect of life for a very great number of people. A person can *live* in bad faith, which does not mean that he does not have abrupt awakenings to cynicism or to good faith, but which implies a constant and particular style of life. Our embarrassment then appears extreme since we can neither reject nor comprehend bad faith.

2. THE UNCONSCIOUS

To escape from these difficulties some have recourse to the unconscious. In the psychoanalytical interpretation, for example, they use the hypothesis of a censor, conceived as a line of demarcation with customs, passport division, currency control, etc., to re-establish the duality of the deceiver and the deceived. Here instinct or, if you prefer, original drives and complexes of drives constituted by our individual history, make up *reality*. An instinct is neither *true* nor *false* since it does not *exist for itself*. It simply *is*, exactly like this table, which is neither true nor false in

2. Sartre's own word, meaning subject to sudden changes or transitions.—Trans.

itself but simply *real.* As for the conscious symbols of the instinct, this interpretation takes them not for appearances but for real psychic facts. Fear, lapses of memory, dreams really exist as concrete facts of consciousness in the same way as the words and the attitudes of the liar are concrete, really existing patterns of behavior. The subject has the same relation to these phenomena as the deceived to the behavior of the deceiver. He observes them in their reality and must interpret them. There is a *truth* in the activities of the deceiver; if the deceived could re-attach them to the situation which the deceiver is in and to his project of the lie, they would become integral parts of truth, by virtue of being lying behavior. Similarly there is a truth in the symbolic acts; it is what the psychoanalyst discovers when he re-attaches them to the historical situation of the patient, to the unconscious complexes which they express, to the blocking of the censor. Thus the subject deceives himself about the *meaning* of his behavior, he apprehends it in its concrete existence but not in its *truth,* simply because he cannot derive it from an original situation and from a psychic constitution which remain alien to him.

By the distinction between the "id" and the "ego," Freud has cut the psychic whole into two. I *am* the ego but I *am not* the id. I hold no privileged position in relation to my unconscious psyche. I *am* my own psychic phenomena insofar as I observe them in their conscious reality. For example I am the impulse to steal this or that book from this bookstall. I co-operate with the impulse; I clarify it, and I decide in terms of it to commit the theft. But I *am* not those psychic facts, insofar as I receive them passively and am obliged to resort to hypotheses about their origin and their true meaning, just as the scientist makes conjectures about the nature and essence of an external phenomenon. This theft, for example, which I interpret as an immediate impulse determined by the rarity, the interest, or the price of the volume which I am going to steal—it is in truth a process derived from self-punishment, which is attached more or less directly to an Oedipus complex. The impulse toward the theft contains a truth which can be reached only by more or less probable hypotheses.

The criterion of this truth will be the number of conscious psychic facts which it explains; from a more pragmatic point of view it will be also the success of the psychiatric cure which it allows. Finally the discovery of this truth will necessitate the co-operation of the psychoanalyst, who appears as the *mediator* between my unconscious drives and my conscious life. The Other appears as being able to effect the synthesis between the unconscious thesis and the conscious antithesis. I can know myself only through the mediation of the other, which means that I am in relation to *my* "id," in the position of the *Other.* If I have a little knowledge of psychoanalysis, I can, under circumstances particularly favorable, try to psychoanalyze myself. But this attempt can succeed only if I distrust every kind of intuition, only if I apply to my case *from the outside,* abstract schemes and rules already learned. As for the results, whether they are obtained by my efforts alone or with the co-operation of a professional psychoanalyst, they will never have the certainty which intuition confers; they will possess simply the always increasing probability of scientific hypotheses. The hypothesis of the Oedipus complex, like the atomic theory, is nothing but an "experimental idea"; as Peirce said, it is not to be distinguished from the set of experiments which it allows to be performed and the results which it enables us to predict. Thus psychoanalysis substitutes for the notion of bad faith, the idea of a lie without a liar; it allows me to understand how it is possible for me to be lied to without lying to myself since it places me in the same relation to myself that the Other is in respect to me; it replaces the duality of the deceiver and the deceived, the essential condition of the lie, by that of the "id" and the "ego." It introduces into my subjectivity the deepest intersubjective structure of the *Mit-sein.* Can this explanation satisfy us?

Considered more closely the psychoanalytic theory is not as simple as it first appears. It is not accurate to hold that the "id" is presented as a thing in relation to the hypothesis of the psychoanalyst, for a thing is indifferent to the conjectures which we make concerning it, while the "id" in contrast is sensitive to them when we approach the truth. Freud in fact reports resistance when at the end of the first period the doctor is approaching the truth. This resistance is objective behavior apprehended from without: the patient shows defiance, refuses to speak, gives fantastic accounts of his dreams, sometimes even removes himself completely from the psychoanalytic treatment. It is a fair question to ask what part of himself can thus resist. It cannot be the "ego," envisaged as a psychic totality of the facts of consciousness; this could not suspect that the psychiatrist is approaching the goal since the ego's relation to the *meaning* of its own reactions is exactly like that of the psychiatrist himself. At the very most it is possible for the ego to appreciate objectively the degree of probability in the hypotheses set forth, as a witness of the psychoanalysis might be able to do, according to the number of subjective facts which they explain. Furthermore, this probability would appear to the ego to border on certainty, which he could not take offense at, since most of the time it is the ego who is committed by a *conscious* decision to the psychoanalytic therapy. Are we to say that the patient is disturbed by the daily revelations which the psychoanalyst makes to him and that he seeks to remove himself, at the same time pretending in his own eyes to wish to continue the treatment? In this case it is no longer possible to resort to the unconscious to explain bad faith; it is there in full consciousness, with all its contradictions. But this is not the way that the psychoanalyst means to explain this resistance; for him it is secret and deep, it comes from afar; it has its roots in the very thing which the psychoanalyst is trying to make clear.

Furthermore it is equally impossible to explain the resistance as emanating from the complex which the psychoanalyst wishes to bring to light. The complex as such is rather the collaborator of the psychoanalyst since it aims at expressing itself in clear consciousness, since it plays tricks on the censor and seeks to elude it. The only level on which we can locate the refusal of the subject is that of the censor. It alone can comprehend the questions or the revelations of the psychoanalyst as approaching more or less near to the real drives which it strives to repress—it alone because it alone *knows* what it is repressing.

If we reject the language and the materialistic mythology of psychoanalysis, we perceive that the censor in order to apply its activity with discernment must know what it is repressing. In fact if we abandon all the metaphors representing the repression as the impact of blind forces, we have to admit that the censor must choose and in order to choose must be aware of so doing. How could it happen otherwise that the censor allows licit sexual impulses to pass through, that it permits needs (hunger, thirst, sleep) to be expressed in clear consciousness? And how are we to explain that it can relax its surveillance, that it can even be deceived by the disguises of the instinct? But it is not sufficient that it discern the condemned drives; it must also apprehend them *as to be repressed,* which implies in it at the very least an awareness of its activity. In a word, how could the censor discern the impulses needing to be repressed without being conscious of discerning them? How can we conceive of a knowledge which is ignorant of itself? To know is to know that one knows, said Alain. Let us say rather: All knowing is consciousness of knowing. Thus the resistance of the patient implies on the level of the censor an awareness of the thing repressed as such, a comprehension of the goal toward which the questions of the psychoanalyst are leading, and an act of synthetic connection by which it compares the *truth* of the repressed complex to the psychoanalytic hypothesis which aims at it. These various operations in their turn imply that the censor is conscious (of) itself. But what type of self-consciousness can the censor have? It must be the consciousness (of) being conscious of the drive to be repressed, but precisely *in order not to be conscious of it.* What does this mean if not that the censor is in bad faith?

Psychoanalysis has not gained anything for us since in order to overcome bad faith, it has established between the unconscious and consciousness an autonomous consciousness in bad faith. The effort to establish a veritable duality, and even a trinity (*Es, Ich,* and *Überich* expressing itself through the censor) has resulted in a mere verbal terminology. The very essence of the reflexive idea of hiding something from oneself implies the unity of one and the same psychic structure and consequently a double activity within unity, tending on the one hand to maintain and locate the thing to be concealed and on the other hand to repress and disguise it. Each of the two aspects of this activity is complementary to the other; that is, it implies the other in its being. By separating consciousness from the unconscious by means of the censor, psychoanalysis has not succeeded in dissociating the two phases of the act, since the libido is a blind conatus toward conscious expression and since the conscious phenomenon is a passive, doctored result. Psychoanalysis has merely localized this double activity of repulsion and attraction on the level of the censor.

Furthermore the problem still remains of accounting for the unity of the total phenomenon (repression of the drive which disguises itself and passes over into symbolic form), of establishing comprehensible connections among its different phases. How can the repressed drive "disguise itself" if it does not include (1) the consciousness of being repressed, (2) the consciousness of having been repressed because it is what it is, (3) a project of disguise? No mechanistic theory of condensation or of transference can explain these modifications by which the drive itself is affected, for the description of the process of disguise implies a veiled appeal to finality. And similarly how are we to account for the pleasure or the anguish which accompanies the symbolic and conscious satisfaction of the drive if consciousness does not include—beyond the censor—an obscure comprehension of the goal to be attained as simultaneously desired and forbidden. By rejecting the conscious unity of the psyche, Freud is obliged to imply everywhere a magic unity linking distant phenomena across obstacles, just as sympathetic magic unites the bewitched person and the wax image fashioned in his likeness. The unconscious drive (*Trieb*) through magic is endowed with the character "repressed" or "condemned," which completely pervades it, colors it, and magically provokes its symbolism. Similarly the conscious phenomenon is entirely colored by its symbolic meaning although it cannot apprehend this meaning by itself in clear consciousness.

Aside from its inferiority in principle, the explanation by magic does not avoid the coexistence—on the level of the unconscious, on that of the censor, and on that of consciousness—of two contradictory, complementary structures which reciprocally imply and destroy each other. Proponents of the theory have hypostatized and "reified" bad faith; they have not escaped it. This is what has inspired a Viennese psychiatrist, Steckel, to depart from the psychoanalytical tradition and to write in *The Frigid Woman:* "Every time that I have been able to carry my investigations far enough, I have established that the core of the psychosis was conscious." Moreover the cases which he reports in his work bear witness to a pathological bad faith which the Freudian doctrine cannot account for. There is the question, for example, of women whom marital disappointment has made frigid; that is, they succeed in hiding from themselves, not complexes deeply sunk in half physiological darkness, but modes of behavior which are objectively discoverable, which they cannot fail to recognize at the moment they perform them. Frequently in fact the husband reveals to Steckel that his wife has given objective signs of pleasure, but the woman when questioned will fiercely deny them. Here we find a pattern of *distraction.* Admissions which Steckel was able to draw out inform us that these pathologically frigid women apply themselves to becoming distracted in advance from the pleasure which they dread; many for example at the time of the sexual act, turn their thoughts away toward their daily occupations, make up their household accounts. Will anyone speak of an unconscious here? Yet if the frigid woman thus distracts her consciousness from the pleasure which she experiences, it is by no means cynically and in full agreement with herself; *it is in order to prove to herself* that she is frigid. We have in fact to deal with a phenomenon of bad faith since the efforts taken in order not to be present to the experienced pleasure imply the recognition that the pleasure is experienced; they imply it *in order to deny it.* But we are no longer on the ground of psycho-analysis. Thus on the one hand the explanation by means of the unconscious, due to the fact that it breaks the psychic unity, cannot account for the facts which at first sight it appeared to explain. And on the other hand, there exists an infinite number of types of behavior in bad faith which explicitly rebuff this kind of explanation because their essence implies that they can appear only in the translucency of consciousness. We find that the problem which we had attempted to resolve is still untouched.

3. PLAY-ACTING

If we wish to get out of our difficulties, we should examine more closely the patterns of bad faith and attempt a description of them. This description will permit us perhaps to define more precisely the conditions under which bad faith is possible; that is, to reply to the question we raised at the outset: "What must be the being of man if he is to be capable of bad faith?"

Take the example of a young woman who has consented to go out with a particular man for the first time. She knows very well the intentions which the man who is speaking to her cherishes regarding her. She knows also that it will be necessary sooner or later for her to make a decision. But she does not want to feel the urgency; she concerns herself only with what is respectful and discreet in the attitude of her companion. She does not apprehend this conduct as an attempt to make what we call "the first advances"; that is, she does not want to see possibilities of temporal development which his conduct presents. She restricts this behavior to what is in the present; she does not wish to read in the phrases which he addresses to her anything other than their explicit meaning. If he says to her, "I find you so attractive!" she disarms this phrase of its sexual implications; she attaches to the conversation and to the behavior of the speaker the immediate meanings which she imagines as objective qualities. The man who is speaking to her appears to her sincere and respectful as the table is round or square, as the wall coloring is blue or gray. The qualities thus attached to the person she is listening to are in this way congealed in a permanence like that of things, which is no other than the projection of the strict present of the qualities into the temporal flux. This is because she does not quite know what she wants. She is profoundly aware of the desire which she inspires, but the desire cruel and naked would humiliate and horrify her. Yet she would find no charm in a respect which would be only respect. In order to satisfy her, there must be a feeling which is addressed wholly to her *personality*—*i.e.,* to her full freedom—and which would be a recognition of her freedom. But at the same time this feeling must be wholly desire; that is, it must address itself to her body as object. This time, then, she refuses to apprehend the desire for what it is; she does not even give it a name; she recognizes it only to the extent that it transcends itself toward admiration, esteem, respect and that it is wholly absorbed in the more refined forms which it produces, to the extent of no longer retaining any prominence except as a sort of warmth and density. But then suppose he takes her hand. This act of her companion risks changing the situation by calling for an immediate decision. To leave the hand there is to consent in herself to flirt, to involve herself. To withdraw it is to break the troubled and unstable harmony which gives the hour its charm. Her aim is to postpone the moment of decision as long as possible. We know what happens next; the young woman leaves her hand there, but she *does not notice* that she is leaving it. She does not notice because it happens by chance that she is at this moment wholly spiritual. She draws her companion up to the most lofty regions of sentimental speculation; she speaks of Life, of her life, she shows herself in her essential aspect—a personality, a consciousness. And during this time the divorce of the body from the soul is accomplished; the hand rests inert between the warm hands of her companion—neither consenting nor resisting—a thing.

We shall say that this woman is in bad faith. But we see immediately that she uses various procedures in order to maintain herself in this bad faith. She has disarmed the actions of her companion by reducing them to being only what they are; that is, to existing in the mode of the in-itself. But she permits herself to enjoy his desire, to the extent that she will apprehend it as not being what it is, will recognize its transcendence. Finally while feeling profoundly the presence of her own body—to the extent of being excited perhaps—she realizes herself as *not being* her own body, and she contemplates it as though from above as a passive object to which events can *happen* but which can neither provoke them nor avoid them because all its possibilities are outside of it. What unity do we find in these various aspects of bad faith? It is a certain art of forming contradictory concepts which unite in themselves both an idea and the negation of that idea. The basic concept which is thus engendered, utilizes the double property of the human being, who is at once a *facticity* and a *transcendence*. These two aspects of human reality are and ought to be capable of a valid co-ordination. But bad faith does not wish either to co-ordinate them or to surmount them in a synthesis. Bad faith seeks to affirm their identity while preserving their differences. It must affirm facticity as *being* transcendence and transcendence as *being* facticity, in such a way that at the instant when a person apprehends the one, he can find himself abruptly faced with the other.

We can find the prototype of formulae of bad faith in certain famous expressions which have been rightly conceived to produce their whole effect in a spirit of bad faith. Take for example the title of a work by Jacques Chardonne, *Love Is Much More than Love* [*L'amour, c'est beaucoup plus que l'amour*]. We see here how unity is established between *present* love in its facticity—"the contact of two epidermises," sensuality, egoism, Proust's mechanism of jealousy, Adler's battle of the sexes, etc.—and love as transcendence—Mauriac's "river of fire," the longing for the infinite, Plato's *eros,* Lawrence's deep cosmic intuition, etc. Here we leave facticity to find ourselves suddenly beyond the present and the factual condition of man, beyond the psychological, in the heart of metaphysics. On the other hand, the title of a play by Sarment, *I Am Too Great for Myself* [*Je suis trop grand pour moi*], which also presents characters in bad faith, throws us first into full transcendence in order suddenly to imprison us within the narrow limits of our actual essence. We find this structure again in the famous sentence: "He has become what he was [*Il est devenu ce qu'il était*]," or in its no less famous opposite: "Eternity at last changes each man into himself [*Tel qu'en lui-même enfin l'éternité le change*]." Of course these various formulae have only the appearance of bad faith; they have been conceived in this paradoxical form explicitly to shock the mind and discountenance it by an enigma. But it is precisely this appearance which is of concern to us. What counts here is that the formulae do not constitute new, solidly structured ideas; on the contrary, they are formed so as to remain in perpetual disintegration and so that we may slide at any moment from naturalistic present to transcendence and vice versa.

We can see the use which bad faith can make of these judgments which all aim at establishing that I am not what I am. If I were only what I *am*, I could, for example, seriously consider an adverse criticism which someone makes of me, question myself scrupulously, and perhaps be compelled to recognize the truth in it. But thanks to transcendence, I escape all that I am. I do not even have to discuss the justice of the reproach. As Susannah says to Figaro, "To prove that I am right would be to recognize that I can be wrong." I am on a plane where no reproach can touch me since what I really am is my transcendence. I flee from myself, I escape myself, I leave my tattered garment in the hands of the fault-finder. But the ambiguity necessary for bad faith comes from the fact that I affirm here that I *am* my transcendence in the mode of being of a thing. It is only thus, in fact, that I can feel that I escape all reproaches. It is in the sense that our young woman purifies the desire of anything humiliating by being willing to consider it only as pure transcendence, which she avoids even naming. But conversely "I Am Too Great for Myself," while showing our transcendence changed into facticity, is the source of an infinity of excuses for our failures or our weaknesses. Similarly our young woman flirting maintains transcendence to the extent that the respect, the esteem manifested by the actions of her admirer are already on the plane of the transcendent. But she arrests this transcendence, she glues [*empâte*] it down with all the facticity of the present; respect is nothing other than respect, it is an arrested transcending which no longer transcends itself toward anything.

But although this *metastable* concept of "transcendence-facticity" is one of the most basic instruments of bad faith, it is not the only one of its kind. We can equally well use another kind of duplicity derived from human reality which we will express roughly by saying that its being-for-itself implies correlatively a being-for-others. Upon any one of my actions it is always possible for two looks to converge, mine and that of the Other. The action will not present exactly the same structure in each case. But as we shall see later, as everyone feels, there is between these two aspects of my being, no difference between appearance and being—as if I were to myself the truth of myself and as if the Other possessed only a deformed image of me. The equal dignity of being, possessed by my being-for-others and by my being-for-myself permits a perpetually disintegrating synthesis and a perpetual game of escape from the for-itself to the for-others and from the for-others to the for-itself. We have seen also the use which our young woman made of our being-in-the-midst-of-the-world—*i.e.*, of our inert presence as a passive object among other objects—in order to relieve herself suddenly from the functions of her being-in-the-world—that is, from the being which makes there to be a world by projecting itself beyond the world toward its own possibilities. Let us note finally the confusing syntheses which play on the nihilating ambiguity of these temporal *ekstases,* affirming at once that I am what I have been (the man who deliberately *arrests himself* at one period in his life and refuses to take into consideration the later changes) and that I am not what I have been (the man who in the face of reproaches or rancor dissociates himself from his past by insisting on his freedom and on his perpetual re-creation). In all these concepts, which have only a transitive role in the reasoning and which are eliminated from the conclusion (like imaginary numbers in the calculations of physicists), we find again the same structure. We have to deal with human reality as a being which is what it is not and which is not what it is.

But what exactly is necessary in order for these concepts of disintegration to be able to receive even a pretense of existence, in order for them to be able to appear for a moment to consciousness, even in a process of evanescence? A quick examination of the idea of sincerity, the antithesis of bad faith, will be very instructive in this connection. Actually sincerity presents itself as a requirement and consequently is not a *state*. Now what is the ideal to be attained in this case? It is necessary that a man be *for himself* only what he *is*. But is this not precisely the definition of the in-itself—or if you prefer—the principle of identity? To posit as an ideal the being of things, is this not to assert at the same time that this being does not belong to human reality and that the principle of identity, far from being a universal axiom universally applied, is only a synthetic principle enjoying a merely regional universality? Thus in order that the concepts of bad faith can delude us at least for a moment, in order that the candor of "pure hearts" (*cf.* Gide, Kessel) can have validity for human reality as an ideal, the principle of identity must not represent a constitutive principle of human reality and human reality must not be necessarily what it is but must be able to be what it is not. What does this mean?

If man is what he is, bad faith is forever impossible and candor ceases to be his ideal and becomes instead his being. But is man what he is? And more generally, how can he *be* what he is when he exists as consciousness of being? If candor or sincerity is a universal value, it is evident that the maxim "one must be what one is" does not serve solely as a regulative principle for judgments and concepts by which I express what I am. It posits not merely an ideal of knowing but an ideal of *being;* it proposes to us an absolute conforming of being with itself as a prototype of being. In this sense it is necessary that we *make ourselves* what we are. But what *are we* then if we have the constant obligation to make ourselves what we are, if our mode of being is having the obligation to be what we are?

Take, for example, this waiter in the café. His movement is quick and studied, a little too precise, a little too rapid. He comes toward the patrons with a step a little too quick. He bends forward a little too eagerly; his voice, his eyes express an interest a little too solicitous for the order of the customer. Finally there he returns, trying to imitate in his walk the inflexible stiffness of some kind of automaton while carrying his tray with the recklessness of a tightrope walker by putting it in a perpetually unstable, perpetually broken equilibrium which he perpetually re-establishes by a light movement of the arm and hand. All his behavior seems to us a game. He is trying to link his movements together as if they were mechanisms, the one regulating the other; his gestures and even his voice seem to be mechanisms; he is imitating the quickness and pitiless rapidity of things. He is playing with himself. But what is he playing? We need not watch long before we can explain it: he is playing *at being* a waiter in a café. There is nothing there to surprise us. A game is a kind of investigation in which one gets one's bearings. The child plays with his body in order to explore it, to take inventory of it; the waiter in the café plays with his condition in order to *realize* it. This obligation is not different from that which is imposed on all tradesmen. Their condition is wholly one of ceremony. The public demands of them that they realize it as a ceremony; there is the dance of the grocer, of the tailor, of the auctioneer, by which they endeavor to persuade their clientele that they are nothing but a grocer, an auctioneer, a tailor. A grocer who dreams is offensive to the buyer, because such a grocer is not wholly a grocer. Etiquette requires that he limit himself to his function as a grocer, just as the soldier at attention makes himself into a soldier-thing with a look straight in front of him, which does not see at all, which is no longer meant to see, since it is the regulation and not the interest of the moment which determines the point on which he must fix his eyes (the look "fixed at ten paces"). There are indeed many precautions to imprison a man in what he is, as if we lived in perpetual fear that he might escape from it, that he might overflow and suddenly elude his condition.

At the same time, from the point of view of his own consciousness, the waiter in the café cannot be immediately a café waiter in the sense that this inkwell *is* an inkwell, or the glass *is* a glass. It is not that he cannot form reflective judgments or concepts concerning his condition. He knows well what it "means": the obligation of getting up at five o'clock, of sweeping the floor of the shop before the restaurant opens, of starting the coffee pot going, etc. He knows the rights which it allows: the right to the tips, the right to belong to a union, etc. But all these concepts, all these judgments refer to the transcendent. It is a matter of abstract possibilities, of rights and duties conferred on a "person possessing rights." And it is precisely this person *whom I have to be* (let us assume that I am the waiter in question) and who I am not. It is not that I do not wish to be this person or that I want this person to be different. But rather there is no common measure between his being and mine. It is a performance [*representation*] for others and for myself, which means that I can be the waiter only by "acting his part." But if I so represent myself, I am not he; I am separated from him as the object from the subject, separated *by nothing,* but this nothing isolates me from him. I cannot be he, I can only play *at being* him; that is, imagine to myself that I am he. And thereby I affect him with nothingness. In vain do I fulfill the functions of a café waiter. I can be the waiter only in the neutralized mode, as the actor is Hamlet, by mechanically making the *typical gestures* of my state and by aiming at myself as an imaginary café waiter through those gestures taken as an "analogue." What I attempt to realize is a being-in-itself of the café waiter, as if it were not just in my power to confer their value and their urgency upon my duties and the rights of my position, as if it were not my free choice to get up each morning at five o'clock or to remain in bed, even though it meant getting fired. As if from the very fact that I sustain this role in existence I did not transcend it on every side, as if I did not constitute myself as one *beyond* my condition. Yet there is no doubt that I *am* in a sense a café waiter—otherwise could I not just as well call myself a diplomat or a reporter? But if I am one, this cannot be in the mode of being-in-itself. I am a waiter in the mode of *being what I am not.*

Furthermore we are dealing with more than mere social positions; I am never any one of my attitudes, any one of my actions. The good speaker is the one who *plays* at speaking, because he cannot *be speaking.* The attentive pupil who wishes to *be* attentive, his eyes riveted on the teacher, his ears open wide, so exhausts himself in playing the attentive role that he ends up by no longer hearing anything. Perpetually absent to my body, to my acts, I am despite myself that "divine absence" of which Valéry speaks. I cannot say either that I *am* here or that I *am* not here, in the sense that we say "that box of matches *is* on the table"; this would be to confuse my "being-in-the world" with a "being-in the midst of the world." Nor that I *am* standing, nor that I *am* seated; this would be to confuse my body with the idiosyncratic totality of which it is only one of the structures. On all sides I escape being and yet—I am.

But take a mode of being which concerns only myself: I am sad. One might think that surely I am the sadness in the mode of being what I am. What is the sadness, however, if not the intentional unity which comes to reassemble and animate the totality of my conduct? It is the meaning of this dull look with which I view the world, of my bowed shoulders, of my lowered head, of the listlessness in my whole body. But at the very moment when I adopt each of these modes of behavior, do I not know that I can also not adopt it? Let a stranger suddenly appear and I will lift up my head, I will assume a lively cheerfulness. What will remain of my sadness except that I complacently promise it an appointment for later after the departure of the visitor? Moreover is not this sadness itself a mode of behavior? Is it not consciousness which affects itself with sadness as a magical recourse against a situation which is too urgent? And in this case even, should we not say that being sad means first to make oneself sad? That may be, someone will say, but after all doesn't giving oneself the being of sadness mean to *receive* this being? It makes no difference from where I receive it. The fact is that a consciousness which affects itself with sadness *is* sad precisely for this reason. But it is difficult to comprehend the nature of consciousness; the being-sad is not a ready-made being which I give to myself as I can give this book to my friend. I do not possess the property of *affecting myself with being.* If I make myself sad, I must continue to make myself sad from beginning to end. I cannot take advantage of the impetus already acquired and allow it to go on its way without re-creating it, nor can I carry it in the manner of an inert body which continues its movement after the initial shock. There is no inertia in consciousness. If I make myself sad, it is because I *am* not sad—the being of the sadness escapes me by and in the very act by which I affect myself with it. The being-in-itself of sadness perpetually haunts my consciousness (of) being sad, but it is as a value which I cannot realize; it stands as a regulative meaning of my sadness, not as its constitutive modality.

Someone may say that my consciousness at least *is,* whatever may be the object or the state of which it makes itself conscious. But how do we distinguish my consciousness (of) being sad from sadness? Is it not all one? It is true in a way that my consciousness *is,* if one means by this that for another it is a part of the totality of being on which judgments can be brought to bear. But it should be noted, as Husserl clearly understood, that my consciousness appears originally to the Other as an absence. It is the object always present as the *meaning* of all my attitudes and all my conduct—and always absent, for it gives itself to the intuition of another as a perpetual question—still better, as a perpetual freedom. When Peter looks at me, I know of course that he is looking at me. His eyes, things in the world, are fixed on my body, a thing in the world—that is the objective fact of which I can say: it *is.* But it is also a fact *in the world.* The meaning of this look is not a fact in the world, and this is what makes me uncomfortable. Although I smile, promise, threaten, nothing I do can get hold of the approbation, the free judgment which I seek;

I know that it is always beyond. I feel it in my actions themselves, which are no longer operations directed toward things. To the extent that they are linked with the other, they are for myself merely *presentations* which await being constituted as graceful or uncouth, sincere or insincere, etc., by an apprehension which is always beyond my efforts to provoke, an apprehension which will be provoked by my efforts only if of itself it lends them force (that is, only insofar as the apprehension allows itself to be provoked from the outside), and *is its own mediator with the transcendent.* Thus the objective fact of the being-in-itself of the consciousness of the Other is posited in order to disappear in negativity and in freedom: consciousness of the Other is as not-being; its being-in-itself "here and now" is not-to-be.

The Encounter with the Other

1. THE LOOK

We have described human reality from the standpoint of negative behavior and from the standpoint of the *cogito*. Following this lead we have discovered that human reality is-for-itself. Is this *all* that it is? Without going outside our attitude of reflective description, we can encounter modes of consciousness which seem, even while themselves remaining strictly in for-itself, to point to a radically different type of ontological structure. This ontological structure is *mine*; . . . I am concerned about myself, and yet this concern for-myself reveals to me a being which is *my* being without being-for-me.

Consider, for example, shame. Here we are dealing with a mode of consciousness which has a structure identical with all those which we have previously described. It is a non-positional self-consciousness, conscious (of) itself as shame; as such, it is an example of what the Germans call *Erlebnis*, and it is accessible to reflection. In addition its structure is intentional; it is a shameful apprehension *of* something and this something is *me*. I am ashamed of what I *am*. Shame therefore realizes an intimate relation of myself to myself. Through shame I have discovered an aspect of *my* being. Yet although certain complex forms derived from shame can appear on the reflective plane, shame is not originally a phenomenon of reflection. In fact no matter what results one can obtain in solitude by the religious *practice* of shame, it is in its primary structure shame *before somebody*. I have just made an awkward or vulgar gesture. This gesture clings to me; I neither judge it nor blame it. I simply live it. I realize it in the mode of for-itself. But now suddenly I raise my head. Somebody was there and has seen me. Suddenly I realize the vulgarity of my gesture, and I am ashamed. It is certain that my shame is not reflective, for the presence of another in my consciousness, even as a catalyst, is incompatible with the reflective attitude; in the field of my reflection I can never meet with anything but the consciousness which is mine. But the Other is the indispensable mediator between myself and me. I am ashamed of myself *as I appear* to the Other.

By the mere appearance of the Other, I am put in the position of passing judgment on myself as on an object, for it is as an object that I appear to the Other. Yet this object which has appeared to the Other is not an empty image in the mind of another. Such an image, in fact, would be imputable wholly to the Other and so could not "touch" me. I could feel irritation, or anger before it as before a bad portrait of myself which gives to my expression an ugliness or baseness which I do not have, but I could not be touched to the quick. Shame is by nature *recognition*. I recognize that I *am* as the Other sees me. There is however no question of a comparison between what I am for myself and what I am for the Other as if I found in myself, in the mode of being of the for-itself, an equivalent of what I am for the Other. In the first place this comparison is not encountered in us as the result of a concrete psychic operation. Shame is an immediate shudder which runs through me from head to foot without any discursive preparation. In addition the comparison is impossible; I am unable to bring about any relation between what I am in the intimacy of the for-itself, without distance, without withdrawal [*recul*], without perspective, and this unjustifiable being-in-itself which I am for the Other. There is no standard here, no table of correlation. Moreover the very notion of *vulgarity* implies an inter-monadic relation. Nobody can be vulgar all by himself!

Thus the Other has not only revealed to me what I was; he has established me in a new type of being which can support new qualifications. This being was not in me potentially before the appearance of the Other, for it could not have found any place in the for-itself. Even if some power had been pleased to endow me with a body wholly constituted before it should be for-others, still my vulgarity and my awkwardness could not lodge there potentially; for they are meanings and as such they transcend the body and at the same time refer to a witness capable of understanding them and to the totality of my human reality. But this new being which appears *for* the other does not reside *in* the Other; I am responsible for it as is shown very well by the educational procedure of making children ashamed of what they are.

Thus shame is shame *of oneself before the Other;* these two structures are inseparable. But at the same time I need the Other in order to realize fully all the structures of my being. The for-itself refers to the for-others. Therefore if we wish to grasp in its totality the relation of man's being to being-in-itself, we cannot be satisfied with the descriptions outlined in the earlier chapters of this work. We must answer two far more formidable questions: first that of the existence of the Other, then the question of my ontological relation to the being of the Other. . . .

I am in a public park. Not far away there is a lawn and along the edge of that lawn there are benches. A man passes by those benches. I see this man; I apprehend him as an object and at the same time as a man. What does this mean? What do I imply when I assert that this object *is a man*?

If I were to think of him as being only a puppet, I should apply to him the categories which I ordinarily use to group temporal-spatial "things." That is, I should apprehend him as being "be-side" the benches, two yards and twenty inches from the lawn, as exercising a certain pressure on the ground, etc. His relation with other objects would be of the purely additive type; this means that I could have him disappear without the relations of the other objects around him being perceptibly *changed*. In short, no new relation would appear *through him* between those things in my universe: grouped and synthesized *from my point of view* into instrumental complexes, they would *from his point of view* disintegrate into a plurality of indifferent relations. Perceiving him as a *man*, on the other hand, is not to apprehend an additive relation between the chair and him; it is to register an organization *without distance* of the things in my universe around that privileged object. To be sure, the lawn remains two yards and twenty inches away from him, but it is also *as a lawn* linked with him in a relation which at once both transcends distance and contains it. Instead of the two terms of the distance being indifferent, interchangeable, and in a reciprocal relation, the distance *is unfolded starting from* the man whom I see and *extending up to* the lawn as the synthetic emergence of a unilateral relation. We are dealing with a relation which is without *parts*, given immediately, inside of which there unfolds a spatiality which is not *my* spatiality; for instead of a grouping *toward me* of the objects, there is now an orientation *which flees from me*.

Of course this relation without distance and without parts is in no way that original relation of the Other to me which I am seeking. In the first place, it concerns only the man and the things in the world. In addition it is still an object of knowledge; I would express it, for example, by saying that this man sees the lawn, or that in spite of the prohibiting sign he is preparing to walk on the grass, etc. Finally it still retains a merely probable character: First, it is *probable* that this object is a man. Second, even granted that he is a man, it remains only probable that he *sees* the lawn at the moment that I perceive him; it is possible that he is dreaming of some project without exactly being aware of what is around him, or that he is blind, etc., etc. Nevertheless this new relation of the object-man to the object-lawn has a particular character; it is simultaneously given to me as a whole, since it is there in the world as an object which I can know (it is, in fact, an objective relation which I express by saying: Peter has glanced at this watch, John has looked out the window, etc.), and at the same time it entirely escapes me. To the extent that the man-as-object is the fundamental term of this relation, to the extent that the relation goes *toward him*, it escapes me. I cannot put myself at the center of it. The distance which unfolds between the lawn and the man across the synthetic emergence of this primary relation is a negation of the distance which I establish—as a pure type of external negation—between these two objects. The distance appears as a pure *disintegration* of the relations which I apprehend between the objects of my universe. It is not I who realize this disintegration; it appears to me as a relation which I aim at emptily across the distances which I originally established between things. It stands as a background of things, a background which on principle escapes me and which is conferred on them from without. Thus the appearance among the objects of *my* universe of an element of disintegration in that universe is what I mean by the appearance of a man in my universe.

The Other is first the permanent flight of things toward a limit which I apprehend as an object at a certain distance from me but which escapes me inasmuch as it unfolds about itself its own distances. Moreover this process of disintegration gains momentum; if there exists between the lawn and the Other a relation which is without distance and which creates distance, then there exists necessarily a relation between the Other and the statue which stands on a pedestal *in the middle of* the lawn, and a relation between the Other and the big chestnut trees which border the walk; there is a total space which is grouped around the Other, and this space is made *with my space;* there is a regrouping in which I participate but which escapes me, a regrouping of all the objects which people my universe. This regrouping does not stop there. The grass is something qualified; it is *this* green grass which exists for the Other; in this sense the very quality of the object, its deep, raw green is in direct relation to this man. This green turns toward the Other an aspect which escapes me. I apprehend the relation of the green to the Other as an objective relation, but I cannot apprehend the green *as* it appears to the Other. Thus suddenly an object has appeared which has stolen the world from me. Everything is in place; everything still exists for me; but everything is traversed by an invisible flight and congealed in the direction of a new object. The appearance of the Other in the world corresponds therefore to a congealed sliding of the whole universe, to a decentralization of the world which undermines the centralization which I am simultaneously effecting.

But *the Other* is still an object *for me*. He belongs to *my distances;* the man is there, twenty paces from me, he is turning his back on me. As such he is again two yards, twenty inches from the lawn, six yards from the statue; hence the disintegration of my universe is contained within the limits of this same universe; we are not dealing here with a flight of the world toward nothingness or outside itself. Rather it appears that the world has a kind of drain hole in the middle of its being and that it is perpetually flowing off through this hole. The universe, the flow, and the drain hole are all once again recovered, reapprehended, and congealed into an object. All this is there *for me* as a partial structure of the world, even though the total disintegration of the universe is involved. Moreover these disintegrations may often be contained within more narrow limits. There, for example, is a man who is reading while he walks. The disintegration of the universe which he represents is purely virtual; he has ears which do not hear, eyes which see nothing except his book. Between his book and him I apprehend an undeniable relation without distance of the same type as that which earlier connected the walker with the grass. But this time the form has closed in on itself. There is a full object for me to grasp. In the midst of the world I can say "man-reading" as I could say "cold stone," "fine rain." I apprehend a closed "Gestalt" in which the *reading* forms the essential quality; for the rest, it remains blind and mute, lets itself be known and perceived as a pure and simple temporal-spatial thing, and seems to be related to the rest of the world by a purely indifferent externality. The quality "man-reading" as the relation of the man to the book is simply a little particular crack in my universe. At the heart of this solid, visible form he makes himself a particular emptying. The form is massive only in appearance; its peculiar meaning is to be—in the midst of my universe, at ten paces from me, at the heart of that massivity—a closely consolidated and localized flight.

None of this enables us to leave the level on which the Other is an *object*. At most we are dealing with a particular type of objectivity akin to that which Husserl designated by the term *absence* without, however, his noting that the Other is defined not as the absence of a consciousness in relation to the body which I see but by the absence of the world which I perceive, an absence discovered at the very heart of my perception of this world. On this level the Other is an object in the world, an object which can be defined by the world. But this relation of flight and of absence on the part of the world in relation to me is only probable. If it is this which defines the objectivity of the Other, then to what original presence of the Other does it refer? Now we can give this answer: if the Other-as-object is defined in connection with the world as the object which *sees* what I see, then my fundamental connection with the Other-as-subject must be able to be referred back to my permanent possibility of *being seen* by the Other. It is in and through the revelation of my being-as-object for the Other that I must be able to apprehend the presence of his being-as-subject. For just as the Other is a probable object for me-as-subject, so I can discover myself in the process of becoming a probable object for only a certain subject. This revelation cannot derive from the fact that *my universe is an object for the Other-as-object,* as if the Other's look after having wandered over the lawn and the surrounding objects came following a definite path to place itself on me. I have observed that I cannot be an object for an object. A radical conversion of the Other is necessary if he is to escape objectivity. Therefore I cannot consider the look which the Other directs on me as one of the possible manifestations of his objective being; the Other cannot look at *me* as he looks at the grass. Furthermore my objectivity cannot itself derive *for me* from the objectivity of the world since I am precisely the one by whom *there is* a world; that is, the one who on principle cannot be an object for himself.

Thus this relation which I call "being-seen-by-another," far from being merely one of the relations signified by the word *man*, represents an irreducible fact which cannot be deduced either from the essence of the Other-as-object, or from my being-as-subject. On the contrary, if the concept of the Other-as-object is to have any meaning, this can be only as the result of the conversion and the degradation of that original relation. In a word, my apprehension of the Other in the world as *probably being* a man refers to my permanent possibility of *being-seen-by-him;* that is, to the permanent possibility that a subject who sees me may be substituted for the object seen by me. "Being-seen-by-the-Other" is the *truth* of "seeing-the-Other." Thus the notion of the Other cannot under any circumstances aim at a solitary, extra-mundane consciousness which I cannot even think. The man is defined by his relation to the world and by his relation to myself. He is that object in the world which determines an internal flow of the universe, an internal hemorrhage. He is the subject who is revealed to me in that flight of myself toward objectivation. But the original relation of myself to the Other is not only an absent truth aimed at across the concrete presence of an object in my universe; it is also a concrete, daily relation which at each instant I experience. At each instant the Other *is looking at me.* It is easy therefore for us to attempt with concrete examples to describe this fundamental relationship which must form the basis of any theory concerning the Other. If the Other is on principle the *one who looks at me*, then we must be able to explain the meaning of the Other's look.

Every look directed toward me is manifested in connection with the appearance of a sensible form in our perceptive field, but contrary to what might be expected, it is not connected with any specific form. Of course what *most often* manifests a look is the convergence of two ocular globes in my direction. But the look will be given just as well on occasion when there is a rustling of branches, or the sound of a footstep followed by silence, or the slight opening of a shutter, or a light movement of a curtain. During an attack, men who are crawling through the brush apprehend as a *look to be avoided,* not two eyes, but a white farmhouse which is outlined against the sky at the top of a little hill. It is obvious that the object thus constituted still manifests the look as being probable. It is only probable that behind the bush which has just moved there is someone hiding who is watching me. But this probability need not detain us for the moment; we shall return to this point later. What is important first is to define the look in itself. Now the bush, the farmhouse are not the look; they only represent the *eye,* for the eye is not at first apprehended as a sensible organ of vision but as the support for the look. They never refer therefore to the actual eye of the watcher hidden behind the curtain, behind a window in the farmhouse. In themselves they are already eyes. On the other hand neither is the look one quality among others of the object which functions as an eye, nor is it the total form of that object, nor a "worldly" relation which is established between that object and me. On the contrary, far from perceiving the look *on* the objects which manifest it, my apprehension of a look turned toward me appears on the ground of the destruction of the eyes which "look at me." If I apprehend the look, I cease to perceive the eyes; they are there, they remain in the field of my perception as pure *presentations,* but I do not make any use of them; they are neutralized, put out of play; they are no longer the object of a thesis but remain in that state of "disconnection" in which the world is put by a consciousness practicing the phenomenological reduction prescribed by Husserl. It is never when eyes are looking at you that you can find them beautiful or ugly, that you can notice their color. The Other's look disguises his eyes; he seems to go *in front of them.* This illusion stems from the fact that eyes as objects of my perception remain at a precise distance which unfolds from me to them (in a word, I am present to the eyes without distance, but they are distant from the place where I "find myself"), whereas the look is upon me without distance while at the same time it holds me at a distance—that is, its immediate presence to me unfolds a distance which removes me from it. I cannot therefore direct my attention on the look without at the same time having my perception decompose and pass into the background. There is produced here something analogous to what I attempted to show elsewhere in connection with the subject of the imagination. We cannot, I said then, perceive and imagine simultaneously; it must be either one or the other. I would add here: we cannot perceive the world and at the same time apprehend a look fastened upon us; it must be either one or the other. This is because to perceive is to *look at*, and to apprehend a look is not to apprehend a look-as-object in the world (unless the look is not directed upon us); it is to be conscious of *being looked at*. The look which the eyes manifest, no matter what kind of eyes they are, is a pure reference to myself. What I apprehend immediately when I hear the branches crackling behind me is not that *there is someone there;* it is that I am vulnerable, that I have a body which can be hurt, that I occupy a place and that I cannot in any case escape from the space in which I am without defense—in short, that I *am seen.* Thus the look is first an intermediary which refers from me to myself. What is the nature of this intermediary? What does *being seen* mean for me?

2. SHAME

Let us imagine that moved by jealousy, curiosity, or vice I have just glued my ear to the door and looked through a keyhole. I am alone and on the level of a non-thetic self-consciousness. This means first of all that there is no self to inhabit my consciousness, nothing therefore to which I can refer my acts in order to qualify them. They are in no way *known;* I *am my* acts and hence they carry in themselves their whole justification. I am a pure consciousness *of* things, and things, caught up in the circuit of my selfness, offer to me their potentialities as the replica of my non-thetic consciousness (of) my own possibilities. This means that behind that door a spectacle is presented as "to be seen," a conversation as "to be heard." The door, the keyhole are at once both instruments and obstacles; they are presented as "to be handled with care"; the keyhole is given as "to be looked through close by and a little to one side," etc. Hence from this moment "I do what I have to do." No transcending view comes to confer upon my acts the character of a *given* on which a judgment can be brought to bear. My consciousness clings to my acts, it *is* my acts; and my acts are commanded only by the ends to be attained and by the instruments to be employed. My attitude, for example, has no "outside"; it is a pure process of relating the instrument (the keyhole) to the end to be attained (the spectacle to be seen), a pure mode of losing myself in the world, of making myself absorbed by things as ink is by a blotter in order that an instrumental complex oriented toward an end may be synthetically detached on the ground of the world. The order is the reverse of causal order. It is the end to be attained which organizes all the moments which precede it. The end justifies the means; the means do not exist for themselves and outside the end.

Moreover the ensemble exists only in relation to a free project of my possibilities. Jealousy, as the possibility which I *am,* organizes this instrumental complex by transcending the complex toward itself. But I *am* this jealousy; I do not *know* it. If I contemplated it instead of making it, then only the worldly complex of instrumentality could teach it to me. This complex with its double and inverted determination (there is a spectacle to be seen behind the door only because I am jealous, but my jealousy is nothing except the simple objective fact that *there is* a sight to *be seen* behind the door)—this we shall call *situation.* This situation reflects to me at once both my facticity and my freedom; on the occasion of a certain objective structure of the world which surrounds me, it refers my freedom to me in the form of tasks to be freely done. There is no constraint here since my freedom gnaws away at my possibles and since correlatively the potentialities of the world indicate and offer only themselves. Moreover I cannot truly define myself as *being* in a situation: first because I am not a positional consciousness of myself; second because I am my own nothingness. In this sense—and since I am what I am not and since I am not what I am—I cannot even define myself as truly *being* in the process of listening at doors. I escape this temporary definition of myself by means of all my transcendence. There as we have seen is the origin of bad faith. Thus not only am I unable to *know* myself, but my very being escapes—although I *am* that very escape from my being—and I am absolutely nothing. There is nothing *there* but a pure nothingness encircling a certain objective complex and throwing it into relief upon the world, but this complex is a real system, a disposition of means in view of an end.

But suddenly I hear footsteps in the hall. Someone is looking at me! What does this mean? It means that I am suddenly affected in my being and that essential modifications appear in my structure—modifications which I can apprehend and fix conceptually by means of the reflective *cogito*.

First of all, I now exist as *myself* for my unreflective consciousness. This irruption of the self has often been described: I see *myself* because *somebody* sees me—as it is usually expressed. This way of putting it is not wholly accurate. Let us look more carefully. So long as we considered the for-itself in its isolation, we were able to maintain that the unreflective consciousness cannot be inhabited by a self; the self was given in the form of an object and only for the reflective consciousness. But here the self comes to haunt the unreflective consciousness. Now the unreflective consciousness is a consciousness *of* the world. Therefore for the unreflective consciousness the self exists on the level of objects-in-the-world; this role which devolved only on the reflective consciousness—the making-present of the self—belongs now to the unreflective consciousness. Only the reflective consciousness has the self directly for an object. The unreflective consciousness does not apprehend the *person* directly or as *its* object; the person is presented to consciousness *insofar as the person is an object for the Other*. This means that all of a sudden I am conscious of myself as escaping myself, not in that I am the foundation of my own nothingness but in that I have my foundation outside myself. I am for myself only as I am a pure reference to the Other.

Nevertheless we must not conclude here that the object is the Other and that the *ego* present to my consciousness is a secondary structure or a meaning of the Other-as-object; the Other is not an object here and cannot be an object, as we have shown, unless at the same time *my* self ceases to be an object-for-the-Other and vanishes. Thus I do not aim at the Other as an object nor at my *ego* as an object for myself; I do not even direct an empty intention toward the *ego* as toward an object presently out of my reach. In fact it is separated from me by a nothingness which I cannot fill since I apprehend it *as not being for me* and since on principle it exists for the *Other.* Therefore I do not aim at it as if it could someday be given me but on the contrary insofar as it on principle flees from me and will never belong to me. Nevertheless I *am that ego;* I do not repudiate it as an alien image, but it is present to me as a self which I *am* without *knowing* it; for I discover it in shame and, in other instances, in pride. It is shame or pride which reveals to me the Other's look and myself at the terminus of that look. It is the shame or pride which makes me *live,* not *know* the situation of being looked at.

Now, shame, as we noted at the beginning of this chapter, is shame of *self;* it is the *recognition* of the fact that I *am* indeed that object which the Other is looking at and judging. I can be ashamed only as my freedom escapes me in order to become a *given* object. Thus originally the relation between my unreflective consciousness and my *ego,* which is being looked at, is a relation not of knowing but of being. Beyond any knowledge which I can have, I am this self which another knows. And this self which I am—this I am in a world which the Other has made alien to me, for the Other's look embraces my being and correlatively the walls, the door, the keyhole. All these instrumental things in the midst of which I am, now turn toward the Other an aspect which on principle escapes me. Thus I am my *ego* for the Other in the midst of a world which flows toward the Other. Earlier we were able to describe as an internal hemorrhage the flow of *my* world toward the Other-as-object. For in effect the flow of blood was trapped and localized by the very fact that I congealed into an object in my world that Other toward which this world was bleeding. Thus not a drop of blood was lost; all was recovered, surrounded, localized although in a being which I could not penetrate. Here in contrast the flow is without limit; it is lost externally; the world flows out of the world and I flow outside myself. The Other's look makes me be beyond my being in this world and puts me in the midst of the world which is at once *this world* and beyond this world. What sort of relations can I enter into with this being which I am and which shame reveals to me?

In the first place there is a relation of being. I *am* this being. I do not for an instant think of denying it; my shame is a confession. I shall be able later to use bad faith so as to hide it from myself, but bad faith is also a confession since it is an effort to flee the being which I am. But I am this being, neither in the mode of "having to be" nor in that of "was"; I do not found it in its being; I cannot produce it directly. But neither is it the indirect, strict effect of my acts as when my shadow on the ground or my reflection in the mirror is moved in correlation with the gestures which I make. This being which I am preserves a certain indeterminacy, a certain unpredictability. And these new characteristics do not come only from the fact that I cannot *know* the Other; they stem also and especially from the fact that the Other is free. Or to be exact and to reverse the terms, the Other's freedom is revealed to me across the uneasy indeterminacy of the being which I am for him. Thus this being is not my possible; it is not always in question at the heart of my freedom. On the contrary, it is the other side of my freedom. It is given to me as a burden which I carry without ever being able to turn back to know it, without even being able to realize its weight. If it is comparable to my shadow, it is like a shadow which is projected on a moving and unpredictable material such that no table of reference can be provided for calculating the distortions resulting from these movements. Yet we still have to do with *my* being and not with an image of my being. We are dealing with my being as it is inscribed in and by the Other's freedom. Everything takes place as if I had a dimension of being from which I was separated by a radical nothingness; and this nothingness is the Other's freedom. The Other has to make my being-for-him *be* insofar as he has to be his being. Thus each of my free acts involves me in a new setting where the very material of my being is the unpredictable freedom of another. Yet by my very shame I claim as mine that freedom of another. I affirm a profound unity of consciousnesses, not that harmony of monads which has sometimes been taken as a guarantee of objectivity but a unity of being; for I accept and wish that others should confer upon me a being which I recognize.

Shame reveals to me that I *am* this being, not in the mode of "was" or of "having to be" but *in-itself.* When I am alone, I cannot realize my "being-seated"; at most it can be said that I simultaneously both am it and am not it. But in order for me to be what I am, it suffices merely that the Other look at me. It is not for myself, to be sure; I myself shall never succeed at realizing this being-seated which I grasp in the Other's look. I shall remain forever a consciousness. But it is for the Other. Once more the nihilating escape of the for-itself is congealed, once more the in-itself closes in upon the for-itself. But once more this metamorphosis is effected at a *distance*. For the Other I *am seated* as this inkwell *is* on the table; for the Other, I *am bending over* the keyhole as this tree *is bent* by the wind. Thus for the Other I have stripped myself of my transcendence. This is because my transcendence becomes for whoever makes himself a witness of it (*i.e.*, determines himself as *not being* my transcendence) a purely observed transcendence, a given transcendence; that is, it acquires a nature by the sole fact that the *Other* confers on it an outside. This is achieved, not by any distortion or by a refraction which the Other would impose on my transcendence through his categories, but by his very being. If there is an Other, whatever or whoever he may be, whatever may be his relations with me, and without his acting upon me in any way except by the pure emergence of his being—then I have an outside, I have a *nature*. My original fall is the existence of the Other. Shame—like pride—is the apprehension of myself as a nature although that very nature escapes me and is unknowable as such. Strictly speaking, it is not that I perceive myself losing my freedom in order to become a *thing*, but my nature is—over there, outside my lived freedom—as a given attribute of this being which I am for the Other.

I grasp the Other's look at the very center of my *act* as the solidification and alienation of my own possibilities. In fear or in anxious or prudent anticipation, I perceive that these possibilities which I *am* and which are the condition of my transcendence are given also to another, given as about to be transcended in turn by his own possibilities. The Other as a look is only that—my transcendence transcended. Of course I still *am* my possibilities in the mode of non-thetic consciousness (of) these possibilities. But at the same time the look alienates them from me. Hitherto I grasped these possibilities thetically on the world and in the world in the form of the potentialities of instruments: the dark corner in the hallway referred to me the possibility of hiding—as a simple potential quality of its shadow, as the invitation of its darkness. This quality or instrumentality of the object belonged to it alone and was given as an objective, ideal property marking its real belonging to that complex which we have called *situation*. But with the Other's look a new organization of complexes comes to superimpose itself on the first. To apprehend myself as seen is, in fact, to apprehend myself as seen *in the world* and from the standpoint of the world. The look does not carve me out in the universe; it comes to search for me at the heart of my situation and grasps me only in irresolvable relations with instruments. If I am seen as seated, I must be seen as "seated-on-a chair," if I am grasped as bent over, it is as "bent-over-the-keyhole," etc. But suddenly the alienation of myself, which is the act of being-looked-at, involves the alienation of the world which I organize. I am seen as seated on this chair with the result that I do not see it at all, that it is impossible for me to see it, that it escapes me so as to organize itself into a new and differently oriented complex—with other relations and other distances in the midst of other objects which similarly have for me a secret aspect.

Thus I who, insofar as I am my possibles, am what I am not and am not what I am—behold now I *am* somebody! And the one who I am—and who on principle escapes me—I am he *in the midst of the world* insofar as he escapes me. Due to this fact my relation to an object or the potentiality of an object decomposes under the Other's look and appears to me in the world as my possibility of utilizing the object, but only as this possibility on principle escapes me; that is, insofar as it is transcended by the Other toward his own possibilities. For example, the potentiality of the dark corner becomes a given possibility of hiding in the corner by the sole fact that the Other can transcend it toward his possibility of illuminating the corner with his flashlight. This possibility is there, and I apprehend it but as absent, as *in the Other;* I apprehend it through my anguish and through my decision to give up that hiding place which is "*too risky.*" Thus my possibilities are present to my unreflective consciousness insofar as the Other *is watching for me.* If I see him ready for anything, his hand in his pocket where he has a weapon, his finger placed on the electric bell and ready "at the slightest movement on my part" to call the police, I apprehend my possibilities from outside and through him at the same time that I *am* my possibilities, somewhat as we objectively apprehend our thought through language at the same time that we think it *in order to* express it in language. This inclination to run away, which dominates me and carries me along and which I *am*—this I read in the Other's watchful look and in that other look—the gun pointed at me. The Other apprehends this inclination in me insofar as he has anticipated it and is already prepared for it. He apprehends it in me insofar as he surpasses it and disarms it. But I do not grasp the actual transcending; I grasp simply the death of my possibility. A subtle death: for my possibility of hiding still remains *my* possibility; inasmuch as I *am* it, it still lives; and the dark corner does not cease to indicate to me its potentiality to me. But if instrumentality is defined as the fact of "being able to be transcended toward———," then my very possibility becomes an instrumentality. My possibility of hiding in the corner becomes the fact that the Other can transcend it toward his possibility of pulling me out of concealment, of identifying me, of arresting me. *For the Other* my possibility is at once an obstacle and a means as all instruments are. It is an obstacle, for it will compel him to certain new acts (to advance toward me, to turn on his flashlight). It is a means, for once I am discovered in this cul-de-sac, I "am caught." In other words every act performed against the Other can on principle be for the Other an instrument which will serve him against me. And I grasp the Other not in the clear vision of what he can make out of my act but in a fear which *lives* all my possibilities as ambivalent. The Other is the hidden death of my possibilities insofar as I live that death as hidden in the midst of the world. The connection between my possibility and the instrument is no more than between two instruments which are adjusted externally to each other to achieve an end which eludes me. *Both* the obscurity of the dark corner and my possibility of hiding there are transcended by the Other when, before I have been able to make a move to take refuge there, he throws the light on the corner. Thus in the jolt I feel when I apprehend the Other's look, suddenly I experience a subtle alienation of all my possibilities, which are now associated with objects of the world, far from me in the midst of the world. . . .

With the Other's look the "situation" escapes me. To use an everyday expression which better expresses our thought, I *am no longer master of the situation.* Or more exactly, I remain master of it, but it has one real dimension by which it escapes me, by which unforeseen reversals cause it *to be* otherwise than it appears for me. To be sure it can happen that in strict solitude I perform an act whose consequences are completely opposed to my anticipations and to my desires; for example I gently draw toward me a small platform holding this fragile vase, but this movement results in tipping over a bronze statuette which breaks the vase into a thousand pieces. Here, however, there is nothing which I could not have foreseen if I had been more careful, if I had observed the arrangement of the objects, etc.—*nothing which on principle escapes me.* The appearance of the Other, on the contrary, causes the appearance in the situation of an aspect which I did not wish, of which I am not master, and which on principle escapes me since it is *for the Other.* This is what Gide has appropriately called "the devil's part." It is the unpredictable but still real *reverse side.*

It is this unpredictability which Kafka's art attempts to describe in *The Trial* and *The Castle.* In one sense everything which K. and the Surveyor are doing belongs strictly to them in their own right, and insofar as they act upon the world the results conform strictly to anticipations; they are successful acts. But at the same time the *truth* of these acts constantly escapes them; the acts have on principle a meaning which is their *true meaning* and which neither K. nor the Surveyor will ever know. Without doubt Kafka is trying here to express the transcendence of the divine; it is for the divine that the human act is constituted in truth. But God here is only the concept of the Other pushed to the limit. We shall return to this point. That gloomy, evanescent atmosphere of *The Trial,* that ignorance which, however, is lived as ignorance, that total opacity which can only be felt as a presentiment across a total translucency—this is nothing but the description of our being-in-the-midst-of-the-world-for-others. . . .

SIMONE DE BEAUVOIR

Simone de Beauvoir was born in Paris on January 9, 1908. An avowed atheist but a cultural conservative, de Beauvoir's father was an upwardly mobile individual who harbored aspirations as an actor, dabbled in the theater, studied law, but ultimately went to work as a legal secretary in the civil service. De Beauvoir's mother was from an aristocratic, staunchly Catholic family, and despite her husband's hostility to religion, she struggled to raise her daughter in the Catholic faith. She succeeded for a time, but at the age of fourteen de Beauvoir had a deconversion experience that left her cold to faith for the rest of her life.

A brilliant student, de Beauvoir began studying philosophy in her high school years. In 1925, she passed her baccalaureate exam in math and philosophy, and soon thereafter she started her studies at the Sorbonne. De Beauvoir wrote a thesis on Gottfried Wilhelm von Leibniz, and at the young age of twenty-one, she took second place to her classmate Jean-Paul Sartre in the highly competitive aggregate exam in philosophy. In the process of cramming for that exam together, de Beauvoir and Sartre became lifelong friends and lovers. For the time, their relationship was highly unconventional.

Sartre and de Beauvoir were candid about the fact that they would never marry, and they made it known that they were involved in an open relationship; open, that is, to the possibility of love and love affairs with others. De Beauvoir had dalliances with both men and women, and she and Sartre entered into triangular relationships with other women. In 1943, with Sartre's approval, de Beauvoir published a fictionalized account of the love triangle among Sartre, Olga Kosakievicz, and herself. The book, *She Came to Stay*, sold very well and launched de Beauvoir on the writing career that she had always aspired to. It was followed by a string of novels and plays.

During the German occupation, the Nazis had de Beauvoir dismissed from her lycée teaching post; nevertheless, she was not a particularly active member of the Resistance. After the war, de Beauvoir wrote articles for and helped edit the prestigious *Les Temps Modernes*, a French literary and political review. In 1949, she published her most influential book, *The Second Sex*. In this work that was, at the time, highly controversial, de Beauvoir argues that men have succeeded in defining themselves as the norm (consider, for example, the use of the masculine pronoun to refer to an unspecified individual) and in the process women are automatically regarded as "the other." In this proto-feminist treatise, de Beauvoir takes the Sartrean position, to be tempered in later years, that women are largely responsible for accepting the chauvinist structure of society. Not surprisingly, the heroines in many of de Beauvoir's novels were women who, like herself, refused to abide by social conventions.

Ironically enough, however, de Beauvoir often referred to herself as Sartre's disciple. And the reader will be able to detect Sartre's presence in our selection from de Beauvoir's *Ethics of Ambiguity* (1947). It is as if de Beauvoir is here trying to provide the promised (but never delivered) sequel on ethics to Sartre's *Being and Nothingness*.

For Sartre, there is no God, no divine plan, no universal moral law, and the French philosopher has often been condemned for the fact that his radical view of human freedom shipwrecks normative ethics. Given Sartre's position, what rational grounds are there for claiming that one action is better than another? De Beauvoir tries to resolve this question for Sartre. While acknowledging that "ethics does not provide recipes" and that we are condemned to ambiguity, de Beauvoir argues, in an almost Kantian fashion, that moral worth resides in the way that we relate ourselves to our own freedom and to the freedom of others. The analysis of freedom is the axial point of de Beauvoir's authorship, and she works this theme out very well in her piquant collection of short stories *The Woman Destroyed*.

After Sartre's death in 1980, de Beauvoir published *Adieu: A Farewell to Sartre*. Shortly before she died in 1986, de Beauvoir also published an intriguing collection of letters from her lifelong companion.

The notion of ambiguity must not be confused with that of absurdity. To declare that existence is absurd is to deny that it can ever be given a meaning; to say that it is ambiguous is to assert that its meaning is never fixed, that it must be constantly won. Absurdity challenges every ethics; but also the finished rationalization of the real would leave no room for ethics; it is because man's condition is ambiguous that he seeks, through failure and outrageousness, to save his existence. Thus, to say that action has to be lived in its truth, that is, in the consciousness of the antinomies which it involves, does not mean that one has to renounce it. In *Plutarch Lied* Pierrefeu rightly says that in war there is no victory which can not be regarded as unsuccessful, for the objective which one aims at is the total annihilation of the enemy and this result is never attained; yet there are wars which are won and wars which are lost. So is it with any activity; failure and success are two aspects of reality which at the start are not perceptible. That is what makes criticism so easy and art so difficult: the critic is always in a good position to show the limits that every artist gives himself in choosing himself; painting is not given completely either in Giotto or Titian or Cézanne; it is sought through the centuries and is never finished; a painting in which all pictorial problems are resolved is really inconceivable; painting itself is this movement toward its own reality; it is not the vain displacement of a millstone turning in the void; it concretizes itself on each canvas as an absolute existence. Art and science do not establish themselves despite failure but through it; which does not prevent there being truths and errors, masterpieces and lemons, depending upon whether the discovery or the painting has or has not known how to win the adherence of human consciousnesses; this amounts to saying that failure, always ineluctable, is in certain cases spared and in others not.

It is interesting to pursue this comparison; not that we are likening action to a work of art or a scientific theory, but because in any case human transcendence must cope with the same problem: it has to found itself, though it is prohibited from ever fulfilling itself. Now, we know that neither science nor art ever leaves it up to the future to justify its present existence. In no age does art consider itself as something which is paving the way for Art: so-called archaic art prepares for classicism only in the eyes of archaeologists; the sculptor who fashioned the Korai of Athens rightfully thought that he was producing a finished work of art; in no age has science considered itself as partial and lacunary; without believing itself to be definitive, it has however, always wanted to be a total expression of the world, and it is in its totality that in each age it again raises the question of its own validity. There we have an example of how man must, in any event, assume his finiteness: not by treating his existence as transitory or relative but by reflecting the infinite within it, that is, by treating it as absolute. There is an art only because at every moment art has willed itself absolutely; likewise there is a liberation of man only if, in aiming at itself, freedom is achieved absolutely in the very fact of aiming at itself. This requires that each action be considered as a finished form whose different moments, instead of fleeing toward the future in order to find there their justification, reflect and confirm one another so well that there is no longer a sharp separation between present and future, between means and ends.

But if these moments constitute a unity, there must be no contradiction among them. Since the liberation aimed at is not a *thing* situated in an unfamiliar time, but a movement which realizes itself by tending to conquer, it can not attain itself if it denies itself at the start; action can not seek to fulfill itself by means which would destroy its very meaning. So much so that in certain situations there will be no other issue for man than rejection. In what is called political realism there is no room for rejection because the present is considered as transitory; there is rejection only if man lays claim in the present to his existence as an absolute value; then he must absolutely reject what would deny this value. Today, more or less consciously in the name of such an ethics, we condemn a magistrate who handed over a communist to save ten hostages and along with him all the Vichyites who were trying "to make the best of things": it was not a matter of rationalizing the present such as it was imposed by the German occupation, but of rejecting it unconditionally. The resistance did not aspire to a positive effectiveness; it was a negation, a revolt, a martyrdom; and in this negative movement freedom was positively and absolutely confirmed.

In one sense the negative attitude is easy; the rejected object is given unequivocally and unequivocally defines the revolt that one opposes to it; thus, all French anti-fascists were united during the occupation by their common resistance to a single oppressor. The return to the positive encounters many more obstacles, as we have well seen in France where divisions and hatreds were revived at the same time as were the parties. In the moment of rejection, the antinomy of action is removed, and means and end meet; freedom immediately sets itself up as its own goal and fulfills itself by so doing. But the antinomy reappears as soon as freedom again gives itself ends which are far off in the future;

then, through the resistances of the given, divergent means offer themselves and certain ones come to be seen as contrary to their ends. It has often been observed that revolt alone is pure. Every construction implies the outrage of dictatorship, of violence. This is the theme, among others, of Koestler's *Gladiators.* Those who, like this symbolic *Spartacus,* do not want to retreat from the outrage and resign themselves to impotence, usually seek refuge in the values of seriousness. That is why, among individuals as well as collectivities, the negative moment is often the most genuine. Goethe, Barrès, and Aragón, disdainful or rebellious in their romantic youth, shattered old conformisms and thereby proposed a real, though incomplete, liberation. But what happened later on? Goethe became a servant of the state, Barrès of nationalism, and Aragón of Stalinist conformism. We know how the seriousness of the Catholic Church was substituted for the Christian spirit, which was a rejection of dead Law, a subjective rapport of the individual with God through faith and charity; the Reformation was a revolt of subjectivity, but Protestantism in turn changed into an objective moralism in which the seriousness of works replaced the restlessness of faith. As for revolutionary humanism, it accepts only rarely the tension of permanent liberation; it has created a Church where salvation is bought by membership in a party as it is bought elsewhere by baptism and indulgences. We have seen that this recourse to the serious is a lie; it entails the sacrifice of man to the Thing, of freedom to the Cause. In order for the return to the positive to be genuine it must involve negativity, it must not conceal the antinomies between means and end, present and future; they must be lived in a permanent tension; one must retreat from neither the outrage of violence nor deny it, or, which amounts to the same thing, assume it lightly. Kierkegaard has said that what distinguishes the pharisee from the genuinely moral man is that the former considers his anguish as a sure sign of his virtue; from the fact that he asks himself, "Am I Abraham?" he concludes, "I am Abraham"; but morality resides in the painfulness of an indefinite questioning. The problem which we are posing is not the same as that of Kierkegaard; the important thing to us is to know whether, in given conditions, Isaac must be killed or not. But we also think that what distinguishes the tyrant from the man of good will is that the first rests in the certainty of his aims, whereas the second keeps asking himself, "Am I really working for the liberation of men? Isn't this end contested by the sacrifices through which I aim at it?" In setting up its ends, freedom must put them in parentheses, confront them at each moment with that absolute end which it itself constitutes, and contest, in its own name, the means it uses to win itself.

It will be said that these considerations remain quite abstract. What must be done, practically? Which action is good? Which is bad? To ask such a question is also to fall into a naive abstraction. We don't ask the physicist, "Which hypotheses are true?" Nor the artist, "By what procedures does one produce a work whose beauty is guaranteed?" Ethics does not furnish recipes any more than do science and art. One can merely propose methods. Thus, in science the fundamental problem is to make the idea adequate to its content and the law adequate to the facts; the logician finds that in the case where the pressure of the given fact bursts the concept which serves to comprehend it, one is obliged to invent another concept; but he can not define *a priori* the moment of invention, still less foresee it. Analogously, one may say that in the case where the content of the action falsifies its meaning, one must modify not the meaning, which is here willed absolutely, but the content itself; however, it is impossible to determine this relationship between meaning and content abstractly and universally: there must be a trial and decision in each case. But likewise just as the physicist finds it profitable to reflect on the conditions of scientific invention and the artist on those of artistic creation without expecting any ready-made solutions to come from these reflections, it is useful for the man of action to find out under what conditions his undertakings are valid. We are going to see that on this basis new perspectives are disclosed.

In the first place, it seems to us that the individual as such is one of the ends at which our action must aim. Here we are at one with the point of view of Christian charity, the Epicurean cult of friendship, and Kantian moralism which treats each man as an end. He interests us not merely as a member of a class, a nation, or a collectivity, but as an individual man. This distinguishes us from the systematic politician who cares only about collective destinies; and probably a tramp enjoying his bottle of wine, or a child playing with a balloon, or a Neapolitan lazzarone loafing in the sun in no way helps in the liberation of man; that is why the abstract will of the revolutionary scorns the concrete benevolence which occupies itself in satisfying desires which have no morrow. However, it must not be forgotten that there is a concrete bond between freedom and existence; to will man free is to will there to *be* being, it is to will the disclosure of being in the joy of existence; in order for the idea of liberation to have a concrete meaning, the joy of existence must be asserted in each one, at every instant; the movement toward freedom assumes its real, flesh and blood figure in the world by thickening into pleasure, into happiness. If the satisfaction of an old man drinking a glass of wine counts for nothing, then production and wealth are only hollow myths; they have meaning only if they are capable of being retrieved in individual and living joy. The saving of time and the conquest of leisure have no meaning if we are not moved by the laugh of a child at play. If we do not love life on our own account and through others, it is futile to seek to justify it in any way.

However, politics is right in rejecting benevolence to the extent that the latter thoughtlessly sacrifices the future to the present. The ambiguity of freedom, which very often is occupied only in fleeing from itself, introduces a difficult equivocation into relationships with each individual taken one by one. Just what is meant by the expression "to love others"? What is meant by taking them as ends? In any event, it is evident that we are not going to decide to fulfill the will of every man. There are cases where a man positively wants evil, that is, the enslavement of other men, and he must then be fought. It also happens that, without harming anyone, he flees from his own freedom, seeking passionately and alone to attain the being which constantly eludes him. If he asks for our help, are we to give it to him? We blame a man who helps a drug addict intoxicate himself or a desperate man commit suicide, for we think that rash behavior of this sort is an attempt of the individual against his own freedom; he must be made aware of his error and put in the presence of the real demands of his freedom. Well and good. But what if he persists? Must we then use violence? There again the serious man busies himself dodging the problem; the values of life, of health, and of moral conformism being set up, one does not hesitate to impose them on others. But we know that this pharisaism can cause the worst disasters: lacking drugs, the addict may kill himself. It is no more necessary to serve an abstract ethics obstinately than to yield without due consideration to impulses of pity or generosity; violence is justified only if it opens concrete possibilities to the freedom which I am trying to save; by practising it I am willy-nilly assuming an engagement in relation to others and to myself; a man whom I snatch from the death which he had chosen has the right to come and ask me for means and reasons for living; the tyranny practised against an invalid can be justified only by his getting better; whatever the purity of the intention which animates me, any dictatorship is a fault for which I have to get myself pardoned. Besides, I am in no position to make decisions of this sort indiscriminately; the example of the unknown person who throws himself into the Seine and whom I hesitate whether or not to fish out is quite abstract; in the absence of a concrete bond with this desperate person my choice will never be anything but a contingent facticity. If I find myself in a position to do violence to a child, or to a melancholic, sick, or distraught person the reason is that I also find myself charged with his upbringing, his happiness, and his health: I am a parent, a teacher, a nurse, a doctor, or a friend ... So, by a tacit agreement, by the very fact that I am solicited, the strictness of my decision is accepted or even desired; the more seriously I accept my responsibilities, the more justified it is. That is why love authorizes severities which are not granted to indifference. What makes the problem so complex is that, on the one hand, one must not make himself an accomplice of that flight from freedom that is found in heedlessness, caprice, mania, and passion, and that, on the other hand, it is the abortive movement of man toward being which is his very existence, it is through the failure which he has assumed that he asserts himself as a freedom. To want to prohibit a man from error is to forbid him to fulfill his own existence, it is to deprive him of life. At the beginning of Claudel's *The Satin Shoe,* the husband of Dona Prouheze, the Judge, the Just, as the author regards him, explains that every plant needs a gardener in order to grow and that he is the one whom heaven has destined for his young wife; beside the fact that we are shocked by the arrogance of such a thought (for how does he know that he is this enlightened gardener? Isn't he merely a jealous husband?) this likening of a soul to a plant is not acceptable; for, as Kant would say, the value of an act lies not in its *conformity* to an external model, but in its internal truth. We object to the inquisitors who want to create faith and virtue from without; we object to all forms of fascism which seek to fashion the happiness of man from without; and also the paternalism which thinks that it has done something for man by prohibiting him from certain possibilities of temptation, whereas what is necessary is to give him reasons for resisting it.

Thus, violence is not immediately justified when it opposes willful acts which one considers perverted; it becomes inadmissible if it uses the pretext of ignorance to deny a freedom which, as we have seen, can be practised within ignorance itself. Let the "enlightened elites" strive to change the situation of the child, the illiterate, the primitive crushed beneath his superstitions; that is one of their most urgent tasks; but in this very effort they must respect a freedom which, like theirs, is absolute. They are always opposed, for example, to the extension of universal suffrage by adducing the incompetence of the masses, of women, of the natives in the colonies; but this forgetting that man always has to decide by himself in the darkness, that he must want beyond what he knows. If infinite knowledge were necessary (even supposing that it were conceivable), then the colonial administrator himself would not have the right to freedom; he is much further from perfect knowledge than the most backward savage is from him. Actually, to vote is not to govern; and to govern is not merely to maneuver; there is an ambiguity today, and particularly in France, because we think that we are not the master of our destiny; we no longer hope to help make history, we are resigned to submitting to it; all that our internal politics does is reflect the play of external forces, no party hopes to determine the fate of the country but merely to foresee the future which is being prepared in the world by foreign powers and to use, as best we can, the bit of indetermination which still escapes their foresight. Drawn along by this tactical realism, the citizens themselves no longer consider the vote as the assertion of their will but as a maneuver, whether one adheres completely to the maneuvering of a party or whether one invents his own strategy; the electors consider themselves not as men who are consulted about a particular point but as forces which are numbered and which are ordered about with a view to distant ends. And that is probably why the French, who formerly were so eager to declare their opinions, take no further interest in an act which has become a disheartening strategy. So, the fact is that if it is necessary not to vote but to measure the weight of one's vote, this calculation requires such extensive information and such a sureness of foresight that only a specialized technician can have the boldness to express an opinion. But that is one of the abuses whereby the whole meaning of democracy is lost; the logical conclusion of this would be to suppress the vote. The vote should really be the expression of a concrete will, the choice of a representative capable of defending, within the general framework of the country and the world, the particular interests of his electors. The ignorant and the outcast also has interests to defend; he alone is "competent" to decide upon his hopes and his trust. By a sophism which leans upon the dishonesty of the serious, one does not merely argue about his formal impotence to choose, but one draws arguments from the content of his choice.

I recall, among others, the naivete of a right-thinking young girl who said, "The vote for women is all well and good in principle, only, if women get the vote, they'll all vote red." With like impudence it is almost unanimously stated today in France that if the natives of the French Union were given the rights of self-determination, they would live quietly in their villages without doing anything, which would be harmful to the higher interests of the Economy. And doubtless the state of stagnation in which they choose to live is not that which a man can wish for another man; it is desirable to open new possibilities to the indolent negroes so that the interests of the Economy may one day merge with theirs. But for the time being, they are left to vegetate in the sort of situation where their freedom can merely be negative: the best thing they can desire is not to tire themselves, not to suffer, and not to work; and even this freedom is denied them. It is the most consummate and inacceptable form of oppression.

However, the "enlightened elite" objects, one does not let a child dispose of himself, one does not permit him to vote. This is another sophism. To the extent that woman or the happy or resigned slave lives in the infantile world of ready-made values, calling them "an eternal child" or "a grown-up child" has some meaning, but the analogy is only partial. Childhood is a particular sort of situation: it is a natural situation whose limits are not created by other men and which is thereby not comparable to a situation of oppression; it is a situation which is common to all men and which is temporary for all; therefore, it does not represent a limit which cuts off the individual from his possibilities, but, on the contrary, the moment of a development in which new possibilities are won. The child is ignorant because he has not yet had the time to acquire knowledge, not because this time has been refused him. To treat him as a child is not to bar him from the future but to open it to him; he needs to be taken in hand, he invites authority, it is the form which the resistance of facticity, through which all liberation is brought about, takes for him. And on the other hand, even in this situation the child has a right to his freedom and must be respected as a human person.

What gives *Emile* its value is the brilliance with which Rousseau asserts this principle. There is a very annoying naturalistic optimism in *Emile*; in the rearing of the child, as in any relationship with others, the ambiguity of freedom implies the outrage of violence; in a sense, all education is a failure. But Rousseau is right in refusing to allow childhood to be oppressed. And in practise raising a child as one cultivates a plant which one does not consult about its needs is very different from considering it as a freedom to whom the future must be opened.

Thus, we can set up point number one: the good of an individual or a group of individuals requires that it be taken as an absolute end of our action; but we are not authorized to decide upon this end *a priori*. The fact is that no behavior is ever authorized to begin with, and one of the concrete consequences of existentialist ethics is the rejection of all the previous justifications which might be drawn from the civilization, the age, and the culture; it is the rejection of every principle of authority. To put it positively, the precept will be to treat the other (to the extent that he is the only one concerned, which is the moment that we are considering at present) as a freedom so that his end may be freedom; in using this conducting-wire one will have to incur the risk, in each case, of inventing an original solution. Out of disappointment in love a young girl takes an overdose of phenobarbital; in the morning friends find her dying, they call a doctor, she is saved; later on she becomes a happy mother of a family; her friends were right in considering her suicide as a hasty and heedless act and in putting her into a position to reject it or return to it freely. But in asylums one sees melancholic patients who have tried to commit suicide twenty times, who devote their freedom to seeking the means of escaping their jailers and of putting an end to their intolerable anguish; the doctor who gives them a friendly pat on the shoulder is their tyrant and their torturer. A friend who is intoxicated by alcohol or drugs asks me for money so that he can go and buy the poison that is necessary to him; I urge him to get cured, I take him to a doctor, I try to help him live; insofar as there is a chance of my being successful,

I am acting correctly in refusing him the sum he asks for. But if circumstances prohibit me from doing anything to change the situation in which he is struggling, all I can do is give in; a deprivation of a few hours will do nothing but exasperate his torments uselessly; and he may have recourse to extreme means to get what I do not give him. That is also the problem touched on by Ibsen in *The Wild Duck*. An individual lives in a situation of falsehood; the falsehood is violence, tyranny: shall I tell the truth in order to free the victim? It would first be necessary to create a situation of such a kind that the truth might be bearable and that, though losing his illusions, the deluded individual might again find about him reasons for hoping. What makes the problem more complex is that the freedom of one man almost always concerns that of other individuals. Here is a married couple who persist in living in a hovel; if one does not succeed in giving them the desire to live in a more healthful dwelling, they must be allowed to follow their preferences; but the situation changes if they have children; the freedom of the parents would be the ruin of their sons, and as freedom and the future are on the side of the latter, these are the ones who must first be taken into account. The Other is multiple, and on the basis of this new questions arise.

One might first wonder for whom we are seeking freedom and happiness. When raised in this way, the problem is abstract; the answer will, therefore, be arbitrary, and the arbitrary always involves outrage. It is not entirely the fault of the district social-worker if she is apt to be odious; because, her money and time being limited, she hesitates before distributing it to this one or that one, she appears to others as a pure externality, a blind facticity. Contrary to the formal strictness of Kantianism for whom the more abstract the act is the more virtuous it is, generosity seems to us to be better grounded and therefore more valid the less distinction there is between the other and ourself and the more we fulfill ourself in taking the other as an end. That is what happens if I am engaged in relation to others. The Stoics impugned the ties of family, friendship, and nationality so that they recognized only the universal form of man. But man is man only through situations whose particularity is precisely a universal fact. There are men who expect help from certain men and not from others, and these expectations define privileged lines of action. It is fitting that the negro fight for the negro, the Jew for the Jew, the proletarian for the proletarian, and the Spaniard in Spain. But the assertion of these particular solidarities must not contradict the will for universal solidarity and each finite undertaking must also be open on the totality of men.

But it is then that we find in concrete form the conflicts which we have described abstractly; for the cause of freedom can triumph only through particular sacrifices. And certainly there are hierarchies among the goods desired by men: one will not hesitate to sacrifice the comfort, luxury, and leisure of certain men to assure the liberation of certain others; but when it is a question of choosing among freedoms, how shall we decide?

Let us repeat, one can only indicate a method here. The first point is always to consider what genuine human interest fills the abstract form which one proposes as the action's end. Politics always puts forward Ideas: Nation, Empire, Union, Economy, etc. But none of these forms has value in itself; it has it only insofar as it involves concrete individuals. If a nation can assert itself proudly only to the detriment of its members, if a union can be created only to the detriment of those it is trying to unite, the nation or the union must be rejected. We repudiate all idealisms, mysticisms, etcetera which prefer a Form to man himself. But the matter becomes really agonizing when it is a question of a Cause which genuinely serves man. That is why the question of Stalinist politics, the problem of the relationship of the Party to the masses which it uses in order to serve them, is in the forefront of the preoccupations of all men of good will. However, there are very few who raise it without dishonesty, and we must first try to dispel a few fallacies.

The opponent of the U.S.S.R. is making use of a fallacy when, emphasizing the part of criminal violence assumed by Stalinist politics, he neglects to confront it with the ends pursued. Doubtless, the purges, the deportations, the abuses of the occupation, and the police dictatorship surpass in importance the violences practised by any other country; the very fact that there are a hundred and sixty million inhabitants in Russia multiplies the numerical coefficient of the injustices committed. But these quantitative considerations are insufficient. One can no more judge the means without the end which gives it its meaning than he can detach the end from the means which defines it. Lynching a negro or suppressing a hundred members of the opposition are two analogous acts. Lynching is an absolute evil; it represents the survival of an obsolete civilization, the perpetuation of a struggle of races which has to disappear; it is a fault without justification or excuse. Suppressing a hundred opponents is surely an outrage, but it may have meaning and a reason; it is a matter of maintaining a regime which brings to an immense mass of men a bettering of their lot. Perhaps this measure could have been avoided; perhaps it merely represents that necessary element of failure which is involved in any positive construction. It can be judged only by being replaced in the ensemble of the cause it serves.

But, on the other hand, the defender of the U.S.S.R. is making use of a fallacy when he unconditionally justifies the sacrifices and the crimes by the ends pursued; it would first be necessary to prove that, on the one hand, the end is unconditioned and that, on the other hand, the crimes committed in its name were strictly necessary. Against the death of Bukharin one counters with Stalingrad; but one would have to know to what effective extent the Moscow trials increased the chances of the Russian victory. One of the ruses of Stalinist orthodoxy is, playing on the idea of necessity, to put the whole of the revolution on one side of the scale; the other side will always seem very light. But the very idea of a total dialectic of history does not imply that any factor is ever determining; on the contrary, if one admits that the life of a man may change the course of events, it is that one adheres to the conception which grants a preponderant role to

Cleopatra's nose and Cromwell's wart. One is here playing, with utter dishonesty, on two opposite conceptions of the idea of necessity: one synthetic, and the other analytic; one dialectic, the other deterministic. The first makes History appear as an intelligible becoming within which the particularity of contingent accidents is reabsorbed; the dialectical sequence of the moments is possible only if there is within each moment an indetermination of the particular elements taken one by one. If, on the contrary, one grants the strict determinism of each casual series, one ends in a contingent and disordered vision of the ensemble, the conjunction of the series being brought about by chance. Therefore, a Marxist must recognize that none of his particular decisions involves the revolution in its totality; it is merely a matter of hastening or retarding its coming, of saving himself the use of other and more costly means. That does not mean that he must retreat from violence but that he must not regard it as justified *a priori* by its ends. If he considers his enterprise in its truth, that is, in its finiteness, he will understand that he has never anything but a finite stake to oppose to the sacrifices which he calls for, and that it is an uncertain stake. Of course, this uncertainty should not keep him from pursuing his goals; but it requires that one concern himself in each case with finding a balance between the goal and its means.

Thus, we challenge every condemnation as well as every *a priori* justification of the violence practised with a view to a valid end. They must be legitimized concretely. A calm, mathematical calculation is here impossible. One must attempt to judge the chances of success that are involved in a certain sacrifice; but at the beginning this judgment will always be doubtful; besides, in the face of the immediate reality of the sacrifice, the notion of chance is difficult to think about. On the one hand, one can multiply a probability infinitely without ever reaching certainty; but yet, practically, it ends by merging with this asymptote: in our private life as in our collective life there is no other truth than a statistical one. On the other hand, the interests at stake do not allow themselves to be put into an equation; the suffering of one man, that of a million men, are incommensurable with the conquests realized by millions of others, present death is incommensurable with the life to come. It would be utopian to want to set up on the one hand the chances of success multiplied by the stake one is after, and on the other hand the weight of the immediate sacrifice. One finds himself back at the anguish of free decision. And that is why political choice is an ethical choice: it is a wager as well as a decision; one bets on the chances and risks of the measure under consideration; but whether chances and risks must be assumed or not in the given circumstances must be decided without help, and in so doing one sets up values. If in 1793 the Girondists rejected the violences of the Terror whereas a Saint-Just and a Robespierre assumed them, the reason is that they did not have the same conception of freedom. Nor was the same republic being aimed at between 1830 and 1840 by the republicans who limited themselves to a purely political opposition and those who adopted the technique of insurrection. In each case it is a matter of defining an end and realizing it, knowing that the choice of the means employed affects both the definition and the fulfillment.

Ordinarily, situations are so complex that a long analysis is necessary before being able to pose the ethical moment of the choice. We shall confine ourselves here to the consideration of a few simple examples which will enable us to make our attitude somewhat more precise. In an underground revolutionary movement when one discovers the presence of a stool-pigeon, one does not hesitate to beat him up; he is a present and future danger who has to be gotten rid of; but if a man is merely suspected of treason, the case is more ambiguous. We blame those northern peasants who in the war of 1914–18 massacred an innocent family which was suspected of signaling to the enemy; the reason is that not only were the presumptions vague, but the danger was uncertain; at any rate, it was enough to put the suspects into prison; while waiting for a serious inquiry it was easy to keep them from doing any harm. However, if a questionable individual holds the fate of other men in his hands, if, in order to avoid the risk of killing one innocent man, one runs the risk of letting ten innocent men die, it is reasonable to sacrifice him. We can merely ask that such decisions be not taken hastily and lightly, and that, all things considered, the evil that one inflicts be lesser than that which is being forestalled.

There are cases still more disturbing because there the violence is not immediately efficacious; the violences of the Resistance did not aim at the material weakening of Germany; it happens that their purpose was to create such a state of violence that collaboration would be impossible; in one sense, the burning of a whole French village was too high a price to pay for the elimination of three enemy officers; but those fires and the massacring of hostages were themselves parts of the plan; they created an abyss between the occupiers and the occupied. Likewise, the insurrections in Paris and Lyons at the beginning of the nineteenth century, or the revolts in India, did not aim at shattering the yoke of the oppressor at one blow, but rather at creating and keeping alive the meaning of the revolt and at making the mystifications of conciliation impossible. Attempts which are aware that one by one they are doomed to failure can be legitimized by the whole of the situation which they create. This is also the meaning of Steinbeck's novel *In Dubious Battle* where a communist leader does not hesitate to launch a costly strike of uncertain success but through which there will be born, along with the solidarity of the workers, the consciousness of exploitation and the will to reject it.

It seems to me interesting to contrast this example with the debate in John Dos Passos' *The Adventures of a Young Man*. Following a strike, some American miners are condemned to death. Their comrades try to have their trial reconsidered. Two methods are put forward: one can act officially, and one knows that they then have an excellent chance of winning their case; one can also work up a sensational trial with the Communist Party taking the affair in hand, stirring up a press campaign and circulating international petitions; but the court will be unwilling to yield to this intimidation. The party will thereby get a tremendous amount of publicity, but the miners will be condemned. What is a man of good will to decide in this case?

Dos Passos' hero chooses to save the miners and we believe that he did right. Certainly, if it were necessary to choose between the whole revolution and the lives of two or three men, no revolutionary would hesitate; but it was merely a matter of helping along the party propaganda, or better, of increasing somewhat its chances of developing within the United States; the immediate interest of the C.P. in that country is only hypothetically tied up with that of the revolution; in fact, a cataclysm like the war has so upset the situation of the world that a great part of the gains and losses of the past have been absolutely swept away. If it is really *men* which the movement claims to be serving, in this case it must prefer saving the lives of three concrete individuals to a very uncertain and weak chance of serving a little more effectively by their sacrifice the mankind to come. If it considers these lives negligible, it is because it too ranges itself on the side of the formal politicians who prefer the Idea to its content; it is because it prefers itself, in its subjectivity, to the goals to which it claims to be dedicated. Besides, whereas in the example chosen by Steinbeck the strike is immediately an appeal to the freedom of the workers and in its very failure is already a liberation, the sacrifice of the miners is a mystification and an oppression; they are duped by being made to believe that an effort is being made to save their lives, and the whole proletariat is duped with them. Thus, in both examples, we find ourselves before the same abstract case: men are going to die so that the party which claims to be serving them will realize a limited gain; but a concrete analysis leads us to opposite moral solutions.

It is apparent that the method we are proposing, analogous in this respect to scientific or aesthetic methods, consists, in each case, of confronting the values realized with the values aimed at, and the meaning of the act with its content. The fact is that the politician, contrary to the scientist and the artist, and although the element of failure which he assumes is much more outrageous, is rarely concerned with making use of it. May it be that there is an irresistible dialectic of power wherein morality has no place? Is the ethical concern, even in its realistic and concrete form, detrimental to the interests of action? The objection will surely be made that hesitation and misgivings only impede victory. Since, in any case, there is an element of failure in all success, since the ambiguity, at any rate, must be surmounted, why not refuse to take notice of it? In the first number of the *Cahiers d'Action* a reader declared that once and for all we should regard the militant communist as "the permanent hero of our time" and should reject the exhausting tension demanded by existentialism; installed in the permanence of heroism, one will blindly direct himself toward an uncontested goal; but one then resembles Colonel de la Roque who unwaveringly went right straight ahead of him without knowing where he was going. Malaparte relates that the young Nazis, in order to become insensitive to the suffering of others, practised by plucking out the eyes of live cats; there is no more radical way of avoiding the pitfalls of ambiguity. But an action which wants to serve man ought to be careful not to forget him on the way; if it chooses to fulfill itself blindly, it will lose its meaning or will take on an unforeseen meaning; for the goal is not fixed once and for all; it is defined all along the road which leads to it. Vigilance alone can keep alive the validity of the goals and the genuine assertion of freedom. Moreover, ambiguity can not fail to appear on the scene; it is felt by the victim, and his revolt or his complaints also make it exist for his tyrant; the latter will then be tempted to put everything into question, to renounce, thus denying both himself and his ends; or, if he persists, he will continue to blind himself only by multiplying crimes and by perverting his original design more and more. The fact is that the man of action becomes a dictator not in respect to his ends but because these ends are necessarily set up through his will. Hegel, in his *Phenomenology*, has emphasized this inextricable confusion between objectivity and subjectivity.

A man gives himself to a Cause only by making it *his* Cause; as he fulfills himself within it, it is also through him that it is expressed, and the will to power is not distinguished in such a case from generosity; when an individual or a party chooses to triumph, whatever the cost may be, it is their own triumph which they take for an end. If the fusion of the Commissar and the Yogi were realized, there would be a self-criticism in the man of action which would expose to him the ambiguity of his will, thus arresting the imperious drive of his subjectivity and, by the same token, contesting the unconditioned value of the goal. But the fact is that the politician follows the line of least resistance; it is easy to fall asleep over the unhappiness of others and to count it for very little; it is easier to throw a hundred men, ninety-seven of whom are innocent, into prison, than to discover the three culprits who are hidden among them; it is easier to kill a man than to keep a close watch on him; all politics makes use of the police, which officially flaunts its radical contempt for the individual and which loves violence for its own sake. The thing that goes by the name of political necessity is in part the laziness and brutality of the police. That is why it is incumbent upon ethics not to follow the line of least resistance; an act which is not destined, but rather quite freely consented to; it must make itself effective so that what was at first facility may become difficult. For want of internal criticism, this is the role that an opposition must take upon itself. There are two types of opposition. The first is a rejection of the very ends set up by a regime: it is the opposition of anti-fascism to fascism, of fascism to socialism. In the second type, the oppositionist accepts the objective goal but criticizes the subjective movement which aims at it; he may not even wish for a change of power, but he deems it necessary to bring into play a contestation which will make the subjective appear as such. Thereby he exacts a perpetual contestation of the means by the end and of the end by the means. He must be careful himself not to ruin, by the means which he employs, the end he is aiming at, and above all not to pass into the service of the oppositionists of the first type. But, delicate as it may be, his role is, nevertheless, necessary. Indeed, on the one hand, it would be absurd to oppose a liberating action with the pretext that it implies crime and tyranny; for without crime and tyranny there could be no liberation of man; one can not escape that dialectic which goes from freedom to freedom through dictatorship and oppression. But, on the other hand, he would be guilty of allowing the liberating movement to harden into a moment which is acceptable only if it passes into its opposite; tyranny and crime must be kept from triumphantly establishing themselves in the world; the conquest of freedom is their only justification, and the assertion of freedom against them must therefore be kept alive.

CONCLUSION

Is this kind of ethics individualistic or not? Yes, if one means by that that it accords to the individual an absolute value and that it recognizes in him alone the power of laying the foundations of his own existence. It is individualism in the sense in which the wisdom of the ancients, the Christian ethics of salvation, and the Kantian ideal of virtue also merit this name; it is opposed to the totalitarian doctrines which raise up beyond man the mirage of Mankind. But it is not solipsistic, since the individual is defined only by his relationship to the world and to other individuals; he exists only by transcending himself, and his freedom can be achieved only through the freedom of others. He justifies his existence by a movement which, like freedom, springs from his heart but which leads outside of him.

This individualism does not lead to the anarchy of personal whim. Man is free; but he finds his law in his very freedom. First, he must assume his freedom and not flee it; he assumes it by a constructive movement: one does not exist without doing something; and also by a negative movement which rejects oppression for oneself and others. In construction, as in rejection, it is a matter of reconquering freedom on the contingent facticity of existence, that is, of taking the given, which, at the start, *is there* without any reason, as something willed by man. A conquest of this kind is never finished; the contingency remains, and, so that he may assert his will, man is even obliged to stir up in the world the outrage he does not want. But this element of failure is a very condition of his life; one can never dream of eliminating it without immediately dreaming of death. This does not mean that one should consent to failure, but rather one must consent to struggle against it without respite.

Yet, isn't this battle without victory pure gullibility? It will be argued that this is only a ruse of transcendance projecting before itself a goal which constantly recedes, running after itself on an endless treadmill; to exist for Mankind is to remain where one is, and it fools itself by calling this turbulent stagnation progress; our whole ethics does nothing but encourage it in this lying enterprise since we are asking each one to confirm existence as a value for all others; isn't it simply a matter of organizing among men a complicity which allows them to substitute a game of illusions for the given world?

We have already attempted to answer this objection. One can formulate it only by placing himself on the grounds of an inhuman and consequently false objectivity; within Mankind men may be fooled; the word "lie" has a meaning by opposition to the truth established by men themselves, but Mankind can not fool itself completely since it is precisely Mankind which creates the criteria of true and false. In Plato, art is mystification because there is the heaven of Ideas; but in the earthly domain all glorification of the earth is true as soon as it is realized. Let men attach value to words, forms, colors, mathematical theorems, physical laws, and athletic prowess; let them accord value to one another in love and friendship, and the objects, the events, and the men immediately *have* this value; they have it absolutely. It is possible that a man may refuse to love anything on earth; he will prove this refusal and he will carry it out by suicide. If he lives, the reason is that, whatever he may say, there still remains in him some attachment to existence; his life will be commensurate with this attachment; it will justify itself to the extent that it genuinely justifies the world.

This justification, though open upon the entire universe through time and space, will always be finite. Whatever one may do, one never realizes anything but a limited work, like existence itself which tries to establish itself through that work and which death also limits. It is the assertion of our finiteness which doubtless gives the doctrine which we have just evoked its austerity and, in some eyes, its sadness. As soon as one considers a system abstractly and theoretically, one puts himself, in effect, on the plane of the universal, thus, of the infinite. That is why reading the Hegelian system is so comforting. I remember having experienced a great feeling of calm on reading Hegel in the impersonal framework of the Bibliothèque Nationale in August 1940. But once I got into the street again, into my life, out of the system, beneath a real sky, the system was no longer of any use to me: what it had offered me, under a show of the infinite, was the consolations of death; and I again wanted to live in the midst of living men. I think that, inversely, existentialism does not offer to the reader the consolations of an abstract evasion: existentialism proposes no evasion. On the contrary, its ethics is experienced in the truth of life, and it then appears as the only proposition of salvation which one can address to men. Taking on its own account Descartes' revolt against the evil genius, the pride of the thinking reed in the face of the universe which crushes him, it asserts that, despite his limits, through them, it is up to each one to fulfill his existence as an absolute. Regardless of the staggering dimensions of the world about us, the density of our ignorance, the risks of catastrophes to come, and our individual weakness within the immense collectivity, the fact remains that we are absolutely free today if we choose to will our existence in its finiteness, a finiteness which is open on the infinite. And in fact, any man who has known real loves, real revolts, real desires, and real will knows quite well that he has no need of any outside guarantee to be sure of his goals; their certitude comes from his own drive. There is a very old saying which goes: "Do what you must, come what may." That amounts to saying in a different way that the result is not external to the good will which fulfills itself in aiming at it. If it came to be that each man did what he must, existence would be saved in each one without there being any need of dreaming of a paradise where all would be reconciled in death.

ALBERT CAMUS

Albert Camus was born on November 7, 1913, in Mondovi, Algeria. His father was killed in 1914 at the Battle of the Marne in World War I, and Camus was raised by a grandmother and his devoted but illiterate mother, who worked as a charwoman. The Camus family lived in a small flat without electricity in a run-down area of Mondovi. Camus's slightly better situated uncle helped him and the family as much as he could.

One of the heroes in Camus's life was a teacher from grade school, Louis Germain. He recognized Camus's keen intelligence and helped him win a scholarship to one of the best high schools in the area. There Camus was exposed to the writings of Plato, Pascal, Augustine, Kierkegaard, Dostoevsky, and Nietzsche.

As a teenager, Camus enjoyed sports such as boxing and soccer. Indeed, in a letter he once remarked, "It was on the playing fields that I learned my only lessons in ethics." Camus also savored the intensely beautiful sun and sea of his beloved Algeria, where he spent many hours splashing in the surf. However, his intensely physical life was curtailed when he contracted tuberculosis at seventeen. Camus was hospitalized for months, and from then on struggled with his health and never had the same vigor again. He became depressed over his weakened physical condition, and on and off, that depression would accompany him through the rest of his days.

In 1933, Camus commenced study at the University of Algeria. Unlike his more privileged fellow students, Camus always had to divide his time between study and work. Some of the jobs that he held were automobile accessories salesman, meteorologist, clerk, and journalist. In 1934, Camus married for the first time. His wife was a heroin addict. As a young husband, he struggled unsuccessfully to help her conquer the addiction. Their painful relationship came to a close within a couple of years, though it was not until 1940 that they would become officially divorced.

Camus joined the Communist Party in 1935 and helped with the party's theater productions. A stellar student at the university, Camus wrote a brilliant master's thesis on Plotinus and Augustine. However, without any further academic prospects, Camus took a job writing for a leftist newspaper in 1939. The paper was forced to shut down a year later, and Camus departed from Algeria for Paris, where he found work for the large-circulation *Paris-Soir*. However, he quit the paper after a few months and began his lapidary *The Stranger*, which along with *The Myth of Sisyphus* was published by the prestigious Gallimard Press in 1942. These two books immediately established his reputation.

During the war, Camus became editor of the influential Resistance newspaper *Combat*. Along with his trenchant editorials, he continued to write novels and plays. At this time, he began stormy friendships with Jean-Paul Sartre, André Gide, and Simone de Beauvoir. He also became a reader for Gallimard, a job that he would keep for many years to come.

Camus had married Francine Faure in 1940, and in 1945, he became the father of twins. That same year his play *Caligula* became a big hit. After the war, Camus continued on for a year as editor of *Combat*, and famous as he now was, he did a lecture tour of America in 1946. In June 1947, Camus published *The Plague*. The period after the war was both intellectually vibrant and tumultuous. While Sartre and many of Camus's Left Bank friends were still communists, Camus saw in this movement the same potential for tyranny that he witnessed with the Nazis. His unwillingness to bow to Marxist ideologies, along with his stance against the use of terrorism by the Algerians in their war for independence with France, culminated in a public break with Sartre.

Camus was the veteran of many political frays, and they took their psychological toll on him. Worse yet, in the fifties he fell in love with Maria Casares, and his domestic situation deteriorated to the point where his wife attempted suicide. The theme of his constant womanizing and his wife's despair are incorporated in his 1957 masterwork *The Fall*. That same year, Camus was awarded the Nobel Prize for literature. Never one to forget his friends, Camus dedicated the prize to Germain, the primary school teacher who helped set Camus on his path.

In the late fifties Camus, who had directed many plays, was planning to take on the directorship of a major theater company. He was also working on an autobiographical novel (*The First Man*) about his youth in Algeria. But fate had other plans. Camus, who once remarked that he could not think of a more meaningless death than perishing in a car crash, died in a highway accident on January 4, 1960. He had the manuscript of his novel with him in the car, which was driven by Michel Gallimard, a relative of his publisher.

Camus's voice was shaped by both his sensuous love of nature and the poverty of his early years. As the reader will glean from our selections from *The Myth of Sisyphus*, Camus tries to affirm life while rejecting both the heaven of religion and the utopian hereafter of the communists. Jacob may have wrestled with God, but Camus tried to wrangle an authentic sense of meaning from a cold and indifferent universe. It is this terrible combination of the human hunger for meaning and the indifference of the universe that casts the formula for Camus's important and related concepts of the absurd and revolt, which may be best expressed together in his famous quip, "There is no fate that cannot be surmounted by scorn."

Profoundly affected by writers as diverse as Dostoevsky, Faulkner, Hemingway, and Malraux, Camus was an exquisite stylist. His novels outshine his philosophical tracts. I strongly recommend reading the bookends of his authorship, namely, *The Stranger* and *The Fall*.

FROM

THE MYTH OF SISYPHUS

An Absurd Reasoning

ABSURDITY AND SUICIDE

There is but one truly serious philosophical problem, and that is suicide. Judging whether life is or is not worth living amounts to answering the fundamental question of philosophy. All the rest—whether or not the world has three dimensions, whether the mind has nine or twelve categories—comes afterwards. These are games; one must first answer. And if it is true, as Nietzsche claims, that a philosopher, to deserve our respect, must preach by example, you can appreciate the importance of that reply, for it will precede the definitive act. These are facts the heart can feel; yet they call for careful study before they become clear to the intellect.

If I ask myself how to judge that this question is more urgent than that, I reply that one judges by the actions it entails. I have never seen anyone die for the ontological argument. Galileo, who held a scientific truth of great importance, abjured it with the greatest ease as soon as it endangered his life. In a certain sense, he did right.* That truth was not worth the stake. Whether the earth or the sun revolves around the other is a matter of profound indifference. To tell the truth, it is a futile question. On the other hand, I see many people die because they judge that life is not worth living. I see others paradoxically getting killed for the ideas or illusions that give them a reason for living (what is called a reason for living is also an excellent reason for dying). I therefore conclude that the meaning of life is the most urgent of questions. How to answer it? On all essential problems (I mean thereby those that run the risk of leading to death or those that intensify the passion of living) there are probably but two methods of thought: the method of La Palisse and the method of Don Quixote. Solely the balance between evidence and lyricism can allow us to achieve simultaneously emotion and lucidity. In a subject at once so humble and so heavy with emotion, the learned and classical dialectic must yield, one can see, to a more modest attitude of mind deriving at one and the same time from common sense and understanding.

Suicide has never been dealt with except as a social phenomenon. On the contrary, we are concerned here, at the outset, with the relationship between individual thought and suicide. An act like this is prepared within the silence of the heart, as is a great work of art. The man himself is ignorant of it. One evening he pulls the trigger or jumps. Of an apartment-building manager who had killed himself I was told that he had lost his daughter five years before, that he had changed greatly since, and that that experience had "undermined" him. A more exact word cannot be imagined. Beginning to think is beginning to be undermined. Society has but little connection with such beginnings. The worm is in man's heart. That is where it must be sought. One

---

* From the point of view of the relative value of truth. On the other hand, from the point of view of virile behavior, this scholar's fragility may well make us smile.

must follow and understand this fatal game that leads from lucidity in the face of existence to flight from light.

There are many causes for a suicide, and generally the most obvious ones were not the most powerful. Rarely is suicide committed (yet the hypothesis is not excluded) through reflection. What sets off the crisis is almost always unverifiable. Newspapers often speak of "personal sorrows" or of "incurable illness." These explanations are plausible. But one would have to know whether a friend of the desperate man had not that very day addressed him indifferently. He is the guilty one. For that is enough to precipitate all the rancors and all the boredom still in suspension.*

But if it is hard to fix the precise instant, the subtle step when the mind opted for death, it is easier to deduce from the act itself the consequences it implies. In a sense, and as in melodrama, killing yourself amounts to confessing. It is confessing that life is too much for you or that you do not understand it. Let's not go too far in such analogies, however, but rather return to everyday words. It is merely confessing that that "is not worth the trouble." Living, naturally, is never easy. You continue making the gestures commanded by existence for many reasons, the first of which is habit. Dying voluntarily implies that you have recognized, even instinctively, the ridiculous character of that habit, the absence of any profound reason for living, the insane character of that daily agitation, and the uselessness of suffering.

What, then, is that incalculable feeling that deprives the mind of the sleep necessary to life? A world that can be explained even with bad reasons is a familiar world. But, on the other hand, in a universe suddenly divested of illusions and lights, man feels an alien, a stranger. His exile is without remedy since he is deprived of the memory of a lost home or the hope of a promised land. This divorce between man and his life, the actor and his setting, is properly the feeling of absurdity. All healthy men having

---

* Let us not miss this opportunity to point out the relative character of this essay. Suicide may indeed be related to much more honorable considerations—for example, the political suicides of protest, as they were called, during the Chinese revolution.

thought of their own suicide, it can be seen, without further explanation, that there is a direct connection between this feeling and the longing for death.

The subject of this essay is precisely this relationship between the absurd and suicide, the exact degree to which suicide is a solution to the absurd. The principle can be established that for a man who does not cheat, what he believes to be true must determine his action. Belief in the absurdity of existence must then dictate his conduct. It is legitimate to wonder, clearly and without false pathos, whether a conclusion of this importance requires forsaking as rapidly as possible an incomprehensible condition. I am speaking, of course, of men inclined to be in harmony with themselves.

Stated clearly, this problem may seem both simple and insoluble. But it is wrongly assumed that simple questions involve answers that are no less simple and that evidence implies evidence. *A priori* and reversing the terms of the problem, just as one does or does not kill oneself, it seems that there are but two philosophical solutions, either yes or no. This would be too easy. But allowance must be made for those who, without concluding, continue questioning. Here I am only slightly indulging in irony: this is the majority. I notice also that those who answer "no" act as if they thought "yes." As a matter of fact, if I accept the Nietzschean criterion, they think "yes" in one way or another. On the other hand, it often happens that those who commit suicide were assured of the meaning of life. These contradictions are constant. It may even be said that they have never been so keen as on this point where, on the contrary, logic seems so desirable. It is a commonplace to compare philosophical theories and the behavior of those who profess them. But it must be said that of the thinkers who refused a meaning to life none except Kirilov who belongs to literature, Peregrinos who is born of legend,* and Jules Lequier who belongs to hypothesis, admitted his logic to

---

* I have heard of an emulator of Peregrinos, a post-war writer who, after having finished his first book, committed suicide to attract attention to his work. Attention was in fact attracted, but the book was judged no good.

the point of refusing that life. Schopenhauer is often cited, as a fit subject for laughter, because he praised suicide while seated at a well-set table. This is no subject for joking. That way of not taking the tragic seriously is not so grievous, but it helps to judge a man.

In the face of such contradictions and obscurities must we conclude that there is no relationship between the opinion one has about life and the act one commits to leave it? Let us not exaggerate in this direction. In a man's attachment to life there is something stronger than all the ills in the world. The body's judgment is as good as the mind's, and the body shrinks from annihilation. We get into the habit of living before acquiring the habit of thinking. In that race which daily hastens us toward death, the body maintains its irreparable lead. In short, the essence of that contradiction lies in what I shall call the act of eluding because it is both less and more than diversion in the Pascalian sense. Eluding is the invariable game. The typical act of eluding, the fatal evasion that constitutes the third theme of this essay, is hope. Hope of another life one must "deserve" or trickery of those who live not for life itself but for some great idea that will transcend it, refine it, give it a meaning, and betray it.

Thus everything contributes to spreading confusion. Hitherto, and it has not been wasted effort, people have played on words and pretended to believe that refusing to grant a meaning to life necessarily leads to declaring that it is not worth living. In truth, there is no necessary common measure between these two judgments. One merely has to refuse to be misled by the confusions, divorces, and inconsistencies previously pointed out. One must brush everything aside and go straight to the real problem. One kills oneself because life is not worth living, that is certainly a truth—yet an unfruitful one because it is a truism. But does that insult to existence, that flat denial in which it is plunged come from the fact that it has no meaning? Does its absurdity require one to escape it through hope or suicide—this is what must be clarified, hunted down, and elucidated while brushing aside all the rest. Does the Absurd dictate death? This problem must be given priority over others, outside all methods of thought and all exercises of the disinterested mind. Shades of meaning, contradictions, the psychology that an "objective" mind can always introduce into all problems have no place in this pursuit and this passion. It calls simply for an unjust—in other words, logical—thought. That is not easy. It is always easy to be logical. It is almost impossible to be logical to the bitter end. Men who die by their own hand consequently follow to its conclusion their emotional inclination. Reflection on suicide gives me an opportunity to raise the only problem to interest me: is there a logic to the point of death? I cannot know unless I pursue, without reckless passion, in the sole light of evidence, the reasoning of which I am here suggesting the source. This is what I call an absurd reasoning. Many have begun it. I do not yet know whether or not they kept to it.

When Karl Jaspers, revealing the impossibility of constituting the world as a unity, exclaims: "This limitation leads me to myself, where I can no longer withdraw behind an objective point of view that I am merely representing, where neither I myself nor the existence of others can any longer become an object for me," he is evoking after many others those waterless deserts where thought reaches its confines. After many others, yes indeed, but how eager they were to get out of them! At that last crossroad where thought hesitates, many men have arrived and even some of the humblest. They then abdicated what was most precious to them, their life. Others, princes of the mind, abdicated likewise, but they initiated the suicide of their thought in its purest revolt. The real effort is to stay there, rather, in so far as that is possible, and to examine closely the odd vegetation of those distant regions. Tenacity and acumen are privileged spectators of this inhuman show in which absurdity, hope, and death carry on their dialogue. The mind can then analyze the figures of that elementary yet subtle dance before illustrating them and reliving them itself.

ABSURD WALLS

Like great works, deep feelings always mean more than they are conscious of saying. The regularity of an impulse or a repulsion in a soul is encountered again in habits of doing or thinking, is reproduced in consequences of which the soul itself knows nothing. Great feelings take with them their own universe, splendid or abject. They light up with their passion an exclusive world in which they recognize their climate. There is a universe of jealousy, of ambition, of selfishness, or of generosity. A universe—in other words, a metaphysic and an attitude of mind. What is true of already specialized feelings will be even more so of emotions basically as indeterminate, simultaneously as vague and as "definite," as remote and as "present" as those furnished us by beauty or aroused by absurdity.

At any streetcorner the feeling of absurdity can strike any man in the face. As it is, in its distressing nudity, in its light without effulgence, it is elusive. But that very difficulty deserves reflection. It is probably true that a man remains forever unknown to us and that there is in him something irreducible that escapes us. But *practically* I know men and recognize them by their behavior, by the totality of their deeds, by the consequences caused in life by their presence. Likewise, all those irrational feelings which offer no purchase to analysis. I can define them *practically*, appreciate them *practically*, by gathering together the sum of their consequences in the domain of the intelligence, by seizing and noting all their aspects, by outlining their universe. It is certain that apparently, though I have seen the same actor a hundred times, I shall not for that reason know him any better personally. Yet if I add up the heroes he has personified and if I say that I know him a little better at the hundredth character counted off, this will be felt to contain an element of truth. For this apparent paradox is also an apologue. There is a moral to it. It teaches that a man defines himself by his make-believe as well as by his sincere impulses. There is thus a lower key of feelings, inaccessible in the heart but partially disclosed by the acts they imply and the attitudes of mind they assume. It is clear that in this way I am defining a method. But it is also evident that that method is one of analysis and not of knowledge. For methods imply metaphysics; unconsciously they disclose conclusions that they often claim not to know yet. Similarly, the last pages of a book are already contained in the first pages. Such a link is inevitable. The method defined here acknowledges the feeling that all true knowledge is impossible. Solely appearances can be enumerated and the climate make itself felt.

Perhaps we shall be able to overtake that elusive feeling of absurdity in the different but closely related worlds of intelligence, of the art of living, or of art itself. The climate of absurdity is in the beginning. The end is the absurd universe and that attitude of mind which lights the world with its true colors to bring out the privileged and implacable visage which that attitude has discerned in it.

All great deeds and all great thoughts have a ridiculous beginning. Great works are often born on a streetcorner or in a restaurant's revolving door. So it is with absurdity. The absurd world more than others derives its nobility from that abject birth. In certain situations, replying "nothing" when asked what one is thinking about may be pretense in a man. Those who are loved are well aware of this. But if that reply is sincere, if it symbolizes that odd state of soul in which the void becomes eloquent, in which the chain of daily gestures is broken, in which the heart vainly seeks the link that will connect it again, then it is as it were the first sign of absurdity.

It happens that the stage sets collapse. Rising, streetcar, four hours in the office or the factory, meal, streetcar, four hours of work, meal, sleep, and Monday Tuesday Wednesday Thursday Friday and Saturday according to the same rhythm—this path is easily followed most of the time. But one day the "why" arises and everything begins in that weariness tinged with amazement. "Begins"—this is important. Weariness comes at the end of the acts of a mechanical life, but at the same time it inaugurates the impulse of consciousness. It awakens consciousness and provokes what follows. What follows is the gradual return into the chain or it is the definitive awakening. At the end of the awakening comes, in time, the consequence: suicide or recovery. In itself weariness has something sickening about it. Here, I must conclude that it is good. For everything begins with consciousness and nothing is worth anything except through it. There is nothing original about these remarks. But they are obvious; that is enough for a while, during a sketchy reconnaissance in the origins of the absurd. Mere "anxiety," as Heidegger says, is at the source of everything.

Likewise and during every day of an unillustrious life, time carries us. But a moment always comes when we have to carry it. We live on the future: "tomorrow," "later on," "when you have made your way," "you will understand when you are old enough." Such irrelevancies are wonderful, for, after all, it's a matter of dying. Yet a day comes when a man notices or says that he is thirty. Thus he asserts his youth. But simultaneously he situates himself in relation to time. He takes his place in it. He admits that he stands at a certain point on a curve that he acknowledges having to travel to its end. He belongs to time, and by the horror that seizes him, he recognizes his worst enemy. Tomorrow, he was longing for tomorrow, whereas everything in him ought to reject it. That revolt of the flesh is the absurd.*

A step lower and strangeness creeps in: perceiving that the world is "dense," sensing to what a degree a stone is foreign and irreducible to us, with what intensity nature or a landscape can negate us. At the heart of all beauty lies something inhuman, and these hills, the softness of the sky, the outline of these trees at this very minute lose the illusory meaning with which we had clothed them, henceforth more remote than a lost paradise. The primitive hostility of the world rises up to face us across millen-

---

* But not in the proper sense. This is not a definition, but rather an enumeration of the feelings that may admit of the absurd. Still, the enumeration finished, the absurd has nevertheless not been exhausted.

nia. For a second we cease to understand it because for centuries we have understood in it solely the images and designs that we had attributed to it beforehand, because henceforth we lack the power to make use of that artifice. The world evades us because it becomes itself again. That stage scenery masked by habit becomes again what it is. It withdraws at a distance from us. Just as there are days when under the familiar face of a woman, we see as a stranger her we had loved months or years ago, perhaps we shall come even to desire what suddenly leaves us so alone. But the time has not yet come. Just one thing: that denseness and that strangeness of the world is the absurd.

Men, too, secrete the inhuman. At certain moments of lucidity, the mechanical aspect of their gestures, their meaningless pantomime makes silly everything that surrounds them. A man is talking on the telephone behind a glass partition; you cannot hear him, but you see his incomprehensible dumb show: you wonder why he is alive. This discomfort in the face of man's own inhumanity, this incalculable tumble before the image of what we are, this "nausea," as a writer of today calls it, is also the absurd. Likewise the stranger who at certain seconds comes to meet us in a mirror, the familiar and yet alarming brother we encounter in our own photographs is also the absurd.

I come at last to death and to the attitude we have toward it. On this point everything has been said and it is only proper to avoid pathos. Yet one will never be sufficiently surprised that everyone lives as if no one "knew." This is because in reality there is no experience of death. Properly speaking, nothing has been experienced but what has been lived and made conscious. Here, it is barely possible to speak of the experience of others' deaths. It is a substitute, an illusion, and it never quite convinces us. That melancholy convention cannot be persuasive. The horror comes in reality from the mathematical aspect of the event. If time frightens us, this is because it works out the problem and the solution comes afterward. All the pretty speeches about the soul will have their contrary convincingly proved, at least for a time. From this inert body on which a slap makes no mark the soul has disappeared. This elementary and definitive aspect of the adventure constitutes the absurd feeling. Under the fatal lighting of that destiny, its uselessness becomes evident. No code of ethics and no effort are justifiable *a priori* in the face of the cruel mathematics that command our condition.

Let me repeat: all this has been said over and over. I am limiting myself here to making a rapid classification and to pointing out these obvious themes. They run through all literatures and all philosophies. Everyday conversation feeds on them. There is no question of reinventing them. But it is essential to be sure of these facts in order to be able to question oneself subsequently on the primordial question. I am interested—let me repeat again—not so much in absurd discoveries as in their consequences. If one is assured of these facts, what is one to conclude, how far is one to go to elude nothing? Is one to die voluntarily or to hope in spite of everything? Beforehand, it is necessary to take the same rapid inventory on the plane of the intelligence.

—

The mind's first step is to distinguish what is true from what is false. However, as soon as thought reflects on itself, what it first discovers is a contradiction. Useless to strive to be convincing in this case. Over the centuries no one has furnished a clearer and more elegant demonstration of the business than Aristotle: "The often ridiculed consequence of these opinions is that they destroy themselves. For by asserting that all is true we assert the truth of the contrary assertion and consequently the falsity of our own thesis (for the contrary assertion does not admit that it can be true). And if one says that all is false, that assertion is itself false. If we declare that solely the assertion opposed to ours is false or else that solely ours is not false, we are nevertheless forced to admit an infinite number of true or false judgments. For the one who expresses a true assertion proclaims simultaneously that it is true, and so on *ad infinitum.*"

This vicious circle is but the first of a series in which the mind that studies itself gets lost in a giddy whirling. The very simplicity of these paradoxes makes them irreducible. Whatever may be the plays on words and the acrobatics of logic, to understand is, above all, to unify. The mind's deepest desire, even in its most elaborate operations, parallels man's unconscious feeling in the face of his universe: it is an insistence upon familiarity, an appetite for clarity. Understanding the world for a man is reducing it to the human, stamping it with his seal. The cat's universe is not the universe of the anthill. The truism "All thought is anthropomorphic" has no other meaning. Likewise, the mind that aims to understand reality can consider itself satisfied only by reducing it to terms of thought. If man realized that the universe like him can love and suffer, he would be reconciled. If thought discovered in the shimmering mirrors of phenomena eternal relations capable of summing them up and summing themselves up in a single principle, then would be seen an intellectual joy of which the myth of the blessed would be but a ridiculous imitation. That nostalgia for unity, that appetite for the absolute illustrates the essential impulse of the human drama. But the fact of that nostalgia's existence does not imply that it is to be immediately satisfied. For if, bridging the gulf that separates desire from conquest, we assert with Parmenides the reality of the One (whatever it may be), we fall into the ridiculous contradiction of a mind that asserts total unity and proves by its very assertion its own difference and the diversity it claimed to resolve. This other vicious circle is enough to stifle our hopes.

These are again truisms. I shall again repeat that they are not interesting in themselves but in the consequences that can be deduced from them. I know another truism: it tells me that man is mortal. One can nevertheless count the minds that have deduced the extreme conclusions from it. It is essential to consider as a constant point of reference in this essay the regular hiatus between what we fancy we know and what we really know, practical assent and simulated ignorance which allows us to live with ideas which, if we truly put them to the test, ought to upset our whole life. Faced with this inextricable contradiction of the mind, we shall fully grasp the divorce separating us from our own creations. So long as the mind keeps silent in the motionless world of its hopes, everything is reflected and arranged in the unity of its nostalgia. But with its first move this world cracks and tumbles: an infinite number of shimmering fragments is offered to the understanding. We must despair of ever reconstructing the familiar, calm surface which would give us peace of heart. After so many centuries of inquiries, so many abdications among thinkers, we are well aware that this is true for all our knowledge. With the exception of professional rationalists, today people despair of true knowledge. If the only significant history of human thought were to be written, it would have to be the history of its successive regrets and its impotences.

Of whom and of what indeed can I say: "I know that!" This heart within me I can feel, and I judge that it exists. This world I can touch, and I likewise judge that it exists. There ends all my knowledge, and the rest is construction. For if I try to seize this self of which I feel sure, if I try to define and to summarize it, it is nothing but water slipping through my fingers. I can sketch one by one all the aspects it is able to assume, all those likewise that have been attributed to it, this upbringing, this origin, this ardor or these silences, this nobility or this vileness. But aspects cannot be added up. This very heart which is mine will forever remain indefinable to me. Between the certainty I have of my existence and the content I try to give to that assurance, the gap will never be filled. Forever I shall be a stranger to myself. In psychology as in logic, there are truths but no truth. Socrates' "Know thyself" has as much value as the "Be virtuous" of our confessionals. They reveal a nostalgia at the same time as an ignorance. They are sterile exercises on great subjects. They are legitimate only in precisely so far as they are approximate.

And here are trees and I know their gnarled surface, water and I feel its taste. These scents of grass and stars at night, certain evenings when the heart relaxes—how shall I negate this world whose power and strength I feel? Yet all the knowledge on earth will give me nothing to assure me that this world is mine. You describe it to me and you teach me to classify it. You enumerate its laws and in my thirst for knowledge I admit that they are true. You take apart its mechanism and my hope increases. At the final stage you teach me that this wondrous and multicolored universe can be reduced to the atom and that the atom itself can be reduced to the electron. All this is good and I wait for you to continue. But you tell me of an invisible planetary system in which electrons gravitate around a nucleus. You explain this world to me with an image. I realize then that you have been reduced to poetry: I shall never know. Have I the time to become indignant? You have already changed theories. So that science that was to teach me everything ends up in a hypothesis, that lucidity founders in metaphor, that uncertainty is resolved in a work of art. What need had I of so many efforts? The soft lines of these hills and the hand of evening on this troubled heart teach me much more. I have returned to my beginning. I realize that if through science I can seize phenomena and enumerate them, I cannot, for all that, apprehend the world. Were I to trace its entire relief with my finger, I should not know any more. And you give me the choice between a description that is sure but that teaches me nothing and hypotheses that claim to teach me but that are not sure. A stranger to myself and to the world, armed solely with a thought that negates itself as soon as it asserts, what is this condition in which I can have peace only by refusing to know and to live, in which the appetite for conquest bumps into walls that defy its assaults? To will is to stir up paradoxes. Everything is ordered in such a way as to bring into being that poisoned peace produced by thoughtlessness, lack of heart, or fatal renunciations.

Hence the intelligence, too, tells me in its way that this world is absurd. Its contrary, blind reason, may well claim that all is clear; I was waiting for proof and longing for it to be right. But despite so many pretentious centuries and over the heads of so many eloquent and persuasive men, I know that is false. On this plane, at least, there is no happiness if I cannot know. That universal reason, practical or ethical, that determinism, those categories that explain everything are enough to make a decent man laugh. They have nothing to do with the mind. They negate its profound truth, which is to be enchained. In this unintelligible and limited universe, man's fate henceforth assumes its meaning. A horde of irrationals has sprung up and surrounds him until his ultimate end. In his recovered and now studied lucidity, the feeling of the absurd becomes clear and definite. I said that the world is absurd, but I was too hasty. This world in itself is not reasonable, that is all that can be said. But what is absurd is the confrontation of this irrational and the wild longing for clarity whose call echoes in the human heart. The absurd depends as much on man as on the world. For the moment it is all that links them together. It binds them one to the other as only hatred can weld two creatures together. This is all I can discern clearly in this measureless universe where my adventure takes place. Let us pause here. If I hold to be true that absurdity that determines my relationship with life, if I become thoroughly imbued with that sentiment that seizes me in face of the world's scenes, with that lucidity imposed on me by the pursuit of a science, I must sacrifice everything to these certainties and I must see them squarely to be able to maintain them. Above all, I must adapt my behavior to them and pursue them in all their consequences. I am speaking here of decency. But I want to know beforehand if thought can live in those deserts.

———

I already know that thought has at least entered those deserts. There it found its bread. There it realized that it had previously been feeding on phantoms. It justified some of the most urgent themes of human reflection.

From the moment absurdity is recognized, it becomes a passion, the most harrowing of all. But whether or not one can live with one's passions, whether or not one can accept their law, which is to burn the heart they simultaneously exalt—that is the whole question. It is not, however, the one we shall ask just yet. It stands at the center of this experience. There will be time to come back to it. Let us recognize rather those themes and those impulses born of the desert. It will suffice to enumerate them. They, too, are known to all today. There have always been men to defend the rights of the irrational. The tradition of what may be called humiliated thought has never ceased to exist. The criticism of rationalism has been made so often that it seems unnecessary to begin again. Yet our epoch is marked by the rebirth of those paradoxical systems that strive to trip up the reason as if truly it had always forged ahead. But that is not so much a proof of the efficacy of the reason as of the intensity of its hopes. On the plane of history, such a constancy of two attitudes illustrates the essential passion of man torn between his urge toward unity and the clear vision he may have of the walls enclosing him.

But never perhaps at any time has the attack on reason been more violent than in ours. Since Zarathustra's great outburst: "By chance it is the oldest nobility in the world. I conferred it upon all things when I proclaimed that above them no eternal will was exercised," since Kierkegaard's fatal illness, "that malady that leads to death with nothing else following it," the significant and tormenting themes of absurd thought have followed one another. Or at least, and this proviso is of capital importance, the themes of irrational and religious thought. From Jaspers to Heidegger, from Kierkegaard to Chestov, from the phenomenologists to Scheler, on the logical plane and on the moral plane, a whole family of minds related by their nostalgia but opposed by their methods or their aims, have persisted in blocking the royal road of reason and in recovering the direct paths of truth. Here I assume these thoughts to be known and lived. Whatever may be or have been their ambitions, all started out from that indescribable universe where contradiction, antinomy, anguish, or impotence reigns. And what they have in common is precisely the themes so far disclosed. For them, too, it must be said that what matters above all is the conclusions they have managed to draw from those discoveries. That matters so much that they must be examined separately. But for the moment we are concerned solely with their discoveries and their initial experiments. We are concerned solely with noting their agreement. If it would be presumptuous to try to deal with their philosophies, it is possible and sufficient in any case to bring out the climate that is common to them.

Heidegger considers the human condition coldly and announces that that existence is humiliated. The only reality is "anxiety" in the whole chain of beings. To the man lost in the world and its diversions this anxiety is a brief, fleeting fear. But if that fear becomes conscious of itself, it becomes anguish, the perpetual climate of the lucid man "in whom existence is concentrated." This professor of philosophy writes without trembling and in the most abstract language in the world that "the finite and limited character of human existence is more primordial than man himself." His interest in Kant extends only to recognizing the restricted character of his "pure Reason." This is to conclude at the end of his analyses that "the world can no longer offer anything to the man filled with anguish." This anxiety seems to him so much more important than all the categories in the world that he thinks and talks only of it. He enumerates its aspects: boredom when the ordinary man strives to quash it in him and benumb it; terror when the mind contemplates death. He too does not separate consciousness from the absurd. The consciousness of death is the call of anxiety and "existence then delivers itself its own summons through the intermediary of consciousness." It is the very voice of anguish and it adjures existence "to return from its loss in the anonymous They." For him, too, one must not sleep, but must keep alert until the consummation. He stands in this absurd world and points out its ephemeral character. He seeks his way amid these ruins.

Jaspers despairs of any ontology because he claims that we have lost "naïveté." He knows that we can achieve nothing that will transcend the fatal game of appearances. He knows that the end of the mind is failure. He tarries over the spiritual adventures revealed by history and pitilessly discloses the flaw in each system, the illusion that saved everything, the preaching that hid nothing. In this ravaged world in which the impossibility of knowledge is established, in which everlasting nothingness seems the only reality and irremediable despair seems the only attitude, he tries to recover the Ariadne's thread that leads to divine secrets.

Chestov, for his part, throughout a wonderfully monotonous work, constantly straining toward the same truths, tirelessly demonstrates that the tightest system, the most universal rationalism always stumbles eventually on the irrational of human thought. None of the ironic facts or ridiculous contradictions that depreciate the reason escapes him. One thing only interests him, and that is the exception, whether in the domain of the heart or of the mind. Through the Dostoevskian experiences of the condemned man, the exacerbated adventures of the Nietzschean mind, Hamlet's imprecations, or the bitter aristocracy of an Ibsen, he tracks down, illuminates, and magnifies the human revolt against the irremediable. He refuses the reason its reasons and begins to advance with some decision only in the middle of that colorless desert where all certainties have become stones.

Of all perhaps the most engaging, Kierkegaard, for a part of his existence at least, does more than discover the absurd, he lives it. The man who writes: "The surest of stubborn silences is not to hold one's tongue but to talk" makes sure in the beginning that no truth is absolute or can render satisfactory an existence that is impossible in itself. Don Juan of the understanding, he multiplies pseudonyms and contradictions, writes his *Discourses of Edification* at the same time as that manual of cynical spiritualism, *The Diary of the Seducer.* He refuses consolations, ethics, reliable principles. As for that thorn he feels in his heart, he is careful not to quiet its pain. On the contrary, he awakens it and, in the desperate joy of a man crucified and happy to be so, he builds up piece by piece—lucidity, refusal, make-believe—a category of the man possessed. That face both tender and sneering, those pirouettes followed by a cry from the heart are the absurd spirit itself grappling with a reality beyond its comprehension. And the spiritual adventure that leads Kierkegaard to his beloved scandals begins likewise in the chaos of an experience divested of its setting and relegated to its original incoherence.

On quite a different plane, that of method, Husserl and the phenomenologists, by their very extravagances, reinstate the world in its diversity and deny the transcendent power of the reason. The spiritual universe becomes incalculably enriched through them. The rose petal, the milestone, or the human hand are as important as love, desire, or the laws of gravity. Thinking ceases to be unifying or making a semblance familiar in the guise of a major principle. Thinking is learning all over again to see, to be attentive, to focus consciousness; it is turning every idea and every image, in the manner of Proust, into a privileged moment. What justifies thought is its extreme consciousness. Though more positive than Kierkegaard's or Chestov's, Husserl's manner of proceeding, in the beginning, nevertheless negates the classic method of the reason, disappoints hope, opens to intuition and to the heart a whole proliferation of phenomena, the wealth of which has about it something inhuman. These paths lead to all sciences or to none. This amounts to saying that in this case the means are more important than the end. All that is involved is "an attitude for understanding" and not a consolation. Let me repeat: in the beginning, at very least.

How can one fail to feel the basic relationship of these minds! How can one fail to see that they take their stand around a privileged and bitter moment in which hope has no further place? I want everything to be explained to me or nothing. And the reason is impotent when it hears this cry from the heart. The mind aroused by this insistence seeks and finds nothing but contradictions and nonsense. What I fail to understand is nonsense. The world is peopled with such irrationals. The world itself, whose single meaning I do not understand, is but a vast irrational. If one could only say just once: "This is clear," all would be saved. But these men vie with one another in proclaiming that nothing

is clear, all is chaos, that all man has is his lucidity and his definite knowledge of the walls surrounding him.

All these experiences agree and confirm one another. The
mind, when it reaches its limits, must make a judgment and
choose its conclusions. This is where suicide and the reply stand.
But I wish to reverse the order of the inquiry and start out from
the intelligent adventure and come back to daily acts. The experiences called to mind here were born in the desert that we must
not leave behind. A least it is essential to know how far they
went. At this point of his effort man stands face to face with the
irrational. He feels within him his longing for happiness and for
reason. The absurd is born of this confrontation between the
human need and the unreasonable silence of the world. This
must not be forgotten. This must be clung to because the whole
consequence of a life can depend on it. The irrational, the human
nostalgia, and the absurd that is born of their encounter—these
are the three characters in the drama that must necessarily end
with all the logic of which an existence is capable.

PHILOSOPHICAL SUICIDE

The feeling of the absurd is not, for all that, the notion of the absurd. It lays the foundations for it, and that is all. It is not limited
to that notion, except in the brief moment when it passes judgment on the universe. Subsequently it has a chance of going further. It is alive; in other words, it must die or else reverberate. So
it is with the themes we have gathered together. But there again
what interests me is not works or minds, criticism of which
would call for another form and another place, but the discovery
of what their conclusions have in common. Never, perhaps, have
minds been so different. And yet we recognize as identical the
spiritual landscapes in which they get under way. Likewise, despite such dissimilar zones of knowledge, the cry that terminates
their itinerary rings out in the same way. It is evident that the
thinkers we have just recalled have a common climate. To say

that that climate is deadly scarcely amounts to playing on words. Living under that stifling sky forces one to get away or to stay. The important thing is to find out how people get away in the first case and why people stay in the second case. This is how I define the problem of suicide and the possible interest in the conclusions of existential philosophy.

But first I want to detour from the direct path. Up to now we have managed to circumscribe the absurd from the outside. One can, however, wonder how much is clear in that notion and by direct analysis try to discover its meaning on the one hand and, on the other, the consequences it involves.

If I accuse an innocent man of a monstrous crime, if I tell a virtuous man that he has coveted his own sister, he will reply that this is absurd. His indignation has its comical aspect. But it also has its fundamental reason. The virtuous man illustrates by that reply the definitive antinomy existing between the deed I am attributing to him and his lifelong principles. "It's absurd" means "It's impossible" but also "It's contradictory." If I see a man armed only with a sword attack a group of machine guns, I shall consider his act to be absurd. But it is so solely by virtue of the disproportion between his intention and the reality he will encounter, of the contradiction I notice between his true strength and the aim he has in view. Likewise we shall deem a verdict absurd when we contrast it with the verdict the facts apparently dictated. And, similarly, a demonstration by the absurd is achieved by comparing the consequences of such a reasoning with the logical reality one wants to set up. In all these cases, from the simplest to the most complex, the magnitude of the absurdity will be in direct ratio to the distance between the two terms of my comparison. There are absurd marriages, challenges, rancors, silences, wars, and even peace treaties. For each of them the absurdity springs from a comparison. I am thus justified in saying that the feeling of absurdity does not spring from the mere scrutiny of a fact or an impression, but that it bursts from the comparison between a bare fact and a certain reality, between an action and the world that transcends it. The absurd is essentially a divorce. It lies in neither of the elements compared; it is born of their confrontation.

In this particular case and on the plane of intelligence, I can therefore say that the Absurd is not in man (if such a metaphor could have a meaning) nor in the world, but in their presence together. For the moment it is the only bond uniting them. If I wish to limit myself to facts, I know what man wants, I know what the world offers him, and now I can say that I also know what links them. I have no need to dig deeper. A single certainty is enough for the seeker. He simply has to derive all the consequences from it.

The immediate consequence is also a rule of method. The odd trinity brought to light in this way is certainly not a startling discovery. But it resembles the data of experience in that it is both infinitely simple and infinitely complicated. Its first distinguishing feature in this regard is that it cannot be divided. To destroy one of its terms is to destroy the whole. There can be no absurd outside the human mind. Thus, like everything else, the absurd ends with death. But there can be no absurd outside this world either. And it is by this elementary criterion that I judge the notion of the absurd to be essential and consider that it can stand as the first of my truths. The rule of method alluded to above appears here. If I judge that a thing is true, I must preserve it. If I attempt to solve a problem, at least I must not by that very solution conjure away one of the terms of the problem. For me the sole datum is the absurd. The first and, after all, the only condition of my inquiry is to preserve the very thing that crushes me, consequently to respect what I consider essential in it. I have just defined it as a confrontation and an unceasing struggle.

And carrying this absurd logic to its conclusion, I must admit that that struggle implies a total absence of hope (which has nothing to do with despair), a continual rejection (which must not be confused with renunciation), and a conscious dissatisfaction (which must not be compared to immature unrest). Everything that destroys, conjures away, or exorcises these requirements (and, to begin with, consent which overthrows divorce) ruins the absurd and devaluates the attitude that may then be proposed. The absurd has meaning only in so far as it is not agreed to.

———

There exists an obvious fact that seems utterly moral: namely, that a man is always a prey to his truths. Once he has admitted them, he cannot free himself from them. One has to pay something. A man who has become conscious of the absurd is forever bound to it. A man devoid of hope and conscious of being so has ceased to belong to the future. That is natural. But it is just as natural that he should strive to escape the universe of which he is the creator. All the foregoing has significance only on account of this paradox. Certain men, starting from a critique of rationalism, have admitted the absurd climate. Nothing is more instructive in this regard than to scrutinize the way in which they have elaborated their consequences.

Now, to limit myself to existential philosophies, I see that all of them without exception suggest escape. Through an odd reasoning, starting out from the absurd over the ruins of reason, in a closed universe limited to the human, they deify what crushes them and find reason to hope in what impoverishes them. That forced hope is religious in all of them. It deserves attention.

I shall merely analyze here as examples a few themes dear to Chestov and Kierkegaard. But Jaspers will provide us, in caricatural form, a typical example of this attitude. As a result the rest will be clearer. He is left powerless to realize the transcendent, incapable of plumbing the depth of experience, and conscious of that universe upset by failure. Will he advance or at least draw the conclusions from that failure? He contributes nothing new. He has found nothing in experience but the confession of his own impotence and no occasion to infer any satisfactory principle. Yet without justification, as he says to himself, he suddenly asserts all at once the transcendent, the essence of experience, and the superhuman significance of life when he writes: "Does not the failure reveal, beyond any possible explanation and interpretation, not the absence but the existence of transcendence?" That existence which, suddenly and through a blind act of human confidence, explains everything, he defines as "the unthinkable unity of the general and the particular." Thus the absurd becomes god (in the broadest meaning of this word) and that inability to understand becomes the existence that illuminates everything. Nothing logically prepares this reasoning. I can call it a leap. And paradoxically can be understood Jaspers's insistence, his infinite patience devoted to making the experience of the transcendent impossible to realize. For the more fleeting that approximation is, the more empty that definition proves to be, and the more real that transcendent is to him; for the passion he devotes to asserting it is in direct proportion to the gap between his powers of explanation and the irrationality of the world and of experience. It thus appears that the more bitterly Jaspers destroys the reason's preconceptions, the more radically he will explain the world. That apostle of humiliated thought will find at the very end of humiliation the means of regenerating being to its very depth.

Mystical thought has familiarized us with such devices. They are just as legitimate as any attitude of mind. But for the moment I am acting as if I took a certain problem seriously. Without judging beforehand the general value of this attitude or its educative power, I mean simply to consider whether it answers the conditions I set myself, whether it is worthy of the conflict that concerns me. Thus I return to Chestov. A commentator relates a remark of his that deserves interest: "The only true solution," he said, "is precisely where human judgment sees no solution. Otherwise, what need would we have of God? We turn toward God only to obtain the impossible. As for the possible, men suffice." If there is a Chestovian philosophy, I can say that it is altogether summed up in this way. For when, at the conclusion of his passionate analyses, Chestov discovers the fundamental absurdity of all existence, he does not say: "This is the absurd," but rather: "This is God: we must rely on him even if he does not correspond to any of our rational categories." So that confusion may not be possible, the Russian philosopher even hints that this God is perhaps full of hatred and hateful, incomprehensible and contradictory; but the more hideous is his face, the more he asserts his power. His greatness is his incoherence. His proof is his inhumanity. One must spring into him and by this leap free oneself from rational illusions. Thus, for Chestov acceptance of the absurd is contemporaneous with the absurd itself. Being aware of it amounts to accepting it, and the whole logical effort of his thought is to bring it out so that at the same time the tremendous hope it involves may burst forth. Let me repeat that this attitude is legitimate. But I am persisting here in considering a single problem and all its consequences. I do not have to examine the emotion of a thought or of an act of faith. I have a whole lifetime to do that. I know that the rationalist finds Chestov's attitude annoying. But I also feel that Chestov is right rather than the rationalist, and I merely want to know if he remains faithful to the commandments of the absurd.

Now, if it is admitted that the absurd is the contrary of hope, it is seen that existential thought for Chestov presupposes the absurd but proves it only to dispel it. Such subtlety of thought is a conjuror's emotional trick. When Chestov elsewhere sets his absurd in opposition to current morality and reason, he calls it truth and redemption. Hence, there is basically in that definition of the absurd an approbation that Chestov grants it. If it is admitted that all the power of that notion lies in the way it runs counter to our elementary hopes, if it is felt that to remain, the absurd requires not to be consented to, then it can be clearly seen that it has lost its true aspect, its human and relative character in order to enter an eternity that is both incomprehensible and satisfying. If there is an absurd, it is in man's universe. The moment the notion transforms itself into eternity's springboard, it ceases to be linked to human lucidity. The absurd is no longer that evidence that man ascertains without consenting to it. The struggle is eluded. Man integrates the absurd and in that communion causes to disappear its essential character, which is opposition, laceration, and divorce. This leap is an escape. Chestov, who is so fond of quoting Hamlet's remark: "The time is out of joint," writes it down with a sort of savage hope that seems to belong to him in particular. For it is not in this sense that Hamlet says it or Shakespeare writes it. The intoxication of the irrational and the vocation of rapture turn a lucid mind away from the absurd. To Chestov reason is useless but there is something beyond reason. To an absurd mind reason is useless and there is nothing beyond reason.

This leap can at least enlighten us a little more as to the true nature of the absurd. We know that it is worthless except in an equilibrium, that it is, above all, in the comparison and not in the terms of that comparison. But it so happens that Chestov puts all the emphasis on one of the terms and destroys the equilibrium. Our appetite for understanding, our nostalgia for the absolute are explicable only in so far, precisely, as we can understand and explain many things. It is useless to negate the reason absolutely. It has its order in which it is efficacious. It is properly that of human experience. Whence we wanted to make everything clear. If we cannot do so, if the absurd is born on that occasion, it is born precisely at the very meeting-point of that efficacious but limited reason with the ever resurgent irrational. Now, when Chestov rises up against a Hegelian proposition such as "the motion of the solar system takes place in conformity with immutable laws and those laws are its reason," when he devotes all his passion to upsetting Spinoza's rationalism, he concludes, in effect, in favor of the vanity of all reason. Whence, by a natural and illegitimate reversal, to the pre-eminence of the irrational.* But the transition is not evident. For here may intervene the notion of limit and the notion of level. The laws of nature may be operative up to a certain limit, beyond which they turn against themselves to give birth to the absurd. Or else, they may justify themselves on the level of description without for that reason being true on the level of explanation. Everything is sacrificed

---

* Apropos of the notion of exception particularly and against Aristotle.

here to the irrational, and, the demand for clarity being conjured away, the absurd disappears with one of the terms of its comparison. The absurd man, on the other hand, does not undertake such a leveling process. He recognizes the struggle, does not absolutely scorn reason, and admits the irrational. Thus he again embraces in a single glance all the data of experience and he is little inclined to leap before knowing. He knows simply that in that alert awareness there is no further place for hope.

What is perceptible in Leo Chestov will be perhaps even more so in Kierkegaard. To be sure, it is hard to outline clear propositions in so elusive a writer. But, despite apparently opposed writings, beyond the pseudonyms, the tricks, and the smiles, can be felt throughout that work, as it were, the presentiment (at the same time as the apprehension) of a truth which eventually bursts forth in the last works: Kierkegaard likewise takes the leap. His childhood having been so frightened by Christianity, he ultimately returns to its harshest aspect. For him, too, antinomy and paradox become criteria of the religious. Thus, the very thing that led to despair of the meaning and depth of this life now gives it its truth and its clarity. Christianity is the scandal, and what Kierkegaard calls for quite plainly is the third sacrifice required by Ignatius Loyola, the one in which God most rejoices: "The sacrifice of the intellect."* This effect of the "leap" is odd, but must not surprise us any longer. He makes of the absurd the criterion of the other world, whereas it is simply a residue of the experience of this world. "In his failure," says Kierkegaard, "the believer finds his triumph."

It is not for me to wonder to what stirring preaching this attitude is linked. I merely have to wonder if the spectacle of the absurd and its own character justifies it. On this point, I know that

---

* It may be thought that I am neglecting here the essential problem, that of faith. But I am not examining the philosophy of Kierkegaard or of Chestov or, later on, of Husserl (this would call for a different place and a different attitude of mind); I am simply borrowing a theme from them and examining whether its consequences can fit the already established rules. It is merely a matter of persistence.

it is not so. Upon considering again the content of the absurd, one understands better the method that inspired Kierkegaard. Between the irrational of the world and the insurgent nostalgia of the absurd, he does not maintain the equilibrium. He does not respect the relationship that constitutes, properly speaking, the feeling of absurdity. Sure of being unable to escape the irrational, he wants at least to save himself from that desperate nostalgia that seems to him sterile and devoid of implication. But if he may be right on this point in his judgment, he could not be in his negation. If he substitutes for his cry of revolt a frantic adherence, at once he is led to blind himself to the absurd which hitherto enlightened him and to deify the only certainty he henceforth possesses, the irrational. The important thing, as Abbé Galiani said to Mme d'Epinay, is not to be cured, but to live with one's ailments. Kierkegaard wants to be cured. To be cured is his frenzied wish, and it runs throughout his whole journal. The entire effort of his intelligence is to escape the antinomy of the human condition. An all the more desperate effort since he intermittently perceives its vanity when he speaks of himself, as if neither fear of God nor piety were capable of bringing him to peace. Thus it is that, through a strained subterfuge, he gives the irrational the appearance and God the attributes of the absurd: unjust, incoherent, and incomprehensible. Intelligence alone in him strives to stifle the underlying demands of the human heart. Since nothing is proved, everything can be proved.

Indeed, Kierkegaard himself shows us the path taken. I do not want to suggest anything here, but how can one fail to read in his works the signs of an almost intentional mutilation of the soul to balance the mutilation accepted in regard to the absurd? It is the leitmotiv of the *Journal*. "What I lacked was the animal which *also* belongs to human destiny. . . . But give me a body then." And further on: "Oh! especially in my early youth what should I not have given to be a man, even for six months . . . what I lack, basically, is a body and the physical conditions of existence." Elsewhere, the same man nevertheless adopts the great cry of hope that has come down through so many centuries and quickened so many hearts, except that of the absurd man. "But for the Christian death is certainly not the end of everything and it implies infinitely more hope than life implies for us, even when that life is overflowing with health and vigor." Reconciliation through scandal is still reconciliation. It allows one perhaps, as can be seen, to derive hope of its contrary, which is death. But even if fellow-feeling inclines one toward that attitude, still it must be said that excess justifies nothing. That transcends, as the saying goes, the human scale; therefore it must be superhuman. But this "therefore" is superfluous. There is no logical certainty here. There is no experimental probability either. All I can say is that, in fact, that transcends my scale. If I do not draw a negation from it, at least I do not want to found anything on the incomprehensible. I want to know whether I can live with what I know and with that alone. I am told again that here the intelligence must sacrifice its pride and the reason bow down. But if I recognize the limits of the reason, I do not therefore negate it, recognizing its relative powers. I merely want to remain in this middle path where the intelligence can remain clear. If that is its pride, I see no sufficient reason for giving it up. Nothing more profound, for example, than Kierkegaard's view according to which despair is not a fact but a state: the very state of sin. For sin is what alienates from God. The absurd, which is the metaphysical state of the conscious man, does not lead to God.* Perhaps this notion will become clearer if I risk this shocking statement: the absurd is sin without God.

It is a matter of living in that state of the absurd. I know on what it is founded, this mind and this world straining against each other without being able to embrace each other. I ask for the rule of life of that state, and what I am offered neglects its basis, negates one of the terms of the painful opposition, demands of me a resignation. I ask what is involved in the condition I recognize as mine; I know it implies obscurity and ignorance; and I am assured that this ignorance explains everything and that

* I did not say "excludes God," which would still amount to asserting.

this darkness is my light. But there is no reply here to my intent, and this stirring lyricism cannot hide the paradox from me. One must therefore turn away. Kierkegaard may shout in warning: "If man had no eternal consciousness, if, at the bottom of everything, there were merely a wild, seething force producing everything, both large and trifling, in the storm of dark passions, if the bottomless void that nothing can fill underlay all things, what would life be but despair?" This cry is not likely to stop the absurd man. Seeking what is true is not seeking what is desirable. If in order to elude the anxious question: "What would life be?" one must, like the donkey, feed on the roses of illusion, then the absurd mind, rather than resigning itself to falsehood, prefers to adopt fearlessly Kierkegaard's reply: "despair." Everything considered, a determined soul will always manage.

—

I am taking the liberty at this point of calling the existential attitude philosophical suicide. But this does not imply a judgment. It is a convenient way of indicating the movement by which a thought negates itself and tends to transcend itself in its very negation. For the existentials negation is their God. To be precise, that god is maintained only through the negation of human reason.* But, like suicides, gods change with men. There are many ways of leaping, the essential being to leap. Those redeeming negations, those ultimate contradictions which negate the obstacle that has not yet been leaped over, may spring just as well (this is the paradox at which this reasoning aims) from a certain religious inspiration as from the rational order. They always lay claim to the eternal, and it is solely in this that they take the leap.

It must be repeated that the reasoning developed in this essay leaves out altogether the most widespread spiritual attitude of our enlightened age: the one, based on the principle that all is reason, which aims to explain the world. It is natural to give a clear view of the world after accepting the idea that it must be clear. That is even legitimate, but does not concern the reason-

---

* Let me assert again: it is not the affirmation of God that is questioned here, but rather the logic leading to that affirmation.

ing we are following out here. In fact, our aim is to shed light upon the step taken by the mind when, starting from a philosophy of the world's lack of meaning, it ends up by finding a meaning and depth in it. The most touching of those steps is religious in essence; it becomes obvious in the theme of the irrational. But the most paradoxical and most significant is certainly the one that attributes rational reasons to a world it originally imagined as devoid of any guiding principle. It is impossible in any case to reach the consequences that concern us without having given an idea of this new attainment of the spirit of nostalgia.

I shall examine merely the theme of "the Intention" made fashionable by Husserl and the phenomenologists. I have already alluded to it. Originally Husserl's method negates the classic procedure of the reason. Let me repeat. Thinking is not unifying or making the appearance familiar under the guise of a great principle. Thinking is learning all over again how to see, directing one's consciousness, making of every image a privileged place. In other words, phenomenology declines to explain the world, it wants to be merely a description of actual experience. It confirms absurd thought in its initial assertion that there is no truth, but merely truths. From the evening breeze to this hand on my shoulder, everything has its truth. Consciousness illuminates it by paying attention to it. Consciousness does not form the object of its understanding, it merely focuses, it is the act of attention, and, to borrow a Bergsonian image, it resembles the projector that suddenly focuses on an image. The difference is that there is no scenario, but a successive and incoherent illustration. In that magic lantern all the pictures are privileged. Consciousness suspends in experience the objects of its attention. Through its miracle it isolates them. Henceforth they are beyond all judgments. This is the "intention" that characterizes consciousness. But the word does not imply any idea of finality; it is taken in its sense of "direction": its only value is topographical.

At first sight, it certainly seems that in this way nothing contradicts the absurd spirit. That apparent modesty of thought that limits itself to describing what it declines to explain, that intentional discipline whence result paradoxically a profound enrichment of experience and the rebirth of the world in its prolixity are absurd procedures. At least at first sight. For methods of thought, in this case as elsewhere, always assume two aspects, one psychological and the other metaphysical.* Thereby they harbor two truths. If the theme of the intentional claims to illustrate merely a psychological attitude, by which reality is drained instead of being explained, nothing in fact separates it from the absurd spirit. It aims to enumerate what it cannot transcend. It affirms solely that without any unifying principle thought can still take delight in describing and understanding every aspect of experience. The truth involved then for each of those aspects is psychological in nature. It simply testifies to the "interest" that reality can offer. It is a way of awaking a sleeping world and of making it vivid to the mind. But if one attempts to extend and give a rational basis to that notion of truth, if one claims to discover in this way the "essence" of each object of knowledge, one restores its depth to experience. For an absurd mind that is incomprehensible. Now, it is this wavering between modesty and assurance that is noticeable in the intentional attitude, and this shimmering of phenomenological thought will illustrate the absurd reasoning better than anything else.

For Husserl speaks likewise of "extra-temporal essences" brought to light by the intention, and he sounds like Plato. All things are not explained by one thing but by all things. I see no difference. To be sure, those ideas or those essences that consciousness "effectuates" at the end of every description are not yet to be considered perfect models. But it is asserted that they are directly present in each datum of perception. There is no longer a single idea explaining everything, but an infinite number of essences giving a meaning to an infinite number of objects. The world comes to a stop, but also lights up. Platonic realism becomes intuitive, but it is still realism. Kierkegaard was

* Even the most rigorous epistemologies imply metaphysics. And to such a degree that the metaphysic of many contemporary thinkers consists in having nothing but an epistemology.

swallowed up in his God; Parmenides plunged thought into the One. But here thought hurls itself into an abstract polytheism. But this is not all: hallucinations and fictions likewise belong to "extra-temporal essences." In the new world of ideas, the species of centaurs collaborates with the more modest species of metropolitan man.

For the absurd man, there was a truth as well as a bitterness in that purely psychological opinion that all aspects of the world are privileged. To say that everything is privileged is tantamount to saying that everything is equivalent. But the metaphysical aspect of that truth is so far-reaching that through an elementary reaction he feels closer perhaps to Plato. He is taught, in fact, that every image presupposes an equally privileged essence. In this ideal world without hierarchy, the formal army is composed solely of generals. To be sure, transcendency had been eliminated. But a sudden shift in thought brings back into the world a sort of fragmentary immanence which restores to the universe its depth.

Am I to fear having carried too far a theme handled with greater circumspection by its creators? I read merely these assertions of Husserl, apparently paradoxical yet rigorously logical if what precedes is accepted: "That which is true is true absolutely, in itself; truth is one, identical with itself, however different the creatures who perceive it, men, monsters, angels or gods." Reason triumphs and trumpets forth with that voice, I cannot deny. What can its assertions mean in the absurd world? The perception of an angel or a god has no meaning for me. That geometrical spot where divine reason ratifies mine will always be incomprehensible to me. There, too, I discern a leap, and though performed in the abstract, it nonetheless means for me forgetting just what I do not want to forget. When farther on Husserl exclaims: "If all masses subject to attraction were to disappear, the law of attraction would not be destroyed but would simply remain without any possible application," I know that I am faced with a metaphysic of consolation. And if I want to discover the point where thought leaves the path of evidence, I have only to reread the parallel reasoning that Husserl voices regarding the mind: "If we could contemplate clearly the exact laws of psychic processes, they would be seen to be likewise eternal and invariable, like the basic laws of theoretical natural science. Hence they would be valid even if there were no psychic process." Even if the mind were not, its laws would be! I see then that of a psychological truth Husserl aims to make a rational rule: after having denied the integrating power of human reason, he leaps by this expedient to eternal Reason.

Husserl's theme of the "concrete universe" cannot then surprise me. If I am told that all essences are not formal but that some are material, that the first are the object of logic and the second of science, this is merely a question of definition. The abstract, I am told, indicates but a part, without consistency in itself, of a concrete universal. But the wavering already noted allows me to throw light on the confusion of these terms. For that may mean that the concrete object of my attention, this sky, the reflection of that water on this coat, alone preserve the prestige of the real that my interest isolates in the world. And I shall not deny it. But that may mean also that this coat itself is universal, has its particular and sufficient essence, belongs to the world of forms. I then realize that merely the order of the procession has been changed. This world has ceased to have its reflection in a higher universe, but the heaven of forms is figured in the host of images of this earth. This changes nothing for me. Rather than encountering here a taste for the concrete, the meaning of the human condition, I find an intellectualism sufficiently unbridled to generalize the concrete itself.

———

It is futile to be amazed by the apparent paradox that leads thought to its own negation by the opposite paths of humiliated reason and triumphal reason. From the abstract god of Husserl to the dazzling god of Kierkegaard the distance is not so great. Reason and the irrational lead to the same preaching. In truth the way matters but little; the will to arrive suffices. The abstract philosopher and the religious philosopher start out from the same disorder and support each other in the same anxiety. But the essential is to explain. Nostalgia is stronger here than knowledge. It is significant that the thought of the epoch is at once one of the most deeply imbued with a philosophy of the non-significance of the world and one of the most divided in its conclusions. It is constantly oscillating between extreme rationalization of reality which tends to break up that thought into standard reasons and its extreme irrationalization which tends to deify it. But this divorce is only apparent. It is a matter of reconciliation, and, in both cases, the leap suffices. It is always wrongly thought that the notion of reason is a one-way notion. To tell the truth, however rigorous it may be in its ambition, this concept is nonetheless just as unstable as others. Reason bears a quite human aspect, but it also is able to turn toward the divine. Since Plotinus, who was the first to reconcile it with the eternal climate, it has learned to turn away from the most cherished of its principles, which is contradiction, in order to integrate into it the strangest, the quite magic one of participation.* It is an instrument of thought and not thought itself. Above all, a man's thought is his nostalgia.

Just as reason was able to soothe the melancholy of Plotinus, it provides modern anguish the means of calming itself in the familiar setting of the eternal. The absurd mind has less luck. For it the world is neither so rational nor so irrational. It is unreasonable and only that. With Husserl the reason eventually has no limits at all. The absurd, on the contrary, establishes its limits since it is powerless to calm its anguish. Kierkegaard independently asserts that a single limit is enough to negate that anguish. But the absurd does not go so far. For it that limit is directed solely at the reason's ambitions. The theme of the irrational, as it

* A.—At that time reason had to adapt itself or die. It adapts itself. With Plotinus, after being logical it becomes æsthetic. Metaphor takes the place of the syllogism.

B.—Moreover, this is not Plotinus' only contribution to phenomenology. This whole attitude is already contained in the concept so dear to the Alexandrian thinker that there is not only an idea of man but also an idea of Socrates.

is conceived by the existentials, is reason becoming confused and escaping by negating itself. The absurd is lucid reason noting its limits.

Only at the end of this difficult path does the absurd man recognize his true motives. Upon comparing his inner exigence and what is then offered him, he suddenly feels he is going to turn away. In the universe of Husserl the world becomes clear and that longing for familiarity that man's heart harbors becomes useless. In Kierkegaard's apocalypse that desire for clarity must be given up if it wants to be satisfied. Sin is not so much knowing (if it were, everybody would be innocent) as wanting to know. Indeed, it is the only sin of which the absurd man can feel that it constitutes both his guilt and his innocence. He is offered a solution in which all the past contradictions have become merely polemical games. But this is not the way he experienced them. Their truth must be preserved, which consists in not being satisfied. He does not want preaching.

My reasoning wants to be faithful to the evidence that aroused it. That evidence is the absurd. It is that divorce between the mind that desires and the world that disappoints, my nostalgia for unity, this fragmented universe and the contradiction that binds them together. Kierkegaard suppresses my nostalgia and Husserl gathers together that universe. That is not what I was expecting. It was a matter of living and thinking with those dislocations, of knowing whether one had to accept or refuse. There can be no question of masking the evidence, of suppressing the absurd by denying one of the terms of its equation. It is essential to know whether one can live with it or whether, on the other hand, logic commands one to die of it. I am not interested in philosophical suicide, but rather in plain suicide. I merely wish to purge it of its emotional content and know its logic and its integrity. Any other position implies for the absurd mind deceit and the mind's retreat before what the mind itself has brought to light. Husserl claims to obey the desire to escape "the inveterate habit of living and thinking in certain well-known and convenient conditions of existence," but the final leap restores in him the eternal and its comfort. The leap does not represent an extreme danger as Kierkegaard would like it to do. The danger, on the contrary, lies in the subtle instant that precedes the leap. Being able to remain on that dizzying crest—that is integrity and the rest is subterfuge. I know also that never has helplessness inspired such striking harmonies as those of Kierkegaard. But if helplessness has its place in the indifferent landscapes of history, it has none in a reasoning whose exigence is now known.

ABSURD FREEDOM

Now the main thing is done, I hold certain facts from which I cannot separate. What I know, what is certain, what I cannot deny, what I cannot reject—this is what counts. I can negate everything of that part of me that lives on vague nostalgias, except this desire for unity, this longing to solve, this need for clarity and cohesion. I can refute everything in this world surrounding me that offends or enraptures me, except this chaos, this sovereign chance and this divine equivalence which springs from anarchy. I don't know whether this world has a meaning that transcends it. But I know that I do not know that meaning and that it is impossible for me just now to know it. What can a meaning outside my condition mean to me? I can understand only in human terms. What I touch, what resists me—that is what I understand. And these two certainties—my appetite for the absolute and for unity and the impossibility of reducing this world to a rational and reasonable principle—I also know that I cannot reconcile them. What other truth can I admit without lying, without bringing in a hope I lack and which means nothing within the limits of my condition?

If I were a tree among trees, a cat among animals, this life would have a meaning, or rather this problem would not arise, for I should belong to this world. I should *be* this world to which I am now opposed by my whole consciousness and my whole insistence upon familiarity. This ridiculous reason is what sets me in opposition to all creation. I cannot cross it out with a stroke of the pen. What I believe to be true I must therefore preserve. What seems to me so obvious, even against me, I must support. And what constitutes the basis of that conflict, of that break between the world and my mind, but the awareness of it? If therefore I want to preserve it, I can through a constant awareness, ever revived, ever alert. This is what, for the moment, I must remember. At this moment the absurd, so obvious and yet so hard to win, returns to a man's life and finds its home there. At this moment, too, the mind can leave the arid, dried-up path of lucid effort. That path now emerges in daily life. It encounters the world of the anonymous impersonal pronoun "one," but henceforth man enters in with his revolt and his lucidity. He has forgotten how to hope. This hell of the present is his Kingdom at last. All problems recover their sharp edge. Abstract evidence retreats before the poetry of forms and colors. Spiritual conflicts become embodied and return to the abject and magnificent shelter of man's heart. None of them is settled. But all are transfigured. Is one going to die, escape by the leap, rebuild a mansion of ideas and forms to one's own scale? Is one, on the contrary, going to take up the heart-rending and marvelous wager of the absurd? Let's make a final effort in this regard and draw all our conclusions. The body, affection, creation, action, human nobility will then resume their places in this mad world. At last man will again find there the wine of the absurd and the bread of indifference on which he feeds his greatness.

Let us insist again on the method: it is a matter of persisting. At a certain point on his path the absurd man is tempted. History is not lacking in either religions or prophets, even without gods. He is asked to leap. All he can reply is that he doesn't fully understand, that it is not obvious. Indeed, he does not want to do anything but what he fully understands. He is assured that this is the sin of pride, but he does not understand the notion of sin; that perhaps hell is in store, but he has not enough imagination to visualize that strange future; that he is losing immortal life, but that seems to him an idle consideration. An attempt is made to get him to admit his guilt. He feels innocent. To tell the truth, that is all he feels—his irreparable innocence. This is what allows him everything. Hence, what he demands of himself is to live *solely* with what he knows, to accommodate himself to what is, and to bring in nothing that is not certain. He is told that nothing is. But this at least is a certainty. And it is with this that he is concerned: he wants to find out if it is possible to live *without appeal*.

———

Now I can broach the notion of suicide. It has already been felt what solution might be given. At this point the problem is reversed. It was previously a question of finding out whether or not life had to have a meaning to be lived. It now becomes clear, on the contrary, that it will be lived all the better if it has no meaning. Living an experience, a particular fate, is accepting it fully. Now, no one will live this fate, knowing it to be absurd, unless he does everything to keep before him that absurd brought to light by consciousness. Negating one of the terms of the opposition on which he lives amounts to escaping it. To abolish conscious revolt is to elude the problem. The theme of permanent revolution is thus carried into individual experience. Living is keeping the absurd alive. Keeping it alive is, above all, contemplating it. Unlike Eurydice, the absurd dies only when we turn away from it. One of the only coherent philosophical positions is thus revolt. It is a constant confrontation between man and his own obscurity. It is an insistence upon an impossible transparency. It challenges the world anew every second. Just as danger provided man the unique opportunity of seizing awareness, so metaphysical revolt extends awareness to the whole of experience. It is that constant presence of man in his own eyes. It is not aspiration, for it is devoid of hope. That revolt is the certainty of a crushing fate, without the resignation that ought to accompany it.

This is where it is seen to what a degree absurd experience is remote from suicide. It may be thought that suicide follows revolt—but wrongly. For it does not represent the logical outcome of revolt. It is just the contrary by the consent it presupposes. Suicide, like the leap, is acceptance at its extreme. Everything is over and man returns to his essential history. His future, his unique and dreadful future—he sees and rushes toward it. In its way, suicide settles the absurd. It engulfs the absurd in the same death. But I know that in order to keep alive, the absurd cannot be settled. It escapes suicide to the extent that it is simultaneously awareness and rejection of death. It is, at the extreme limit of the condemned man's last thought, that shoelace that despite everything he sees a few yards away, on the very brink of his dizzying fall. The contrary of suicide, in fact, is the man condemned to death.

That revolt gives life its value. Spread out over the whole length of a life, it restores its majesty to that life. To a man devoid of blinders, there is no finer sight than that of the intelligence at grips with a reality that transcends it. The sight of human pride is unequaled. No disparagement is of any use. That discipline that the mind imposes on itself, that will conjured up out of nothing, that face-to-face struggle have something exceptional about them. To impoverish that reality whose inhumanity constitutes man's majesty is tantamount to impoverishing him himself. I understand then why the doctrines that explain everything to me also debilitate me at the same time. They relieve me of the weight of my own life, and yet I must carry it alone. At this juncture, I cannot conceive that a skeptical metaphysics can be joined to an ethics of renunciation.

Consciousness and revolt, these rejections are the contrary of renunciation. Everything that is indomitable and passionate in a human heart quickens them, on the contrary, with its own life. It is essential to die unreconciled and not of one's own free will. Suicide is a repudiation. The absurd man can only drain everything to the bitter end, and deplete himself. The absurd is his extreme tension, which he maintains constantly by solitary effort, for he knows that in that consciousness and in that day-to-day revolt he gives proof of his only truth, which is defiance. This is a first consequence.

———

If I remain in that prearranged position which consists in draw-ing all the conclusions (and nothing else) involved in a newly discovered notion, I am faced with a second paradox. In order to remain faithful to that method, I have nothing to do with the problem of metaphysical liberty. Knowing whether or not man is free doesn't interest me. I can experience only my own free-dom. As to it, I can have no general notions, but merely a few clear insights. The problem of "freedom as such" has no mean-ing. For it is linked in quite a different way with the problem of God. Knowing whether or not man is free involves knowing whether he can have a master. The absurdity peculiar to this problem comes from the fact that the very notion that makes the problem of freedom possible also takes away all its meaning. For in the presence of God there is less a problem of freedom than a problem of evil. You know the alternative: either we are not free and God the all-powerful is responsible for evil. Or we are free and responsible but God is not all-powerful. All the scholastic subtleties have neither added anything to nor subtracted any-thing from the acuteness of this paradox.

This is why I cannot get lost in the glorification or the mere definition of a notion which eludes me and loses its meaning as soon as it goes beyond the frame of reference of my individual experience. I cannot understand what kind of freedom would be given me by a higher being. I have lost the sense of hierarchy. The only conception of freedom I can have is that of the pris-oner or the individual in the midst of the State. The only one I know is freedom of thought and action. Now if the absurd can-cels all my chances of eternal freedom, it restores and magnifies, on the other hand, my freedom of action. That privation of hope and future means an increase in man's availability.

Before encountering the absurd, the everyday man lives with aims, a concern for the future or for justification (with regard to whom or what is not the question). He weighs his chances, he counts on "someday," his retirement or the labor of his sons. He still thinks that something in his life can be directed. In truth, he acts as if he were free, even if all the facts make a point of contradicting that liberty. But after the absurd, everything is upset. That idea that "I am," my way of acting as if everything has a meaning (even if, on occasion, I said that nothing has)—all that is given the lie in vertiginous fashion by the absurdity of a possible death. Thinking of the future, establishing aims for oneself, having preferences—all this presupposes a belief in freedom, even if one occasionally ascertains that one doesn't feel it. But at that moment I am well aware that that higher liberty, that freedom *to be,* which alone can serve as basis for a truth, does not exist. Death is there as the only reality. After death the chips are down. I am not even free, either, to perpetuate myself, but a slave, and, above all, a slave without hope of an eternal revolution, without recourse to contempt. And who without revolution and without contempt can remain a slave? What freedom can exist in the fullest sense without assurance of eternity?

But at the same time the absurd man realizes that hitherto he was bound to that postulate of freedom on the illusion of which he was living. In a certain sense, that hampered him. To the extent to which he imagined a purpose to his life, he adapted himself to the demands of a purpose to be achieved and became the slave of his liberty. Thus I could not act otherwise than as the father (or the engineer or the leader of a nation, or the post-office sub-clerk) that I am preparing to be. I think I can choose to be that rather than something else. I think so unconsciously, to be sure. But at the same time I strengthen my postulate with the beliefs of those around me, with the presumptions of my human environment (others are so sure of being free, and that cheerful mood is so contagious!). However far one may remain from any presumption, moral or social, one is partly influenced by them and even, for the best among them (there are good and bad presumptions), one adapts one's life to them. Thus the absurd man realizes that he was not really free. To speak clearly, to the extent to which I hope, to which I worry about a truth that might be individual to me, about a way of being or creating, to the extent to which I arrange my life and prove thereby that I accept its having a meaning, I create for myself barriers between which I confine my life. I do like so many bureaucrats of the mind and heart who only fill me with disgust and whose only vice, I now see clearly, is to take man's freedom seriously.

The absurd enlightens me on this point: there is no future. Henceforth this is the reason for my inner freedom. I shall use two comparisons here. Mystics, to begin with, find freedom in giving themselves. By losing themselves in their god, by accepting his rules, they become secretly free. In spontaneously accepted slavery they recover a deeper independence. But what does that freedom mean? It may be said, above all, that they *feel* free with regard to themselves, and not so much free as liberated. Likewise, completely turned toward death (taken here as the most obvious absurdity), the absurd man feels released from everything outside that passionate attention crystallizing in him. He enjoys a freedom with regard to common rules. It can be seen at this point that the initial themes of existential philosophy keep their entire value. The return to consciousness, the escape from everyday sleep represent the first steps of absurd freedom. But it is existential *preaching* that is alluded to, and with it that spiritual leap which basically escapes consciousness. In the same way (this is my second comparison) the slaves of antiquity did not belong to themselves. But they knew that freedom which consists in not feeling responsible.* Death, too, has patrician hands which, while crushing, also liberate.

Losing oneself in that bottomless certainty, feeling henceforth sufficiently remote from one's own life to increase it and take a broad view of it—this involves the principle of a liberation. Such new independence has a definite time limit, like any freedom of action. It does not write a check on eternity. But it takes the place of the illusions of *freedom*, which all stopped with death. The divine availability of the condemned man before whom the prison doors open in a certain early dawn, that unbelievable disinterestedness with regard to everything except for

---

* I am concerned here with a factual comparison, not with an apology of humility. The absurd man is the contrary of the reconciled man.

the pure flame of life—it is clear that death and the absurd are here the principles of the only reasonable freedom: that which a human heart can experience and live. This is a second consequence. The absurd man thus catches sight of a burning and frigid, transparent and limited universe in which nothing is possible but everything is given, and beyond which all is collapse and nothingness. He can then decide to accept such a universe and draw from it his strength, his refusal to hope, and the unyielding evidence of a life without consolation.

———

But what does life mean in such a universe? Nothing else for the moment but indifference to the future and a desire to use up everything that is given. Belief in the meaning of life always implies a scale of values, a choice, our preferences. Belief in the absurd, according to our definitions, teaches the contrary. But this is worth examining.

Knowing whether or not one can live *without appeal* is all that interests me. I do not want to get out of my depth. This aspect of life being given me, can I adapt myself to it? Now, faced with this particular concern, belief in the absurd is tantamount to substituting the quantity of experiences for the quality. If I convince myself that this life has no other aspect than that of the absurd, if I feel that its whole equilibrium depends on that perpetual opposition between my conscious revolt and the darkness in which it struggles, if I admit that my freedom has no meaning except in relation to its limited fate, then I must say that what counts is not the best living but the most living. It is not up to me to wonder if this is vulgar or revolting, elegant or deplorable. Once and for all, value judgments are discarded here in favor of factual judgments. I have merely to draw the conclusions from what I can see and to risk nothing that is hypothetical. Supposing that living in this way were not honorable, then true propriety would command me to be dishonorable.

The most living; in the broadest sense, that rule means nothing. It calls for definition. It seems to begin with the fact that the notion of quantity has not been sufficiently explored. For it can account for a large share of human experience. A man's rule of conduct and his scale of values have no meaning except through the quantity and variety of experiences he has been in a position to accumulate. Now, the conditions of modern life impose on the majority of men the same quantity of experiences and consequently the same profound experience. To be sure, there must also be taken into consideration the individual's spontaneous contribution, the "given" element in him. But I cannot judge of that, and let me repeat that my rule here is to get along with the immediate evidence. I see, then, that the individual character of a common code of ethics lies not so much in the ideal importance of its basic principles as in the norm of an experience that it is possible to measure. To stretch a point somewhat, the Greeks had the code of their leisure just as we have the code of our eight-hour day. But already many men among the most tragic cause us to foresee that a longer experience changes this table of values. They make us imagine that adventurer of the everyday who through mere quantity of experiences would break all records (I am purposely using this sports expression) and would thus win his own code of ethics.* Yet let's avoid romanticism and just ask ourselves what such an attitude may mean to a man with his mind made up to take up his bet and to observe strictly what he takes to be the rules of the game.

Breaking all the records is first and foremost being faced with the world as often as possible. How can that be done without contradictions and without playing on words? For on the one hand the absurd teaches that all experiences are unimportant, and on the other it urges toward the greatest quantity of experiences. How, then, can one fail to do as so many of those men I was speaking of earlier—choose the form of life that brings us the most possible of that human matter, thereby introducing a scale of values that on the other hand one claims to reject?

---

* Quantity sometimes constitutes quality. If I can believe the latest restatements of scientific theory, all matter is constituted by centers of energy. Their greater or lesser quantity makes its specificity more or less remarkable. A billion ions and one ion differ not only in quantity but also in quality. It is easy to find an analogy in human experience.

But again it is the absurd and its contradictory life that teaches us. For the mistake is thinking that that quantity of experiences depends on the circumstances of our life when it depends solely on us. Here we have to be over-simple. To two men living the same number of years, the world always provides the same sum of experiences. It is up to us to be conscious of them. Being aware of one's life, one's revolt, one's freedom, and to the maximum, is living, and to the maximum. Where lucidity dominates, · the scale of values becomes useless. Let's be even more simple. Let us say that the sole obstacle, the sole deficiency to be made good, is constituted by premature death. Thus it is that no depth, no emotion, no passion, and no sacrifice could render equal in the eyes of the absurd man (even if he wished it so) a conscious life of forty years and a lucidity spread over sixty years.* Madness and death are his irreparables. Man does not choose. The absurd and the extra life it involves *therefore do not depend on man's will,* but on its contrary, which is death.† Weighing words carefully, it is altogether a question of luck. One just has to be able to consent to this. There will never be any substitute for twenty years of life and experience.

By what is an odd inconsistency in such an alert race, the Greeks claimed that those who died young were beloved of the gods. And that is true only if you are willing to believe that entering the ridiculous world of the gods is forever losing the purest of joys, which is feeling, and feeling on this earth. The present and the succession of presents before a constantly conscious soul is the ideal of the absurd man. But the word "ideal" rings false in this connection. It is not even his vocation, but merely the third consequence of his reasoning. Having started from an anguished awareness of the inhuman, the meditation on

---

* Same reflection on a notion as different as the idea of eternal nothingness. It neither adds anything to nor subtracts anything from reality. In psychological experience of nothingness, it is by the consideration of what will happen in two thousand years that our own nothingness truly takes on meaning. In one of its aspects, eternal nothingness is made up precisely of the sum of lives to come which will not be ours.

† The will is only the agent here: it tends to maintain consciousness. It provides a discipline of life, and that is appreciable.

the absurd returns at the end of its itinerary to the very heart of the passionate flames of human revolt.*

———

Thus I draw from the absurd three consequences, which are my revolt, my freedom, and my passion. By the mere activity of consciousness I transform into a rule of life what was an invitation to death—and I refuse suicide. I know, to be sure, the dull resonance that vibrates throughout these days. Yet I have but a word to say: that it is necessary. When Nietzsche writes: "It clearly seems that the chief thing in heaven and on earth is to *obey* at length and in a single direction: in the long run there results something for which it is worth the trouble of living on this earth as, for example, virtue, art, music, the dance, reason, the mind—something that transfigures, something delicate, mad, or divine," he elucidates the rule of a really distinguished code of ethics. But he also points the way of the absurd man. Obeying the flame is both the easiest and the hardest thing to do. However, it is good for man to judge himself occasionally. He is alone in being able to do so.

"Prayer," says Alain, "is when night descends over thought." "But the mind must meet the night," reply the mystics and the existentials. Yes, indeed, but not that night that is born under closed eyelids and through the mere will of man—dark, impenetrable night that the mind calls up in order to plunge into it. If it must encounter a night, let it be rather that of despair, which remains lucid—polar night, vigil of the mind, whence will arise perhaps that white and virginal brightness which outlines every object in the light of the intelligence. At that degree, equivalence encounters passionate understanding. Then it is no longer even a question of judging the existential leap. It resumes its place

* What matters is coherence. We start out here from acceptance of the world. But Oriental thought teaches that one can indulge in the same effort of logic by choosing *against* the world. That is just as legitimate and gives this essay its perspectives and its limits. But when the negation of the world is pursued just as rigorously, one often achieves (in certain Vedantic schools) similar results regarding, for instance, the indifference of works. In a book of great importance, *Le Choix*, Jean Grenier establishes in this way a veritable "philosophy of indifference."

amid the age-old fresco of human attitudes. For the spectator, if he is conscious, that leap is still absurd. In so far as it thinks it solves the paradox, it reinstates it intact. On this score, it is stirring. On this score, everything resumes its place and the absurd world is reborn in all its splendor and diversity.

But it is bad to stop, hard to be satisfied with a single way of seeing, to go without contradiction, perhaps the most subtle of all spiritual forces. The preceding merely defines a way of thinking. But the point is to live.

THE MYTH OF SISYPHUS

The gods had condemned Sisyphus to ceaselessly rolling a rock to the top of a mountain, whence the stone would fall back of its own weight. They had thought with some reason that there is no more dreadful punishment than futile and hopeless labor.

If one believes Homer, Sisyphus was the wisest and most prudent of mortals. According to another tradition, however, he was disposed to practice the profession of highwayman. I see no contradiction in this. Opinions differ as to the reasons why he became the futile laborer of the underworld. To begin with, he is accused of a certain levity in regard to the gods. He stole their secrets. Ægina, the daughter of Æsopus, was carried off by Jupiter. The father was shocked by that disappearance and complained to Sisyphus. He, who knew of the abduction, offered to tell about it on condition that Æsopus would give water to the citadel of Corinth. To the celestial thunderbolts he preferred the benediction of water. He was punished for this in the underworld. Homer tells us also that Sisyphus had put Death in chains. Pluto could not endure the sight of his deserted, silent empire. He dispatched the god of war, who liberated Death from the hands of her conqueror.

It is said also that Sisyphus, being near to death, rashly wanted to test his wife's love. He ordered her to cast his unburied body into the middle of the public square. Sisyphus woke up in the underworld. And there, annoyed by an obedience so contrary to human love, he obtained from Pluto permission to return to earth in order to chastise his wife. But when he had seen again the face of this world, enjoyed water and sun, warm stones and the sea, he no longer wanted to go back to the infernal darkness. Recalls, signs of anger, warnings were of no avail. Many years more he lived facing the curve of the gulf, the sparkling sea, and the smiles of earth. A decree of the gods was necessary. Mercury came and seized the impudent man by the collar and, snatching him from his joys, led him forcibly back to the underworld, where his rock was ready for him.

You have already grasped that Sisyphus is the absurd hero. He *is*, as much through his passions as through his torture. His scorn of the gods, his hatred of death, and his passion for life won him that unspeakable penalty in which the whole being is exerted toward accomplishing nothing. This is the price that must be paid for the passions of this earth. Nothing is told us about Sisyphus in the underworld. Myths are made for the imagination to breathe life into them. As for this myth, one sees merely the whole effort of a body straining to raise the huge stone, to roll it and push it up a slope a hundred times over; one sees the face screwed up, the cheek tight against the stone, the shoulder bracing the clay-covered mass, the foot wedging it, the fresh start with arms outstretched, the wholly human security of two earth-clotted hands. At the very end of his long effort measured by skyless space and time without depth, the purpose is achieved. Then Sisyphus watches the stone rush down in a few moments toward that lower world whence he will have to push it up again toward the summit. He goes back down to the plain.

It is during that return, that pause, that Sisyphus interests me. A face that toils so close to stones is already stone itself! I see that man going back down with a heavy yet measured step toward the torment of which he will never know the end. That hour like a breathing-space which returns as surely as his suffering, that is the hour of consciousness. At each of those moments when he leaves the heights and gradually sinks toward the lairs of the gods, he is superior to his fate. He is stronger than his rock.

If this myth is tragic, that is because its hero is conscious. Where would his torture be, indeed, if at every step the hope of succeeding upheld him? The workman of today works every day in his life at the same tasks, and this fate is no less absurd. But it is tragic only at the rare moments when it becomes conscious. Sisyphus, proletarian of the gods, powerless and rebellious, knows the whole extent of his wretched condition: it is what he thinks of during his descent. The lucidity that was to constitute his torture at the same time crowns his victory. There is no fate that cannot be surmounted by scorn.

—

If the descent is thus sometimes performed in sorrow, it can also take place in joy. This word is not too much. Again I fancy Sisyphus returning toward his rock, and the sorrow was in the beginning. When the images of earth cling too tightly to memory, when the call of happiness becomes too insistent, it happens that melancholy rises in man's heart: this is the rock's victory, this is the rock itself. The boundless grief is too heavy to bear. These are our nights of Gethsemane. But crushing truths perish from being acknowledged. Thus, Œdipus at the outset obeys fate without knowing it. But from the moment he knows, his tragedy begins. Yet at the same moment, blind and desperate, he realizes that the only bond linking him to the world is the cool hand of a girl. Then a tremendous remark rings out: "Despite so many ordeals, my advanced age and the nobility of my soul make me conclude that all is well." Sophocles' Œdipus, like Dostoevsky's Kirilov, thus gives the recipe for the absurd victory. Ancient wisdom confirms modern heroism.

One does not discover the absurd without being tempted to write a manual of happiness. "What! by such narrow ways—?" There is but one world, however. Happiness and the absurd are two sons of the same earth. They are inseparable. It would be a mistake to say that happiness necessarily springs from the absurd discovery. It happens as well that the feeling of the absurd springs from happiness. "I conclude that all is well," says Œdipus, and that remark is sacred. It echoes in the wild and limited universe of man. It teaches that all is not, has not been, exhausted. It drives out of this world a god who had come into it with dissatisfaction and a preference for futile sufferings. It makes of fate a human matter, which must be settled among men.

All Sisyphus' silent joy is contained therein. His fate belongs to him. His rock is his thing. Likewise, the absurd man, when he contemplates his torment, silences all the idols. In the universe suddenly restored to its silence, the myriad wondering little voices of the earth rise up. Unconscious, secret calls, invitations from all the faces, they are the necessary reverse and price of victory. There is no sun without shadow, and it is essential to know the night. The absurd man says yes and his effort will henceforth be unceasing. If there is a personal fate, there is no higher destiny, or at least there is but one which he concludes is inevitable and despicable. For the rest, he knows himself to be the master of his days. At that subtle moment when man glances backward over his life, Sisyphus returning toward his rock, in that slight pivoting he contemplates that series of unrelated actions which becomes his fate, created by him, combined under his memory's eye and soon sealed by his death. Thus, convinced of the wholly human origin of all that is human, a blind man eager to see who knows that the night has no end, he is still on the go. The rock is still rolling.

I leave Sisyphus at the foot of the mountain! One always finds one's burden again. But Sisyphus teaches the higher fidelity that negates the gods and raises rocks. He too concludes that all is well. This universe henceforth without a master seems to him neither sterile nor futile. Each atom of that stone, each mineral flake of that night-filled mountain, in itself forms a world. The struggle itself toward the heights is enough to fill a man's heart. One must imagine Sisyphus happy.

RALPH ELLISON

Named after Emerson, Ralph Waldo Ellison was born in Oklahoma on March 1, 1914. At that time, Oklahoma was a strange mix of southern and frontier culture, but it was also a place where there was a strong and fiercely independent black community. Whites, blacks, and Native Americans mixed freely. Like Camus, Nietzsche, Sartre, and Unamuno, Ellison lost his bright and energetic father when he was very young. Though the family was poor, his mother was intellectually vibrant and socially active and did everything she could do to nurture the minds of her two sons, Ralph and Henry.

At an early age, Ellison was a passionate jazz buff and an accomplished trumpet player. He earned a scholarship to study music and music theory at Tuskegee Institute. Late in his undergraduate studies, there was a mix-up with his scholarship, and Ellison moved to New York to try to earn money for school by working as a musician. However, it was high noon in the Great Depression, and trumpet players were not in much demand. Ellison found work as a clerk and receptionist with a psychiatrist in Harlem.

During this time, Ellison struck up intense and important friendships with Langston Hughes and Richard Wright. In addition to his classic, *Native Son,* Wright had penned the existential novel *The Outsider.* He encouraged Ellison to write and helped bring him under the spell of Kierkegaard and Dostoevsky. Wright was also instrumental in getting Ellison hired by the Federal Writing Project. In 1938, Ellison was commissioned by the project to conduct a series of interviews with African Americans. Many of the words that he recorded would later resonate in his fiction.

With the support of Wright and others, Ellison began publishing in the late 1930s. In 1942, he became managing editor of the *Negro Quarterly.* He wanted to aid in the war effort but not, as he put it, "in a Jim Crow way," so from 1943–45, Ellison signed on as a cook in the Merchant Marines. In 1945, while on a sick leave, Ellison began the work that would make him a very visible figure in the literary world, *Invisible Man*. The book, which was published in 1952, won the National Book Award and has become widely regarded as one of the most significant novels of the twentieth century.

After securing his literary station, Ellison taught at Bard, Rutgers, the University of Chicago, and other institutions of higher learning. He published many essays and worked endlessly on his second novel but never finished it to his satisfaction. Constructed from the work in progress, *Juneteenth* was published after Ellison's death on April 16, 1994.

As an established author, Ellison was always getting into trouble for insisting that there was no separate African-American identity; rather, "we are all notes in a long and improvised tune that draws from many sources white, black, and native American." Ironically enough, however, Ellison's identity as an African-American author is so strong that it has been convenient for scholars to forget that his work is also squarely in the existential tradition. Ellison wrote, "The problem of becoming an artist is related to that of becoming a man, of becoming visible." Like Camus, whom he read closely, Ellison was consumed with the task of trying to find an authentic way of being in an absurd world. And if that task does not bespeak an existential frame of mind, then nothing does.

INVISIBLE MAN

Prologue

I am an invisible man. No, I am not a spook like those who haunted Edgar Allan Poe; nor am I one of your Hollywood-movie ectoplasms. I am a man of substance, of flesh and bone, fiber and liquids—and I might even be said to possess a mind. I am invisible, understand, simply because people refuse to see me. Like the bodiless heads you see sometimes in circus side-shows, it is as though I have been surrounded by mirrors of hard, distorting glass. When they approach me they see only my surroundings, themselves, or figments of their imagination—indeed, everything and anything except me.

Nor is my invisibility exactly a matter of a biochemical accident to my epidermis. That invisibility to which I refer occurs because of a peculiar disposition of the eyes of those with whom I come in contact. A matter of the construction of their *inner* eyes, those eyes with which they look through their physical eyes upon reality. I am not complaining, nor am I protesting either. It is sometimes advantageous to be unseen, although it is most often rather wearing on the nerves. Then too, you're constantly being bumped against by those of poor vision. Or again, you often doubt if you really exist. You wonder whether you aren't simply a phantom in other people's minds. Say, a figure in a nightmare which the sleeper tries with all his strength to destroy. It's when you feel like this that, out of resentment, you begin to bump people back. And, let me confess, you feel that way most of the time. You ache with the need to convince yourself that you do exist in the real world, that you're a part of all the sound and anguish, and you strike out with your fists, you curse and you swear to make them recognize you. And, alas, it's seldom successful.

One night I accidentally bumped into a man, and perhaps because of the near darkness he saw me and called me an insulting name. I sprang at him, seized his coat lapels and demanded that he apologize. He was a tall blond man, and as my face came close to his he looked insolently out of his blue eyes and cursed me, his breath hot in my face as he struggled. I pulled his chin down sharp upon the crown of my head, butting him as I had seen the West Indians do, and I felt his flesh tear and the blood gush out, and I yelled, "Apologize! Apologize!" But he continued to curse and struggle, and I butted him again and again until he went down heavily, on his knees, profusely bleeding. I kicked him repeatedly, in a frenzy because he still uttered insults though his lips were frothy with blood. Oh yes, I kicked him! And in my outrage I got out my knife and prepared to slit his throat, right there beneath the lamplight in the deserted street, holding him in the collar with one hand, and opening the knife with my teeth—when it occurred to me that the man had not *seen* me, actually; that he, as far as he knew, was in the midst of a walking nightmare! And I stopped the blade, slicing the air as I pushed him away, letting him fall back to the street. I stared at him hard as the lights of a car stabbed through the darkness. He lay there, moaning on the asphalt; a man almost killed by a phantom. It unnerved me. I was both disgusted and ashamed. I was like a drunken man myself, wavering about on weakened legs. Then I was amused: Something in this man's thick head had sprung out and beaten him within an inch of his life. I began to laugh at this crazy discovery. Would he have awakened at the point of death? Would Death himself have freed him for wakeful living? But I didn't linger. I ran away into the dark, laughing so hard I feared I might rupture myself. The next day I saw his picture in the *Daily News,* beneath a caption stating that he had been "mugged." Poor fool, poor blind fool, I thought with sincere compassion, mugged by an invisible man!

Most of the time (although I do not choose as I once did to deny the violence of my days by ignoring it) I am not so overtly violent. I remember that I am invisible and walk softly so as not to awaken the sleeping ones. Sometimes it is best not to awaken them; there are few things in the world as dangerous as sleepwalkers. I learned in time though that it is possible to carry on a fight against them without their realizing it. For instance, I have been carrying on a fight with Monopolated Light & Power for some time now. I use their service and pay them nothing at all, and they don't know it. Oh, they suspect that power is being drained off, but they don't know where. All they know is that according to the master meter back there in their power station a hell of a lot of free current is disappearing somewhere into the jungle of Harlem. The joke, of course, is that I don't live in Harlem but in a border area. Several years ago (before I discovered the advantages of being invisible) I went through the routine process of buying service and paying their outrageous rates. But no more. I gave up all that, along with my apartment, and my old way of life: That way based upon the fallacious assumption that I, like other men, was visible. Now, aware of my invisibility, I live rent-free in a building rented strictly to whites, in a section of the basement that was shut off and forgotten during the nineteenth century, which I discovered when I was trying to escape in the night from Ras the Destroyer. But that's getting too far ahead of the story, almost to the end, although the end is in the beginning and lies far ahead.

The point now is that I found a home—or a hole in the ground, as you will. Now don't jump to the conclusion that because I call my home a "hole" it is damp and cold like a grave; there are cold holes and warm holes. Mine is a warm hole. And remember, a bear retires to his hole for the winter and lives until spring; then he comes strolling out like the Easter chick breaking from its shell. I say all this to assure you that it is incorrect to assume that, because I'm invisible and live in a hole, I am dead. I am neither dead nor in a state of suspended animation. Call me Jack-the-Bear, for I am in a state of hibernation.

My hole is warm and full of light. Yes, *full* of light. I doubt if there is a brighter spot in all New York than this hole of mine, and I do not exclude Broadway. Or the Empire State Building on a photographer's dream night. But that is taking advantage of you. Those two spots are among the darkest of our whole civilization—pardon me, our whole *culture* (an important distinction, I've heard)— which might sound like a hoax, or a contradiction, but that (by contradiction, I mean) is how the world moves: Not like an arrow, but a boomerang. (Beware of those who speak of the *spiral* of history; they are preparing a boomerang. Keep a steel helmet handy.) I know; I have been boomeranged across my head so much that I now can see the darkness of lightness. And I love light. Perhaps you'll think it strange that an invisible man should need light, desire light, love light. But maybe it is exactly because I *am* invisible. Light confirms my reality, gives birth to my form. A beautiful girl once told me of a recurring nightmare in which she lay in the center of a large dark room and felt her face expand until it filled the whole room, becoming a formless mass while her eyes ran in bilious jelly up the chimney. And so it is with me. Without light I am not only invisible, but formless as well; and to be unaware of one's form is to live a death. I myself, after existing some twenty years, did not become alive until I discovered my invisibility.

That is why I fight my battle with Monopolated Light & Power. The deeper reason, I mean: It allows me to feel my vital aliveness. I also fight them for taking so much of my money before I learned to protect myself. In my hole in the basement there are exactly 1,369 lights. I've wired the entire ceiling, every inch of it. And not with fluorescent bulbs, but with the older, more-expensive-to-operate kind, the filament type. An act of sabotage, you know. I've already begun to wire the wall. A junk man I know, a man of vision, has supplied me with wire and sockets. Nothing, storm or flood, must get in the way of our need for light and ever more and brighter light. The truth is the light and light is the truth. When I finish all four walls, then I'll start on the floor. Just how that will go, I don't know. Yet when you have lived invisible as long as I have you develop a certain ingenuity. I'll solve the problem. And maybe I'll invent a gadget to place my coffee pot on the fire while I lie in bed, and even invent a gadget to warm my bed—like the fellow I saw in one of the picture magazines who made himself a gadget to warm his shoes! Though invisible, I am in the great American tradition of tinkers. That makes me kin to Ford, Edison and Franklin. Call me, since I have a theory and a concept, a "thinker-tinker." Yes, I'll warm my shoes; they need it, they're usually full of holes. I'll do that and more.

Now I have one radio-phonograph; I plan to have five. There is a certain acoustical deadness in my hole, and when I have music I want to *feel* its vibration, not only with my ear but with my whole body. I'd like to hear five recordings of Louis Armstrong playing and singing "What Did I Do to Be so Black and Blue"—all at the same time. Sometimes now I listen to Louis while I have my favorite dessert of vanilla ice cream and sloe gin. I pour the red liquid over the white mound, watching it glisten and the vapor rising as Louis bends that military instrument into a beam of lyrical sound. Perhaps I like Louis Armstrong because he's made poetry out of being invisible. I think it must be because he's unaware that he *is* invisible. And my own grasp of invisibility aids me to understand his music. Once when I asked for a cigarette, some jokers gave me a reefer, which I lighted when I got home and sat listening to my phonograph. It was a strange evening. Invisibility, let me explain, gives one a slightly different sense of time, you're never quite on the beat. Sometimes you're

ahead and sometimes behind. Instead of the swift and impercep-
tible flowing of time, you are aware of its nodes, those points
where time stands still or from which it leaps ahead. And you slip
into the breaks and look around. That's what you hear vaguely in
Louis' music.

Once I saw a prizefighter boxing a yokel. The fighter was swift
and amazingly scientific. His body was one violent flow of rapid
rhythmic action. He hit the yokel a hundred times while the
yokel held up his arms in stunned surprise. But suddenly the
yokel, rolling about in the gale of boxing gloves, struck one blow
and knocked science, speed and footwork as cold as a well-digger's
posterior. The smart money hit the canvas. The long shot got the
nod. The yokel had simply stepped inside of his opponent's sense
of time. So under the spell of the reefer I discovered a new
analytical way of listening to music. The unheard sounds came
through, and each melodic line existed of itself, stood out clearly
from all the rest, said its piece, and waited patiently for the other
voices to speak. That night I found myself hearing not only in
time, but in space as well. I not only entered the music but descended, like Dante, into its depths. And *beneath the swiftness of the
hot tempo there was a slower tempo and a cave and I entered it and looked
around and heard an old woman singing a spiritual as full of Weltschmerz
as flamenco, and beneath that lay a still lower level on which I saw a beautiful girl the color of ivory pleading in a voice like my mother's as she stood
before a group of slaveowners who bid for her naked body, and below that I
found a lower level and a more rapid tempo and I heard someone shout:*

*"Brothers and sisters, my text this morning is the 'Blackness of Black-
ness.'"*

*And a congregation of voices answered: "That blackness is most black,
brother, most black . . ."*

"In the beginning . . ."

"At the very start," they cried.

". . . there was blackness . . ."

"Preach it . . ."

". . . and the sun . . ."

"The sun, Lawd . . ."

"*. . . was bloody red . . .*"

"*Red . . .*"

"*Now black is . . .*" *the preacher shouted.*

"*Bloody . . .*"

"*I said black is . . .*"

"*Preach it, brother . . .*"

"*. . . an' black ain't . . .*"

"*Red, Lawd, red: He said it's red!*"

"*Amen, brother . . .*"

"*Black will git you . . .*"

"*Yes, it will . . .*"

"*Yes, it will . . .*"

"*. . . an' black won't . . .*"

"*Naw, it won't!*"

"*It do . . .*"

"*It do, Lawd . . .*"

"*. . . an' it don't.*"

"*Halleluiah . . .*"

"*. . . It'll put you, glory, glory, Oh my Lawd, in the* WHALE'S BELLY.*"

"*Preach it, dear brother . . .*"

"*. . . an' make you tempt . . .*"

"*Good God a-mighty!*"

"*Old Aunt Nelly!*"

"*Black will make you . . .*"

"*Black . . .*"

"*. . . or black will un-make you.*"

"*Ain't it the truth, Lawd?*"

And at that point a voice of trombone timbre screamed at me, "*Git out of here, you fool! Is you ready to commit treason?*"

And I tore myself away, hearing the old singer of spirituals moaning, "*Go curse your God, boy, and die.*"

I stopped and questioned her, asked her what was wrong.

"*I dearly loved my master, son,*" *she said.*

"*You should have hated him,*" *I said.*

"*He gave me several sons,*" *she said,* "*and because I loved my sons I learned to love their father though I hated him too.*"

"*I too have become acquainted with ambivalence,*" *I said.* "*That's why I'm here.*"

"*What's that?*"

"*Nothing, a word that doesn't explain it. Why do you moan?*"

"*I moan this way 'cause he's dead,*" *she said.*

"*Then tell me, who is that laughing upstairs?*"

"*Them's my sons. They glad.*"

"*Yes, I can understand that too,*" *I said.*

"*I laughs too, but I moans too. He promised to set us free but he never could bring hisself to do it. Sill I loved him . . .*"

"*Loved him? You mean . . . ?*"

"*Oh yes, but I loved something else even more.*"

"*What more?*"

"*Freedom.*"

"*Freedom,*" *I said.* "*Maybe freedom lies in hating.*"

"*Naw, son, it's in loving. I loved him and give him the poison and he withered away like a frost-bit apple. Them boys woulda tore him to pieces with they homemade knives.*"

"*A mistake was made somewhere,*" *I said,* "*I'm confused.*" *And I wished to say other things, but the laughter upstairs became too loud and moan-like for me and I tried to break out of it, but I couldn't. Just as I was leaving I felt an urgent desire to ask her what freedom was and went back. She sat with her head in her hands, moaning softly; her leather-brown face was filled with sadness.*

"*Old woman, what is this freedom you love so well?*" *I asked around a corner of my mind.*

She looked surprised, then thoughtful, then baffled. "*I done forgot, son. It's all mixed up. First I think it's one thing, then I think it's another. It gits my head to spinning. I guess now it ain't nothing but knowing how to say what I got up in my head. But it's a hard job, son. Too much is done happen to me in too short a time. Hit's like I have a fever. Ever' time I starts to walk my head gits to swirling and I falls down. Or if it ain't that, it's the boys; they gits to laughing and wants to kill up the white folks. They's bitter, that's what they is . . .*"

"*But what about freedom?*"

"*Leave me 'lone, boy; my head aches!*"

I left her, feeling dizzy myself. I didn't get far.

Suddenly one of the sons, a big fellow six feet tall, appeared out of no-where and struck me with his fist.

"What's the matter, man?" I cried.

"You made Ma cry!"

"But how?" I said, dodging a blow.

"Askin' her them questions, that's how. Git outa here and stay, and next time you got questions like that, ask yourself!"

He held me in a grip like cold stone, his fingers fastening upon my windpipe until I thought I would suffocate before he finally allowed me to go. I stumbled about dazed, the music beating hysterically in my ears. It was dark. My head cleared and I wandered down a dark narrow passage, thinking I heard his footsteps hurrying behind me. I was sore, and into my being had come a profound craving for tranquillity, for peace and quiet, a state I felt I could never achieve. For one thing, the trumpet was blaring and the rhythm was too hectic. A tom-tom beating like heart-thuds began drowning out the trumpet, filling my ears. I longed for water and I heard it rushing through the cold mains my fingers touched as I felt my way, but I couldn't stop to search because of the footsteps behind me.

"Hey, Ras," I called. "Is it you, Destroyer? Rinehart?"

No answer, only the rhythmic footsteps behind me. Once I tried cross-ing the road, but a speeding machine struck me, scraping the skin from my leg as it roared past.

Then somehow I came out of it, ascending hastily from this underworld of sound to hear Louis Armstrong innocently ask-ing,

> *What did I do*
> *To be so black*
> *And blue?*

At first I was afraid; this familiar music had demanded action, the kind of which I was incapable, and yet had I lingered there beneath the surface I might have attempted to act. Nevertheless, I know now that few really listen to this music. I sat on the chair's edge in a soaking sweat, as though each of my 1,369 bulbs had every one become a klieg light in an individual setting for a third degree with Ras and Rinehart in charge. It was exhausting—as though I had held my breath continuously for an hour under the terrifying serenity that comes from days of intense hunger. And yet, it was a strangely satisfying experience for an invisible man to hear the silence of sound. I had discovered unrecognized compulsions of my being—even though I could not answer "yes" to their promptings. I haven't smoked a reefer since, however; not because they're illegal, but because to *see* around corners is enough (that is not unusual when you are invisible). But to hear around them is too much; it inhibits action. And despite Brother Jack and all that sad, lost period of the Brotherhood, I believe in nothing if not in action.

Please, a definition: A hibernation is a covert preparation for a more overt action.

Besides, the drug destroys one's sense of time completely. If that happened, I might forget to dodge some bright morning and some cluck would run me down with an orange and yellow street car, or a bilious bus! Or I might forget to leave my hole when the moment for action presents itself.

Meanwhile I enjoy my life with the compliments of Monopolated Light & Power. Since you never recognize me even when in closest contact with me, and since, no doubt, you'll hardly believe that I exist, it won't matter if you know that I tapped a power line leading into the building and ran it into my hole in the ground. Before that I lived in the darkness into which I was chased, but now I see. I've illuminated the blackness of my invisibility— and vice versa. And so I play the invisible music of my isolation. The last statement doesn't seem just right, does it? But it is; you hear this music simply because music is heard and seldom seen, except by musicians. Could this compulsion to put invisibility down in black and white be thus an urge to make music of invisibility? But I am an orator, a rabble rouser—Am? I *was,* and perhaps shall be again. Who knows? All sickness is not unto death, neither is invisibility.

I can hear you say, "What a horrible, irresponsible bastard!"

And you're right. I leap to agree with you. I am one of the most irresponsible beings that ever lived. Irresponsibility is part of my invisibility; any way you face it, it is a denial. But to whom can I be responsible, and why should I be, when you refuse to see me? And wait until I reveal how truly irresponsible I am. Responsibility rests upon recognition, and recognition is a form of agreement. Take the man whom I almost killed: Who was responsible for that near murder—I? I don't think so, and I refuse it. I won't buy it. You can't give it to me. *He* bumped *me, he* insulted *me*. Shouldn't he, for his own personal safety, have recognized my hysteria, my "danger potential"? He, let us say, was lost in a dream world. But didn't *he* control that dream world—which, alas, is only too real!—and didn't *he* rule me out of it? And if he had yelled for a policeman, wouldn't *I* have been taken for the offending one? Yes, yes, yes! Let me agree with you, I was the irresponsible one; for I should have used my knife to protect the higher interests of society. Some day that kind of foolishness will cause us tragic trouble. All dreamers and sleepwalkers must pay the price, and even the invisible victim is responsible for the fate of all. But I shirked that responsibility; I became too snarled in the incompatible notions that buzzed within my brain. I was a coward . . .

But what did *I* do to be so blue? Bear with me.

About the Editor

GORDON MARINO earned his bachelor of arts from Columbia University, his master's degree in philosophy from the University of Pennsylvania, and his doctorate from the University of Chicago, Committee on Social Thought. Marino was research fellow at the Kierkegaard Biblioteket in Copenhagen for three years. He is coeditor of *The Cambridge Companion to Kierkegaard* and author of *Kierkegaard in the Present Age*. Marino's essays have appeared in *The Atlantic Monthly, The New York Times Magazine, The Wall Street Journal,* and many other periodicals. He is currently Professor of Philosophy, the Boldt Distinguished Chair in the Humanities, Director of the Hong Kierkegaard Library, and assistant football coach at St. Olaf College in Northfield, Minnesota.

MODERN LIBRARY IS ONLINE AT WWW.MODERNLIBRARY.COM

MODERN LIBRARY ONLINE IS YOUR GUIDE TO CLASSIC LITERATURE ON THE WEB

THE MODERN LIBRARY E-NEWSLETTER

Our free e-mail newsletter is sent to subscribers, and features sample chapters, interviews with and essays by our authors, upcoming books, special promotions, announcements, and news.

To subscribe to the Modern Library e-newsletter, send a blank e-mail to: **sub_modernlibrary@info.randomhouse.com** or visit **www.modernlibrary.com**

THE MODERN LIBRARY WEBSITE

Check out the Modern Library website at
www.modernlibrary.com for:

- The Modern Library e-newsletter
- A list of our current and upcoming titles and series
- Reading Group Guides and exclusive author spotlights
- Special features with information on the classics and other paperback series
- Excerpts from new releases and other titles
- A list of our e-books and information on where to buy them
- The Modern Library Editorial Board's 100 Best Novels and 100 Best Nonfiction Books of the Twentieth Century written in the English language
- News and announcements

Questions? E-mail us at **modernlibrary@randomhouse.com**
For questions about examination or desk copies, please visit
the Random House Academic Resources site at
www.randomhouse.com/academic